THE EMERGENCE OF SOCIAL WELFARE
AND SOCIAL WORK

THE EMERGENCE OF SOCIAL WELFARE AND SOCIAL WORK

Neil Gilbert and Harry Specht
UNIVERSITY OF CALIFORNIA, BERKELEY

F. E. PEACOCK PUBLISHERS, INC.   ITASCA, ILLINOIS 60143

To Barbara and Riva

CONTENTS

W, D.
+
P. S.

INTRODUCTION

Social welfare is an emerging institution; social work is an emerging profession. Both are mechanisms created to cope with the problems of social change and the exigencies of life in modern industrial society. All industrialized societies devote some significant part of their resources to social welfare, and all have developed some sort of professional practice that is similar to American and British social work.[1] Thus, while the institution and the profession are relatively young, nevertheless they represent prominent social inventions that influence the conditions of life in modern society.

As social designs, the profession and the institution represent relatively new ideas that are changing rapidly in response to the needs and values of the community. Just during this century, social welfare in the United States has undergone dramatic changes. At the turn of the century it was organized almost exclusively as a private activity supported by the charitable impulse. Until the 1930s only state and local governments participated with charitable organizations in the support of welfare programs. Since the 1930s the federal government has assumed an increasingly larger role in social welfare.[2] At present it is the major source of social welfare funds, and expenditures for social welfare constitute the largest item in the federal budget.[3]

The growth and development of the profession of social work in this century has been just as dramatic. Until the late 1800s the profession did not exist in any organizational or scientific sense. Essentially, up to that time, social work involved various forms of charitable activity voluntarily offered as a matter of individual conscience.[4] By 1915 there was sufficient development of the organizational, ethical, scientific, and theoretical aspects of a profession for the National Conference of Charities and Corrections that year to seriously debate the question "Is Social Work a Profession?" In a presentation responding to this question, Dr. Abraham Flexner analyzed the criteria of a profession and concluded that social work was hardly eligible to claim professional status.[5] Despite this assessment, by the 1920s several schools of education for social work had been established, and a number of professional organizations had been founded. By midcentury a unified national organization of professional social workers had been formed (the National Association of Social Workers), as well as an accrediting body for educational programs conferring degrees in social work (the Council on Social Work Education). Currently in the United States there are well over 200 accredited schools offering degrees in social work at the bachelor's, master's, and doctoral levels; in addition, there are several professional journals devoted to these subjects.[6]

Along with the phenomenal growth of the institution and the profession, another change is currently taking place. That is, social welfare and social work are coming to be seen as programs and services that are necessary and important to everyone, not only the poor, the sick, and the handicapped. These developments, of course, are neither smooth nor uncontested, as the readings in this book will reveal.

Our intention in this book is to introduce students to important sets of ideas associated with the unfolding of social welfare and social work. The readings in Part I are concerned with ideas about the changing nature of the responsibility society assumes for the welfare of its members, the role of public and private efforts in these collective endeavors, the functions of social welfare and how they fit into the institutional structure of modern society, and the directions in which this institution appears to be headed. The readings in Part II bring in the analysis and interpretation of needs and problems that emanate from existing social arrangements. These readings were selected to provide examples of how ideas derived from sociological critiques operate as an intellectual stimulus to institutional and professional developments. Part III deals with conceptions of the nature and development of professionalism in social work, the organizational context in which practice takes place, and the directions in which professional practice seems headed.

To set the framework for this book, we will briefly review the relationships among the topics around which the readings are organized: social welfare, sociological critique, and social work.

THE INSTITUTION AND PROFESSIONAL PRACTICE

The institution of social welfare is much older than the profession of social work. The institution serves as a mechanism for mutual support which expresses the collective responsibility of the community for helping its members. It consists of a series of programmatic arrangements for meeting needs through the allocation of income and services outside of other institutional channels, such as the family and the market.[7] These programmatic arrangements are run by people from many professions, including public health, nursing, city planning, public administration, teaching, and social work. Among these professional groups social work is most strongly identified with the institution of social welfare because it provides the greatest amount of manpower for the diverse areas of social welfare programming. In addition, social work training is geared primarily to the broad range of social welfare programs unlike (on the one hand) city planning and public administration, where much of the training is concerned with planning and management of the physical side of urban development or (on the other hand) nursing, public health, and teaching, where training tends to be focused around a limited number of programmatic arrangements within the overall institution.

Social welfare programs can be distinguished broadly in terms of arrangements concerned with income maintenance and social services. Historically, programs for income maintenance developed first because social welfare emerged as an institution concerned with problems of economic dependency and insecurity. The history of social welfare as an institution can be read in large part as the history of the development of labor legislation. That this system of mutual support evolved in relation to the need to earn a living is not too surprising, because this is one of man's foremost needs. Social work, too, began with a concern for problems of economic dependency, but it rapidly expanded its purview to include many other social problems. The reason for this, we think, is that there is little need for an enduring professional service in connection with the provision of economic supports.

In most societies, security of family income is the first area around which social welfare provisions are established; and once these monetary provisions are established as a fiscal transaction, it requires only certain kinds of professional administrative and management personnel for eligibility determination and delivery of benefits. Thus, while income maintenance is among the most compelling of human needs, it is also the least fruitful one around which to develop direct personal services. However, many of the problems that are attendant upon financial deprivation and other social dislocations (such as family disorganization and juvenile delinquency) are rich fields for the development of direct professional services. Therefore, even though financial need may be the original cause of many problems, social work as a profession has tended to develop its professional methodologies to intervene in problems that mainly require individual and institutional adjustments.

The profession of social work provides services to those in need within the institutional framework of social welfare. These services include counseling, education, advocacy, information giving, and referral. But the relationship between the profession and the institution is more complex than that of an agent carrying forward the institutional agenda. The profession also has responsibilities for creating, maintaining, and reforming the institutional context within which it operates.

This dual responsibility is, on the one hand, to directly aid clients in need and, on the other hand, to attend to the institutional structure within which these services are offered. This duality is a source of confusion and strain in the profession. The strain is reflected in the inescapable realities of practice which confront professionals with difficult moral dilemmas. Should society's resources be devoted to helping people who have been damaged by the inequities and inadequacies of the social system or to finding ways to change the system so that its inequities and inadequacies are eliminated? Is the remedial function of social work a disservice to the poor and needy because it helps the system to survive by carting away and repairing the wounded, particularly those who are the greatest nuisances— thereby retarding social change?

These dilemmas are, essentially, insoluble. Some of the confusion that surrounds this dual responsibility is reflected in the names given to schools engaged in the education of professional social workers, such as School of Social Welfare (University of California, Berkeley), School of Applied Social Sciences (Western Reserve University), School of Social Service Administration (University of Chicago), School of Social Work (University of Alabama), Graduate School of Social Service (Indiana University), and School of Social Policy and Community Service (State University of New York at Buffalo). If we add to this partial list of names for master's degree programs in social work the many names of departments that offer undergraduate majors in social work (e.g., Sociology, Social Work, Social

Services, Social Welfare and Correction, Behavioral Sciences, Health and Social Services, Urban Life, and Social Science), the reader can begin to sense the difficulties that exist in sorting out the basic terminology of the field.

By and large, regardless of the names, the educational programs we have mentioned are concerned with training practitioners to provide direct services to those in need. With few exceptions the training of social welfare specialists—practitioners prepared to deal with activities related to the development and reform of the institution—has not been emphasized in the United States as an important area separate from the training of social workers for direct services. (An outstanding exception is the Florence Heller School for Advanced Studies in Social Welfare at Brandeis University. However, this school offers training only at the doctoral level.) The situation is considerably different in the United Kingdom, where training for "social administration" (the equivalent of what we refer to as social welfare) is clearly differentiated from social work practice and is recognized as an important field of study in its own right.

This situation appears to be changing in the United States. Recently, schools of social work have begun to organize their programs along lines designated as "clinical track" and "social change track," "direct service" and "indirect service," and the "micro-level" and "macro-level" of practice. Thus the dual responsibility of the profession in relation to the institution, which has long been recognized in theory, seems to be gaining a formal role in the structure of professional training.

PROFESSIONAL PRACTICE AND SOCIOLOGICAL CRITIQUE

In its efforts to provide for mutual support, the institution of social welfare is concerned both with rehabilitation of individuals who have personal problems and with the reform of society's need-meeting structures. In practice, social workers are engaged in both rehabilitation and reform activities.

Rehabilitation activities include counseling, education, advocacy, information giving, and referral. These activities are the major subject matter of social casework, group work, and those aspects of community organization in which direct services are provided to community groups. Currently there has been great interest in the profession in the development of a "generalist" approach which integrates these different methodologies of direct services.[8] The largest numbers of professional social workers will always be needed to provide these direct services. These are personally engaging activities and constitute the sort of work that will be an attractive career for those who enjoy being involved with others and the sharing of intimate, sometimes troubling, personal experiences.

Reform activities are concerned with bringing about a better adjustment between human needs and social resources by creating organizational arrangements through which society can deal with recognized social problems, deviancies, and maladjustments. These activities are the major subject matter of the indirect services—community organization, planning, administration, and evaluation—for which the social welfare specialist is trained. A smaller, but currently growing, number of professional social workers undertake these functions. Generally the work here is drier and less personally engaging than in the direct services, involving as it does an orientation toward research, policy analysis, and program development.

There is another type of activity which is closely related to social reform and which has a substantial influence upon its direction. This activity involves the description and analysis of social problems. We call it "sociological critique" in the sense that it seeks to assess patterns of human interaction to explain where and why social institutions fail. While many academic disciplines contribute to these activities, the mainstream of the intellectual force flows from sociology. Auguste Comte, Karl Marx, Ferdinand Tönnies, Max Weber, and Hênri de Saint-Simon are some of the early sociologists who provided analyses of society, critiques that enabled people to consider alternative means for organizing their communities. As noted in the first textbook of American sociology: "Sociology was born of the modern ardor to improve society."[9]

During the period following World War I through the 1920s, social work was considered by many to be "applied social science." Since that period the relationship between social work and sociology in the United States has declined as the sociological orientation has moved away from application and toward the theoretical aspects of problem analysis. However, the relationship is still quite evident on the undergraduate level in social work education because many programs offering an undergraduate major or a degree in social work are located in departments of sociology and social science. The situation is somewhat different in the United Kingdom and Germany, where the influence of sociology on social work at all educational levels is very strong, with sociologists exercising intellectual hegemony over the social work profession.

Because sociological critique has an influential bearing on social work practice, it is important to recognize the distinctions between these two types of activities. Sociological critique points up what is wrong with society. Its function is not to refine the operation of the welfare system but, rather, to be dissatisfied with what is. The intellectual analyses of many social critics may be backed up by strong personal commitments. Some who are engaged in social-critiquing activities are not satisfied with being merely academic; they participate actively in experimenting with and attempting to implement their ideas for social reform. Richard Cloward, Frances Fox Piven, Frank Riessman, Michael Harrington, Nathan Glazer, and Daniel Moynihan are among those who combine the academic and theoretical orientation of sociological critique with efforts at practical application. But for the most part this combination is more the exception than the rule. The university offers the major possibility of permanent careers for those engaged in research and analysis of social problems. To some degree the insulation of the academic environment is necessary to allow sociological critique to be objective and fearless of reprisals from institutional spheres that might be offended.

There are elements of tension and reciprocity in the relationships between sociological critique and social welfare and social work practice. The institution of social welfare and the profession of social work constitute important sources of data for the study of social problems. Many social work practitioners are intellectually and emotionally drawn to sociological critique because it often expresses the problems and frustrations experienced in practice. The ideas of sociological critique provide a source of innovation and change in social welfare programs and social work technology. Many students come to the field of social work stimulated by the ideas of sociological critique they encounter in their undergraduate work in the social sciences. For these students, the reciprocal elements between sociological critique and social work practice often stand out more sharply than the conflicts.

But with this reciprocity there is also a built-in strain between social work practice and sociological critique, because social work practitioners invariably have to come to grips with the implications of sociological critique. The descriptions and cause-effect analysis of social problems such as poverty, juvenile delinquency, and mental illness suggest new programs and technologies for improving social welfare. But it is the social work practitioner's job to apply these ideas in practice. And here is where there are at least three potential sources of tension. First, there are usually competing theories generated by sociological critique that have different implications for rehabilitation and reform activities in social work practice. Second, sociological critique often yields assessments of practice that are less than flattering. A social worker who has devoted a life's career to developing his professional skill will not be enthusiastic about analyses that suggest his function is socially irrelevant or, worse, oppressive and reactionary. Finally, when ideas of sociological critique are transformed into new programs and methodologies, they often fall short of expectation and the new arrangements quickly become the target of new sociological critique, leaving the practitioner wondering whether he can ever do anything right.

Thus, the interaction among reform, rehabilitation, and sociological critique is a source of both vigor and conflict in the emergence of social work and social welfare. While each of these activities may stimulate and inspire the others, not infrequently each may also disappoint and frustrate the aspirations of the others.

SELECTION OF READINGS

In preparing the chapters of this book and selecting readings we have addressed an audience with a social science background. Our readers, we expect, have mastered introductory materials in history, economics, sociology, and psychology, and they may already be acquainted with some of the authors from whom we have selected readings.

We tended to select articles that deal with subject matter at a high level of generalization. For example, the paper by Gideon Sjoberg, Richard Brymer, and Buford Farris, "Bureaucracy and the Lower Class" (Reading 21) deals with the broad moral questions that underlie more specific social work issues such as community control and self-determination for ethnic subcommunities. Similarly, rather than deal with specific programs like negative income tax and revenue sharing, we have selected Richard Titmuss's "The Role of Redistribution in Social Policy" (Reading 5) and George Hoshino's "Britain's Debate on Universal or Selective Services" (Reading 10) because they deal with general welfare issues. Our basic criterion in picking readings was whether they analyzed or described major ideas that illuminate the interesting and universal aspects of the emergence of social welfare and social work.

The book is organized in three sections, with an introduction to each of the seven chapters. The readings in Part I, "Social Welfare," focus upon the evolution of social welfare from three perspectives: (1) as it emerged in the transition from preindustrial society, (2) the place of social welfare in the institutional context of modern society, and (3) the directions in which social welfare seems to be headed.

The articles presented in the first chapter analyze the development of social welfare in the context of the great social, political, and economic changes in the transition from preindustrial society. As these changes occurred, new institutional arrangements were required to perform necessary societal functions, such as mutual aid, production, distribution, and social control, which had previously been centered in the traditional network of social relationships. How and where the evolving institution of social welfare fits into the overall framework of these new institutional patterns—its primary or core functions in modern society—are issues that have received varying interpretations. The articles in the second chapter offer a series of divergent views concerning the primary functions served by the institution of social welfare.

Whatever conceptual problems and disagreements exist in defining the functional boundaries of the institution precisely, they are not due to a lack of concrete, ongoing, social welfare activity in society. While the functional boundaries are vague, we can distinguish the broad shape, content, and direction of contemporary social welfare. This is the purpose of the third chapter. The articles here deal with some of the important features of contemporary social welfare activities and where they are headed. The relationships between public and private efforts in the provision of services, the shape of social insurance programs, and trends in service delivery are reviewed.

The readings in Part II, "Sociological Critique," consist of examples of social problem analyses that have influenced the direction of social work. The readings here examine causes and potential social welfare solutions of the problems of alienation, mental illness, race relations, poverty, and juvenile delinquency.

The readings in Part III, "Social Work," are organized in three chapters. Chapter five is concerned with the emergence of social work as a profession. The papers included in this chapter reflect the ongoing concern of social work with the attributes of a profession and the dilemmas and problems of professionalism in social work.

Most social workers practice in agencies (which are usually bureaucracies), and most social work services are financed by large governmental and voluntary agencies. Chapter six is devoted to discussion of the organizational context of social work practice.

The final chapter attempts to give some idea of the present status of the profession. In addition, the readings in this chapter deal with the major directions social work seems to be taking in this decade.

NOTES

1. For example, the following table is a list of the expenditures made for social security in 1963, by rank, in the 24 highest expenditure countries.

Countries Spending More than 5 Percent of GNP on Social Security in 1963, by Rank of Expenditure

Rank	Country	Percent	Rank	Country	Percent
1	Czechoslovakia	16.9	13	Norway	10.6
2	Austria	15.9	14	Yugoslavia	10.5
3	West Germany	15.3	15	USSR	10.2
4	France	14.6	16	Canada	9.8
5	Belgium	13.8	17	Finland	9.5
6	Luxembourg	13.8	18	Portugal	9.3
7	Sweden	13.5	19	Ireland	9.1
8	Italy	12.8	20	Australia	8.0
9	Netherlands	12.7	21	Switzerland	7.4
10	New Zealand	11.9	22	Iceland	7.2
11	Denmark	11.9	23	United States	6.2
12	United Kingdom	11.2	24	Japan	5.2

Source: Gaston V. Rimlinger, *Welfare Policy and Industrialization in Europe, America, and Russia* (New York: John Wiley & Sons, Inc., 1971), p. 333. Data from International Labour Organization, *The Cost of Social Security, 1960–1963* (preliminary), reported in Walter Galenson, "Social Security and Economic Development," *Industrial and Labor Relations Review*, 21 (July 1968): 568–69.

Also see Neil Gilbert and Harry Specht, *Dimensions of Social Welfare Policy* (Englewood Cliffs, N. J.: Prentice-Hall, Inc., 1974), pp. 2–4; Robert Pruger and Leonard Miller, *Income Maintenance Programs*, Module 23 (New York: MSS Modular Publications, Inc., 1974), pp. 1–38; U.S. Department of Health, Education, and Welfare, *Social Security Programs throughout the World, 1971*, Research Report No. 40 (Washington, D.C.: U.S. Government Printing Office, 1971).

2. Gaston V. Rimlinger, *Welfare Policy and Industrialization in Europe, America, and Russia* (New York: John Wiley & Sons, Inc., 1971), pp. 193–244; Ida C. Merriam and Alfred M. Skolnik, *Social Welfare Expenditures under Public Programs in the United States,*

1929–66 (Washington, D.C.: U.S. Government Printing Office, 1968); Social Security Administration, *Social Security Programs in the United States* (Washington, D.C.: U.S. Government Printing Office, 1968); and Alfred M. Skolnik and Sophie R. Dales, "Social Welfare Expenditures, Fiscal Year 1974," *Social Security Bulletin,* 38 (January 1975): 4–18.

3. Skolnik and Dales, "Social Welfare Expenditures."

4. See Howard Goldstein, *Social Work Practice: A Unitary Approach* (Columbia: University of South Carolina Press, 1973), pp. 20–55, and Reading 15, Harriet Bartlett, "Early Trends."

5. Abraham Flexner, "Is Social Work a Profession?" *Proceedings of the National Conference of Charities and Corrections* (Chicago, 1915), pp. 576–90.

6. *Colleges and Universities with Approved Undergraduate Social Work Programs, and Graduate Schools of Social Work* (New York: Council on Social Work Education, 1973). Professional journals for social work and social welfare include: *Social Work, Social Service Review, Social Work Today* (British), *Journal of Social Policy* (British), and *Journal of Education for Social Work.*

7. "Income" and "services" is a shorthand expression of the types of social provision allocated through social welfare arrangements. For a more detailed analysis of social provisions see Neil Gilbert and Harry Specht, *Dimensions of Social Welfare Policy* (Englewood Cliffs, N.J.: Prentice-Hall, Inc., 1974), pp. 81–102.

8. Development of a unitary method of social work practice is discussed in Reading 24, Allen Pincus and Anne Minahan, "Toward a Model for Teaching a Basic First-Year Course in Methods of Social Work Practice."

9. Lewis Coser, *The Functions of Social Conflict* (New York: Free Press, 1956), p. 17.

Part I

SOCIAL WELFARE

Chapter One

EMERGENCE OF THE INSTITUTION

The origin of social welfare in Western society has many roots, some of which extend far back to the religious teachings of the ancient Christians and Jews, which stressed compassion and charity for the poor. However, it is in the transition from preindustrial to industrial society that the main root from which contemporary social welfare arrangements have grown can be found. The institution of social welfare, as we know it today, emerged out of society's varied efforts to cope with changes in economic and social relationships fostered by the breakdown of feudalism, the Reformation, and the emergence of a capitalist orientation by the end of the Middle Ages. This was a tumultuous period during which traditional forms of social relationships and values were overwhelmed by the forces of change. In the process they were transformed to accommodate to the reality of social existence in an industrial society.

What was this reality? Social theorists of the 19th century distinguished many elements in the transformation of community life that marked the shift from preindustrial to industrial society. The French sociologist Émile Durkheim analyzed the change in the basis of social cohesion, which he described as moving from mechanical solidarity to organic solidarity. In a peasant community the integration of the individual—his sense of being a part of the whole—

derived from the likeness that was all about him in work, values, and beliefs. This likeness was reinforced by tradition and produced a form of mechanical solidarity described by Durkheim as follows:

> The social molecules which can be coherent in this way can act together only in the measure that they have no actions of their own, as the molecules of inorganic bodies. That is why we propose to call this type of solidarity mechanical. The term does not signify it is produced by mechanical and artificial means. We call it that only by analogy to the cohesion which unites the elements of an inanimate body, as opposed to that which makes a unity out of the elements of a living body.[1]

As the division of labor necessary to perform industrial tasks increased, a new form of social cohesion emerged which was based upon the interdependence of people. The sense of social solidarity that came from likeness was replaced by what Durkheim referred to as organic solidarity. Community life became highly diversified, like an organism with numerous units performing different functions, all of which are required to keep the system in working order.

The German sociologist Ferdinand Tönnies sought to capture the essence of the transformation of community life by analyzing this phenomenon in terms of what has become a classic typology: Gemeinschaft and Gesellschaft. These polar ideal types are logical constructs which attempt to extract the core elements of the phenomena under investigation. Gemeinschaft reflects elements of the social system of peasant or tribal communities, and Gesellschaft the corresponding elements in urban communities. Some of the characteristics of these community types are summarized in Table 1.

According to Tönnies, Gemeinschaft social relationships are based

TABLE 1
Characteristics of Tribal and Urban Communities

	Gemeinschaft	Gesellschaft
Social structure	Simple	Complex
Relationships	Private—Family	Public—Strangers
Self-expression	Conformity	Individualism
Social control	Religion—Custom	Law
Ownership	Communal	Private property
Will to associate (basis of human relationships)	Natural (relationships are ends in themselves)	Rational (relationships are means to ends)
Payment for service	Usage of land and commodities	Money

upon the idea of a natural distribution which determines and is in turn supported by a sacred sense of tradition. Thus:

> The relationship between community and feudal lords, and more especially that between the community and its members, is based not upon contracts, but upon understanding, like that within the family. The village community, even where it encompasses also the feudal lord, is like one individual household in its necessary relationship to the land.[2]

As the feudal society began to crumble, so did the "individual household," and with it went the stability and security it had provided for its members. While imposing a strong order of constraint on individual freedom, feudalism offered a form of social insurance against unemployment, disaster, old age, and other exigencies of life. With its collapse, individual freedom increased, along with uncertainty and hardship. New social arrangements were required to mitigate these hardships, to reduce uncertainty, and to stabilize community life. It is in this context that the institution of social welfare emerged.

The readings in this chapter describe the early types of social arrangements devised to deal with the problems of economic insecurity and social control that resulted from a declining feudal economy and a rising capitalist state. The beginning of social welfare as we know it today can be traced to the development of the English Poor Law of 1601.[3] English poor law embodied the conflicting strains between the desire to reinforce the feudal structure and the increasing assumption by government of responsibility for the poor. The various statutes that were codified in the Poor Law of 1601 amounted to more than government relief to substitute for the system of mutual support that had been provided under feudal custom. The law also served as a mechanism for social control by requiring registration of need, distinguishing between the impotent and the nonimpotent poor, and securing work for those strong enough to be in the labor force. To a lesser degree, the poor laws also served a socialization function by authorizing local officials to assume responsibility for apprenticing the children of the poor so they might become industrious, self-supporting citizens. However, as a cornerstone of the modern institution of social welfare, the most prominent feature of Elizabethan poor law was its endorsement of the principle of public obligation for the economic well-being of the people.

A number of statutes followed the Poor Law of 1601. Some were repressive measures, such as those embodied in the Law of Settlement of 1662, which buttressed the Act of 1531 in restricting the movement of the poor from their parishes. Another such measure provided for establishment of the workhouse in 1772, the wretched conditions of which were considered both a necessary discipline for the poor and a deterrent to the choice of public relief by the able-bodied. Other statutes were positive efforts to deal with relief for the poor, such as the Gilbert Act of 1782, which sought to provide assistance to the able-bodied poor in their own homes and to mitigate the demoralizing effects of the workhouse system. One of the pivotal experiments in relief tried during this period (and certainly the most absorbing one) was the well-intentioned effort to provide a guaranteed minimum wage. This effort and its consequences are analyzed by Karl Polyani in Reading 1, "Speenhamland, 1795," which is an excellent introductory analytic perspective on social welfare. Polyani shows how the unintended but nonetheless devasting effects of Speenhamland prepared the way for the Poor Law Reform of 1834, under which public responsibility for the able-bodied poor was considerably diminished and extremely harsh conditions were imposed upon those who sought public relief. With the Industrial Revolution almost completed, public protection against economic risk was at its nadir, and the able-bodied were left to fend for themselves in the open marketplace.

Reading 2, "The Changing Balance of Status and Contract in Assistance Policy," by Samuel Mencher, provides an overview of the development of assistance policy from the preindustrial poor laws through contemporary arrangements for social security. Mencher's framework for examining assistance policies in the light of the changing social relationships that marked the transition from the feudal period to modern times draws attention to three elements: (1) the growth of contractual relationships which culminated in the Poor Law Reform of 1834, (2) the rise of new status relationships reflected in relief policy toward the end of the 19th century, and (3) the mixture of status and contract relationships characteristic of government responsibility for relief in the capitalist welfare state.

While the institution of social welfare is composed primarily of programs under public auspices, voluntary or private efforts account for a substantial proportion of social welfare activities. Public programs in the United States evolved more slowly than those in England, leaving the voluntary sector in this country with an important role in carrying out welfare functions. The voluntary sector developed out of two streams of activity that often intermixed: philanthropic endeavors of the upper classes, and self-help efforts at the grass roots. The latter approach is described in Reading 3, "In Fellow Feeling," by Oscar Handlin. Handlin offers a penetrating account of the experience of immigrants who came to the United States in the 19th century and adjusted to urban life in a foreign land. One of these adjustments involved the creation of new social arrangements among the immigrants as they banded together for mutual protection and assistance in coping with the uncertainties of a strange and unstable environment. The formation of these voluntary associations is one of the unique and stirring features of the emergence of social welfare in the United States.

NOTES

1. Émile Durkheim, *The Division of Labor in Society,* trans. George Simpson (New York: Free Press, paperback ed., 1965), p. 130.
2. Ferdinand Tönnies, *Community and Society (Gemeinschaft and Gesellschaft),* trans. and ed. Charles Loomis (New York: Harper Torchbooks, 1963), p. 59.
3. Karl de Schweinitz, *England's Road to Social Security* (Philadelphia: University of Pennsylvania Press, 1961), pp. 20–29.

1   Speenhamland, 1795

KARL POLANYI

Eighteenth century society unconsciously resisted any attempt at making it a mere appendage of the market. No market economy was conceivable that did not include a market for labor; but to establish such a market, especially in England's rural civilization, implied no less than the wholesale destruction of the traditional fabric of society. During the most active period of the Industrial Revolution, from 1795 to 1834, the creating of a labor market in England was prevented through the Speenhamland Law.

The market for labor was, in effect, the last of the markets to be organized under the new industrial system, and this final step was taken only when market economy was set to start, and when the absence of a market for labor was proving a greater evil even to the common people themselves than the calamities that were to accompany its introduction. In the end the free labor market, in spite of the inhuman methods employed in creating it, proved financially beneficial to all concerned.

Yet it was only now that the crucial problem appeared. The economic advantages of a free labor market could not make up for the social destruction wrought by it. Regulation of a new type had to be introduced under which labor was again protected, only this time from the working of the market mechanism itself. Though the new protective institutions, such as trade unions and factory laws, were adapted, as far as possible, to the requirements of the economic mechanism, they nevertheless interfered with its self-regulation and, ultimately, destroyed the system.

In the broad logic of this development the Speenhamland Law occupied a strategic position.

In England both land and money were mobilized before labor was. The latter was prevented from forming a national market by strict legal restrictions on its physical mobility, since the laborer was practically bound to his parish. The Act of Settlement of 1662, which laid down the rules of so-called parish serfdom, was loosened only in 1795. This step would have made possible the setting up of a national labor market had not in the very same year the Speenhamland Law or "allowance system" been introduced. The tendency of this law was to the opposite; namely, towards a powerful reinforcement of the paternalistic system of labor organization as inherited from the Tudors and Stuarts. The justices of Berkshire, meeting at the Pelikan Inn, in Speenhamland, near Newbury, on May 6, 1795, in a time of great distress, decided that subsidies in aid of wages should be granted in accordance with a scale dependent upon the price of bread, so that a minimum income should be assured to the poor *irrespective of their earnings*. The magistrates' famous recommendation ran: When the gallon loaf of bread of definite quality "shall cost 1 shilling, then every poor and industrious person shall have for his support 3 shillings weekly, either procured by his own or his family's labor, *or an allowance from the poor rates*, and for the support of his wife and every other of his family, 1 shilling, 6 pence; when the gallon loaf shall cost 1/6, then 4 shillings weekly, plus 1/10; on every pence which the bread price raises above 1 shilling he shall have 3 pence for himself and 1 pence for the others." The figures varied somewhat in various counties, but in most cases the Speenhamland *scale* was adopted. This was meant as an emergency measure, and was informally introduced. Although commonly called a law, *the scale itself was never enacted.* Yet very soon it became the law of the land over most' of the countryside, and later even in a number of manufacturing districts; actually it introduced no less a social and economic innovation than the "right to live," and until abolished in 1834, it effectively prevented the establishment of a competitive labor market. Two years earlier, in 1832, the middle class had forced its way to power, partly in order to remove this obstacle to the new capitalistic economy. Indeed, nothing could be more obvious than that the wage system imperatively demanded the withdrawal of the "right to live" as proclaimed in Speenhamland—under the new regime of the economic man, nobody would work for a wage if he could make a living by doing nothing.

Another feature of the reversal of the Speenhamland method was less obvious to most nineteenth century writers, namely, that the wage system had to be made universal in the interest also of the wage earners themselves, even though this meant depriving them of their legal claim to subsistence. The "right to live" had proved a deathtrap.

The paradox was merely apparent. Allegedly, Speenhamland meant that the Poor Law was to be administered liberally—actually, it was turned into the opposite of its original intent. Under Elizabethan Law the poor were forced to work at whatever wages they could get and only those who could obtain no work were entitled to relief; relief in *aid of wages* was neither intended nor given. Under the Speenhamland Law a man was relieved even if he was in employment, as long as his wages amounted to less than the family income granted to him by the scale. Hence, no laborer had any material interest in satisfying his employer, his income being the same whatever wages he earned; this was different only in case standard wages, *i.e.*, the wages actually paid, exceeded the scale, an occurrence which was not the rule in the countryside since the employer could obtain labor at almost any wages; however little he paid, the subsidy from the rates brought the workers' income up to scale. Within a few years the productivity of labor began to sink to that of pauper labor, thus providing an added reason for employers not to raise wages above the scale. For, once the intensity of labor, the care and efficiency with which it was performed, dropped below a definite level, it became indistinguishable from "boondoggling" or the semblance of work maintained for the sake of appearances. Though in principle work was still enforced, in practice outdoor relief became general and even when relief was administered in the poorhouse the enforced occupation of the inmates now hardly deserved the name of work. This amounted to the abandonment of Tudor legislation not for the sake of less but of more paternalism. The extension of outdoor relief, the introduction of aid-in-wages supplemented by separate allowances for wife and children, each item rising and falling with the bread price, meant a dramatic re-entry in regard to labor of that same regulative principle that was being rapidly eliminated in regard to industrial life as a whole.

No measure was ever more universally popular.[1] Parents were free of the care of their children, and children were no more dependent upon parents; employers could reduce wages at will and laborers were safe from hunger whether they were busy or slack; humanitarians applauded the measure as an act of mercy even though not of justice and the selfish gladly consoled themselves with the thought that though it was merciful at least it was not liberal; and even ratepayers were slow to realize what would happen to the rates under a system which proclaimed the "right to live" whether a man earned a living wage or not.

In the long run the result was ghastly. Although it took some time till the self-respect of the common man sank to the low point where he preferred poor relief to wages, his wages which were subsidized from public funds were bound eventually to be bottomless, and to force him upon the rates. Little by little the people of the countryside were pauperized; the adage, "once on the rates, always on the rates" was a true saying. But for the protracted effects of the allowance system, it would be impossible to explain the human and social degradation of early capitalism.

The Speenhamland episode revealed to the people of the leading country of the century the true nature of the social adventure on which they were embarking. Neither the rulers nor the ruled ever forgot the lessons of that fool's paradise; if the Reform Bill of 1832 and the Poor Law Amendment of 1834 were commonly regarded as the starting point of modern capitalism, it was because they put an end to the rule of the benevolent landlord and his allowance system. The attempt to create a capitalistic order without a labor market had failed disastrously. The laws governing such an order had asserted themselves, and manifested their radical antagonism to the principle of paternalism. The rigor of these laws had become apparent and their violation had been cruelly visited upon those who had disobeyed them.

Under Speenhamland society was rent by two opposing influences, the one emanating from paternalism and protecting labor from the dangers of the market system; the other organizing the elements of production, including land, under a market system, and thus divesting the common people of their former status, compelling them to gain a living by offering their labor for sale, while at the same time depriving their labor of its market value. A new class of employers was being created, but no corresponding class of employees could constitute itself. A new gigantic wave of enclosures was mobilizing the land and producing a rural proletariat, while the "maladministration of the Poor Law" precluded them from gaining a living by their labor. No wonder that the contemporaries were appalled at the seeming contradiction of an almost miraculous increase in production accompanied by a near starvation of the masses. By 1834, there was a general conviction—with many thinking people a passionately held conviction—that anything was preferable to the continuance of Speenhamland. Either machines had to be demolished, as the Luddites had tried to do, or a regular labor market had to be created. Thus was mankind forced into the paths of a utopian experiment.

This is not the place to expatiate upon the economics of Speenhamland; there will be occasion for that later on. On the face of it the "right to live" should have stopped wage labor altogether. Standard wages should have gradually dropped to zero, thus putting the actual wage bill wholly on the parish, a procedure which would have made the absurdity of the arrangement manifest. But this was an essentially precapitalistic age, when the common people were still traditionally minded, and far from being directed in their behavior by monetary motives alone. The great majority of the countryfolk were occupier-owners or lifeholders, who preferred any kind of existence to the status of pauper, even if it was not deliberately burdened by irksome or ignominious disabilities, as subsequently happened. If laborers had been free to combine for the furtherance of their interests, the allowance system might, of course, have had a contrary effect on standard wages: for trade union action would have been greatly helped by the relief of the unemployed implied in so liberal an administration of the Poor

Law. That was presumably one of the reasons for the unjust Anti-Combination Laws of 1799–1800, which would be otherwise hardly explicable since the Berkshire magistrates and members of Parliament were both, on the whole, concerned about the economic condition of the poor, and after 1797 political unrest had subsided. Indeed, it might be argued that the paternalistic intervention of Speenhamland called forth the Anti-Combination Laws, a further intervention, but for which Speenhamland might have had the effect of raising wages instead of depressing them as it actually did. In conjunction with the Anti-Combination Laws, which were not revoked for another quarter century, Speenhamland led to the ironical result that the financially implemented "right to live" eventually ruined the people whom it was ostensibly designed to succor.

To later generations nothing could have been more patent than the mutual incompatibility of institutions like the wage system and the "right to live," or, in other words, than the impossibility of a functioning capitalistic order as long as wages were subsidized from public funds. But the contemporaries did not comprehend the order for which they were preparing the way. Only when a grave deterioration of the productive capacity of the masses resulted—a veritable national calamity which was obstructing the progress of machine civilization—did the necessity of abolishing the unconditional right of the poor to relief impose itself upon the consciousness of the community. The complicated economics of Speenhamland transcended the comprehension of even the most expert observers of the time; but the conclusion appeared only the more compelling that aid-in-wages must be inherently vicious, since it miraculously injured even those who received it.

The pitfalls of the market system were not readily apparent. To realize this clearly we must distinguish between the various vicissitudes to which the laboring people were exposed in England since the coming of the machine: first, those of the Speenhamland period, 1795 to 1834; second, the hardships caused by the Poor Law Reform, in the decade following 1834; third, the deleterious effects of a competitive labor market after 1834, until in the 1870's the recognition of the trade unions offered sufficient protection. Chronologically, Speenhamland antedated market economy; the decade of the Poor Law Reform Act was a transition to that economy. The last period—overlapping the former—was that of market economy proper.

The three periods differed sharply. Speenhamland was designed to prevent the proletarianization of the common people, or at least to slow it down. The outcome was merely the pauperization of the masses, who almost lost their human shape in the process.

The Poor Law Reform of 1834 did away with this obstruction to the labor market: the "right to live" was abolished. The scientific cruelty of that Act was so shocking to public sentiment in the 1830's and 1840's that the vehement contemporary protests blurred the picture in the eyes of posterity. Many of the most needy poor, it was true, were left to their fate as outdoor relief was withdrawn, and among those who suffered most bitterly were the "deserving poor" who were too proud to enter the workhouse which had become an abode of shame. Never perhaps in all modern history has a more ruthless act of social reform been perpetrated; it crushed multitudes of lives while merely pretending to provide a criterion of genuine destitution in the workhouse test. Psychological torture was coolly advocated and smoothly put into practice by mild philanthropists as a means of oiling the wheels of the labor mill. Yet the bulk of the complaints were really due to the abruptness with which an institution of old standing was uprooted and a radical transformation rushed into effect. Disraeli denounced this "inconceivable revolution" in the lives of the people. However, if money incomes alone had counted, the condition of the people would have soon been deemed improved.

The problems of the third period went incomparably deeper. The bureaucratic atrocities committed against the poor during the decade following 1834 by the new centralized Poor Law authorities were merely sporadic and as nothing compared to the all-round effects of that most potent of all modern institutions, the labor market. It was similar in scope to the threat Speenhamland offered, with the significant difference that not the absence but the presence of a competitive labor market was now the source of danger. If Speenhamland had prevented the emergence of a working class, now the laboring poor were being formed into such a class by the pressure of an unfeeling mechanism. If under Speenhamland the people had been taken care of as none too precious beasts deserved to be, now they were expected to take care of themselves, with all the odds against them. If Speenhamland meant the snug misery of degradation, now the laboring man was homeless in society. If Speenhamland had overworked the values of neighborhood, family, and rural surroundings, now man was detached from home and kin, torn from his roots and all meaningful environment. In short, if Speenhamland meant the rot of immobility, now the peril was that of death through exposure.

Not until 1834 was a competitive labor market established in England; hence, industrial capitalism as a social system cannot be said to have existed before that date. Yet almost immediately the self-protection of society set in: factory laws and social legislation, and a political and industrial working class movement sprang into being. It was in this attempt to stave off the entirely new dangers of the market mechanism that protective action conflicted fatally with the self-regulation of the system. It is no exaggeration to say that the social history of the nineteenth century was determined by the logic of the market system proper after it was released by the Poor Law Reform Act of 1834. The starting point of this dynamic was the Speenhamland Law.

If we suggest that the study of Speenhamland is the study of the birth of nineteenth century civilization, it is not its economic and social effect that we have exclusively in mind, nor even the determining influence of these effects upon modern political history, but the fact that, mostly unknown to the present generation, our social consciousness was cast in its mold. The figure of the pauper, almost forgotten since, dominated a discussion the imprint of which was as powerful as that of the most spectacular events in history. If the French Revolution was indebted to the thought of Voltaire and Diderot, Quesnay and Rousseau, the Poor Law discussion formed the minds of Bentham and Burke, Godwin and Malthus, Ricardo and Marx, Robert Owen and John Stuart Mill, Darwin and Spencer, who shared with the French Revolution the spiritual parentage of nineteenth century civilization. It was in the decades following Speenhamland and the Poor Law Reform that the mind of man turned towards his own community with a new anguish of concern: the revolution which the justices of Berkshire had vainly attempted to stem and which the Poor Law Reform eventually freed shifted the vision of men towards their own collective being as if they had overlooked its presence before. A world was uncovered the very existence of which had not been suspected, that of the laws governing a complex society. Although the emergence of society in this new and distinctive sense happened in the economic field, its reference was universal.

The form in which the nascent reality came to our consciousness was political economy. Its amazing regularities and stunning contradictions had to be fitted into the scheme of philosophy and theology in order to be assimilated to human meanings. The stubborn facts and the inexorable brute laws that appeared to abolish our freedom had in one way or another to be reconciled to freedom. This was the mainspring of the metaphysical forces that secretly sustained the positivists and utilitarians. Unbounded hope and limitless despair looking towards unexplored regions of human possibilities were the mind's ambivalent response to these awful limitations. Hope—the vision of perfectibility—was distilled out of the nightmare of population and wage laws, and was embodied in a concept of progress so inspiring that it appeared to justify the vast and painful dislocations to come. Despair was to prove an even more powerful agent of transformation.

Man was forced to resign himself to secular perdition: he was. doomed either to stop the procreation of his race or to condemn himself wittingly to liquidation through war and pestilence, hunger and vice. Poverty was nature surviving in society; that the limitedness of food and the unlimitedness of men had come to an issue just when the promise of a boundless increase of wealth burst in upon us made the irony only the more bitter.

Thus was the discovery of society integrated with man's spiritual universe; but how was this new reality, society, to be translated into terms of life? As guides to practice the moral principles of harmony and conflict were strained to the utmost, and forced into a pattern of all but complete contradiction. Harmony was inherent in economy, it was said, the interests of the individual and the community being ultimately identical—but such harmonious self-regulation required that the individual respect economic law even if it happened to destroy him. Conflict, also, seemed inherent in economy, whether as competition of individuals or as struggle of classes—but such conflict, again, might turn out to be only the vehicle of a deeper harmony immanent in present, or perhaps future, society.

Pauperism, political economy, and the discovery of society were closely interwoven. Pauperism fixed attention on the incomprehensible fact that poverty seemed to go with plenty. Yet this was only the first of the baffling paradoxes with which industrial society was to confront modern man. He had entered his new abode through the door of economics, and this adventitious circumstance invested the age with its materialist aura. To Ricardo and Malthus nothing seemed more real than material goods. The laws of the market meant for them the limit of human possibilities. Godwin believed in unlimited possibilities and hence had to deny the laws of the market. That human possibilities were limited, not by the laws of the market, but by those of society itself was a recognition reserved to Owen who alone discerned behind the veil of market economy the emergent reality: society. However, his vision was lost again for a century.

Meanwhile, it was in relation to the problem of poverty that people began to explore the meaning of life in a complex society. The induction of political economy into the realm of the universal happened in two opposite perspectives, that of progress and perfectibility on the one hand, determinism and damnation on the other; its translation into practice was also achieved in two opposite ways, through the principle of harmony and self-regulation on the one hand, competition and conflict on the other. Economic liberalism and the class concept were preformed in these contradictions. With the finality of an elemental event, a new set of ideas entered our consciousness.

ANTECEDENTS AND CONSEQUENCES

The Speenhamland system was originally no more than a makeshift. Yet few institutions have shaped the fate of a whole civilization more decisively than this, which had to be discarded before the new era could begin. It was the typical product of an age of transformation and deserves the attention of any student of human affairs today.

Under the mercantile system the labor organization of England rested on the Poor Law and the Statute of Artificers. Poor Law, as applied to the laws of 1536 to 1601, is admittedly a misnomer; actually these laws, and subsequent amendments, formed half of the labor code of England; the other half consisted of the Statute of Artificers of 1563. The latter dealt with the employed; the Poor Law, with what we would call the unemployed and unemployable (apart from the aged and children). To these measures were added later, as we saw, the Act of Settlement of 1662 concerning the legal abode of the people which restricted their mobility to the utmost. (The neat distinction between employed, unemployed, and unemployable is, of course, anachronistic since it implies the existence of a modern wage system which was absent for another 250 years or so; we use these terms for the sake of simplicity in this very broad presentation.)

Labor organization, according to the Statute of Artificers, rested on three pillars: enforcement of labor, seven years' apprenticeship, and yearly wage assessments by public officials. The law—this should be emphasized—applied to agricultural laborers as much as to artisans, and was enforced in rural districts as well as in towns. For about eighty years the Statute was strictly executed; later the apprenticeship clauses fell partly into desuetude, being restricted to the traditional crafts; to the new industries like cotton they simply did not apply; yearly wage assessments, based on the cost of living, also were in abeyance in a large part of the country after the Restoration (1660). Formally, the assessment clauses of the Statute were repealed only in 1813, the wage clauses in 1814. However, in many respects the apprenticeship rule survived the Statute; it is still the general practice in the skilled trades in England. The enforcement of labor in the countryside was discontinued little by little. Still it can be said that for the two and a half centuries in question the Statute of Artificers laid down the outlines of a national organization of labor based on the principles of regulation and paternalism.

The Statute of Artificers was thus supplemented by the Poor Laws, a most confusing term in modern ears, to which "poor" and "pauper" sound much alike. Actually, the gentlemen of England judged all persons poor who did not command an income sufficient to keep them in leisure. "Poor" was thus practically synonymous with "common people," and the common people comprised all but the landed classes (hardly any successful merchant failed to acquire landed property). Hence the term "poor" meant all people who were in need and all the people, if and when they were in need. This, of course, included paupers, but not them alone. The aged, the infirm, the orphans had to be taken care of in a society which claimed that within its confines there was a place for every Christian. But over and above, there were the able-bodied poor, whom we would call the unemployed, on the assumption that they could earn their living by manual work if only they could find employment. Beggary was severely punished; vagrancy, in case of repetition, was a capital offense. The Poor Law of 1601 decreed that the able-bodied poor should be put to work so as to earn their keep, which the parish was to supply; the burden of relief was put squarely on the parish, which was empowered to raise the necessary sums by local taxes or rates. These were to be levied upon all householders and tenants, rich and nonrich alike, according to the rental of the land or houses they occupied.

The Statute of Artificers and the Poor Law together provided what

might be called a Code of Labor. However, the Poor Law was administered locally; every parish—a tiny unit—had its own provisions
for setting the able-bodied to work; for maintaining a poorhouse;
for apprenticing orphans and destitute children; for caring for the
aged and the infirm; for the burial of paupers; and every parish had
its own scale of rates. All this sounds grander than it often was;
many parishes had no poorhouses; a great many more had no
reasonable provisions for the useful occupation of the able-bodied;
there was an endless variety of ways in which the sluggardliness of
the local rate-payers, the indifference of the overseers of the poor,
the callousness of the interests centering on pauperism vitiated the
working of the law. Still, by and large, the nearly sixteen thousand
Poor Law authorities of the country managed to keep the social
fabric of village life unbroken and undamaged.

Yet under a national system of labor, the local organization of
unemployment and poor relief was a patent anomaly. The greater
the variety of local provisions for the poor, the greater the danger
to the well-kept parish that it would be swamped by the professional pauper. After the Restoration the Act of Settlement and
Removal was passed to protect the "better" parishes from the in-
flux of paupers. More than a century later, Adam Smith inveighed
against this Act because it immobilized the people, and thus prevented them from finding useful employment as it prevented the
capitalist from finding employees. Only with the good will of the
local magistrate and the parish authorities could a man stay in any
other but his home parish; everywhere else he was liable to expul-
sion even though in good standing and employed. The legal status
of the people was therefore that of freedom and equality subject
to incisive limitations. They were equal before the law, and free as
to their persons. But they were not free to choose their occupations
or those of their children; they were not free to settle where they
pleased; and they were forced to labor. The two great Elizabethan
Statutes and the Act of Settlement together were a charter of liberty
to the common people as well as a seal of their disabilities.

The Industrial Revolution was well on the way, when in 1795,
under the pressure of the needs of industry, the Act of 1662 was
partially repealed, parish serfdom was abolished, and the physical
mobility of the laborer was restored. A labor market could now be
established on a national scale. But in the very same year, as we
know, a practice of Poor Law administration was introduced which
meant the reversal of the Elizabethan principle of enforced labor.
Speenhamland ensured the "right to live"; grants in aid-of-wages

were made general; family allowances were superadded; and all this was to be given in outdoor relief, *i.e.*, without committing the recipient to the workhouse. Although the scale of relief was exiguous, it was enough for bare subsistence. This was a return to regulationism and paternalism with a vengeance just when, it would seem, the steam engine was clamoring for freedom and the machines were crying out for human hands. Yet the Speenhamland Law coincided in time with the withdrawal of the Act of Settlement. The contradiction was patent: the Act of Settlement was being repealed because the Industrial Revolution demanded a national supply of laborers who would offer to work for wages, while Speenhamland proclaimed the principle that no man need fear to starve and that the parish would keep him and his family however little he earned. There was stark contradiction between the two industrial policies; what else but a social enormity could be expected from their simultaneous continued application?

But the generation of Speenhamland was unconscious of what was on its way. On the eve of the greatest industrial revolution in history, no signs and portents were forthcoming. Capitalism arrived unannounced. No one had forecast the development of a machine industry; it came as a complete surprise. For some time England had been actually expecting a permanent recession of foreign trade when the dam burst, and the old world was swept away in one indomitable surge towards a planetary economy.

However, not until the 1850's could anybody have said so with assurance. The key to the comprehension of the Speenhamland magistrates' recommendation lay in their ignorance of the wider implications of the development they were facing. In the retrospect it may seem as if they had not only attempted the impossible, but had done so by means the inner contradictions of which should have been apparent at the time. Actually, they were successful in achieving their aim of protecting the village against dislocation, while the effects of their policy were all the more disastrous in other, unforeseen directions. Speenhamland policy was the outcome of a definite phase in the development of a market for labor power and should be understood in the light of the views taken of that situation by those in the position to shape policy. From this angle the allowance system will appear as a device contrived by squirearchy to meet a situation in which physical mobility could no longer be denied to labor, while the squire wished to avoid such unsettlement of local conditions, including higher wages, as was involved in the acceptance of a free national labor market.

The dynamic of Speenhamland was thus rooted in the circumstances of its origin. The rise in rural pauperism was the first symptom of the impending upheaval. Yet nobody seemed to have thought so at the time. The connection between rural poverty and the impact of world trade was anything but obvious. Contemporaries had no reason to link the number of the village poor with the development of commerce in the Seven Seas. The inexplicable increase in the number of the poor was almost generally put down to the method of Poor Law administration, and not without some good cause. Actually, beneath the surface, the ominous growth of rural pauperism was directly linked with the trend of general economic history. But this connection was still hardly perceptible. Scores of writers probed into the channels by which the poor trickled into the village, and the number as well as the variety of reasons adduced for their appearance was amazing. And yet only a few contemporary writers pointed to those symptoms of the dislocations which we are used to connect with the Industrial Revolution. Up to 1785 the English public was unaware of any major change in economic life, except for a fitful increase of trade and the growth of pauperism.

Where do the poor come from? was the question raised by a bevy of pamphlets which grew thicker with the advancing century. The causes of pauperism and the means of combating it could hardly be expected to be kept apart in a literature which was inspired by the conviction that if only the most apparent evils of pauperism could be sufficiently alleviated it would cease to exist altogether. On one point there appears to have been general agreement, namely, on the great variety of causes that accounted for the fact of the increase. Amongst them were scarcity of grain; too high agricultural wages, causing high food prices; too low agricultural wages; too high urban wages; irregularity of urban employment; disappearance of the yeomanry; ineptitude of the urban worker for rural occupations; reluctance of the farmers to pay higher wages; the landlords' fear that rents would have to be reduced if higher wages were paid; failure of the workhouse to compete with machinery; want of domestic economy; incommodious habitations; bigoted diets; drug habits. Some writers blamed a new type of large sheep; others, horses which should be replaced by oxen; still others urged the keeping of fewer dogs. Some writers believed that the poor should eat less, or no, bread, while others thought that even feeding on the "best bread should not be charged against them." Tea impaired the health of many poor, it was thought, while "home-

brewed beer" would restore it; those who felt most strongly on this
score insisted that tea was no better than the cheapest dram. Forty
years later Harriet Martineau still believed in preaching the advantages of dropping the tea habit for the sake of relieving pauperism.[2] True, many writers complained of the unsettling effects of enclosures; a number of others insisted on the damage done to rural
employment by the ups and downs of manufacturers. Yet on the
whole, the impression prevails that pauperism was regarded as a
phenomenon *sui generis*, a social disease which was caused by a
variety of reasons, most of which became active only through the
failure of the Poor Law to apply the right remedy.

The true answer almost certainly was that the aggravation of
pauperism and the higher rates were due to an increase in what we
would today call invisible unemployment. Such a fact would not be
obvious at a time when even employment was, as a rule, invisible,
as it necessarily was up to a point under cottage industry. Still
there remain these questions: how to account for this increase in
the number of the unemployed and underemployed? and why did
the signs of imminent changes in industry escape the notice even
of observant contemporaries?

The explanation lies primarily in the excessive fluctuations of
trade in early times which tended to cover up the absolute increase
in trade. While the latter accounted for the rise in employment, the
fluctuations accounted for the much bigger rise in unemployment.
But while the increase in the general level of employment was slow,
the increase in unemployment and underemployment would tend
to be fast. Thus the building up of what Friedrich Engels called the
industrial reserve army outweighed by much the creation of the
industrial army proper.

This had the important consequence that the connection between
unemployment and the rise of total trade could be easily overlooked. While it was often remarked that the rise in unemployment
was due to the great fluctuations in trade, it escaped notice that
these fluctuations formed part of an underlying process of even
greater amplitude, namely, a general growth of commerce increasingly based on manufactures. For the contemporaries, there
seemed to be no connection between the mainly urban manu-
factories and the great increase of the poor in the countryside.

The increase in the aggregate of trade naturally swelled the
volume of employment while territorial division of labor combined
with sharp fluctuations of trade was responsible for the severe dislocation of both village and town occupations, which resulted in

the rapid growth of unemployment. The distant rumor of large wages made the poor dissatisfied with those which agriculture could afford, and it created a dislike for that labor as poorly recompensed. The industrial regions of that age resembled a new country, like another America, attracting immigrants by the thousands. Migration is usually accompanied by a very considerable remigration. That such a reflux towards the village must have taken place seems to find support also in the fact that no absolute decrease of the rural population was noted. Thus a cumulative unsettling of the population was proceeding as different groups were drawn for varying periods into the sphere of commercial and manufactural employment, and then left to drift back to their original rural habitat.

Much of the social damage done to England's countryside sprang at first from the dislocating effects of trade directly upon the countryside itself. The Revolution in Agriculture definitely antedated the Industrial Revolution. Both enclosures of the common and consolidations into compact holdings, which accompanied the new great advance in agricultural methods, had a powerfully unsettling effect. The war on cottages, the absorption of cottage gardens and grounds, the confiscation of rights in the common deprived cottage industry of its two mainstays: family earnings and agricultural background. As long as domestic industry was supplemented by the facilities and amenities of a garden plot, a scrap of land, or grazing rights, the dependence of the laborer on money earnings was not absolute; the potato plot or "stubbing geese," a cow or even an ass in the commons made all the difference; and family earnings acted as a kind of unemployment insurance. The rationalization of agriculture inevitably uprooted the laborer and undermined his social security.

On the urban scene the effects of the new scourge of fluctuating employment were, of course, manifest. Industry was generally regarded as a blind alley occupation. "Workmen who are today fully employed may be tomorrow in the streets begging for bread . . . ," wrote David Davies and added: "Uncertainty of labor conditions is the most vicious result of these new innovations." "When a Town employed in a Manufactory is deprived of it, the inhabitants are as it were struck with a palsy, and become instantly a rent-charge upon the Parish; but the mischief does not die with that generation . . ." For in the meantime division of labor wreaks its vengeance: the unemployed artisan returns in vain to his village for "the weaver can turn his hand to nothing." The fatal irreversibility of urbanization hinged upon this simple fact which Adam Smith foresaw when he described the industrial worker as intellectually the inferior of the poorest tiller of the soil, for the latter can usually take himself to any job. Still, up to the time Adam Smith published his *Wealth of Nations* pauperism was not increasing alarmingly.

In the next two decades the picture suddenly changed. In his *Thoughts & Details on Scarcity*, which Burke submitted to Pitt in 1795, the author admitted that in spite of the general progress there had been a "last bad cycle of twenty years." Indeed, in the decade following upon the Seven Years' War (1763) unemployment increased noticeably, as the rise in outdoor relief showed. It happened for the first time that a boom in trade was remarked to have been accompanied by signs of growing distress of the poor. This apparent contradiction was destined to become to the next generation of Western humanity the most perplexing of all the recurrent phenomena in social life. The specter of overpopulation was beginning to haunt people's minds. William Townsend warned in his *Dissertation on the Poor Laws*: "Speculation apart, it is a fact, that in England, we have more than we can feed, and many more than we can profitably employ under the present system of law." Adam Smith, in 1776, had been reflecting the mood of quiet progress. Townsend, writing only ten years later, was already conscious of a groundswell.

However, many things had to happen before (only five years later) a man as removed from politics, as successful, and as matter-of-fact as the Scotch bridgebuilder, Telford, could burst forth with the bitter complaint that little change is to be expected from the ordinary course of government, and that revolution was the only hope. A single copy of Paine's *Rights of Man* mailed by Telford to his home village caused a riot to break out there. Paris was catalyzing the European fermentation.

In Canning's conviction the Poor Law saved England from a revolution. He was primarily thinking of the 1790's and the French Wars. The new outburst of enclosures further depressed the standards of the poor in the countryside. J. H. Clapham, an apologist of these enclosures, conceded that the "coincidence of the area in which wages were most systematically augmented from the rates with the area of maximum recent enclosures is striking." In other words, but for aid-in-wages the poor would have sunk below the starvation level in wide areas of rural England. Rick burning was rampant. The Popgun Plot found wide credence. Rioting was frequent; rumors of rioting very much more so. In Hampshire—and not there alone—the Courts threatened death for any attempt at "forcibly lowering the price of commodities, either at market or on the road"; yet simultaneously, the magistrates of that same county urgently pressed for the general granting of subsidies to wages. Clearly, the time for preventive action had come.

But why, of all courses of action, was that one chosen which appeared later as the most impracticable of all? Let us consider the situation and the interests involved. Squire and parson ruled the village. Townsend summed up the situation by saying that the landed gentleman keeps manufactures "at a convenient distance" because "he considers that manufactures fluctuate; that the benefit which he is to derive from them will not bear proportion with the burthen which it must entail upon his property. . . ." The burden consisted mainly in two seemingly contradictory effects of manufactures, namely, the increase in pauperism and the rise in wages. But the two were contradictory only if the existence of a competitive labor market was assumed, which would, of course, have tended to diminish unemployment by reducing the wages of the employed. In the absence of such a market—and the Act of Settlement was still in force—pauperism and wages might rise simultaneously. Under such conditions the "social cost" of urban unemployment was mainly borne by the home village to which the out-of-work would often repair. High wages in the towns were a still greater burden on rural economy. Agricultural wages were more than the farmer could carry, though less than the laborer could subsist on. It seems clear that agriculture could not compete with town wages. On the other hand, there was general agreement that the Act of Settlement should be repealed, or at least loosened, so as to help labor to find employment and the employers to find laborers. This, it was felt, would increase the productivity of labor all around and, incidentally, diminish the real burden of wages. But the immediate question of the wage differential between town and village would obviously become even more pressing for the village by allowing wages to "find their own level." The flux and reflux of industrial employment alternating with spasms of unemployment would dislocate rural communities more than ever. A dam had to be erected to protect the village from the flood of rising wages. Methods had to be found which would protect the rural setting against social dislocation, reinforce traditional authority, prevent the draining off of rural labor, and raise agricultural wages without overburdening the farmer. Such a device was the Speenhamland Law. Shoved into the turbulent waters of the Industrial Revolution, it was bound to create an economic vortex. However, its social implications met squarely the situation, as it was judged by the ruling village interest —the squire's.

From the point of view of Poor Law administration Speenhamland was a grievously retrogressive step. The experience of 250 years had shown that the parish was too small a unit for Poor Law administration, since no treatment of this matter was adequate which failed to distinguish between the able-bodied unemployed on the one hand, the aged, infirm, and children on the other. It was as if a township today attempted to deal singlehanded with unemployment insurance, or as if such an insurance were mixed up with the care for the aged. Accordingly, only in those short periods, when the administration of the Poor Law was both *national* and *differentiated* could it be more or less satisfactory. Such a period was that from 1590 to 1640, under Burleigh and Laud, when the Crown handled the Poor Law through the justices of peace, and an ambitious scheme of erecting poorhouses, together with the enforcement of labor, was initiated. But the Commonwealth (1642–60) destroyed again what was now denounced as the personal rule of the Crown, and the Restoration, ironically enough, completed the work of the Commonwealth. The Act of Settlement of 1662 restricted the Poor Law to the parish basis, and legislation paid but scant attention to pauperism up to the third decade of the eighteenth century. In 1722, at last, efforts at differentiation set in; workhouses were to be built by unions of parishes, as distinct from local poorhouses; and occasional outdoor relief was permitted, as the workhouse would now provide a test of need. In 1782, with Gilbert's Act, a long step was taken to expand the units of administration by encouraging the setting up of parish unions; at that time it was urged that parishes find employment for the able-bodied in the neighborhood. Such a policy was to be supplemented by the granting of outdoor relief and even of aid-in-wages, in order to diminish the cost of relief to the able-bodied. Although the setting up of unions of parishes was permissive, not mandatory, it meant an advance toward the larger unit of administration and the differentiation of the various categories of the relieved poor. Thus in spite of the deficiencies of the system, Gilbert's Act represented an attempt in the right direction, and as long as outdoor relief and aid-in-wages were merely subsidiary to positive social legislation, they need not have been fatal to a rational solution. Speenhamland put a stop to reform. By making outdoor relief and aid-in-wages *general*, it did not (as has been falsely asserted) follow up the line of Gilbert's Act, but completely reversed its tendency and actually demolished the whole system of the Elizabethan Poor Law. The laboriously established distinction between workhouse and poorhouse became meaningless; the various categories of paupers and able-bodied unemployed now tended to fuse into one indiscriminate mass of dependent poverty. The opposite of a process of differentiation set in: the workhouse merged into the poorhouse, the poorhouse itself tended more and more to disappear; and the parish was again made the sole and final unit in this veritable masterpiece of institutional degeneration.

The supremacy of squire and parson was even enhanced in consequence of Speenhamland, if such a thing was at all possible. The "undistinguishing benevolence of power," of which the overseers of the poor complained, was at its best in that role of "Tory socialism" in which the justices of peace swayed the benevolent power, while the brunt of the rates was borne by the rural middle class. The bulk of yeomanry had long vanished in the vicissitudes of the Agricultural Revolution, and the remaining lifeholders and occupying-proprietors tended to merge with the cottagers and scrap-holders into one social stratum in the eyes of the potentate of the countryside. He did not too well distinguish between needy people, and people who happened to be in need; from the lofty heights from which he was watching the struggling life of the village there seemed to be no hard and fast line separating the poor from the destitute, and he may have been not unduly surprised to learn in a bad year that a small farmer was going "on the rates," after having been ruined by their disastrous level. Surely such cases were not frequent, but their very possibility emphasized the fact that many ratepayers were themselves poor. On the whole, the relationship of the ratepayer and the pauper was somewhat similar to that of the employed and the unemployed of our times under various schemes of insurance which make the employed bear the burden of keeping the temporarily unemployed. Still, the typical ratepayer was usually not eligible for poor relief, and the typical agricultural laborer paid no rates. Politically, the squire's pull with the village poor was strengthened by Speenhamland while that of the rural middle class was weakened.

The craziest aspect of the system was its economics proper. The question "Who paid for Speenhamland?" was practically unanswerable. Directly, the main burden fell, of course, on the ratepayers.

But the farmers were partly compensated by the low wages they had to pay their laborers—a direct result of the Speenhamland system. Moreover, the farmer was frequently remitted a part of his rates, if he was willing to employ a villager who would otherwise fall on the rates. The consequent overcrowding of the farmer's kitchen and yard with unnecessary hands, some of them not too keen performers, had to be set down on the debit side. The labor of those who were actually on the rates was to be had even more cheaply. They had often to work as "roundsmen" at alternating places, being paid only their food, or being put up for auction in the village "pound," for a few pence a day. How much this kind of indentured labor was worth is another question. To top it all, aids-in-rent were sometimes allowed to the poor, while the unscrupulous proprietor of the cottages made money by rack-renting the unsanitary habitations; the village authorities were likely to close an eye as long as the rates for the hovels continued to be turned in. That such a tangle of interests would undermine any sense of financial responsibility and encourage every kind of petty corruption is evident.

Still, in a broader sense, Speenhamland paid. It was started as aid-in-wages, ostensibly benefiting the employees, but actually using public means to subsidize the employers. For the main effect of the allowance system was to depress wages below the subsistence level. In the thoroughly pauperized areas, farmers did not care to employ agricultural laborers who still owned a scrap of land, "because none with property was eligible for parish relief and the standard wage was so low that, without relief of some sort, it was insufficient for a married man." Consequently, in some areas only those people who were on the rates had a chance of employment; those who tried to keep off the rates and earn a living by their own exertions were hardly able to secure a job. Yet in the country at large the great majority must have been of the latter sort and on each of them employers as a class made an extra profit since they benefited from the lowness of wages, without having to make up for it from the rates. In the long run, a system as uneconomical as that was bound to affect the productivity of labor and to depress standard wages, and ultimately even the "scale" set by the magistrates for the benefit of the poor. By the 1820's the scale of bread was actually being whittled down in various counties, and the wretched incomes of the poor were reduced even further. Between 1815 and 1830 the Speenhamland scale, which was fairly equal all over the country, was reduced by almost one-third (this fall also was practically universal). Clapham doubts whether the total burden of the rates was as severe as the rather sudden outburst of complaints would have made one believe. Rightly. For although the rise in the rates was spectacular and in some regions must have been felt as a calamity, it seems most probable that it was not so much the burden itself as rather the economic effect of aid-in-wages on the productivity of labor that was at the root of the trouble. Southern England, which was most sorely hit, paid out in poor rates not quite 3.3 per cent of its income—a very tolerable charge, Clapham thought, in view of the fact that a considerable part of this sum "ought to have gone to the poor in wages." Actually, total rates were falling steadily in the 1830's, and their relative burden must have even more quickly decreased in view of the growing national welfare. In 1818 the sums actually spent on the relief of the poor totaled near eight million pounds; they fell almost continuously until they were less than six million in 1826, while national income was rising rapidly. And yet the criticism of Speenhamland became more and more violent owing to the fact, so it appears, that the dehumanization of the masses began to paralyze national life, and notably to constrain the energies of industry itself.

Speenhamland precipitated a social catastrophe. We have become accustomed to discount the lurid presentations of early capitalism as "sob-stuff." For this there is no justification. The picture drawn by Harriet Martineau, the perfervid apostle of Poor Law Reform, coincides with that of the Chartist propagandists who were leading the outcry against the Poor Law Reform. The facts set out in the famous Report of the Commission on the Poor Law (1834), advocating the immediate repeal of the Speenhamland Law, could have served as the material for Dickens' campaign against the Commission's policy. Neither Charles Kingsley nor Friedrich Engels, neither Blake nor Carlyle, was mistaken in believing that the very image of man had been defiled by some terrible catastrophe. And more impressive even than the outbursts of pain and anger that came from poets and philanthropists was the icy silence with which Malthus and Ricardo passed over the scenes out of which their philosophy of secular perdition was born.

Undoubtedly, the social dislocation caused by the machine and the circumstances under which man was now condemned to serve it had many results that were unavoidable. England's rural civilization was lacking in those urban surroundings out of which the later industrial towns of the Continent grew.[3] There was in the new

towns no settled urban middle class, no such nucleus of artisans
and craftsmen, of respectable petty bourgeois and townspeople as
could have served as an assimilating medium for the crude laborer
who—attracted by high wages or chased from the land by tricky
enclosers—was drudging in the early mills. The industrial town of
the Midlands and the North West was a cultural wasteland; its
slums merely reflected its lack of tradition and civic self-respect.
Dumped into this bleak slough of misery, the immigrant peasant, or
even the former yeoman or copyholder was soon transformed into
a nondescript animal of the mire. It was not that he was paid too
little, or even that he labored too long—though either happened
often to excess—but that he was now existing under physical conditions which denied the human shape of life. Negroes of the African
forest who found themselves caged, panting for air in the hull of a
slave trader might have felt as these people felt. And yet all this
was not irremediable. As long as a man had a status to hold on to,
a pattern set by his kin or fellows, he could fight for it, and regain
his soul. But in the case of the laborer this could happen only in one
way: by his constituting himself the member of a new class. Unless
he was able to make a living by his own labor, he was not a worker
but a pauper. To reduce him artificially to such a condition was the
supreme abomination of Speenhamland. This act of an ambiguous
humanitarianism prevented laborers from constituting themselves
an economic class and thus deprived them of the only means of
staving off the fate to which they were doomed in the economic
mill.

Speenhamland was an unfailing instrument of popular demorali-
zation. If a human society is a self-acting machine for maintaining
the standards on which it is built, Speenhamland was an automaton
for demolishing the standards on which any kind of society could be
based. Not only did it put a premium on the shirking of work and
the pretense of inadequacy, but it increased the attraction of pauperism precisely at the juncture when a man was straining to escape
the fate of the destitute. Once a man was in the poorhouse (he
would usually land there if he and his family had been for some
time on the rates) he was trapped, and could rarely leave it. The
decencies and self-respect of centuries of settled life wore off quickly
in the promiscuity of the poorhouse, where a man had to be cautious
not to be thought better off than his neighbor, lest he be forced to
start out on the hunt for work, instead of "boon-doggling" in the
familiar fold. "The poor-rate had become public spoil. . . . To
obtain their share the brutal bullied the administrators, the profli-

gate exhibited their bastards which must be fed, the idle folded
their arms and waited till they got it; ignorant boys and girls married upon it; poachers, thieves and prostitutes extorted it by intimidation; country justices lavished it for popularity, and Guardians
for convenience. This was the way the fund went. . . ." "Instead
of the proper number of laborers to till his land—laborers paid by
himself—the farmer was compelled to take double the number,
whose wages were paid partly out of the rates; and these men,
being employed by compulsion on him, were beyond his control—
worked or not as they chose—let down the quality of his land, and
disabled him from employing the better men who would have toiled
hard for independence. These better men sank down amongst the
worst; the rate paying cottager, after a vain struggle, went to the
pay table to seek relief. . . ." Thus Harriet Martineau.[4] Bashful
later-day liberals ungratefully neglected the memory of this outspoken apostle of their creed. Yet even her exaggerations, which
they now feared, put the highlights in the right place. She herself
belonged to that struggling middle class, whose genteel poverty
made them only the more sensitive to the moral intricacies of the
Poor Law. She understood and clearly expressed the need of society
for a new class, a class of "independent laborers." They were the
heroes of her dreams, and she makes one of them—a chronically
unemployed laborer who refuses to go on relief—say proudly to a
colleague who decides to go on the rates: "Here I stand, and defy
anybody to despise me. I could set my children into the middle of
the church aisle and dare anyone to taunt at them about the place
they hold in society. There may be some wiser; there may be many
richer; but there are none more honorable." The big men of the
ruling class were still far from comprehending the need for this new
class. Miss Martineau pointed to "the vulgar error of the aristocracy,
of supposing only one class of society to exist below that wealthy
one with which they are compelled by their affairs to have business." Lord Eldon, she complained, like others who must know better, "included under one head ['the lower classes'] everybody below
the wealthiest bankers—manufacturers, tradesmen, artisans, laborers and paupers. . . ."[5] But it was the distinction between these
last two, she passionately insisted, that the future of society depended upon. "Except the distinction between sovereign and subject, there is no social difference in England so wide as that between
the independent laborer and the pauper; and it is equally ignorant,
immoral, and impolitic to confound the two," she wrote. This, of

course, was hardly a statement of fact; the difference between the two strata had become nonexistent under Speenhamland. Rather it was a statement of policy based upon a prophetic anticipation. The policy was that of the Poor Law Reform Commissioners; the prophecy looked to a free competitive labor market, and the consequent emergence of an industrial proletariat. The abolishment of Speenhamland was the true birthday of the modern working class, whose immediate self-interest destined them to become the protectors of society against the intrinsic dangers of a machine civilization. But whatever the future had in store for them, working class and market economy appeared in history together. The hatred of public relief, the distrust of state action, the insistence on respectability and self-reliance, remained for generations characteristics of the British worker.

The repeal of Speenhamland was the work of a new class entering on the historical scene, the middle classes of England. Squirearchy could not do the job these classes were destined to perform: the transformation of society into a market economy. Dozens of laws were repealed and others enacted before that transformation was on the way. The Parliamentary Reform Bill of 1832 disfranchised the rotten boroughs and gave power in the Commons once and for all to commoners. Their first great act of reform was the abolishing of Speenhamland. Now that we realize the degree to which its paternalist methods were merged with the life of the country, we will understand why even the most radical supporters of reform hesitated to suggest a shorter period than ten or fifteen years for the transition. Actually, it took place with an abruptness which makes nonsense of the legend of English gradualism fostered at a later time when arguments against radical reform were sought. The brutal shock of that event haunted for generations the daydreams of the British working class. And yet the success of this lacerating operation was due to the deep-seated convictions of the broad strata of the population, including the laborers themselves, that the system which to all appearances supported them was in truth despoiling them, and that the "right to live" was the sickness unto death.

The new law provided that in the future no outdoor relief should be given. Its administration was national and differentiated. In this respect also it was a thoroughgoing reform. Aid-in-wages was, of course, discontinued. The workhouse test was reintroduced, but in a new sense. It was now left to the applicant to decide whether he was so utterly destitute of all means that he would voluntarily repair to a shelter which was deliberately made into a place of horror. The workhouse was invested with a stigma; and staying in it was made a psychological and moral torture, while complying with the requirements of hygiene and decency—indeed, ingeniously using them as a pretense for further deprivations. Not the justices of peace, nor local overseers, but wider authorities—the guardians—were to administer the law under dictatorial central supervision. The very burial of a pauper was made an act by which his fellow men renounced solidarity with him even in death.

In 1834 industrial capitalism was ready to be started, and Poor Law Reform was ushered in. The Speenhamland Law which had sheltered rural England, and thereby the laboring population in general, from the full force of the market mechanism was eating into the marrow of society. By the time of its repeal huge masses of the laboring population resembled more the specters that might haunt a nightmare than human beings. But if the workers were physically dehumanized, the owning classes were morally degraded. The traditional unity of a Christian society was giving place to a denial of responsibility on the part of the well-to-do for the conditions of their fellows. The Two Nations were taking shape. To the bewilderment of thinking minds, unheard-of wealth turned out to be inseparable from unheard-of poverty. Scholars proclaimed in unison that a science had been discovered which put the laws governing man's world beyond any doubt. It was at the behest of these laws that compassion was removed from the hearts, and a stoic determination to renounce human solidarity in the name of the greatest happiness of the greatest number gained the dignity of secular religion.

The mechanism of the market was asserting itself and clamoring for its completion: human labor had to be made a commodity. Reactionary paternalism had in vain tried to resist this necessity. Out of the horrors of Speenhamland men rushed blindly for the shelter of a utopian market economy.

NOTES

1. Meredith, H. O., *Outlines of the Economic History of England,* 1908.
2. Martineau, H., *The Hamlet,* 1833.
3. Professor Usher puts the date of the beginning of general urbanization about 1795.

4. Martineau, H., *History of England During the Thirty Years' Peace* (1816–1846), 1849.

5. Martineau, H., *The Parish*, 1833.

2   The Changing Balance of Status and Contract in Assistance Policy

SAMUEL MENCHER

The effect of assistance on dependency has probably been the most persistent problem of social policy since the period of the Reformation. Although the nature of assistance[1] and the concept of dependency have changed markedly during the last four centuries, the expectation, or, more accurately, the fear, has persisted that any effort resulting in benefits beyond those obtainable through the normal economic institutions of society will discourage maximum assumption of responsibility and inevitably decrease the total welfare of society. With increasing knowledge of the social and psychological components of behavior, the concept of dependency has been increasingly broadened, but the ultimate criterion for assistance policy has remained within the economic sphere.

The extent to which individuals may be expected to be independent or to rely on their own resources has varied, but within its own norms each society has struggled with the effects of further redistribution of its economic wealth. For example, contemporary society accepts the cost of schooling as a common responsibility, but the foster placement of children continues to be chargeable to the parents' account. The major problems of society, however, have concerned direct financial aid rather than the provision of objects or services, for, as Pigou notes, the latter tend to be "neutral" in their effect on incentive for income.[2] Since the goal of assistance policy has been to increase the individual's desire or ability for self-support, or at least certainly not to discourage it, assistance policy has struggled primarily with issues related to the productive or potentially productive individual.

Reprinted from *The Social Service Review*, 35 (March 1961): 17–32, by permission of the University of Chicago Press. © 1961 by The University of Chicago.

Thus dependency, for practical purposes, involves the inability or unwillingness of the able-bodied members of the population to provide for themselves and for those considered to be their legal or natural dependents. From the first, the poor law programs of England and western Europe after the Reformation, and even before, distinguished between the "impotent" and the "employable" poor. Though the definition of the classes has changed, there has been continuous acceptance of social responsibility for the "impotent" poor. Basic issues of assistance policy in regard to this group have arisen only as the employable group has been affected. For example, to what extent should the employable groups be held responsible for impotent individuals attached to them? To what extent should individuals who are at any time incapable of employment, whatever the reason, be expected to provide from their previous earnings for their present incapacity or lack of employment?

The purpose of this paper is to analyze the concepts and theories which form the background of contemporary thinking about the relationship of assistance and dependency. This analysis will be presented primarily in terms of the continuing conflict between "status" and "contract" relationships since the period of the Reformation. The concepts of status and contract are broadly derived from Sir Henry Maine.[3] Status, as used here, refers to relationships which are determined essentially by membership in the group, whether it is the family, the community, society as a whole, or any particular institution of society, such as a religious or commercial organization. In a status society, rights and responsibilities are inherent in the relationship of the individual to the social unit. The term "contract" will refer to relationships which are specifically and purposefully entered into, and rights and responsibilities are determined by their acceptance in free exchange.

The distinction between the impotent and the employable illustrates well the difference between status and contract. The continued assistance of the impotent has been on a status basis. No matter what the pressures toward a contract society, extenuating circumstances have resulted in the protection of members of the group, such as children or the handicapped, who are considered incapable of managing their own affairs and cannot therefore be held responsible according to the contract code of society. It is the employable group, however, whose assistance has been directly affected by the attitudes of society toward dependency according to the emphasis on status or contract relationships in particular periods.

From the point of view of status and contract, assistance policy since the Reformation may be roughly divided into three periods. (1) the growth of a contract society between the Reformation and the early nineteenth century; (2) the revival of status relationships in the nineteenth century; and (3) the mixture of status and contract in the twentieth century. Naturally, as in all social phenomena, sharp distinctions tend to be more academic than actual. In the three periods, overlappings occur particularly in the continuance of traditional modes and in the development of new practices. While much of the evidence presented will be related to the English scene, the analysis pertains generally to both British and American assistance policy.

I

The factor most sharply distinguishing the modern from the medieval period has been the changed emphasis on work and effort. Certainly in the four centuries since the Reformation the dominant goal of Western society has been the increasing of man's productivity. However, this emphasis on work and productivity, so integral to contemporary life as to make almost banal any reference to it, represented a fundamental break with earlier eras. The relatively sudden and great attention given to work as reflected in all the institutions of society following the Reformation indicates the significant and revolutionary nature of the change.[4] On the religious side, work became the duty of man before God, and, on the temporal side, labor became more than the means of man's satisfying his own needs; it enriched the wealth of the community and nation. Work had never previously achieved a similar position as a universal value.

In the static feudal economy of the medieval period, the gains that could be obtained from increased productivity, whether in agriculture or in industry, were relatively of little consequence. The feudal society was essentially self-sufficient and non-enterprising. The new economy, ushered in first by the Commercial Revolution and then by the Industrial Revolution, had virtually no limits to its expansion.

The increased wealth, approved by social and religious sanctions, flowing from commerce and industry was directly related to increased effort. The medieval concept of labor as the basis of value was inherited by the new society, and its leading theorist and exponent, Adam Smith, assumed labor to be the "real measure of the exchangeable value of all commodities."[5] However, while labor may have been considered the basis of economic value in the Middle Ages, economic value itself was of much less significance than in the period commencing with the Reformation.

Support from the newly arising religious institutions was especially important if the emphasis on labor and property was to take firm hold. The medieval Church had hardly given sufficient encouragement to devotion to labor or the accumulation of property to satisfy the needs of a commercial society. The new economy of the Reformation had to overcome not only a static feudal economy but also a system of religious values which, in effect, subordinated temporal to spiritual interests. The medieval Church's emphasis on poverty and other-worldliness conflicted sharply with the demands of the developing economy. It cast doubt on the value of wordly labor and questioned the intrinsic right of property. The fundamental weakness of the Church's charitable policy, according to a nineteenth-century Protestant historian of Catholic charity, was its failure to appreciate the importance of work and property, for "a healthy charity is only possible where healthy moral views of work and property prevail."[6]

Since the Reformation, much has been made of the "demoralizing" effect of the Church's indiscriminate almsgiving, which, in reality, was not so great as to justify the amount of attention given it.[7] This demoralizing influence was the threat to a society founded on work and property of a system of charity which permitted other ways of obtaining a livelihood than through productive labor. This criticism, applied to a system of charity flourishing in an era before the ultimate value of work and property was recognized, has, however, remained a classic gauge of the effectiveness of welfare programs since that time.

The medieval Church's approach to work and property and its related philosophy of charity was particularly important for assistance policies after the Reformation, because the Church, either directly through its own institutions or through its influence on lay society, had established the tradition of charitable help. If the emerging society was to continue the practice of philanthropy it must be organized in such a fashion as to distinguish clearly the new relationship between work and property, on the one hand, and charity, on the other.

The emerging commercial society must not only change existing notions of the importance of work but must also take into account the existing attitudes toward labor itself. For several centuries before the Reformation, efforts had been made to enforce the laborer's attachment to his place of employment. While some of these efforts were no doubt motivated by a desire to maintain a ready supply of local labor, they were also indicative of the generally slack attitude of the working population and of the need for strong measures of control.[8] The increasing severity of legislation for this purpose reflects the ineffectiveness of such a policy.

The laboring classes, breaking away from feudalism, sought to escape from the obligation of work as from other feudal requirements. For the most part, they did not have a lengthy experience as small landholders or craftsmen to develop habits of effort and workmanship. The craft guilds, the main institution for medieval and Renaissance workmanship, had only a limited membership, and their exclusiveness prevented any wide diffusion of their influence.[9] The agricultural classes were soon dispossessed of their rights as small property holders as the movement toward enclosure and large-scale farming developed. If the lower classes found no stimulus within their own lives to obtain satisfaction from work, they saw little in the lives of their betters to provide an impression of work as a pleasurable activity. As Veblen has so cogently observed, freedom from work has been a traditional mark of upper-class status. During no period was this more true than during the period preceding the Reformation.

The new entrepreneur classes who proclaimed with such gusto the importance of work as the only acceptable way of living and attaining God's grace did not, however, foster an appreciation of work as an agreeable activity in itself. Work for them was a task and a duty, and its very unpleasantness symbolized its sacredness. Work was a discipline, not a satisfaction. For the classical economist, work could be equated with the renunciation of leisure and freedom of choice. While the entrepreneur classes found sufficient incentive directly from their material gains and ultimately from being among God's chosen, there was little to motivate the laboring classes. Their status was low; they had little to gain from the new religious philosophies; and the work tasks assigned to them were both unpleasant and poorly rewarded.

Finally, the laboring classes saw no advantage in the emphasis on freedom or laissez faire which marked the new economy. The transition from a status society of established and fixed relationships to a contract society of fluid agreements based on material gain presented few advantages to the lower classes. In this arrangement, the worker was stripped of the security formerly provided by the status system and was forced to rely solely on the market value of his labor. However, the development of an open economy was vitally important to the entrepreneur classes, and the possibility that the lower classes might "depend" on the previous guaranties of support through status in a manorial or religious community would hinder the free operation of the new society.

The poor laws of England and western Europe of the sixteenth century must be viewed against the background of an emerging contract society seeking to establish an assistance policy consistent with an emphasis on work both as a value in itself and as a source of economic value. The sixteenth-century poor laws attempted to meet the new needs and to remedy the previous assistance policies by the following reforms:

1. An organized community system of relief was substituted for informal or status-oriented approaches. Through providing a clear, tax-supported method of assistance, the new acts helped make obsolete the earlier habits of philanthropy which provided little social control over labor. Some of the sixteenth-century legislation in England and on the Continent even made specific reference to the prohibition of private philanthropy outside the community-administered program. The Sorbonne authorities disapproved of these measures because they conflicted with the Catholic ethic of charity, and it is likely that the English provisions were also too radical a departure from traditional status practices to be effective, as they were not included in the eventual codification of the poor laws under Elizabeth.

2. The sixteenth-century acts made a clear distinction between the "employable" and the "impotent" poor. The distinction was vital for any effective administration of assistance in a contract society. Thus, those exempted from the contract system and those responsible to it were defined. Individuals unable to market their labor value were still to be protected by the community or, in other words, to be maintained in a status relationship.

The Elizabethan poor law, like the systems of assistance on the Continent around the time of the Reformation, provided for the finding of work for the employable who were not engaged in labor. This provision was to be the source of much controversy by the beginning of the nineteenth century. While recognizing work as the only basis of livelihood for the able-bodied, it continued the traditional status responsibility of the community for all the poor. The possibility of confusing work and assistance was also present, and this threatened the core of the new contract society.

3. The mutual liability for support of parents and children was

extended by the Elizabethan poor law to grandparents. This measure had dual significance. By expanding the responsibility of the employable or those with previous income from employment, it narrowed the sphere of community responsibility and increased the numbers dependent on the contract system of wages. By enforcing family responsibility it helped stabilize the labor market.

Societies faced with the problem of social control of labor frequently have resorted to incentives outside the immediate work situation. The feudal economy provided serfs with their own small plots of land, and even slave economies encouraged the growth of family life. In the sixteenth century, when one of the main problems was irregularity of attachment to the labor market, the enforcement and extension of family responsibility might well act as a leavening force on the lower classes who had neither the possession of property nor the personal investment in a skill to stabilize their work interest.[10]

Thus the English poor law established by the beginning of the seventeenth century the basic policies of (1) work as the only approved source of livelihood for those defined as employable and (2) the separation of the employable from any reliance on the community's provision of assistance. The law, however, was not entirely consistent. If aid were extended to the employable because of their membership in the community, then work ceased to be the only measure of their value, and contract was not the only basis of livelihood. Not, however, until some two centuries later, were the contradictions in both the letter and the spirit of the law fully faced.

During the period before 1834, the poor law system showed many deviations from the emphasis on work and contract. The Elizabethan poor law, as already noted, while not accepting responsibility for the relief of the able-bodied poor, had empowered the parishes to provide work for the employable. This early policy, reflecting the mercantilist philosophy of the time, eventually culminated in the Speenhamland practice of the late eighteenth and early nineteenth centuries of subsidizing wages with relief. The clear distinction between work and assistance, so important to a contract society, was thus dimmed.[11]

The doctrine of laissez faire or the complete acceptance of contract relationships in assistance policy reached its ultimate expression in the poor law reform in 1834. Although their strategy might differ, the goal of such leading advocates of reform as Sir George Nicholls and Nassau Senior was the total abolition of any benefits for the employable group.[12] The most ardent proponents of reform would have done away with the poor law entirely, for, from their point of view, there was no risk befalling the able-bodied or his dependents for which he should not have provided during his period of employment.[13] In effect, the Commission of 1834 concluded that a system of assistance founded on status privileges was far inferior to the normal rigors of the economic market. The investigations of this Commission, along with conditions considered prevalent under pre-Reformation philanthropy, have provided strong foundations for the classic argument of the relationship of assistance and dependency.

However, the succeeding history of poor law administration indicates a failure of the effort to force the employable poor to remain totally dependent on the contract value of their own labor or conversely totally independent of any status right to social support. Able-bodied poor continued to resort to public relief, and succeeding poor law commissions were constantly faced with the growth of relief rolls. What is pertinent is not that the Commission of 1834 and the later commissions and boards did not understand the causes of poverty, or failed to apply appropriate remedies to it, but rather that, despite their strenuous efforts, the poor law remained a resource for the able-bodied.

As suggested above, traditional paternalism continued to frustrate any system which refused to recognize the dependency of the poor on the wealthier elements of the community. Of more significance was the fact that, by the time the doctrine of laissez faire had become completely accepted, it was no longer fully applicable. The concepts of natural rights and of individualism, like the labor theory of value, had their roots in the "handicraft and petty trade" era before the growth of large-scale manufacture and commerce.[14] An assistance policy, therefore, founded on an out-moded scheme of social and economic relationships had little likelihood of success. The poor law guardians continued to provide, albeit poorly, outdoor relief to the able-bodied and their families. The doctrine of status, recognizing the dependence of the individual on the resources of the group, was maintained in practice, if not in theory.

The Reform Act of 1834 may be considered the high-water mark of the doctrine of contract as applied to assistance programs in England. The doctrine of contract was reinforced by closely associated economic and social theories. Thus assistance was criticized, not only because it upset the natural harmony of the economic market, but because it reduced the wealth of the nation both by withdrawing labor from productive work and by providing goods to nonproductive members of society. Since, in the minds of some nineteenth-century classical economists, the only justification for consumption was the creation of further wealth, the assistance recipient was viewed as a drain on the resources of the nation.[15]

This approach to consumption, however, meant that employed labor itself was considered to require only sufficient subsistence to make possible its continued engagement in production. Any further compensation would have led to unproductive consumption. Thus the principle of "less eligibility" established by the Commission of 1834 meant that, in reality, those dependent on the assistance system would receive less than was necessary for subsistence. Here again, as with denying assistance to the able-bodied, the contract aspects of the program were thwarted by the traditional status elements in poor law administration. While the entrepreneur of the early Industrial Revolution might look upon labor as an abstract and easily replaceable unit in production, the poor law guardians continued to see assistance recipients as persons or families and frequently indulged them beyond the budgetary limits established by the poor law boards.

The adoption of the principle of less eligibility also reflected the utilitarian pleasure-pain psychology of the period. According to the utilitarian view, behavior is motivated by the seeking after pleasure and the avoidance of pain, and if through the practice of less eligibility idleness could be made sufficiently unpleasant or painful in comparison with work, then work, no matter how undesirable, would be preferred over idleness. Since the conditions of the working class in the beginning of the nineteenth century were especially poor, and the estimate of their character by the influential elements of society was particularly low, a strong policy was required to motivate the lower classes toward work.[16] This the Act of 1834 attempted to do not only through the principle of less eligibility but also through the application of the workhouse test.

Finally, the contract view of the dependency of the poor received much support from what may be termed the pessimistic social and economic theories of the period. Both Malthus and Ricardo stressed the inevitability of poverty and subsistence wages. The laws of population and economics and the miserliness of nature condemned the lower classes to constant poverty. In fact, there was little room for help since any relief would eventually only make heavier the burden of the working population.

II

The second major phase in assistance policy had its inception during the period of poor law reform in the early part of the nineteenth century and continued in England until the beginning of the twentieth century. In the United States its duration was somewhat longer. This second phase was marked by a renewal of status relationships, with the foundation of an established contract society. The nineteenth-century resurgence of status in assistance policy differed in several important respects from earlier practices. These differences were largely influenced by changes in the role and philosophy of both the upper and lower classes and in the concept of the nature and purpose of society itself.

Although the dominant development of the previous period was directed toward the establishment of a contract scheme of relationships, elements of the previous status system continued to be active. However, during the period of emphasis on contract relationships, the concept of status was gradually transformed. In the earlier period, the giving of assistance to the poor was the recognition of a natural relationship between the wealthy and the deprived classes. Whether because of traditional feudal or local rights or because of a religious duty of sharing with the poor, charity was a mutual relationship the acceptance of which required no special behavior on the part of the recipient, unless it was to pray for the salvation of his benefactor. In fact, the advantage of the relationship, according to later critics, fell to the wealthy to whom the poor were merely a convenient object of pity. As for the poor, the complaint was made in the beginning of the sixteenth century that many "wolde not take almes as a free benefyte with thankes: but lordly claymed it as it had been a trybute due unto them by lawe."[17] All that was desired in this period of transition from the feudal to the commercial society was described in the following:

> The poor man agayne loueth the ryche man as hys benefactoure of whom he hath his lyuynge and by whose ayde he is holpen him he thanketh for all he hathe to him he gyveth manye blessynges and good prayers as a token of gratytude and he rendereth theym hertely and as lyberally as he can. For no other cause dyd nature mengle poore and ryche togyther but that poore men shulde receyve benefytes of ryche men.[18]

This was far less than the status relationships of nineteenth-century charity sought to accomplish. True, gratitude has been one of the main elements of charitable giving since the disruption of the medieval system when status endowed definite rights. Any system of status relationships which involved voluntary giving and which did not result in automatic benefits to the giver required at least some such justification as gratitude or recognition on the part of the recipient. In the nineteenth century, however, gratitude alone was not sufficient; gratitude was merely the sign of "worthiness" or readiness to be helped.

While for some patrons of nineteenth-century charity the satisfaction of gratitude was sufficient, these brought upon their philanthropy the same disrepute as had come to characterize pre-Reformation assistance. However, the new approach to status relationships in assistance sought to accomplish what, in the eyes of its supporters, had not been achieved either by the traditional status pattern as exemplified by public relief or by the emphasis on contract. The voluntary nature of giving in accord with the contract motif involved a discretion and selectivity which would counteract any expectation of assistance as an obligation of the rich to the poor.[19] However, in return for the voluntary self-sacrifice of the rich there were to be obligations on the part of the poor: " 'We are willing to give up the life we care for,' Arnold Toynbee said, but we ask 'one thing in return' "—a change in the way of life of the poor.[20]

The new system of status relationships in assistance, introduced by such men as Chalmers, thus differed from the old in recognizing the possibility of change in the poor. This represented a significant shift from the philosophy of all previous assistance policies. Whether denying assistance under the principles of contract relationships or extending it in the traditional pre-Reformation pattern, there had been no expectation of effecting any change in the poor themselves. The poverty of their condition was sufficient evidence of the unworthiness of the poor under early Protestant doctrine.

Whatever conflict there may have been between the contract position of the earlier Protestant ethic and the status approach of the nineteenth century, the ultimate goal for the lower classes was the same—the self-maintenance of the able-bodied poor. The new philanthropists abhorred any assistance policies that might encourage the able-bodied poor to prefer social support to independent effort. If anything, the supporters of the new status philanthropy, as exemplified by the leaders of the Charity Organization

Society, were the most ardent opponents of any system of assistance providing the able-bodied poor with any status claim on the wealth of the community. They sought when possible to protect the poor from the "demoralizing" experience of public assistance, but they were equally critical of private efforts that encouraged status dependency. The COS preserved its own resources for those poor who demonstrated the potential of meeting the commitments of a contract society and relegated to the public authorities those who could not manage without status support.

At the same time the new philanthropy was employing status relationships founded upon the unequal social position of master and servant to effect the independence of the working class, the position of the working class, and to some extent the nature of work itself, had begun to change. Partly as a result of the evangelical faith and interest in the improvement of their condition and partly as a result of forces within the working class itself, the working class achieved a position of respectability in the latter half of the nineteenth century that it had not had previously. A statement such as that made by the economist Alfred Marshall before the Royal Commission on the Aged Poor in 1893 would have seemed inconceivable before the Commission of 1834:

> I am convinced that the leaders of the working men would be as firm as anyone in insisting that scamps and lazy people should be put to a severe discipline; . . . in fact I believe that probably the professional tramp is even more odious to large classes of working men than he is to the rest of society.[21]

In fact, one of Marshall's main criticisms of the work of the Commission was that it had not taken pains to sound out labor's views on the problems of the poor.

Meanwhile a changed attitude toward labor had been growing among employers themselves. George Friedmann compares the attitude toward labor prevalent in the early period of the Industrial Revolution with America's "debauch" of its natural resources. As with other resources, an interest in conserving labor resources occurred. He wrote:

> Toward the close of the century, it became evident that the supply of labor was not inexhaustible, and that it was expensive, all the more so as the workers were organizing both to defend their value on the labor market and the elementary

guarantees of their well-being. Social legislation was devised and refined.[22]

Other important and closely related changes which were to effect reforms in assistance policy were an "optimistic" view of the economic potential of society as contrasted with the pessimism of Malthus and Ricardo and a belief that the purpose of society was to provide satisfactions for its members. While work maintained its place as the most important human function, it ceased to be the only end of life and became more closely related to other social goals.

During the second half of the nineteenth century, the industrial economy of England, America, and western Europe flourished with boundless vigor. The preoccupation was no longer with the sufficiency of production, but rather with the development of markets to absorb current production and to make possible its continued growth. The superfluity of goods lent to a concentration on "consumption and selling" and the satisfactions to be obtained from the products of industry.

The concern of the economist with maximizing satisfactions paralleled the growing interest in conserving human resources. While the emphasis on satisfaction resulted in a welfare economics to a large extent founded on utilitarian ethics, the emphasis on human resources resulted in a social policy to be effected by political action. Thus Alfred Marshall, as a formulator of the new economics, stated that additional income for the poor increases the "total happiness" more than an "equal amount" for the rich "because the happiness which an additional shilling brings to a poor man is much greater than that which it brings to a rich one."[23] As a contributor toward government policy, he commented:

> That a man ought not to be allowed to live in a bad home, that extreme poverty ought to be regarded, not indeed as a crime, but a thing so detrimental to the State that it should not be endured, and that everybody who, whether through his own fault or not, was in effect incapable of keeping together a home that contributed to the well-being of the State, that person should, under the authority of the State, pass into a new form of life.[24]

The new economics and the new view of the role of the state in the latter part of the nineteenth century were laying a foundation for a status system of assistance vastly different from that espoused by the growing movement of private philanthropy of the same period. The individual-centered private philanthropy sought through the instrument of the master-servant status relationship to remove the individual from reliance on society. The new economics concerned itself with the satisfactions of individuals as they affected the total welfare of the community.[25] While these approaches differed in this respect, both agreed in aiming toward the financial responsibility of each individual for himself and his dependents. The new philosophy of state intervention, however, recognized the individual's reliance on society as a resource if his contract relationships were to be adequately fulfilled.

Although there were important differences between the two approaches to assistance policy as evidenced in the Poor Law Commission of 1905—one emphasizing voluntary, personal, and unequal status relationships and the other, common social responsibility —they both assumed that assistance, unless carefully controlled, would be preferred by those eligible to independent effort. There was greater understanding of the causes of dependency than in earlier eras, and it was recognized that all the evils previously attributed to assistance policies alone were the result of many influences. However, the belief remained that, whatever may have caused individuals to need assistance, the provision of assistance itself was sufficient to keep them in a state of dependency. After all, work was still considered an unpleasant responsibility which all would avoid if it were possible.

It is noteworthy that both the Webbs, who supported a highly organized program of state services, and the leaders of the COS, who looked askance at state intervention, opposed pension systems.[26] Both feared the temptation to rely on status benefits, particularly on the part of the working class. When the Webbs spoke of "universal provision" it was largely in regard to services, for the Webbs had almost as little faith in the moral responsibility of the lower classes for work and independence as did the members of the COS.[27]

Thus, by the beginning of the twentieth century there was a shift away from the strict contract position of assistance policy, although the new practices rested, in many respects, on the same tenets as the old. The view of work as a commodity and of the worker merely as a purveyor of a commodity had been undermined, and the distinction between the working class and the society which it served had also been dissolved to a large extent. In effect, some return to a status system had taken place, but not sufficiently for the worker to rely for his economic security on the wealth of society.

However, behind this general position were several factors, already noted, which presaged the development of the third phase of assistance policy: (1) the growth of a strong labor movement concerned with the security of its members, (2) the shifting emphasis in industry from exclusively technological concerns to the human problem of personnel, and (3) the increasing recognition that sound economic and social policy depended on more than productivity and that other factors must be taken into account to assure the economic welfare of society.

III

The third or most recent phase of assistance policy, like those preceding it, has been marked by the inclusion of earlier principles and practices and by the development of new modes reflecting the contemporary scene. The search for an acceptable system of relationships between the employable worker and society, the major concern of assistance policy since the Reformation, has resulted in a new compromise between the principles of contract and status.

The growing importance of the labor movement drew the attention of society to ways of satisfying the needs and demands of the working class for economic security. The solution, however, could not be found, as it was to some extent in the nineteenth century, through status relationships reflecting inequality of social position. Any scheme giving the worker status rights to security must necessarily reflect the equality being achieved by the working class in society as a whole. No system of assistance, however, could guarantee this equality if it conflicted sharply with the contract mores. Exemption from contract relationships involved *ipso facto* some degree of inferiority. Justice according to the contract mores meant the protection of the individual's or the group's bargaining position in a contract relationship, not the guaranty of any assumed rights to a share of the social resources.

Any satisfactory scheme of assistance in twentieth-century England and the United States must, therefore, bridge the gap between contract and status relationships. It must provide the security of status rights without conflicting fundamentally with the contract mores. Thus the major innovation in England and America was social insurance, which represented a suitable compromise between the principles of status and contract. Employability and attachment to work were the core of eligibility for social insurance. The contract relationship of employment was extended to include protection against the risks of injury, sickness, age, survivorship, and even lack of employment. Though the public assistance programs affecting the able-bodied, which had somehow managed to weather the opposition of four centuries, continued, the goal was to replace them with the new insurances. The presence of the insurances would make reliance on assistance based on status relationships even more invidious.

The new programs themselves had, of course, strong status elements. Their establishment or promotion by public institutions rather than by private corporations and their implicit guaranty of security by society indicated a considerable shift from the philosophy that any interference with the responsibility of the able-bodied for their own financial security would lessen their desire for work and independence and consequently have dire effects on the welfare of society as a whole. Although the pessimistic predictions of Malthus and Ricardo had long been discarded, and new social and economic theories had replaced the emphasis on labor value and laissez faire, the fear of the consequences of any status share in the wealth of society remained. The acceptance of the social insurances indicated that the pressures toward a status relationship had taken precedence over, though they had not replaced, the insistence on contract.

The insurances, however, as already noted, were careful to include safeguards for the contract system. The insurances were available only to the employed and their dependents; they required a real attachment to the labor market; they did not provide enough benefits either to compete with wages from employment or to make possible even a minimal standard of living without additional "independent" provision; and, at least in the United States, they aimed to reflect differences in habits of industry and skill. The requirements for benefits, principally the contribution of the worker and/or his employer, gave a sense of contract right. It was this contract right that needed to be controlled so as not to become a status right.

Although in principle the new programs emphasized the responsibility of society as a whole for the welfare of the individual, in practice the core of status relationships developed around the employment situation itself. The employer's contribution to the insurances was symbolic of the employer's or, more generally, the economic institution's responsibility for the welfare of the contributors to production. While employers may have been concerned basically with obtaining maximum work effort, the twentieth-century business organization proceeded from the premise that the best way of obtaining the worker's contribution was through viewing him as a member of a social unit rather than as an abstract commodity.

Labor, too, particularly in the United States, viewed the business organization as the major source of economic security. Some labor leaders even opposed the development of public social security programs and preferred a system of welfare benefits based on agreements between labor and management. Paralleling the growth of public programs was a vast extension of welfare benefits under employer and union aegis to which employers made a large contribution. While these programs formally arose out of the contract relationship between employers and employees, in fact they reflected the recognition on the part of both groups of the status responsibilities of business organizations toward their employees.

It may seem paradoxical that the very institutions which were originally responsible for introducing and enforcing the contract concept should offer the most clear-cut example of status recognition. However, it may be noted that historically those institutions which have had the major role in society have generally provided the focus for status relationships. In a work-centered culture, therefore, it is not surprising that economic institutions should assume this function.

Concomitant with the new relationships on the economic scene, important but less obvious changes were taking place in the meaning of work itself. The position of respectability achieved by labor, the changing view of labor by management, the concept of the plant as a social institution, were all indicative of the changing nature of work. Whatever the specific factors, such as the shorter work week or improved working conditions, work was no longer the same unpleasant sacrifice defined by the classical economists nor were workers the same "sturdy beggars" of the early poor laws. After some four centuries, work became part of the normal pattern of western culture and at least for the working class was freed to some extent from the compulsive sense of duty with which it was originally introduced.[28]

The significance of work to the economy of society also changed perceptibly. Regardless of its moral justification, work in a scarcity economy was essential to provide for the immediate needs of society. As western nations, and particularly America, moved to an economy of abundance, the relative importance of work diminished. The advantages to be obtained from additional work decreased, and increased productivity often created embarrassing problems of distribution. As machine technology improved to the point of automation, the relationship of the wealth of a nation to the quantity of its human labor power became more and more obscured.

The shift in emphasis from production to consumption by the economists of the latter part of the nineteenth century was given further impetus by the new economics of the Keynesian school. The theory of full employment stressed the value of keeping the economy at its full productive capacity. However, the means of achieving full production were largely dependent on consumer demand. Consumer capacity thus became of focal importance to the economic welfare of society. Since Keynesian economics questioned the automatic adjustment of the factors of the economy, the development of consumer capacity became an important function of governmental policy.

This approach to economic welfare was significant for assistance policy. While assistance policy has been largely concerned with the avoidance of any practice that might deter the worker from attachment to the normal labor market, the new emphasis on stimulating consumption indicated that the primary concern was with maintaining the worker's capacity to consume rather than with maintaining his sense of responsibility to the contract relationships of the labor market. In essence, the theory of full employment reinforced the status relationship of the able-bodied worker in society by combining his roles of worker and consumer. Beveridge, in applying Keynesian economics to assistance policy, stated:

> The redistribution of income that is involved in abolishing want by Social Insurance and children's allowances will of itself be a potent force in helping to maintain demand for the products of industry, and so in preventing mass unemployment.[29]

For Beveridge, full employment was a social as well as an economic doctrine. Full employment freed the worker from the threat of poverty and at the same time made more possible the selection of personally satisfying work.

Thus, full employment emphasized the combined status responsibility of society for both insuring sufficient consumer income and providing adequate employment opportunities. In effect, this was a radical reversal of the contract view of society with its foundation in laissez faire and individual responsibility and with its reliance on economic pressures to maintain attachment to work—a tedious duty to be avoided at the slightest pretext.

A new concept of status relationships of the worker to his place of employment and to society has, thus, taken its place alongside, and to some extent has superseded, the effort to maintain contract principles in assistance policy. The social insurances have come to be determined more by their "social" than by their "insurance" aspects, as benefits have tended to reflect need more than contributions. The "social assistance" programs, such as family allowances and universal non-contributory old age pensions, in some western nations have recognized status relationships without reference to contract rights based on employment.

CONCLUSIONS

The development of assistance policy has been examined from the point of view of status-contract relationships for the purpose of understanding the basis of contemporary programs. It has been suggested that the most realistic indicator of assistance policy is the treatment of the able-bodied or employable worker. Assistance policy has been divided into three phases and attitudes toward work; the position of the laboring class and the relationship of work and the worker to society have been related to the concepts of status and contract in assistance policy. The three periods described are: (1) the development of contract relationships between the poor laws of the Reformation and the poor law reform of 1834 in England, (2) the revival of status relationships during the nineteenth century, and (3) the mixture of contract and status in the twentieth century.

It is clear that none of the above periods represents a "pure culture" of the status or contract type. In each, the declining or ascending elements of one or the other are present. However, the resolution of the status-contract balance reached in assistance policy at any one time often reflects attitudes and developments that have already passed their zenith in society generally. For example, contemporary assistance policies place an emphasis on work and the position of the laboring class which more accurately reflects nineteenth- than twentieth-century conditions. There is present in both private and public welfare a contract philosophy that questions any right beyond what has been contracted for in the economic market and a fear of status relationships which must be controlled to avoid the ubiquitous potentiality of dependency. The resulting practices vary from the negative pressures of utilitarian pleasure-pain psychology to the patronizing loss of dignity through personal controls.[30]

At this point it seems that few factors remained to support the original sixteenth-century equation of assistance and dependence; yet the fear of dependency has continued to be one of the besetting concerns of contemporary society and sources of opposition to assistance policies. The concept of dependency has outstripped the original emphasis on independent contract for labor value. Freudian psychology, so influential in professional social work, has emphasized the basically dependent nature of man.[31] Independence has almost replaced work as a value, and any program which tends to "relieve" man from the vicissitudes of life is viewed both as a symptom of and a stimulus to dependency. To the extent that the current concept of dependency is merely a "putting of old wine into new bottles," it needs to be re-examined in light of its historical roots.

NOTES

1. The term "assistance" is used broadly throughout this paper for all programs, whether public or private, which provide financial support.

2. A. C. Pigou, *The Economics of Welfare* (4th ed.; London: Macmillan & Co., 1950), pp. 720 ff.

3. Sir Henry Sumner Maine, *Ancient Law* (London: John Murray, 1906).

4. Erich Fromm, *Escape from Freedom* (New York: Rinehart & Co., 1941), p. 93.

5. Adam Smith, *The Wealth of Nations* (New York: Modern Library, 1937), p. 30.

6. Gerhard Uhlhorn, *Christian Charity in the Ancient Church* (New York: Charles Scribner's Sons, 1883), p. 126.

7. W. J. Ashley, *An Introduction to English Economic History and Theory* (4th ed.; London: Longman's, Green & Co., 1914), Part II, p. 312.

8. *Ibid.*, p. 338.

9. Emil Lederer, "Labour," *Encyclopedia of Social Sciences* (New York: Macmillan Co., 1932), VIII, 616.

10. It is interesting to note that the status responsibilities of the worker were increased at the same time that those of society were lessened. This has remained as one of the conflict points of con-

temporary assistance policy, for there is an inherent contradiction in the expectation of status responsibility in a contract-oriented society.

11. Reinhard Bendix, *Work and Authority in Industry* (New York: John Wiley & Sons, 1956), p. 60.

12. Thomas Mackay, *A History of the English Poor Law* (New York: G. P. Putnam's Sons, 1899), III, 33 ff.

13. *Ibid.*, pp. 153–54.

14. Thorstein Veblen, *The Instinct of Workmanship* (New York: B. W. Huebsch, 1922), pp. 340–41.

15. See Nassau William Senior, *An Outline of the Science of Political Economy* (London: Allen & Unwin, 1938), pp. 55–56.

16. Lewis Mumford, *Technics and Civilization* (New York: Harcourt, Brace & Co., 1934), pp. 172–73.

17. "The Ypres Scheme of Poor Relief," trans. William Marshall (1535), in *Some Early Tracts on Poor Relief*, ed. F. R. Salter (London: Methuen & Co., 1926), p. 42.

18. *Ibid.*, p. 70.

19. See Beatrice Webb, *My Apprenticeship* (New York: Longman's, Green & Co., 1926), pp. 191–92.

20. As quoted in *My Apprenticeship*, p. 177.

21. Alfred Marshall, *Official Papers* (London: Macmillan & Co., 1926), p. 210.

22. George Friedmann, *Industrial Society* (Glencoe, Ill.: Free Press, 1955), p. 29.

23. Alfred Marshall, *Principles of Economics* (8th ed.; London: Macmillan & Co., 1927), p. 474.

24. Marshall, *Official Papers*, pp. 244–45.

25. I. M. D. Little, *A Critique of Welfare Economics* (2d ed.; Oxford: Clarendon Press, 1957), pp. 72–73.

26. Mary Richmond, prominent in the COS in the United States, was also critical of pension systems. See "Motherhood and Pensions" in *The Long View* (New York: Russell Sage Foundation, 1930), pp. 350–64.

27. It should be noted that reformers of welfare policy have frequently been members of the middle class with a highly refined sense of guilt. See *Beatrice Webb's Diaries, 1912–1924*, ed. Margaret I. Cole (London: Longman's, Green & Co., 1952), p. 70.

28. See David Riesman, "Some Observations on Changes in Leisure Attitudes," in *Individualism Reconsidered* (Glencoe, Ill.: Free Press, 1954), particularly pp. 208–9; also Eugene A. Friedmann and Robert J. Havighurst, *The Meaning of Work and Retirement* (Chicago: University of Chicago Press, 1954).

29. William H. Beveridge, *Full Employment in a Free Society* (New York: W. W. Norton & Co., 1945), pp. 255–56.

30. See Grace F. Marcus, *Some Aspects of Relief in Family Casework* (New York: Charity Organization Society, 1929). Although

this interesting study was conducted some thirty years ago, it is still applicable to current relief practices. See also J. P. Kahn, "Attitudes toward Recipients of Public Assistance," *Social Casework*, XXXVI (October, 1955), 364–65.

31. Lucille Austin has deprecated the tendency in casework to overstress the "pull toward dependency," as follows: "It is easy to see how this concept of dependency gave reinforcement to earlier sociological ideas that dependency was enticing and careful efforts had to be made to guard against it. As those concepts were tested in practice, questions were raised about their validity. Experience showed that many people achieved independence in spite of obstacles and maintained it with pleasure" ("The Place of Relief in the Treatment of Dependency," in *Relief Practice in a Family Agency* [New York: Family Welfare Association of America, 1942], p. 26).

3   In Fellow Feeling

OSCAR HANDLIN

Strangers in the immediate world about them, the immigrants often recognized, in dismay, the loneliness of their condition. Their hesitant steps groped around the uncertain hazards of new places and exposed them ever to perilous risks. No one could enjoy the satisfaction of confidence in his own unaided powers.

In their loneliness and helplessness, the immigrants reached for some arm to lean upon. There came a time, they knew, when a man was like a stray dog, driven away by all folk, glad to be caressed by any kindly hand. At many steps in his life's journey he came to points beyond which he could not go on alone; unaided he was doomed. Then it was well if help could come from others like him.

Consequently, the newcomers took pains early to seek out those whom experience made their brothers; and to organize each others' support, they created a great variety of formal and informal institutions. Then, at last, they came to know how good it was that brothers should dwell together.

From *The Uprooted* by Oscar Handlin, pp. 170–79, 189–200, by permission of the author and of Little, Brown and Co. in association with the Atlantic Monthly Press. Copyright © 1951 by Oscar Handlin.

The peasants, in their coming, did not bring with them the social patterns of the Old World. These could not be imposed on the activities of the New. The energies expended in reconstructing the churches revealed the forbidding proportions of the task of transplantation; and the environment, in any case, was hostile to the preservation of village ways. What forms ultimately developed among immigrants were the products of American conditions.

The crowded tenement neighborhoods spontaneously generated associations. Here people could not help meeting one another, their lives were so much in the open, so much shared. The sounds of joy and sorrow traveling up the airshaft united all the residents of the house; the common situation that cut these men off from the rest of the city itself united them. Within the ghetto could grow understanding, then sympathy, and in time co-operation.

Each building acquired a kind of organization, as families learned each other's character, got to know who could be depended on for what, and as they worked together in the necessary care of common facilities. When a crisis came, of sudden childbirth, of illness, of fire, it was the concern of all. In the warm summer evenings while their elders sat on the steps below, the young people would go up to the relative spaciousness of the roof, sometimes sleep the night there on the pebbled tar. Or groups together would venture on trips away, picnics in the park, rides on the ferryboat, or walks across the bridge. It was hard to believe, but true, that so much pleasure should come of talk. She spoke, next door, of events in an unknown place, of the misfortunes of someone else's family in someone else's village; and her tale had emotional force, as if it put into another setting familiar incidents and, by supplying them with generality, gave them meaning. So, strangers became friends. No need to ask what antecedents; the ability to communicate with each other was bond enough.

Down by the corner was, invariably, a place where the men could meet, talk without the constraint of woman's presence. At first some accommodating grocer measured out the spirits in a back room to small groups of convivial acquaintances. But after 1850 more rigid licensing laws had the effect of discouraging such informal establishments. Instead the saloon acquired a certain pre-eminence. But this was not the gaudy uptown emporium with which the readers of temperance tracts were familiar—a front for gambling and vice. Rather, its doors swung open upon modest groups of workingmen who cautiously invested nickels for beer and dimes for whisky for the warmth of companionship. In some places, indeed, the gathering point was not a saloon but a coffeehouse, or, later, a candy store; the site was less important than the coming together.

Here for a time would also be the setting of such occasions as needed the community for celebration. They remembered what affairs had been those weddings in the old home; why a week had not been too long, nor the whole village too many. In this land they had not the space in the crowded flats to welcome the immediate families. But there was gaiety in the room behind the bar where, flushed with temporary happiness, they paced off the once-familiar steps—only an evening, yes, and an early rising for work tomorrow, but a joy nevertheless, one to be long anticipated and long remembered. After a while these parties acquire importance enough to justify their own, more appropriate, premises. A hall is fitted out for the purpose; and if too long a period elapses with no wedding to make it merry, then some enterprising group is sure to contrive the pretext for a dance.

In the tenement, on the corner, in the hall, in none of these neighborhood encounters is there any rigid organization. These are spontaneous expressions of the desire to be not alone, to find understanding through communication with others. Yet, without design, the gatherings acquire form. Usage determines the proper ways of behavior; certain rules of propriety are established; and intimate little rituals develop. Each individual is known to his fellows. He has a reputation and plays a role; and whether he is the butt of laughter or the subject of respect, he is a person of character. That has great value to those who, outside the group, are anonymous integers in an alien society.

To these associations which were their own, and not those of strangers, they turned in the moments of trouble. Now and again the hat went round and the tinkle of reluctant coins recalled the imminent peril of all. But then, disasters were so frequent and so terrible it was an elementary precaution that some among these people should band together to accumulate the funds with which they could give mutual aid to each other. With this added function, the group achieved a more formal structure. To administer its affairs, to safeguard its cash, to allocate its benefits, it needed the services of officers. When those appeared the mutual aid society had evolved.

Although life itself was full of problems, the first concern of these societies was death. The dread transition to the mystery of the world beyond had always been laden with meaningful implications. Since this was not merely an end to mortal flesh, but the beginning also of another existence, they had at home reckoned it of particular im-

portance that a man be laid away in the sacred ground of the ceme-
tery among his friends and relatives. For these awesome proceedings tradition prescribed the precise rites; the dread consequences of
failure or omission no one could foretell. Although the actual task
of interring the body was regarded with disgust and assigned to
some degraded individual, nevertheless the whole village had participated in this last communal duty to its members.

Here the forms were in danger. The isolated man might be buried
by strangers, improperly, in an unhallowed place, far from his kin,
forever to lie in desolate loneliness. More than anything in life itself,
the immigrants wished security in death; and the first task of the
mutual aid society was to provide that assurance. The cost was high
here for what was almost free back there, and only the common
action of the society adequate to meet it. Funerals became events of
great neighborhood ceremonial importance, and the undertaker no
longer a pariah but a person of consequence.

Once the dead were taken care of, for whom eternity was the
concern, then there was time to think of the living. As the groups
grew stronger, as they acquired reserves and financial stability,
they could expand their functions in a variety of directions. Suppose
a man was hurt in the foundry; suppose it crushed his chest, or
broke his arm, or tore his leg away, what then? As easily as a blind
hen found grain, he got compensation from the company. Yet a wife
and the children had to be fed and himself he needed care.

In the village, such assistance had been among the obligations of
the family. It was vain to rely upon such flimsy support here, however. Few households had the resources to take care of their own
when illness struck, or accident; fewer still to extend aid to relatives
or neighbors. The wiser course was to unite in precautionary saving.
Let each one contribute monthly or weekly a fixed sum which would
accumulate as a whole and upon which each could draw when
necessary under the terms of an agreed-on plan. In illness as in
death, the mutual benefit society came increasingly to be the main
reliance of all immigrants.

The associations themselves met with a various fortune. They
thrived or foundered, depending partly upon the honesty, prudence,
and skill of the officers and partly upon the welfare of the members.
Some societies, hopefully inaugurated, quickly came to grief when a
treasurer absconded or through ignorance confounded his accounts
or through unwise investments lost the savings. Others closed their
affairs when depression or even just seasonal slack stopped the flow
of dues and, at the same time, stepped up the requests for benefits.

Perhaps the largest number maintained the precarious balance of income and expenditure through the lifetime at least of their founders.

On the other hand, a few flourished beyond any initial expectation. The presence of a handful of successful members would attract new recruits through the hope of favors or the prestige of belonging. With so heavy a social premium on joining, such organizations felt free to charge what fees they liked; yet growing wealthy, they found few calls from within for assistance. They were likely then to turn their attention to the improvident many who still needed help.

No doubt it was true that no one could be forced to aid the needy. But men were not beasts to be left to perish from want. The associations with funds to spare took on the obligation of relieving the misery of more newly arrived immigrants; the longer-settled but poor they tided over with loans or outright gifts; and the victims of accident or of personal maladjustment they helped with advice and what charity they could.

In addition, some groups through benevolence were induced to construct and maintain the philanthropic institutions the new conditions of living made necessary. The traditional duties of supporting the infirm were too onerous to be borne here by individuals. It was well enough in the peasant hut to find a corner for the old man or woman, to share what food there was. Or, the parentless could slip without difficulty into an uncle's household. And what attention the ill received, they received at home. In the crowded immigrant quarters such cares were enough to disrupt the family's precarious stability. Yet the prospect of confinement in the refuge maintained by the state or municipal government was frightening. The grandparents shuddered at the thought of spending their last days among uncomprehending strangers; orphans sent to such an asylum would surely grow away from the group; and the sick often preferred the possibility of death within the safety of their own houses to the unknown risks of the alien hospital. The old obligation therefore became a new one, not to find space in the flat or time from work for the accommodation of those who needed care, but rather to establish and support their own hospital, orphanage, and home for the aged to perform the task.

As the successful societies took on additional charitable functions, they acquired a variety of forms. In the early intimate days of the life of each, constitutional questions were of very slight concern. The organization then operated after the manner of the old village council, by discussion in which the weight accorded any opinion depended upon the respect accorded the individual who held it. Some associations then advanced to the respectability of a constitution and bylaws, copied in each case from some neighboring body, but derived ultimately from a common ancestry, the American corporation, board of directors, president, treasurer, secretary. Still others assumed the structure of the fraternal secret society. After 1850 particularly, Knights and Orders of many sorts flourished in a bewildering Gothic variety.

The magnetic element at the core of all, however, was always the opportunity for sociability. With the occasional association dedicated to intellectual and physical self-improvement, these provided the means by which like men got to know each other. The balls and picnics had the additional virtue of raising money; but their true end was sociability. And the event that excited greatest enthusiasm was the parade, a procession which enabled the group to display before the whole world the evidence of its solidarity, which enabled the individual to demonstrate that he belonged, was a part of a whole.

Sometimes, in the half-light of a brisk spring late afternoon when the parade was over or on the way home at night in the heady good cheer after the ball, a man would think, as he came up the steps of his house, *What if all this did not exist that I could be part of it, what if I were then alone among the teeming thousands on this block, had none to talk with, none to know and be known by!* The thought alone would inspire him with determination to keep safe the community he was creating.

All around were threats to its integrity. Everywhere in the United States were laws that prescribed a minimum schooling for the children. The State itself sponsored educational institutions into which youngsters were drawn without cost, there to be brought up by aliens, taught alien ways in an alien language, generally by teachers of an alien religion. From this sore spot might spread a hostile influence that could undermine the health of the whole immigrant community. You could sense that danger in the derisive name-calling of the schoolyard, in the unbending severity of the principal, in the bloody fights of the boys on the way.

The alternative was to devise voluntary schools that would serve to strengthen rather than to weaken the coherence of the group. To do so involved a difficult and discouraging task. There was no precedent in the European experience of the newcomers. None of the countries from which these people emigrated had had an educational system that reached down to the peasantry. What efforts had been made in that direction were entirely State-supported.

Yet with devotion and at the expense of considerable sacrifice the immigrants attempted to construct autonomous schools which would leave in their own hands the training of their young. They raised funds and paid out fees for the sake of saving the children. But the measure of their success was not impressive. Among the Germans, Poles, Italians, Jews, and most other groups only a handful of institutions survived in a limited number of places. The Irish Catholics were somewhat better rewarded for their troubles. The earliest Catholic colleges had been directed at training for the priesthood and the earliest convent schools had attracted only an upper-class clientele. But as Irish influence became weightier in the Church the number of elementary schools set up to provide for the children of immigrants increased rapidly. Even within this group, however, parochial schools served only a minority by the end of the period of immigration. The expense was too great to be shouldered fully at once; yet delay established the children within the influence of the public institutions.

Fortunately the school was only one of several means of education. The labor of several hundred parents together could not maintain a building and teachers; but in the nineteenth century, several hundred subscribers could support a newspaper. Shortly after its arrival every group of immigrants found a medium of expression in a press of its own, edited to satisfy its own needs, and published in its own language.

.   .   .   .   .

The men who acquired here new modes of fellowship to replace the old ones destroyed by emigration earned thereby some sense of security against complete isolation. But their efforts, no matter how strenuous, could not forestall changes. The whole of American society was changing. These little immigrant islands within it could not withstand the trend.

Everything in the neighborhood was so nice, they would later say, until the others came. The others brought outlandish ways and unintelligible speech, foreign dress and curious foods, were poor, worked hard, and paid higher rents for inferior quarters. Gradually the older comers saw the new arrivals filter into the district, occupy house after house that became vacant before their advance, until the whole configuration of the place was transformed.

So the tenement regions of the cities became the homes of group after group of immigrants. Through the dark halls and crowded rooms moved the Irish and the Germans, the Italians and the Poles, and all the other wandering peoples, each in turn to make a way of life there. But not permanently; each was in time displaced by its successor.

Movement away from the tenement areas did not immediately destroy the associational life that had proliferated there. Often there was a vigorous continuity. In New York City, for instance, the Germans moved in a straight line northward along the East Side of the island and the Irish did the same on the West Side. Old institutions were transplanted to new settings and, as the suburbs fell before the immigrant advance, they took on some of the aspects of the neighborhoods of first settlement. Still, each removal, in the mind of the individual, raised afresh the question of his affiliations, offered him the opportunity to re-examine the question of where he belonged. This mobility gave all organizations a transient quality, prevented any from becoming fixed, rigid, customary.

Under such circumstances the immigrant societies themselves were bound to change. They had been spontaneous in their organization, but once set up, drifted out of the control of the mass of members. With growth a select leadership appeared; it took skill beyond the capacity of the ordinary laborer to manage the affairs of an insurance association or to edit a newspaper or direct a theater. And the interests and points of view of the leadership were not always the same as those of its following.

The man who took command of the immigrant group sometimes sprang from within the ranks of the newcomers. He had laid hands on the money to open a grocery or to take on contracts and had added by shrewdness and effort to his original store. The fellows who had come off the ship with him still toiled away for their uncertain daily bread, but he was successful, had faced the American environment and had mastered it. At home perhaps he had been only a swineherd, his father a landless cottier without respectable status in the village. But family dignity counted for nothing here. He merited consideration who had acquired a secure existence and had shown thereby his capacity to deal with the New World. The prestige of social office confirmed the leadership of such individuals.

Yet this person who had elevated himself above the others in the group had also thereby imperceptibly separated himself from them. Sure, there was a feeling of personal importance, of self-exaltation at the rise. At the family table there was a lavish spread of food

and at the meetings of the Order there could be the munificent ges-
tures of hospitality and donations. The insecurities were of another
quality.

The laborer after all dealt mostly with others like himself. But the
immigrant become businessman was thrown in with all sorts of people, salesmen, government officials, bankers; and, as the old saying
had it, *Who goes among crows must croak like them, who gets
among goats must jump like them*. It was necessary to get along
with strangers, to win the esteem of influential outsiders. He who
rose must learn to wear American clothing, let his fingernails grow
like a gentleman, cultivate conformity in language and name, and
still not drift so far away as to lose the respect of his own group.
Such were the burdens of leadership.

The weight was even heavier for those who aspired to direct an
immigrant group without having originated within the group itself.
Antedating the mass movement from Europe, and continuing through
the nineteenth century along with it, was a much tinier migration of
political refugees, displaced by the recurrent revolutions on the continent. Repercussions of the French Revolution brought some; from
Ireland came exiles after the disturbances of 1798, 1803, and 1848;
from Germany came those dissatisfied with Metternich's repressions
in the 1820's and with the failure of 1848; from Poland came the
unsuccessful rebels of 1830 and 1863; and from eastern Europe
came handfuls of socialists unsafe at home after 1880. The Land of
Liberty was the universal refuge for dissentients everywhere.

These people in the Old World had had nothing to do with the
peasantry; and in the New continued to stand apart. They were disposed to be apathetic if not hostile to religion; they were radical
rather than conservative in politics; and they were liberal rather
than traditional in their attitudes toward social institutions. Such
substantial differences brought them closer in point of view to the
native Americans than to the mass of newcomers. Yet only a few
entered so readily into the society they found in the United States
as to make for themselves independent careers here.

The most were driven back to the immigrant communities, which
welcomed the services they could perform. They were literate, indeed often well-educated. They could talk and write, make favorable impressions as representatives of the group. Often such men
acquired positions of responsible leadership without yet being integrated into the organizations they led. Suspended between the
American society to which they spoke and the immigrant society

which supported them, they felt the unremitting pressure to reconcile the two.

The same compulsion was heaviest of all when it fell upon those whom the circumstances of nativity gave affiliations in both the greater and the lesser society. One came a young child and went some terms to the public schools. Another cried as a newborn infant in the stifling tenement room and played ball on the street among the passing draymen's teams. They entered manhood with the American ideals absorbed from school and street, not strangers but familiar to the life about them.

Yet often the opportunities lay among their father's folk. There name and religion were advantages not disadvantages. There the accents of the old language, the acquaintance with the ways of the old neighborhood, were assets not liabilities. No young man in business or politics could afford to overlook connections within the immigrant group. For their part, the older people saw an attractiveness in these their youth who bore so much the aspects of Americans. The foreign-born would not always follow their native sons, but were willing to have them lead.

It was significant that immigrant associational activity drew its direction from men who somehow stood apart, from men who had this in common, that they were concerned with using their positions to make an impression in the general society. With that end in view they could not be content with the local club as it had remained under the original founders; a radical transformation was indispensable.

Confederation of existing organizations was the simplest step. After 1850 there were determined efforts within each immigrant group to create one or more national unions that would draw together the scattered societies. After 1880 such efforts achieved a measure of success; Alliances, Leagues, Orders covered the country, and the earlier parochial associations sank to the status of mere branches. In discussion the arguments for combination were plausible enough: funds would be more secure, influence more pervasive. But the men who listened and hesitantly acquiesced knew better, though they knew not how to say it: not they would go to conventions, sit on committees, be consulted by important personages. No, and the intimate meanings of the old meetings would disappear. Still, they were feeble in debate and could not hold out.

Nor could they long resist appeals that awakened attachments to the place of their birth. In the Old World all the nationalist currents of the nineteenth century had passed them by; indeed these people did not even identify themselves in such terms. And certainly emigration involved a rejection of the Old Country. Only in America, as strangers, had they learned from the inevitable contrasts with others to be aware of their own distinctive character.

Their American offspring turned this group-consciousness into nationalism. The sons of the immigrants had no memory of Old Country places, no recollection of the village solidarity. By actual membership in the group and by participation in its activities, they knew they were Irish or German or Italian or Polish. But that affiliation had meaning for them only as a kind of patriotism; and they projected onto their fathers' native lands the kinds of loyalty that, in the United States, seemed proper to a fatherland. Fervently they enlisted in movements to create new states or to support the policies of existing ones. Therein they received the support of the nationalistic émigrés already involved in similar causes and also the approbation of other Americans swayed by the common sympathy of the nineteenth century for oppressed nationalities.

No other form of immigrant association received such universal approval from outside the group. Who would be so stubborn as to remain unconvinced, to abstain from an activity that involved, at once, the renewal of ties with the place of one's birth and the acclaim of the whole country? For almost a century the Irish in America were wrapped up in the struggle for the independence of the Emerald Isle, a struggle for a time so intense as to produce armed invasions of the nearest British territory in Canada. The attitude of German-Americans to the Empire in 1870, of Italian-Americans to the Kingdom, of central and eastern Europeans to the successor republics of 1918, and of the Jews to Zionism, partook of the same quality.

Still a third assault was launched upon the original integrity of immigrant society, this one less successful. The men of radical ideas exiled to the United States attempted to enlist the newcomers in organizations directed against the existing order. Partly the revolutionaries were betrayed by their own ideology: they would never get to realize that the most oppressed economic order was not necessarily the most likely to rebel. The immigrant was an exploited unskilled laborer; they persisted in the hope they might turn his vague discontent into specific radical directions. In any case, the radicals were agitators by profession. Chance had thrown them in with a class with which they were not familiar. They would try to make converts all the same.

Between 1850 and 1880 an exotic agglomeration of socialists, anarchists, and freethinkers labored to find support within the immigrant associations. Though, as intellectuals, they made their voices heard with more volume than their numbers justified, they were hardly in a position to boast of their achievements after thirty years of trying.

After 1880, the radicals were inclined to capitalize on the neglect of the immigrants by the American labor movement. Recognizing the solidarity of these groups, the socialists attempted to enlist the foreign-born through such special agencies as the United German Trades and the United Hebrew Trades. Similarly, after 1900, the I.W.W. set up separate nationality locals and recognized the particular languages of the immigrants in order to gain support among them. But the deep-rooted conservatism of these people proved an insuperable obstacle to such proselytizing. At most the radicals raised disruptive, confusing issues or split the leadership; they could not arouse the enthusiasm of the masses.

Indeed the immigrant who had been at home in his own mutual aid society was dismayed by all these efforts to turn his joining into something else. The national alliances took on the appearance of power and wealth. Nationalistic agitation whipped up a display of emotions. In the Turners, in the Sokols, in the Zouaves—intricate patriotic associations—men deployed in fixed, rigid lines. But the touch of intimate friendliness, the sense of dwelling with one's brothers, vanished. Disappointed, he often dropped out; secession after secession continually reproduced the neighborhood societies which, after all, gave him what he wanted.

Only time went on and even these were not the same.

The will is not to change. But change comes. New words and ways insidiously filter in. *Someone speaks and you can only look at him on the street there, miserable in your lack of English.* Now phrases will be remembered, become familiar, enter into usage, be confounded with the old language. Someday the trolley signs will have a meaning and you will be interpreter for someone greener still.

The old coat disintegrates. Its rugged homespun had come along; its solid virtues had taken the strain of the full way since the old tailor had put his labored stitches into it. The new is one of many, indistinguishable from the rest. Cheaper, it transforms the wearer;

coming out the factory gate he is now also one of many, indistinguishable from the rest.

In New York a German mutual aid society debates the disposition of its funds. The Hildise Bund collects the periodic dues from its members but is concerned lest some sudden press for benefits or some mishap with investments leave it unprepared to pay. In 1868 the association enters into an arrangement by which a local insurance company underwrites the risk. That is the beginning of the business of industrial life insurance that makes the Metropolitan Life the largest in the world. Ultimately the company will bypass the society. Immigrant agents write policies for their countrymen; at lesser cost, with greater security, they perform the old mutual aid functions.

In many other ways, it was tempting to establish compromises with the economies of the wider American institutions. The ruinous expense of separate school systems among some groups was evaded by leaving to the public system the general secular subjects, adding to them outside instruction in religion and language. Disgruntled boys went off to afternoon or vacation *Svenska Skolan* or *Talmud Torah* to acquire in supplementary classes the learning their parents valued.

The parents themselves were sometimes tempted to follow along after their American children's manner. By this means the immigrant press was subtly undermined, though it continued yet to show the signs of growth. As long as the flow of newcomers continued, circulation figures soared. The sheets expanded, and weeklies turned into dailies.

Yet many an editor could see the signs of a change. The boys grew up and would not take the trouble to read in the foreign language. Instead they turned to newspapers in the more familiar English, newspapers being molded to their tastes by perspicacious men alive to the potentialities of this new public. Before the end of the nineteenth century the signs were unmistakable. From St. Louis, Joseph Pulitzer had brought to New York a rich experience as publisher of a German newspaper; the enormous expansion of the circulation of his *World* took its start from the attractiveness of the paper to the second generation of German-Americans. The contemporaneous activities of William Randolph Hearst stood in the same relationship to Irish-Americans.

These mass journals assimilated many characteristics of the immigrant press. They emphasized the sensational and dramatic at the expense of pure news; they devoted space to the doings of the local associations and of local personages; the serial story was at home in their pages; and they stood ready to advise their readers in the most intimate manner. Finally, they catered consistently to the nationalistic emotions of the organized immigrant movements. All this a mass circulation enabled them to do cheaply and lavishly. It was no wonder that even some in the first generation were inclined to lay down their pennies for these papers, simple in language, big with headlines, and fat with pictures.

On the stage where the demands of literacy were still less pressing, the process was already further advanced. From the start there had been a liberal exchange of plays and personalities between the immigrant and American theaters. The hard-pressed Yiddish dramatist who turned out a script a week did not hesitate to borrow plot or characters elsewhere successful; and an individual like Barney Williams had already given a broader currency to the Irish comic. All were absorbed onto the developing vaudeville stage. There the young people, and often their elders as well, could see in successive turns the laughable antics of the recognizably Irish, or German, or Jewish, or Italian; and these the more attractive because interspersed with the trickery of acrobats and magicians and flavored with the lilt of song and dance.

No doubt immigrant impresarios attempted to compete, just as immigrant editors made the effort to rival Hearst and Pulitzer in sensationalism—in both cases in vain. The mass medium that reached the greatest numbers commanded the greatest resources. Once the peak of new arrivals passed, immigrant press and stage alike began to weaken. And already the nickel shows where dim pictures flickered on a screen foreshadowed a medium more popular still that would complete the process.

There was a cost. The whole purpose of the new press and the new entertainment was to reach the widest audience; the means, to reach the most universal common denominator. Steadily the distinctive characteristics were rubbed down, the figures became generalized and blurred. Eternally Maggie continued the pursuit of Jiggs and the Inspector the Katzenjammer Kids; but not so much, and ever less, did these evoke the response of recognition as Irish or German. More often, upon the scene walked unidentifiable men of uncertain paternity, men of vague and colorless names who lived remote lives. Tears and laughter still might come but without the former meaning.

Generalization had wiped out the awareness of their own particular situation the immigrants had once recognized in those pages, on that stage.

In the strange world of lonely men, the immigrants had reached out to each other, eager in the desire to have brothers with whom they could dwell. In the fluid and free life of America, they found the latitude to join with one another, to contrive institutions through which they could act, means of expression that would speak for them.

But the same fluidity and freedom ultimately undermined the societies, the press, and the theater, that at the start they encouraged. While the immigrants, through those institutions, were adjusting to the American environment, the American environment was adjusting to their presence. An open society offered ample scope for mutual give-and-take.

Those who had themselves made the crossing, who recalled from their own experience the meaning in their lives of the first coming-together with friends, would struggle to preserve the old associations. But their sons were not likely to make the attempt. And they themselves would often taste the sadness of defeat.

Chapter Two

THE SOCIETAL CONTEXT OF
SOCIAL WELFARE

The institution of social welfare is unlike other major societal institutions on at least two counts: It is broader in scope, and it is less
well established. Upon reflection, this statement should stimulate
some curiosity. If it is not as well established as other institutions,
how did social welfare get to be so broad in scope? To understand
why this state of affairs characterizes the institution we must consider how the idea of social welfare fits the concept of a social
institution.

Social institutions are networks of relationships that are widely
accepted as the normal way to carry out essential societal functions
such as child rearing, production and distribution of commodities,
and social control. These networks of relationships are concretely
manifest in organizational forms with which we are all familiar: the
church, the university, and the political party, to name a few. Thus,
the concept "institution" is often used on two levels of abstraction;
for example, we may speak both of a religious institution, such as
St. John's church, and of *the* institution of religion, or the "Church."
In the former sense, institution refers to a single organizational unit,
while in the latter it implies the sum of organizational units that
carry the primary responsibility for performing an essential function.

Social institutions are not limited to performing single functions.

On the contrary, a given institution usually serves many functions. The church, for instance, engages in socialization and in recreational and sometimes even political activities, though its main function is that of an agency which fulfills spiritual needs. While the major social institutions may perform many important functions, they are distinguished and achieve normative acceptance primarily on the basis of their core function. The crux of the issue regarding the institution of social welfare, therefore, is the question: What is or should be the core function of social welfare.

The readings in the preceding chapter indicated some of the functions performed by social welfare arrangements, such as redistribution of income, social control of the poor, assistance for the aged and disabled, socialization of the children of the poor, and general provisions for social security. But which of these functions distinguishes social welfare activities from those of familial, religious, political, and economic institutions? Is the core function security, control, redistribution, socialization, assistance, or something else?

One answer to these questions is to view the institution of social welfare as consisting of a series of arrangements necessary to compensate for the imperfections and limitations of other major social institutions in meeting human needs. According to this view, social welfare serves all of the functions noted above under the general rubric of "mutual support."

> Mutual support functions come into play when individuals are not able to meet their needs through the major institutions which operate to carry out the other social functions we have described. This may occur for a wide variety of reasons such as sickness, loss of a wage earner, or inadequate functioning of the economic institutions. In technologically underdeveloped societies, mutual support activities are carried out primarily by the family. As societies have become more complex, other groups, organizations, and agencies develop to carry out mutual support activities, such as the church, voluntary agencies, and government. *The institution of social welfare is that pattern of relationships which develops in society to carry out mutual support functions.*[1]

This definition of the function of social welfare helps to explain why the institution is broader in scope than others, because mutual support activities cut across a wide range of institutional sectors. These activities are relative to and dependent upon the extent to which human needs are met through the primary activities of religious, familial, political, and economic institutions at any given point in time. The relative and diffuse quality of mutual support activities complicates efforts to delineate the institution of social welfare as a separate and distinct entity.

There are a number of reasons why the institution of social welfare is less well established than the other major social institutions. First, as noted above, it is difficult to discern a core function for the pattern of relationships designated as social welfare that is distinct from functions served by older established institutions. Second, there is a fair amount of disagreement concerning the question of whether mutual support activities are a true representation of the main purpose of social welfare. Many critics have observed that beneath the humanitarian facade of mutual support, social welfare arrangements are essentially devices for the social control of the poor and underprivileged.[2] And finally, the institution of social welfare is not established on as firm ground as other institutions because there are divergent views within society concerning the desirability of mutual support activities. Many people view these activities as nothing more than temporary corrective arrangements for meeting needs that are not at the time being served through the regular or "normal" institutional channels.

These comments suggest some of the conceptual problems and disagreements that surround the idea of social welfare. The readings in this chapter present varying perspectives on the primary functions of social welfare, the structure of the institution, and how social welfare activities fit into the institutional framework of democratic-capitalist societies.

In Reading 4, "Conceptions of Social Welfare," Harold L. Wilensky and Charles N. Lebeaux identify the "residual" and "institutional" views of social welfare. With the institutional view, social welfare is perceived to be an established pattern of activities serving important and legitimate functions in modern society. This view is gaining increased popular endorsement over the residual conception. With the latter perspective, social welfare activities are considered to be temporary substitutes for meeting needs through traditionally preferred institutional channels such as the family and the market economy.

Wilensky and Lebeaux also describe a series of essential features that distinguishes social welfare activities. Among these features is the absence of the profit motive as the dominant program purpose. Within this context it is interesting to compare Richard Titmuss's views in "The Role of Redistribution in Social Policy" (Reading 5) with those of Wilensky and Lebeaux on the issue of whether industrial pension plans should be considered in the category of social welfare arrangements. Wilensky and Lebeaux are more equivocal than Titmuss in their analysis of whether industrial pensions are a form of social welfare or part of the conditions of employment in the market economy. Emphasizing the redistributive functions of social welfare arrangements, Titmuss argues that conceptual frameworks for analyzing social welfare arrangements have been too narrow and tend to exclude arrangements that benefit the middle and upper classes more than the poor. For Titmuss, the analysis of the redistributive effects of social welfare would include what he refers to as "fiscal welfare" (e.g., income tax deductions) and "occupational welfare" (i.e., private pensions and other benefits connected with employment), as well as the forms of direct public provisions of services and cash that constitute the prevalent conception of social welfare.

Another reflection on the institutional versus the residual status of social welfare is offered in Reading 6, "The Societal Function of Social Welfare," by Martin Wolins. Wolins distinguishes between "type B welfare programs," which substitute for and are perceived as less desirable than "type A welfare programs," which consist of established need-meeting arrangements that have achieved institutional status. He traces the development of several social welfare arrangements that have moved from residual to institutional status and analyzes the dynamics of this change. While noting that the movement from type B to type A welfare constitutes a measure of social reform, Wolins stresses the historically conservative function of social welfare as a device designed to help maintain stability and control in an industrial society.

Most social welfare activities are conducted under government auspices. Thus, any case for expanding the institution of social welfare is, in part, a case for increasing the range of governmental interventions into other institutional sectors such as the family and the market economy. What are the proper functions of government? Under what conditions are government interventions in the market economy justified? These questions are addressed from the viewpoint of classical liberal economics in Reading 7, "The Role of Government in a Free Society," by Milton Friedman. According to Friedman, much of what we would consider social welfare activity is justified on paternalistic grounds, where government intervention is warranted to protect people who cannot be held responsible for their own well-being. This viewpoint, of course, envisions social welfare as being concerned with the limited function of handling arrangements for the incompetent. Friedman notes that social security programs, among a host of other government activities, are not justified in terms of the criteria for government intervention outlined in his article. From Friedman's perspective, social welfare has a circumscribed and residual function in our society.

NOTES

1. Neil Gilbert and Harry Specht, *Dimensions of Social Welfare Policy* (Englewood Cliffs, N.J.: Prentice-Hall, Inc., 1974), p. 5.
2. For example, see Frances Fox Piven and Richard Cloward, *Regulating the Poor* (New York: Pantheon Books, 1971), and Betty Mandell, "Welfare and Totalitarianism: Part I. Theoretical Issues," *Social Work*, 16 (January 1971): 17–25.

4   Conceptions of Social Welfare

HAROLD L. WILENSKY and CHARLES N. LEBEAUX

What is meant by social welfare? Is it relief, and just for the poor? Is social insurance included? What of public recreation and parks? And if these are social welfare, why not public highways and the Tennessee Valley Authority? How about private industry's pension plans? And what of fee-charging social agencies and the "private practice" of social work?

We are not concerned here with formulating a view of what social welfare ought ideally to involve, but rather with its existing outlines and trends in the United States. Specifically, we will: (1) point out what seem to be the currently dominant concepts of welfare, and (2) state some criteria for delineating social welfare.

From Harold L. Wilensky and Charles N. Lebeaux, *Industrial Society and Social Welfare* (New York: Free Press, 1965), pp. 138–47. Reprinted with permission of the authors and of Macmillan Publishing Company. Copyright © 1958 by Russell Sage Foundation.

CURRENT CONCEPTIONS

Two conceptions of social welfare seem to be dominant in the United States today: the *residual* and the *institutional*. The first holds that social welfare institutions should come into play only when the normal structures of supply, the family and the market, break down. The second, in contrast, sees the welfare services as normal, "first line" functions of modern industrial society. These are the concepts around which drives for more or for less welfare service tend to focus. Not surprisingly, they derive from the ethos of the society in which they are found. They represent a compromise between the values of economic individualism and free enterprise on the one hand, and security, equality, and humanitarianism on the other. They are rather explicit among both social welfare professionals and the lay public.

The residual formulation is based on the premise that there are two "natural" channels through which an individual's needs are properly met: the family and the market economy. These are the preferred structures of supply. However, sometimes these institutions do not function adequately: family life is disrupted, depressions occur. Or sometimes the individual cannot make use of normal channels because of old age or illness. In such cases, according to this idea, a third mechanism of need fulfillment is brought into play— the social welfare structure. This is conceived as a residual agency, attending primarily to emergency functions, and is expected to withdraw when the regular social structure—the family and the economic system—is again working properly. Because of its residual, temporary, substitute characteristic, social welfare thus conceived often carries the stigma of "dole" or "charity."

The residual concept was more popular in the United States before the Great Depression of 1929 than it is now. That it is consistent with the traditional American ideology of individual responsibility and by-your-own-bootstrap progress is readily apparent. But it does not reflect the radical social changes accompanying advanced industrialization, or fully account for various aspects of contemporary social welfare activity.

The second major formulation of social welfare is given in a widely used social work textbook as "the organized system of social services and institutions, designed to aid individuals and groups to attain satisfying standards of life and health. It aims at personal and social relationships which permit individuals the fullest development of their capacities and the promotion of their well-being in harmony with the needs of the community."[1] (1: p. 4). This definition of the "institutional" view implies no stigma, no emergency, no "abnormalcy." Social welfare becomes accepted as a proper, legitimate function of modern industrial society in helping individuals achieve self-fulfillment. The complexity of modern life is recognized. The inability of the individual to provide fully for himself, or to meet all his needs in family and work settings, is considered a "normal" condition; and the helping agencies achieve "regular" institutional status.

While these two views seem antithetical, in practice American social work has tried to combine them, and current trends in social welfare represent a middle course. Those who lament the passing of the old order insist that the second ideology is undermining individual character and the national social structure. Those who bewail our failure to achieve utopia today, argue that the residual conception is an obstacle which must be removed before we can produce the good life for all. In our view, neither ideology exists in a vacuum; each is a reflection of . . . broader cultural and societal conditions . . . ; and with further industrialization the second is likely to prevail.

CRITERIA FOR DELINEATING SOCIAL WELFARE

Keeping in mind this ideological dualism, we can now look at the substance of social welfare. What are the main distinguishing characteristics of activities which fall within the range of welfare practice in America today?[2]

1. *Formal Organization.* Social welfare activities are formally organized. Handouts and individual charity, though they may increase or decrease welfare, are not organized. Likewise, services and help extended within such mutual-aid-relationships as family, friends and neighbors, kinship groups, and the like are not included in the definition of social welfare structure. It is recognized that there is a continuum running from the most informal to the most formal, and that in-between cases—the mutual-aid welfare services of a small labor union, church, or fraternal society—cannot be precisely classified. The distinction is clear in principle, however, and important.

Modern social welfare has really to be thought of as help given to the stranger, not to the person who by reason of personal bond commands it without asking. It assumes a degree of social distance between helped and helper. In this respect it is a social response to the shift from rural to urban-industrial society. Help given within the family or friendship group is but an aspect of the underlying relationship. Welfare services are a different kind of "help." We must think here of the regular, full-time, recognized agencies that carry on the welfare business.

2. *Social Sponsorship and Accountability.* Social auspice—the existence of socially sanctioned purposes and methods, and formal accountability—is the crucial element in social welfare service versus comparable service under profit-making auspices. If mobilization of resources to meet needs is not accomplished by the family or through the market economy, some third type of organization must be provided, and this is typically the society as a whole acting through government (city, state, federal), or a smaller collectivity operating through a private social agency. (2: p. 13.)

Some mechanism for expressing the public interest and rendering the service accountable to the larger community is an essential part of social sponsorship. For public welfare services in a democratic society, the mechanism is simply the representative structure of government. For voluntary agencies accountability is typically, though less certainly, achieved through a governing board. That some of these boards are self-perpetuating, unresponsive to changing needs and isolated from constituencies, does not deny the principle of accountability, any more than oligarchy denies it in the public welfare arena. The principle is acknowledged in privately as well as publicly sponsored organizations.

3. *Absence of Profit Motive as Dominant Program Purpose.* Just as the needs-service cycle within the family is excluded from the concept of social welfare, so generally are those needs which arise and are fulfilled within the bounds of the free enterprise system. The services and goods produced by the market economy and purchased by individuals with money derived from competitive participation in that economy are not social welfare. Profitable and most fee-for-service activities are excluded. But there are cases difficult to classify.

Social welfare objectives can be intimately associated with what is basically profit-making enterprise, as when a private business provides recreation facilities, pension plans, or nurseries for its employees. The view may be taken, on the one hand, that since such services attend human wants quite peripheral to the purpose of the organization, they neither share in nor alter the nature of the underlying profit-making activity. The latter remains nonwelfare, while the

former are essentially social welfare programs under business auspices. This view gains support from the observation that separate
structures for the administration of welfare services often develop
within the business enterprise, and constitute a kind of "social auspice." An industrial pension plan, for instance, usually has a trust
fund separate from the financial operations of the company; a separate office with its own physical facilities will be set up to administer it; the policy-making group—board or committee—will often
have employee or union representation, especially if the plan is collectively bargained; and its operation will likely come under some
degree of government regulation.

On the other hand, the view may be taken that industry-sponsored
welfare programs are simply part of the conditions of employment,
a substitute for wages. Industries provide restrooms and run recreational programs to compete for a labor supply and maintain employee morale and efficiency. Pensions, in this view, are a kind of
deferred wage. Programs are often administered not through separate administrative offices, but by the business accounting or personnel office. Even when separate administrative structures are
created, this does not alter the underlying program purpose of facilitating production.[3]

Thus, the degree to which an industrial welfare program may
be considered social welfare varies inversely with extent of emphasis on a contractual relationship between two parties seeking
a mutually rewarding arrangement, and directly with extent of social sponsorship and control. It is clear, nevertheless, that industrial
welfare programs affect the development of social welfare institutions. The Supplemental Unemployment Benefits scheme, for instance, creates pressure for expanded unemployment insurance,
and private pension plans are integrated with OASI in planning for
retirement. . . .

Some aspects of professional fee-for-service practice are also
difficult to classify. Most Americans probably would think—and
without derogatory implication—that professions as well as trades
are primarily ways of making a living (often a kind of small business), and thus nonwelfare in nature. Yet it is a fact that many individual professional practitioners—physicians, lawyers, and den-
tists particularly—observe what appears to be a semi-social welfare
practice of scaling fees according to ability to pay. Fee-scaling in
private practice, however, is often a professional norm, part of a
formal code of ethics. As such, its meaning and nature derive from
a different context—professionalism—and it can be seen as a de-

vice by which a group with a monopoly of an indispensable service protects its fee-taking privilege. Where the professional "charges what the traffic will bear," there is no ambiguity, and his activity is clearly nonwelfare in nature.

To the extent that the private practice of social casework resembles other fee-for-service professions, it, too, is rather clearly outside the field of social welfare. Solo practice of social work is as yet so little developed, however, that it cannot be seen how close it will hew to the model of the other professions.

4. *Functional Generalization: An Integrative View of Human Needs.* Since almost any of the gamut of culturally conditioned human needs may be unmet and since human capacities which can be developed are many, welfare services to meet needs and enhance capacities will be varied. Placing babies in foster homes, operating a recreation program, administering social insurance, developing medical service in a rural community—the substantive activities here have little in common; a great variety of activities may take on a social welfare aspect. From the standpoint of the welfare structure as a whole, these activities are properly described as "functionally generalized"; that is, welfare services are found attached to, or performing in place of, medical institutions, the family, education, industry—wherever there is "unmet need." It will be noticed that this concept is closely related to that of residuality discussed above; what other institutions do not do, it is the job of welfare to do. To the extent that it is the function of social welfare to come in and "pick up the pieces" in any area of need, it must lack attachment to any given area.

From this characteristic derives, in part at least, the comprehensive view of human needs and personality that distinguishes social work from other professions. An international study by the United Nations of training for social work concludes that social work seeks to assist

> . . . individuals, families and groups in relation to the many social and economic forces by which they are affected, and differs in this respect from certain allied activities, such as health, education, religion, etc. The latter . . . tend to exclude all save certain specific aspects of the socio-economic environment from their purview. . . . The social worker, on the other hand, cannot exclude from his consideration any aspect of the life of the person who seeks help in solving problems of social adjustment . . . [or any] of the community's

social institutions that might be of use to the individual . . .
(2: p. 13)

Individual agencies are, of course, specialized and limited in function; but the welfare field is inclusive. It is because social welfare is
"functionally generalized" that we exclude the school system, which
tends to be segmental in its approach to its clientele.

5. *Direct Concern with Human Consumption Needs.*   Finally, how
are government welfare services to be distinguished from other government services, since all are socially sponsored? It is possible to
place governmental activities on a continuum which ranges from
services primarily concerned with the functional requisites of the
society and only indirectly with the fate of the individual, to those
which provide direct services to meet immediate consumption needs
of individuals and families. At the "indirect" end of this continuum,
following the analysis of Hazel Kyrk, are government activities "inherent in the nature of the state . . . such as the national defense,
the preservation of law and order, the administration of justice, the
exercise of regulatory functions. . . ." Intermediate are road building, flood control, forest conservation, and other such services, "the
benefits of which are so remote in time or diffused among the population that they will not be privately provided." At the direct services
end are those where "specific beneficiaries can be identified, although there are also general benefits. . . . Schools and universities, recreational facilities, libraries, museums, concerts, school books
and lunches, subsidized housing, medical and hospital services. In
this last group of services described are those which are distinctly
for consumer use and enjoyment." (3: pp. 148–149)[4]

In the last group fall the welfare services. Of course, social welfare programs serve the needs of both the larger social structure
and the individual consumer. The unemployment compensation program in the United States, for example, has been designed as an
anti-depression weapon as well as a means of alleviating the individual distress accompanying unemployment. But it is the latter,
rather than the former, aspect of the program which from the
present point of view qualifies it as a social welfare activity.

A nineteenth century view of government in the United States
saw its functions restricted to "activities inherent in the nature of
the state." The veto of Dorothea Dix's mental hospital bill in 1854,
it will be remembered, was based on President Pierce's belief that
the life conditions of individuals were no proper concern of government. Today many government services are directed specifically to

individuals, and it is these which tend to be identified as social welfare.

It is thus an additional distinguishing attribute of social welfare programs that they tend to be aimed directly at the individual and his consumer interests, rather than at the general society and producer interests; that they are concerned with human resources as opposed to other kinds of resources. Soil conservation, subsidy of the merchant marine, development of water power resources, much as these redound ultimately to human welfare, are not typically defined as social welfare; but feeding the hungry, finding homes for dependent children, even provision of recreational facilities are so defined. This is the point of the stipulation in the definition of welfare given by Kraus,[5] that welfare services have "direct effects on welfare and health of individuals and families," and of Cassidy's definition of the social services as "those organized activities that are primarily and directly concerned with the conservation, the protection, and the improvement of human resources." (5: p. 13)

In sum, the major traits which, taken together, distinguish social welfare structure in America (made explicit here as criteria to define the field of analysis) are:

1. Formal organization
2. Social sponsorship and accountability
3. Absence of profit motive as dominant program purpose
4. Functional generalization: integrative, rather than segmental, view of human needs
5. Direct focus on human consumption needs

The major weakness in definition occurs in the area of socially sponsored, nonprofit services which affect nearly everyone in the society. It would seem, for instance, that public education might be classed among the social services, as it is in England (and by a few American welfare experts, for example, Ida C. Merriam). In the U.S. there is apparently a tendency to exclude from the welfare category any service, no matter how identified with welfare it may have been in origin, which becomes highly developed, widespread in its incidence among the population, and professionally staffed by persons other than social workers. Helen Witmer notes social insurance as an example of a welfare service which has tended to move out of the welfare area after it became a "usual institutional arrangement." (6: pp. 484–486) This seems to be consistent with the residual conception and its view of the welfare services as emergency, secondary, peripheral to the main show. As the residual conception becomes weaker, as we believe it will, and the institutional conception increasingly dominant, it seems likely that distinctions between welfare and other types of social institutions will become more and more blurred. Under continuing industrialization all institutions will be oriented toward and evaluated in terms of social welfare aims. The "welfare state" will become the "welfare society," and both will be more reality than epithet.

REFERENCES

1. Walter A. Friedlander, *Introduction to Social Welfare* (New York: Prentice-Hall, 1955), p. 4.
2. United Nations, Department of Social Affairs, *Training for Social Work: An International Survey* (New York: Columbia University Press, 1950), p. 13.
3. Hazel Kyrk, *The Family in the American Economy* (Chicago: University of Chicago Press, 1953), pp. 148–149.
4. Alexander S. Vucinich, *Soviet Economic Institutions: The Social Structure of Production Units* (Stanford, Calif.: Stanford University Press, 1952) pp. 9–10.
5. Harry M. Cassidy, *Social Security and Reconstruction in Canada* (Boston: Bruce Humphries, Inc., 1943), p. 13.
6. Helen L. Witmer, *Social Work: An Analysis of a Social Institution* (New York: Farrar and Rinehart, 1942), pp. 484–486.

NOTES

1. This is a typically vague definition of the "institutional" view. Contemporary definitions of welfare are fuzzy because cultural values regarding the social responsibilities of government, business, and the individual are now in flux. The older doctrines of individualism, private property and free market, and of minimum government provided a clear-cut definition of welfare as "charity for unfortunates." The newer values of social democracy—security, equality, humanitarianism—undermine the notion of "unfortunate classes" in society. All people are regarded as having "needs" which *ipso facto* become a legitimate claim on the whole society. Business and government as channels to supply these needs have vastly broadened their responsibilities. Both the older and newer doctrines coexist today, creating conflicts and ambiguities in values which are reflected in loose definitions of social welfare.

2. All institutions, of course, undergo change over time, both in form and function. However, some continuing identity is usually clear. Thus, the historical continuity and interconnection of social welfare institutions can be traced—from hospitals first designed as a place for the poor to die, to modern community hospitals serving the health needs of all; from sandpiles for the children of working mothers, to the tennis courts and baseball tournaments of a modern recreation program; from poorhouses to Social Security.

3. It is true that men's motives vary; and businessmen are not an exception. What we are talking about here is not individual motives but organizational purposes. Many business leaders may acquire a sense of trusteeship going beyond their obligations to the shareholders. Thus, multi-plant companies have been known to avoid shutdown of an unprofitable unit because of major disruption to the local community. But one cannot say that the enterprise purpose is to save declining communities, any more than one can call dropping 50 cents in a blind man's hat Aid to the Blind.

4. An interesting parallel to the distinction Kyrk makes here has been noted with respect to Soviet state institutions where, since "everything is government," it might also be expected that everything would be social welfare. Sociologist Vucinich observes, however, that in the U.S.S.R.: "Soviet experts in jurisprudence make a sharp distinction between social institutions . . . and Soviet enterprises. Institutions (post offices, telegraphic services, scientific laboratories, schools, and the like) are, in the economic sense, nonproductive units which draw their funds from the state budgets and are not considered independent juridical persons. Enterprises, on the other hand, have their 'own' budgets . . . their 'own' basic capital (machines, tools, etc.) and working capital." (4: pp. 9–10).

5. At a meeting of the United States Committee of the International Conference of Social Work, New York City, June 17, 1955.

5   The Role of Redistribution in Social Policy

RICHARD M. TITMUSS

In the literature of the West, concepts and models of social policy are as diverse as contemporary concepts of poverty. Historically, the two have indeed had much in common. They certainly share di-

From Social Security Bulletin, 28 (June 1965): pp. 14–20.

versity. There are today those at one end of the political spectrum who see social policy as a transitory minimum activity of minimum government for a minimum number of poor people; as a form of social control for minority groups in a "natural" society; as a way of resolving the conflict between the religious ethic of compassion and undiluted individualism. In this view social policy is not good business. Statistical estimates of the national income per capita look healthier if the infant mortality rate rises. At the other end of the political spectrum there are writers like Macbeath who has comprehensively stated that "Social policies are concerned with the right ordering of the network of relationships between men and women who live together in societies, or with the principles which should govern the activities of individuals and groups so far as they affect the lives and interests of other people."[1]

Somewhere between these extreme visionary notions lives a conventional, textbook, definition of social policy.[2] The social services or social welfare, the labels we have for long attached to describe certain areas of public intervention such as income maintenance and public health, are seen as the main ingredients of social policy. They are obvious, direct and measurable acts of government, undertaken for a variety of political reasons, to provide for a range of needs, material and social, and predominantly dependent needs, which the market does not or cannot satisfy for certain designated sections of the population. Typically, these direct services are functionally organised in separate and specialised ministries, departments or divisions of government, central and local. They are seen as the "social policy department." What they do is thought to be explicitly redistributive; they politically interfere with the pattern of claims set by the market. They assign claims from one set of people who are said to produce or earn the national product to another set of people who may merit compassion and charity but not economic rewards for productive service. In short, they are seen as uncovenanted benefits for the poorer sections of the community. And because these separate functional units of social service are accountable to the public their activities are, in large measure, quantifiable. We can thus measure the size of the presumed burden (as it is conventionally called) on the economy.

This, I propose to argue, is a very limited and inadequate model of the working of social policy in the second half of the twentieth century. In its distance from the realities of today it is about as helpful (or unhelpful) as some recent models of economic man maximising his acquisitive drives. Later, I attempt to support and

illustrate this statement by examining some of the lessons of experience of nearly 20 years of so-called "Welfare Statism" in Britain.
First, however, I want to briefly consider one or two of the factors
which have contributed to this limited concept of social policy—particularly in relation to its role as a redistributive agent.

Perhaps the most important causative factor in Britain has to do
with the heritage of the poor law (or public assistance). Less than
60 years ago social policy was, in the eyes of the middle and upper
classes, poor law policy. This model of "welfare use" was part of a
political philosophy which saw society as an adjunct of the market.[3]
As Karl Polyani puts it, "Instead of economy being embedded in
social relations, social relations are embedded in the economic system."[4] The essential, though financially reluctant, role of the poor
law was to support industrialism and the attempt in the nineteenth
century to establish a completely competitive, self-regulating market
economy founded on the motive of individual gain. It thus had to
create a great many rules of expected behaviour; about work and
non-work, property, savings, family relationships, cohabitation, men-
in-the-house, and so forth.[5] Poverty, as Disraeli once said, was de-
clared a crime by industrialism. Laws about poverty became associated with laws about crime.

This system, which legally survived in Britain until 1948, inevitably involved personal discrimination. The stigmata of the poor law
test, moral judgments by people about other people and their behaviour, were a condition of redistribution. The requirements of poor
law and public assistance administration were, we can now see, remarkably attuned to the characteristics of bureaucracy drawn by
Weber and others.[6] It was theoretically a neat and orderly world
of eligible and ineligible citizens; of approved and disapproved patterns of dependency; of those who could manage change and those
who could not. From its operation for over a century Britain inherited in 1948 a whole set of administrative attitudes, values and
rites, essentially middle-class in structure, and moralistic in application. The new social service bottles of 1948 had poured into them
much of the old wine of discrimination and prejudice. It has taken
nearly two decades of sustained programmes of new recruitment,
training, retraining and intraining, and the appointment of social
workers to the public services, to eradicate part of this legacy of
administrative behaviour.[7]

The history of the poor law and public assistance is thus still important to an understanding of social policy concepts today. If one
disregards the social costs of industrialism, of allowing a large part

of the disservices of technological progress to lie where they fall, then the system (of public assistance) was clearly redistributive. It directly benefited the explicit poor. Those in the greatest need did receive some benefit. But with the limited instruments of policy and administrative techniques to hand in the past, the system could only function by operating punitive tests of discrimination; by strengthening conceptions of approved and disapproved dependencies; and by a damaging assault on the recipients of welfare in terms of their sense of self-respect and self-determination. Within the established pattern of commonly held values, the system could only be redistributive by being discriminatory and socially divisive.

All this is now well documented in the archives of social inquiry and is somewhat ancient history. Equally well-known is the story of society's response to the challenge of poverty during the past 30 years or so: the discovery that this system of public aid was administratively grossly inefficient; the discovery that it could not by its very nature absorb the new dimensions of social and psychological knowledge and that, therefore, it could not function effectively both as a redistributive agent and as an agent to prevent social breakdown; and the discovery that the system was fundamentally inconsistent with the need to grant to all citizens, irrespective of race, religion or color, full and equal social rights.[8]

Gradually in Britain, as we tried to learn these lessons, we began to discard the use of discriminatory and overtly redistributive services for second-class citizens. The social services on minimum standards for all citizens crept apologetically into existence. In common with other countries we invented contributory national insurance or social security and provided benefits as of right. The actuary was called in to replace the functions of the public assistance relieving officer. Free secondary education for all children, irrespective of the means of their parents, was enacted in 1944 as part of a comprehensive educational system. Public housing authorities were called upon in 1945 to build houses for people and not just for working-class people. A limited and second-class health insurance scheme for workingmen was transformed, in 1948, into a comprehensive and free-on-demand health service for the whole population.[9]

All these and many other changes in the direct and publicly accountable instruments of social policy led to the notion that, in the year 1948, the "Welfare State" had been established in Britain. While there was general political consensus on this matter there was, on the other hand, much confusion and debate about cause and effect.[10] There were many, for instance, who thought that these policy changes were brought about for deliberately redistributive reasons and that the effects would be significantly egalitarian. This, perhaps, was understandable. Direct welfare in the past had in fact been redistributive (considered apart from the effects of the fiscal system). Therefore it was natural to assume that more welfare in the future would mean more redistribution in favour of the poor. There were others however (among whom I count myself), who believed that the fundamental and dominating historical processes which led to these major changes in social policy were connected with the demand for one society; for non-discriminatory services for all without distinction of class, income or race; for services and re- lations which would deepen and enlarge self-respect; for services which would manifestly encourage social integration. From some perspectives these major changes in policy could be regarded as ideological pleas to the middle- and upper-income classes to share in the benefits (as well as the costs) of public welfare.

Built into the public model of social policy in Britain since 1948 there are two major roles or objectives: the redistributive objective and the non-discriminatory objective. To move towards the latter it was believed that a prerequisite was the legal enactment of uni- versal (or comprehensive) systems of national insurance, education, medical care, housing and other direct services.

What have we learnt in the past 15 years about the actual func- tioning of these services? What has universalism in social welfare achieved? Clearly, I cannot give you a full account of all aspects of this development during a period when, for 13 of these years, the Government in power was not, in the early stages at least, entirely committed to the concept of the "Welfare State." I shall therefore concentrate my conclusions, brief and inadequate though they are, on the theme of redistribution.

Up to this point I have dealt only with what I sometimes call the "Iceberg Phenomena of Social Welfare." That is, the direct public provision of services in kind (e.g. education and medical care) and the direct payment of benefits in cash (e.g. retirement pensions and family allowances).

I now turn to consider two other major categories of social policy which have been developing and extending their roles in Britain and other countries over much the same period of time as the category we call "the social services." Elsewhere, I have described the former as "Fiscal Welfare" and "Occupational Welfare."[11] These are the indirect or submerged parts of the "Iceberg of Social Policy."

In both categories a remarkable expansion has taken place in Britain during the past 20 years.

All three categories of social policy have a great deal in common in terms of redistribution. They are all concerned with changing the individual and family pattern of current and future claims on resources set by the market, set by the possession of accumulated past rights, and set by the allocations made by government to provide for national defence and other non-market sectors. Social welfare changes the pattern of claims by, for instance, directly providing in-kind education or mental hospital care either free or at less than the market cost. Fiscal welfare changes the pattern of claims by taking less in tax (and thus increasing net disposable income) when a taxpayer's child is born, when its education is prolonged, when men have ex-wives to maintain, when taxpayers reach a specified age, and so on. An individual's pattern of claims on resources is today greatly varied through fiscal welfare policy by his or her change in circumstances, family responsibilities, and opportunities available (and taken) for prolonged education, home ownership and so on. In Britain, the United States and other countries the tax system has recently been regarded as an alternative in certain areas to the social security system; as a policy instrument to be used to provide higher incomes for the aged, for large families, for the blind and other handicapped groups, and for meeting part of the costs of education which today may last for up to 20 years or more.[12]

Occupational welfare, provided by virtue of employment status, achievement and record, may take the form of social security provisions in cash or in kind. Such provisions are legally approved by government and, as in the case of fiscal welfare, they may be seen as alternatives to extensions in social welfare. Their cost falls in large measure on the whole population. It is thus, like social welfare and fiscal welfare, a major redistributive mechanism.

In Britain, occupational welfare may include: pensions for employees; survivors benefits; child allowances; death benefits; health and welfare services; severance pay and compensation for loss of office (analogous these days to compensation for loss of property rights); personal expenses for travel, entertainment and dress; meal vouchers; cars and season tickets; residential accommodation; holiday expenses; children's school fees at private schools; sickness benefits; medical expenses; education and training grants and benefits ranging from "obvious forms of realizable goods to the most intangible forms of amenity"[13] expressed in a form that is neither money nor convertible into money.

A substantial part of these occupational welfare benefits can be interpreted—again like fiscal welfare—as social policy recognition of dependencies; the long dependencies of old age, childhood and widowhood, and such short-term dependencies as sickness and the loss of job rights.

The populations to which these three categories of welfare relate differ, but a substantial section of people may be eligible for benefits in respect of all three. In Britain, most of the social welfare services (except national assistance and university education) are universalist and citizen-based; they are open to all without a test of means. Thus, access to them does not depend upon achieved or inherited status. Fiscal welfare relates to a smaller population; only to those who pay direct taxes and not those who pay property taxes and social security contributions. Occupational welfare relates to the employed population and, at present, predominantly favours white-collar and middle-class occupations. Benefits are thus related to achievement.

All three categories of welfare are, as we have seen, redistributive; they change the pattern of claims on current and future resources. They function redistributively as separate, self-contained systems and they do so also in relation to the whole economy. Here is one example. Many private pension schemes, which include manual and non-manual workers, tend to redistribute claims on resources from lower-paid to higher-paid employees. This happens because the lower-paid workers change jobs more frequently; in doing so they do not have credited to them the full amount of pension contributions or premiums. It is estimated in Britain that the cost of full preservation of pension rights for all employees in the private sector (an objective in the present Government's proposals for the reform of social security) could add 15 to 25 percent to the actuarial costs of private schemes.[14] Moreover, as at present organised, the cost to the Treasury (the whole community) of private pension schemes substantially exceeds the Treasury contribution to social security pensions for the whole population. The pensions of the rich are more heavily subsidised by the community than the pensions of the poor.[15]

This in part happens because occupational welfare and fiscal welfare benefits are fundamentally based on the principles of achievement, status and need. If there is need, then the higher the income the higher is the welfare benefit. By contrast, social welfare benefits generally take account only of needs—the need for medical care, for education and so on irrespective of income or status.

I have now described in very general terms three categories of social policy redistribution—with particular reference to their operation in Britain. At present, they are publicly viewed as virtually distinct systems. What goes on within and as a result of one system is ignored by the others. They are appraised, criticised or applauded as abstracted, independent, entities. Historically, they have developed different concepts of poverty or subsistence; different criteria for determining approved dependencies; different standards of moral values in determining eligibility for welfare. Some examples will illustrate this point.

The social policy definition of subsistence as developed in the fiscal system for determining exemption from taxation, income needs in old age, and so on, differs markedly from the definition used in public assistance.[16] In some areas of policy the fiscal definition of poverty is employed, as, for instance, in determining grants to university students.[17] In other and similar areas of policy the public assistance definition is employed—as, for instance, in determining aid for poor parents of 16-year-old children at school.[18] It is odd, when you come to think of it, that dependency at age 16 is assessed at a lower standard of assistance than dependency at 18 or even 23 (in the case of medical students and graduates).

We have in fact two standards of poverty for determining aid from the community; both highly subjective and unscientific; both employed to assist dependent states; a working-class standard and a middle-class standard. The former has been investigated, studied, measured and argued about for long by sociologists, social workers and economists, and made the subject of many books and doctoral theses. By contrast, the latter has been virtually ignored.

One further example of double standards operating in different categories of welfare may be selected from a large field—this one to illustrate the role of moral values in social policy.

In the category of social welfare, cash aid from public funds for unsupported mothers, and their children may be stopped if it is believed that cohabitation is taking place. This is an event—or a relationship—that can rarely be legally proved. It is hardly a scientific fact. We have in Britain a cohabitation regulation;[19] you have a man-in-the-house regulation.[20] They amount to the same thing; they cannot be spelt out in precise operational terms. Their application in practice depends in large measure, therefore, on hearsay and moral judgement.

The same problem of to give or not to give aid arises in the category of fiscal welfare. As an example I quote from a memorandum by Lord Justice Hodson to a Royal Commission on Marriage and Divorce: "A super-tax payer may, and quite frequently nowadays does, have a number of wives living at the same time since after divorce his ex-wives are not treated as one with him for tax purposes he can manage quite nicely since he is permitted" (a social policy decision) "to deduct all his wives' maintenance allowances from his gross income for tax purposes leaving his net income comparatively slightly affected."[21]

In both instances redistribution takes place; the community renders aid in these situations of need and dependency. But while the decision to help the public assistance mother may involve judgements about moral behaviour, in the case of the taxpayer the decision is automatic and impersonal. The logic of the double standard is not apparent. If one is socially acceptable and approved behaviour then why not the other?

Now I must begin to draw these reflections together. What have been the lessons of experience in Britain about the actual functioning of these three categories of welfare during the past 15 years? Obviously, I cannot give you more than a fragment of an answer, and even this involves over-simplifying to a dangerous degree. To analyse and measure the redistributive effects of this process of the social division of welfare would be an immensely complex task —even if the essential statistical data were available which, in many areas, they are not. All I can offer are a few generalised conclusions.

The major positive achievement which has resulted from the creation of direct, universalist, social services in kind has been the erosion of formal discriminatory barriers. One publicly approved standard of service, irrespective of income, class or race, replaced the double standard which invariably meant second-class services for second-class citizens. This has been most clearly seen in the National Health Service. Despite strict controls over expenditure on the Service by Conservative Governments for many years it has maintained the principle of equality of access by all citizens to all branches of medical care. Viewed solely in terms of the welfare objective of non-discriminatory, non-judgemental service this is the signal achievement of the National Health Service. In part this is due to the fact that the middle-classes, invited to enter the Service in 1948, did so and have since largely stayed with the Service. They have not contracted out of socialised medical care as they have done in other fields like secondary education and retirement pensions. Their continuing participation, and their more articulate demands for improvements, have been an important factor in a general rise in standards of service—particularly in hospital care.[22]

But, as some students of social policy in Britain and the United States are beginning to learn, equality of access is not the same thing as equality of outcome. We have to ask statistical and sociological questions about the utilisation of the high-cost quality sectors of social welfare and the low-cost sectors of social welfare. We have to ask similar questions about the ways in which professional people (doctors, teachers, social workers and many others) discharge their roles in diagnosing need and in selecting or rejecting patients, clients and students for this or that service. In the modern world, the professions are increasingly becoming the arbiters of our welfare fate; they are the key-holders to equality of outcome; they help to determine the pattern of redistribution in social policy.

These generalisations apply particularly when services in kind are organised on a universalist, free-on-demand basis. When this is so we substitute, in effect, the professional decision-maker for the crude decisions of the economic marketplace. And we also make much more explicit—an important gain in itself—the fact that the poor have great difficulties in manipulating the wider society, in managing change, in choosing between alternatives, in finding their way around a complex world of welfare.

We have learnt from 15 years' experience of the Health Service that the higher income groups know how to make better use of the Service; they tend to receive more specialist attention; occupy more of the beds in better equipped and staffed hospitals; receive more elective surgery; have better maternity care; and are more likely to get psychiatric help and psychotherapy than low income groups—particularly the unskilled.[23]

These are all factors which are essential to an understanding of the redistributive role played by one of the major direct welfare services in kind. They are not arguments against a comprehensive free-on-demand service. But they do serve to underline one conclusion. Universalism in social welfare, though a needed prerequisite towards reducing and removing formal barriers of social and economic discrimination, does not by itself solve the problem of how to reach the more-difficult-to-reach with better medical care, especially preventive medical care.

Much the same kind of general conclusion can be drawn from Britain's experience in the field of education. Despite reforms and expansion during the past 15 years it is a fact that the proportion of male undergraduates who are the sons of manual workers is today about 1 percent lower than it was between 1928 and 1947. Although we have doubled the number of University students the proportion coming from working-class homes has remained fairly constant at just over a quarter.[24]

The major beneficiaries of the high-cost sectors of the educational system in "The Welfare State" have been the higher income groups. They have been helped to so benefit by the continued existence of a prosperous private sector in secondary education (partly subsidised by the State in a variety of ways including tax deductibles), and by developments since 1948 in provisions for child dependency in the category of fiscal welfare.[25] Take, for example, the case of two fathers each with two children, one earning $60,000 a year, the other $1,500 a year. In combining the effect of direct social welfare expenditures for children and indirect fiscal welfare expenditures for children the result is that the rich father now gets thirteen times more from the State than the poor father in recognition of the dependent needs of childhood.

Housing is another field of social policy which merits analysis from the point of view of redistribution. Here we have to take account of the complex interlocking effects of local rate payments, public housing subsidies, interest rates, tax deductibles for mortgage interest and other factors. When we have done so we find that the subsidy paid by the State to many middle-class families buying their own homes is greater than that received by poor tenants of public housing (local government) schemes.[26]

These are no more than illustrations of the need to study the redistributive effects of social policy in a wider frame of reference. Hitherto, our techniques of social diagnosis and our conceptual frameworks have been too narrow. We have compartmentalised social welfare as we have compartmentalised the poor. The analytic model of social policy that has been fashioned on only the phenomena that are clearly visible, direct and immediately measurable is an inadequate one. It fails to tell us about the realities of redistribution which are being generated by the processes of technological and social change and by the combined effects of social welfare, fiscal welfare and occupational welfare.

How far and to what extent should redistribution take place through welfare channels on the principle of achieved status, inherited status or need? This is the kind of question which, fundamentally, is being asked in Britain today. And it is being directed, in particular, at two major areas of social policy—social security and housing. Both these instruments of change and redistribution have been neglected for a decade or more. We have gone in search of new gods or no gods at all. It is time we returned to consider their roles afresh and with new vision. Perhaps we might then entitle our journey "Ways of Extending the Welfare State to the Poor."

NOTES

1. A. Macbeath, *Can Social Policies Be Rationally Tested?* Oxford University Press, London, 1957.

2. For some discussion of the problems of definitions see H. L. Wilensky and C. N. Lebeaux, *Industrial Society and Social Welfare*, Russell Sage Foundation, New York, 1958; *Social Welfare Statistics of the Northern Countries*, Report No. 9, Stockholm, 1964; Gunnar Myrdal, *Beyond the Welfare State*, Yale University Press, 1960; and Richard M. Titmuss, *Essays on the "Welfare State,"* Allen and Unwin, Ltd., 1958.

3. See, for example, A. V. Dicey, *Law and Opinion in England During the Nineteenth Century*, London, 1905.

4. Karl Polyani, *Origins of Our Time*, Beacon Paperbacks (No. 45), London, 1945, page 63.

5. *Reports of the Royal Commission on the Poor Laws*, His Majesty's Stationery Office, London, 1909.

6. H. H. Gerth and C. W. Mills, *From Max Weber: Essays in Sociology*, Oxford University Press, New York, 1946.

7. See, for example, *Annual Reports of the National Assistance Board, 1950–63*, Her Majesty's Stationery Office, London, and *Seventh and Eighth Reports on the Work of the Children's Department*, Home Office, Her Majesty's Stationery Office, London, 1955 and 1961.

8. Illustrated in the recommendations of the Beveridge Report (*Social Insurance and Allied Services*, Cmd. No. 6404), His Majesty's Stationery Office, London, 1942.

9. M. P. Hall, *The Social Services of Modern England*, Routledge, London, 1952.

10. Richard M. Titmuss, *Income Distribution and Social Change*, chapter 9, Allen and Unwin, Ltd., London, 1962.

11. Richard M. Titmuss, *Essays on the "Welfare State,"* Allen and Unwin, Ltd., London, second edition, 1963.

12. *Reports of the Royal Commission on the Taxation of Profits and Income, 1952–55*, Her Majesty's Stationery Office, London, 1955.

13. *Final Report of the Royal Commission on Taxation*, Cmd.

9474, Her Majesty's Stationery Office, London, 1955, page 68. See also A. Rubner, *Fringe Benefits,* Putnam, London, 1962.

14. See references in Richard M. Titmuss, *Income Distribution and Social Change,* chapter 7, and *British Tax Review,* Jan.–Feb. 1964.

15. Richard M. Titmuss, *The Irresponsible Society,* Fabian Tract No. 323, London, 1959.

16. *Reports of the Royal Commission on the Taxation of Profits and Income,* 1952–55, Her Majesty's Stationery Office, London, 1955.

17. Ministry of Education, *Grants to Students,* Cmd. No. 1051, Her Majesty's Stationery Office, London, 1960.

18. *Report of the Working Party on Educational Maintenance Allowances,* Her Majesty's Stationery Office, London, 1957.

19. National Insurance Act, 1946, section 17 (2) and *Digest of Commissioner's Decisions,* Her Majesty's Stationery Office, London, 1946–64.

20. See *Report of the Public Welfare Crisis Committee,* Metropolitan Washington Chapter of the National Association of Social Workers, Washington, 1963.

21. J. Hudson, *Royal Commission on Marriage and Divorce,* M D P/1952/337, Her Majesty's Stationery Office, London, 1952.

22. A. Lindsey, *Socialized Medicine in England and Wales,* University of North Carolina Press, 1962.

23. Richard M. Titmuss, *Essays on the "Welfare State,"* appendix on the National Health Service, second edition, Allen and Unwin, Ltd., London, 1963.

24. *Robbins Report on Higher Education,* appendix 2, volumes A and B, Her Majesty's Stationery Office, London, 1964.

25. *The Economist,* London, Oct. 26, 1963.

26. D. Nevitt, *Essays on Housing,* Occasional Papers on Social Administration (No. 9), Codicote Press, London, 1964.

6   The Societal Function of Social Welfare

MARTIN WOLINS

INTRODUCTION

Rarely has social work had the buoyancy that it exhibits in the 1960's. The profession is large and strong, making regular gains in popular standing. Recently, there have also been major advances

Reprinted with permission of the author from *New Perspectives: The Berkeley Journal of Social Welfare,* 1 (Spring 1967): 1–18.

in social welfare programs. Although we may not have achieved either the welfare state or a state of complete welfare there is a recognition that welfare measures are a part of modern society. Yet their exact functions are unclear, the expectations uncertain.

Ask a client what he wants from welfare and he is likely to place emphasis on three attributes: It should, he would say, relieve his immediate distress; impose no conditions which lower status; and assure the flow of help as long as needed. In expressing such requirements, the client addresses the two other actors involved—the community and the social agency. Their aims, while coinciding to some extent with his own, do so quite imperfectly. Exercising its humanitarian functions and, in part, salving its guilt, the community is prepared to relieve distress. However, the community also expects its welfare program to improve society by returning recipients to productive endeavors and to protect its institutions against individual or collective violation.

Between the client and the community is the social agency—the administrator of welfare programs. To be useful it must serve as a buffer and a link. A welfare program must tie together donor community and recipient individual. This is clear and is often made explicit in various pronouncements of welfare planning organizations. Less advertised is the other side of this function—keeping the demanding recipient and grudging donor from expressing their mutual dissatisfaction directly. The agency also provides the substance and services to meet needs. It attempts to return the client to productivity by striking a balance in the program between stigma and comfort. Additionally, it may work to reduce the stigmatizing attributes of programs under its control.

Like any system of action, the social welfare agency—the field upon which the forces of client and community interact—is in continuous flux. Contributing to the instability are built-in conflicts between client and agency, agency and community, client and community, as well as internal disagreements within each of them. The humanitarian within the community says: "You are not well and we will bind your wounds." The utilitarian says: "Every consumer except the sick, aged, and young is obligated to produce." The community may speak of rehabilitation and give much attention to this function in the agency, but the latter, although it accepts the mandate, may lack the tools, knowledge, skill, power, or even staff time to bring it about. And the client may add to the conflict by being quite content to remain a permanent recipient of "temporary" assistance.

The obvious complexity of the welfare position in society, the lack of clarity and the apparent conflict between protagonists compels us to attempt to understand it. There are, of course, various ways of analyzing the welfare establishment—historically, programmatically, clinically.[1] The present effort is somewhat different. It is an attempt to explain welfare by posing the question: "Why is it there?" and *answering the question in terms of systemic rather than individual needs.* This approach precludes a look at some needs that are not as yet coercive upon the system, nor does it cover in any way adequately the possibility of a system deliberately introducing needs and satisfiers because "it's right." Looking upon society as completely utilitarian in its objectives, i.e., trying to get the maximum stability at the minimum cost of concessions to deviants and reformers, the paper fails to take into account the occasional nobility of the human spirit which makes a society rise above the demands of its disadvantaged and willingly, dutifully grant them privileges. But the attempt is to explain welfare from a "conservative" point of view, looking more at what has been and is rather than what could or should be its function in society.

Like any model, this one will sound pretentious and definitive. It is not intended to be the former and it cannot be the latter. On the contrary, it is submitted as one way of approaching welfare which is right only insofar as it poses meaningful questions, good only insofar as it explains relationships, fruitful to the extent that it produces research which supports or refutes its views. *The hard stance of the paper should not deceive the reader. It is taken because only a firm position can be disputed.* In some instances it is bolstered by facts at the author's disposal, but sometimes it is an attempt to distill from experience and the literature some insights that are beyond immediate verification, but, hopefully, not unverifiable.

THE OBJECTIVES OF SOCIAL WELFARE

Social welfare is a device for maintaining or strengthening the *existing* social structure of an industrial society. It has served that function for several centuries, sometimes more or less effectively disguised. Historically, humanistic and moralistic protestations have been many, but the veneer of generosity has been thin indeed. While love of one's fellow man may have been a motive for some individual reformers and welfare leaders, while it may have rung from pulpits and activated muckraking movements, it has not been the force that has moved men in power.

England had the earliest substantial welfare legislation in the Western world. The basis for the first poor law was national catastrophe in the form of the plague of 1348 which reduced the labor force. Resulting legal actions to eliminate vagrancy by confining vagrants and other poor to rural employment provided working hands, security for the poor, and reduced a threat to the crown from unattached masses.[2] While numerous additions to and alterations of poor laws took place during the following four centuries, the next substantial change in program was the result of revolutionary rumbles on the Continent and of the Napoleonic Wars. The Speenhamland Act of 1795 was designed to save the poor and aid the landowners at a single stroke. A masterful job of farm subsidy —perhaps the first of its kind—it was, appropriately, criticized by Adam Smith as not fitting the laissez-faire principles of the burgeoning economy. Nevertheless, it relieved the pressures upon the existing power structure. By contrast, the French monarchy was not as farsighted.

The history of welfare in Bismarck's German Empire indicates that it performed a similar conservative function. Welfare legislation arose from political necessity and not humanitarian predispositions. One historian analyzing this period points out that years passed before Bismarck realized ". . . that all could not be well with the social system under which hundreds of thousands of the most patient people in the world were flocking to the banner inscribed 'Proletarians of all countries unite.' . . . His solicitude for the working classes was an acquired solicitude. . . . He passed social laws because they were necessary; social reform was never to him a passion, but always a policy."[3]

Massive welfare legislation came to America in 1929–1933. Earlier depressions were somehow surmounted without major organized welfare programs, but this was the *great* depression. The number of dissidents could be counted in various statistics: marchers on Washington, unemployed, increasing memberships in left and right wing parties. Hoover's attempt to hold the finger in the economic dike failed, and a flood of reform and major welfare legislation poured out of Washington in the first two years of the New Deal. Whether Harry Hopkins really said, "We'll tax and tax, spend and spend, and elect and elect," or the Republican opposition invented it is of little import.[4] Welfare legislation was a way of reducing discontent, electing its proponents, and keeping the major attributes of the social system substantially unchanged.

Voluntary welfare efforts, while more outspokenly humanitarian, also had a strong conservative overtone. Thus, Friedlander, in describing the development of the Charity Organization Societies in the United States, writes that "the founders of these societies represented the 'bourgeois benevolence,' wealthy citizens who felt morally obligated to alleviate the suffering of the poor and *hoped thus to minimize political unrest and industrial strife.*"[5] (Emphasis added.)

It may seem incredible that social welfare should have such major importance. After all, even when it is liberally calculated, the social welfare effort in the United States amounts to only a small fraction of the gross national product.[6] Social welfare holds its importance not by virtue of size or power but owing to several conditions of present-day society. First, an admission that even under ideal circumstances some members will not have their basic needs met. Second, a recognition that pressures build up for orderly modification of the social structure or provision of some alternative ways for needs to be satisfied. Third, an understanding which has, in part, come from Freudian psychology, that needs *will* be met at the expense of the orderly functioning of society, if necessary, when other alternatives are difficult or blocked. Thus the welfare apparatus becomes indispensable. It can stand as a more or less gray area between the clearly right and the patently wrong ways of meeting need. It can be a system of sanctioned deviancy. To explain its functioning we will begin with human needs and the institutional provisions for meeting them.

NEEDS AND INSTITUTIONAL WAYS TO MEET THEM

Need

"A need is a construct . . . which stands for a force . . . to transform in a certain direction an existing, unsatisfying situation."[7] Need, then, may be thought of as a tension state in the human organism which demands reduction. Not all needs have the same order of priority. The organic usually prevail over the social. Hunger and thirst, when sufficiently severe, can displace all other tensions to the point of eradication, but when these are satisfied, other tension states (needs)—sex, alienation, for example, become expressed with a substantial urgency. It appears that the needs are arranged in a kind of imperfect order along an organic-superorganic continuum, with a certain basic uniformity, modified by social impact on the priority of tensions.

It is common in social work to speak of need-meeting. There is no dispute that needs must be met, but are they being met directly by social welfare or other institutions? It seems not. The individual has certain predispositions for resolving particular tensions. And while needs may or may not be social, predispositions always are. It is obviously appropriate to speak of hunger as a universal tension, but beefsteak or steamed taro root are not universal satisfiers. The vegetarian has no need disposition[8] for beefsteak, and the meat lover is not disposed towards taro root as a means of hunger reduction. Similarly, sex may be a universal tension state, but the need dispositions it generates are clearly varied. Need dispositions, these "needs for," are commonly the object of societal and social welfare concern. Their social origin makes the need dispositions changeable and somewhat elusive.

Need-Meeting Social Institutions

Needs, need dispositions, and their satisfactions provide reason and objective to the whole of human organization. What other *raison d'etre* can one ascribe to the existence of the family, the tribe, the office, the factory, the city, the nation? Relative to need the gamut of social institutions can be classed into several categories. These are groupings of individuals who perform specialized functions which are quite different in purpose, motive and mode of operation. The most important for our discussion are the family, the business organization, the informal friendship group, and the polity.[9]

"The family is a social group characterized by common residence, economic cooperation, and reproduction. It includes adults of both sexes, at least two of whom maintain a socially approved sexual relationship, and one or more children, own or adopted of the sexually cohabiting adults."[10] For the sake of brevity let us call this type of arrangement the *F System*. It differs from the other systems in several respects. First, it was historically the progenitor of all the others and did carry the sexual, reproductive, economic, and educational functions Murdock has assigned to it. It also performed some other functions such as the conduct of religious activity, and the care of the sick and aged. Second, the family, even where its functions are most restricted, has retained the sanctioned functions of sex and reproduction that only in the most unusual circumstances have been formally assigned elsewhere. Third, unlike the others, this system is motivated primarily by forces of affection. Only secondarily do reciprocity and social demand, major factors in other systems, become important with regard to family operation.

A second arrangement operates for financial gain. Let us designate it as the E System. It has the major characteristics of the marketplace: Goods are produced only in anticipation of profit; there is intense competition among producers for the consumers' resources; consumers control the fate of producers by having a choice of the goods they will buy. Claims to goods are directly related to the potential consumer's productivity and hence to his income.

The third system type is the informal (I System) type. Its functions are less clearly defined than are those of the others. Membership in it or use of it is voluntary. The system has a generally transitory character in contrast to the stability of the others. Its motive force is reciprocity. An individual becomes involved and contributes because he anticipates some kind of gain in the form of social status, psychic satisfaction, or even economic benefit, although these benefits may not be the stated objectives of informal association.

The final and fourth system type has been designated as the polity (P System) type. It is formal, legal, and includes all of government as well as chartered voluntary organizations not motivated by profit. Several attributes of this system merit particular attention. First, it is to a large extent non-voluntary. Participation is not a matter of choice but is required by law or as a civic duty. Second, the degree of reciprocity is either small or not apparent. Rarely does the contributor to the effort see direct benefits to himself resulting from his contribution. More important, there is no relationship between productivity and the right to demand goods and services. Third, there is no competition in producing goods and services, hence, economic wastefulness can occur, and since this is accompanied by freedom from the profit motive, goods and services may be produced for which there is no demand.[11] Fourth, conditions prevalent in industrial society have led to continual expansion of the P System at the expense of F and E Systems and to some extent even at the expense of the I System.

The "Normal" Need-Meeting Process

Needs are met providing the rules of the system are observed. The family will meet needs if the affective climate is good and if a modicum of reciprocity can be assumed. Similarly, an E System will meet needs when financial resources are brought forth. To have his needs met the individual uses a proper approach to a social institution. Each time the approach is rewarded and a need is met, the rightness of the procedure and of the institution is confirmed. Repeated satisfactions endow the arrangement for need-meeting with the attribute of normality. Within the given social context it becomes "normal" to meet the hunger need through the E System, the sexual need through the F System, the illness need through the P System (as in national health insurance in England or through Medicare in the United States).

If the problems of distribution and productivity are surmounted and a pattern of need-meeting is established, the conviction of its normality leads to a perception of the obvious nature of the mechanism and its rationale. Instead of being a *way* of resolving the tensions of the individual in society, it becomes *the way*, and acquires a "sacredness" which other, possibly more rational alternative approaches, are unlikely to have ascribed to them.

A major issue of social policy in all industrial societies is the division of need-meeting responsibilities between the various system types. There are basic differences of opinion about the "normal" way to meet a need. Several issues are involved. Principal among them are: (1) the distribution of need-meeting resources, and (2) assurance of reciprocity of productivity. With the advent of industrialized society and specialization of functions, need-meeting functions have left the family. The question arose whether they should be assigned to an E or P System. Care of the ill is a good example. Education is another. Both were at first assigned exclusively to the E Systems and their distribution was patently unequal. To some extent the inequality remains in education, even though it is now mostly a P type function. To a much larger extent it is present in the distribution of medical care. Location of a service in the E or the P Systems makes a great deal of difference in reciprocity demands. E provides service only if the client can pay. P demands little in the way of reciprocity using need and legal membership in the system as criteria of eligibility. Understandably, the E system for need-meeting is favored by those who hold a "rugged individualist," conservative point of view, and the P system is promoted by those of a liberal, welfare state, social responsibility persuasion.

In their extreme forms these points of view are embodied in the doctrines of Adam Smith, on the one hand, and Karl Marx, on the other. The first predicts the greatest social good will arise when every person acts purely in his own self-interest within a laissez-faire market economy. If he cannot produce and pay, his need is not met. The second seems to detach production from consumption by calling for a society built on the principles of "from each according to his ability; to each according to his need."

FAILURES OF PERSONS AND SYSTEMS

Personal Malfunctions

Normal need-meeting imposes demands upon the person and the system. Both must have a capacity to reach out to each other when need arises, and this requires: (1) recognition of the need, (2) knowledge of the rules under which it is met, (3) ability to observe them, and (4) systemic readiness to respond. Any one or all of these may be absent owing to personal or systemic dysfunction.

The individual may fail to perceive a need because it is overshadowed by other, more salient discomforts. Or, while recognizing a need, he may not know the appropriate satisfier. Having recognized a need and the appropriate satisfier, the person may not know the rules for obtaining it. Very often such failure to know the rules is encountered when need is to be met in a culture foreign to the person. The new immigrant, the lower-class member who must function in a middle-class value system are disadvantaged in this way. Not knowing the rules, they may attempt to have their needs relieved by resorting to satisfiers or procedures considered inappropriate.

Knowing "the way" may not suffice. One has to have the skill and resources to activate the system, but these may be reduced by various kinds of physical, emotional, social, and economic handicaps. They may also become inadequate or ill-suited by virtue of value differences between the culture of the person with a need and the one within which satisfaction is to occur.

Institutional Malfunction

Even when a system operates well, there will always be some members who fail to know its rules or who are unable or unwilling to fulfill its requirements. But there is no assurance that the systems of our major concern—E, F, and P—will recognize need in their members and stand ready to meet it. That is, they may not operate well. Failure to recognize or acknowledge need may be due to many causes, but evidence of it abounds.

Example in New York: *The New York Times*, January 1, 1964. "At 30 degrees there was no heat in an apartment with a woman and six children. . . . The Harlem rent strike spread last night from 58 to 167 buildings. . . . Jesse Gray, the organizer of the strike, announced that about 1,500 more tenants in 109 buildings had decided to withhold January's rent. . . ."

Example in Indonesia: *The New York Times*, January 19, 1964. "Since Indonesia gained her freedom they have practically accepted a subsistence level of living in return for the largest armed forces in Southeast Asia (now more than 500,-000) and Sukarno's promise to lead their revolution . . . to glory."

Recognition of need and the system's responsibility for meeting it may, however, not be enough. Natural calamities that disorganize the system may prevent need-meeting. Depressions, overpopulation, racial discrimination and social niggardliness may impair or inhibit the provision of need-satisfiers for all.

Need must be met. Tension states within the organism must be reduced. Failing that, the person or institution or both are in jeopardy. When failure to meet need takes place, the individual and systemic adjustments may be either in the direction of conformity with the existing mores or not. Social welfare is a systemic provision whose purpose has been to make it more likely that personal and institutional change will be of the former type.

Available Alternatives

One may actually speak here of three ways of need-meeting: (a) Procedures essentially in conformity with the established order of things (as previously discussed); (b) actions to meet need completely out of conformity and judged to be criminal; and (c) behavior classified between these two points—*acceptable deviancy.*

The unacceptable procedures are important in the scheme of the present discussion only because they always seem to be lurking in the background, ready to be used. Like Freud's *Id,* they underlie the personal and institutional structure and are repressed appropriately by the presence of sanctions and alternatives. When they fail to be repressed, the society is rent by drives to change the existing order. Failing that, individual disregard for the established rules emerges.

Usually, sudden, violent, and massive change does not take place. Institutions are altered by other means when their capacity to meet need becomes obviously inadequate. Such changes are known as social and economic reforms. They are adjustments to long-developing inadequacies in the social system. Because the failure to meet needs is massive, and affects obviously respectable persons, the malfunction is seen as admittedly systemic and the change is seen as socially good. It is progress to abolish old-law tenements, to develop a workmen's compensation act, to spread the system of education to broader masses of the public, or to introduce compulsory vaccination against smallpox. The individual beneficiary from such changes is seen as meriting the benefits by virtue of his membership status. He is a worker, a tenant, a child, a resident in the area where the new benefit applies. He may or may not be required to contribute in order that resources will be available to pay for the new service, but no stigma attaches to his beneficiary status. While such new programs may, and usually do, have a profound impact on the F, I and E Systems, their locus is, clearly, in P.

Type B Welfare Services

In a liberal sense the massive programs mentioned above are social welfare. Perhaps they should be thought of as *social welfare type A*. Also in P, but with quite different attributes, is *social welfare type B*.[12] Unlike participation in the need-meeting transactions of all other systems and other parts of P, derivation of benefits here requires a recognition of special circumstances that warrant special privilege. One who wishes to become a social welfare (type B) beneficiary must become subject to a set of rules established for acceptable deviants. Such rules have been defined by Parsons relative to the status of a sick person:

1. The individual is exempt from meeting some of his usual social responsibilities.
2. He is exempt from responsibility for his own conditions, even when it may be the result of his own actions.

3. The position is undesirable and the individual may occupy it only upon acceptance of this definition.
4. The sick person is responsible for doing his utmost to get better, including seeking out and using technically competent help.[13]

When a person does not have his needs met through the "normal" procedures of society—and the number of such people is sufficiently small so that their dilemma may be defined in personal rather than systemic terms—he is compelled to redefine his status and become a welfare client or a criminal. Obviously, society prefers the former solution. Assuming the client status will, in some instances, carry with it all of the attributes Parsons ascribes to the sick. In most, it will lack the second privilege—exemption from responsibility for the condition that led to the unmet need. Certain physical or emotional disabilities leading to the use of type B welfare services may have all four of the Parsonian qualities, but economic difficulties generally will not. For example, childlessness will not be thought of as the fault of a couple coming to an agency to adopt, but unemployment resulting in an application for financial assistance will be considered the result of "laziness," "shiftlessness," or other self-imposed, undesirable but escapable attributes. Thus, type B welfare programs will be stigmatizing and the role definition of recipients will include personal responsibility and a strong proscription of secondary gain. It is intended that the type B welfare recipient should derive no special advantages from his condition.

Since the status described and the role appropriate to it are unusual, unclear and somewhat unpalatable, social welfare agencies become involved in defining and facilitating them. That is, they function to help a recipient use the service so as to promote his *legitimate* deviance. But that is not their sole function. They must also serve as substitutes for the usual need-meeting institutions and continually work at affecting the societal view of a particular program entrusted to them.

At this point several terms related to type B welfare require elaboration. They are: *problem, less-eligibility* and *social work*. The client who is compelled to meet his needs through the workings of a social institution not normally used for that purpose is perceived as having a problem. Hunger satisfied through the "employment-salary-grocery store" route is seen as different from the "hunger-Christmas basket" sequence or even the "hunger-welfare payment-grocery store" chain of events. The difference is not due to the satisfaction of the hunger need, which takes place in any of the three ways, but in the social perception of the relative desirability of the three procedures. A person who meets his needs through the less desirable channels is defined as having a *problem*. Problems prevent acceptable need-meeting and stand in the way of the client's leaving the role of legitimate deviant.

The problem arises, of course, because the channels open to the client have been defined as *less-eligible*,[14] i.e., less good than the usual, normal way of meeting need. Thus, the client is hung up on the horns of a dilemma, facing, on the one hand, the discomfort of his need and, on the other, the more or less severe disapproval of the only way (other than crime) open to him for meeting it. The disapproval is there intentionally. It is a built-in discomfort for the client of a type B welfare service. It is intended to goad him into "doing his utmost to get better," or in this case seek a more acceptable way for meeting his needs.

Social work is there to help him. One of the major functions of social work has been to help people with problems. This means to aid clients whose needs are met in this gray area of less-eligibility which stands between the acceptable and the proscribed avenues of need-meeting.

When a client approaches a welfare service, his first expression is of an unmet need. The agency's response may well have to be meeting that need. In effect, then, the agency may serve as a substitute for any E, F, I, or P system. But that is not all. If it were not a threat to the existing social structure, provision of alternatives for need-meeting that do not require the reciprocity of productivity of the E system or the affection of the F system, would reduce the need and create no problem. Since much need-meeting does threaten the existing way of doing things in the society, the agency also works with the client's "problem." If the client fails to acknowledge having one, the agency is duty bound to convince him otherwise. The client is thus put in a state of tension which is *low* enough so that he does not reject welfare in favor of a totally proscribed way of reducing his need, and yet *high* enough so that he continually strives to leave his acceptable-deviant role. In relation to the client the agency has two purposes. Its short-range objective is to meet need. Its long-range objective is restoration of "normal" need-meeting capability. This is called *rehabilitation*, which again ascribes a "rightness" to the usual arrangement.

Under stress, the social welfare program is reduced to attempts at meeting short-range objectives only. For this reason the means of short-range need reduction become important in terms of their appropriateness in a rehabilitative process. Procedures for substituting have thus come to be ranked for desirability. If the client is to be re-introduced into the E systems for example, it is not only a matter of a hand-out so as to hold body and soul together. A welfare check is more utilitarian than a food basket, since the former requires that the recipient relate to the system at least on the consumption end, while the latter does not.

This relatedness to the system of society occupies the welfare agency which attempts, when resources permit, to provide the client with personal therapy, in order to help him bridge the gap between his own capabilities and the functional requirements of society. When the gap is too great to be surmounted at one time the welfare agency may also provide half-way structures. In relation to E Systems there may be sheltered workshops for handicapped persons or subsidized employment opportunities in industry for welfare recipients. Clients whose F System functioning has been impaired and who may have been hospitalized may be treated in a half-way house before returning to their families. Children may thus move from institutions to group home to foster home to residence with their own parents.

Throughout the rehabilitation process there is a recognition of a basic premise in need-meeting through normal channels. Every successful repetition reinforces the system and testifies to its rightness. By the same token, failure of person or system becomes a source of distrust between them. Each successive failure increases the gap between the individual and the normal need-meeting structure. In order to re-establish their relationship, successful operations must be assured. If these are unlikely to occur in the "real world," then they must be made to happen initially in more sheltered settings. These will give the client confidence and reassure the members of the appropriate system of his readiness to return to their fold as a fully functioning member.

By providing temporary relief and long-term treatment the welfare agency channels its clients back into the "normal" stream of society. At least it is intended to do so. It also serves as a backstop for the "hindermost," preventing their inevitably resorting to illicit need-meeting procedures in the event the usual, approved channels are, for reasons of personal or systemic failure, not open to them. The effective welfare agency is aware of the second, systemic, reason for possible failure and works not only with the client but also with the E, F, I or P Systems. It may, for example, become involved with employers in an attempt to modify working conditions in order that persons handicapped in some way may continue to be employed. Similarly, a welfare agency may intercede with the family in behalf of a deviant member and involve other members in treatment. It may work with peer groups. It may pressure governmental and voluntary organizations into some flexibility of policy and procedure.

MOVING FROM B TO A WELFARE

Aside from its efforts to adjust the institutional structures to individuals with problems, the welfare agency may be concerned with the functioning of the system in its normal, customary way. It may be sensitive to massive systemic failure or breakdown in intersystemic-linkage which leave in their wake a welfare clientele. When this occurs, social welfare has acted with the systems—not for individual flexibility, but for social reform. A classic example of such action was the famous Pittsburgh Survey which produced evidence of serious malfunctioning of the E System in industrial accident cases and led to the enactment of workmen's compensation laws.[15]

Workmen's compensation and other insurances like unemployment, railroad, and OASDI retirement pensions bring us to the issue of less-eligibility again. As noted briefly earlier, this is no longer an economic concept. In fact, some welfare recipients now have higher cash incomes than the insured, retired, or even employed persons.[16] The concept is now one of attitude. When Old Age Security recipients in California were asked to comment about AFDC, their reaction was that the program was relief. AFDC clients were living off of the society—quite different from themselves, pensioners on OAS. The public generally seems to agree with this view. A less-eligibility label is not necessarily attached to all services given outside of the usual structures. It is a matter of perception, definition. Both OAS and AFDC have the same legislative base, the same financing provisions, the same categorical eligibility criteria, but one is seen as and therefore becomes a "pension,"—the other is "relief."

Yet there is an obvious relationship between programs like AFDC, OAS, and OASDI. All are in P and are characterized by an absence of a direct contributory requirement, but the stigma attached to them varies. OAS has moved from B to A, but the AFDC program remains a B type. Such de-stigmatization has also occurred in education, medical care, and other programs. In each case need-reducing procedures were in E and F, but when these became inadequate "less-eligible" services were instituted, followed by subsequent integration into P without stigma.

The Public School

"During the colonial period there had been two systems of education, just as there had been two systems of poor relief. Families that could afford it sent their children to tuition schools. . . . [The poor might have studied] in the common schools, where their parents could escape from the burden of the school-rate, or part-tuition, by declaring themselves to be paupers. In general the common schools were a minimum provision, associated with boors, paupers, and servants."[17] So the common (later, public) school started as a less-eligibility institution which has evolved over time into the generally accepted P-type system that it is today.

The Voluntary Hospital

Webster's *New International Dictionary*, second edition, 1960, defines a hospital in part as "an institution or place in which patients or injured persons are given medical or surgical care, often in whole or in part at public expense or by charity." To anyone who has heard of Medicare or who has recently been in a hospital, paid up to $50 a day for care, and had a substantial portion of it met by medical insurance, this definition no doubt sounds archaic. Yet the definition was correct no more than a half century ago, and its outmoded ring is a mark of the change in function *and* public image that the voluntary, private, community hospital has experienced. Like the school, the hospital was the result of F System inadequacy. So long as the family could care for the ill person better than anyone else, he stayed at home, if he had one. When the family could not provide, another system took over. The hospital arose out of a less-eligibility base. As it proved its worth in treatment of certain illnesses and prevention of infection, the financially able began to use it. To accommodate them and relate services to fees, the hospital then became in part an E-type system (some hospitals—the proprietary—became wholly so) and in part a less-eligibility system in P.

It became common to see charity and private wards under the same institutional roof, but with markedly different services and social appraisal. With the advent of medical insurances the community hospital increasingly resembles a P-type system, partly financed out of general funds, and showing a decreasing relationship between ability to pay and services.

Adoption

Even in its most "streamlined" form the family is expected to augment its membership by natural procreation. While the adoption of children has a long and interesting history, only lately, and in the Anglo-Saxon world, has it become a major social phenomenon. The number of children adopted in the United States has steadily increased both in absolute number and in proportion to births. At the same time, the perception of the adopted and adopting has undergone marked change. Whereas in the early days parents often went to great length to hide the adopted status of a child, this is no longer the case. Being adopted is an honorable and thoroughly acceptable way of joining a family. The process of de-stigmatization may even have gone a bit further than acceptability: The Chosen Baby,[18] for example sounds more like a term of distinction than simple approval and normality.

It is important to note that ways other than adoption through a child welfare agency exist and are sanctioned. Our current perception of these alternative ways of adoption is still a mark of the conflict between E and P ways of doing things. While we prohibit full-blown E-type arrangements in adoption, we still, as a society, approve independent and fee-for-service mediated adoptions that resemble E System operations in many respects. The trend, however, is clearly toward making adoption an exclusive P-type program without stigma.

Old Age Security

The Social Security Act of 1935 provided a system of retirement insurance (OASI) and relief benefits for three categories of dependents—the aged, the children, and the blind.[19] In the original legislation, these three categorical assistance programs are markedly similar with respect to criteria for eligibility, sources of financing, provisions for administration, and rights of recipients. Yet over the past thirty years, the two large categories—aid to aged and aid to dependent children, have had remarkably different public acceptability. In California, for example, the very title of the aged program is indicative of its high status. It is called Old Age Security. The initials make it easy to confuse with OASDI. Payments under the two programs may well be of the same magnitude. Relative responsibility in OAS is a dead letter. Social work involvement with the OAS recipients is minimal. And since contributions (if any) to OASDI were made long before the receipt of payments and in part by the employer (i.e., consuming public), what difference is there between the insurance and assistance program? No wonder the recipients, the public at large, the press, and increasingly even the politicians treat this program as an established part of the P System![20]

By contrast, what has been the fate of the AFDC program? This program too has grown but, unlike OAS, it has retained less-eligibility characteristics. Recipients are "on relief," they are looked at with disapproval by the public, press, and the legislature. The welfare agencies charged with administering the program insist that these families accept social work service as a matter of obligation rather than ask for it as a right. The amount of the grant per person is lower than in OAS[21] while the public resentment is much greater. While charity of purpose and means seems to have surrounded aid to the aged, confusion, conflict, uncertainty and meanness have been the lot of the children's program. Even the issue of mother's employment has fluctuated from "con" in the Depression to "pro" during the war years, to apparent ambivalence now.[22]

A review of the four cases should yield some general rules about the processes of transition from less-eligibility to unstigmatized P, or from B to A welfare. There seem to be several requirements:

1. The program should be able to provide clear evidence of being effective. This exists in the case of the hospital and OAS and, to a lesser degree, in education and adoption. It is questionable in AFDC if the task is defined as economic self-sufficiency of the children upon reaching maturity.
2. The program should conform to existing values or be presented to appear as if it does. The community hospital is explained as a means of maintaining and promoting the general health and welfare. Public education can be explained in terms of the general achievement orientation of the American society and

its belief in science and reason, and the greater productivity achieved through education. By the same token, old age assistance can be explained as a reward for past services to society, hence freeing the recipient and his family from any obligations to reciprocate in the present or the future. Adoption, insofar as it is relevant to the major interests of society, is probably explainable in terms of emphasis shifts in certain American subgroups from status ascription to achievement. Thus, for example, in the more traditional, less mobile segments of the society (e.g., the South, the Catholics) adoption is less well accepted than among northern Protestants or big-city Jews.[23] The stigma attached to aid to indigent children can be attributed to fears of tampering with the incentive structure. "If you start giving them something for nothing, then why should they learn to work?" the proverbial taxpayer asks. And the question appears to apply to both the mothers and children.

3. A program should affect large numbers of people in order to become acceptable. Furthermore, the magnitude of the program should be apparent. For this reason, the mere fact that some four million children are receiving benefits under AFDC pushes the program toward acceptability. By contrast, the scattered general assistance recipients who are visible singly or in small community groups are more likely to continue being stigmatized. It is easier to ascribe malfunction to the person if it seems to be an occasional occurrence in society rather than a matter of massive failure. Four million failures are somewhat difficult to rationalize in other than systemic terms! Recent public statements on the magnitude of poverty are, therefore, likely to reduce stigma of assistance programs.

4. Ability of recipients to act as upright, law-abiding citizens. This implies the power to organize for political action, to seek redress of grievances in court, to bargain collectively—in brief, to have or to act as if they have the full rights of citizens. An adoption is more acceptable because it is approved by the judiciary. Receipt of aged assistance is more honorable because the aged are organized, lobby in state and national capitals, and their leaders run for public office. (This is aside from the obvious *political* power such organization gives them.) But the AFDC client has no lobby, and rarely exercises the few rights he has. Even his family relationships are char-

acterized as illegal or, at best, extra-legal by virtue of the high illegitimacy rate among recipients of aid.

ACCOMPLISHMENTS OF AND ALTERNATIVES TO SOCIAL WELFARE

Assuming that the functions of social welfare organizations operating in type B are temporary substitutions for the established need-meeting arrangements, rehabilitation, i.e., return of clients to "normal" need-meeting channels, and conversion of programs to type A: How well have they done?

The capability of welfare agencies for *temporary substitution* has been increasing quite rapidly. This has been true for problems that arise in the E, F, and I Systems. Problems of economic dependency have been dealt with by massive expansion of public assistance. While grants are still inadequate, and many persons fail to have basic necessities met, the failures can be remedied. More vexing is the uncertainty as to what the substitution is to accomplish. If substitution is an object unto itself as in OAS, for example, the criteria of achievement are readily detectable. But this is not so with substitution that is one aspect of a long-term rehabilitative process such as AFDC claims to be.

Problems of the family are dealt with only partially. Childlessness may be relieved temporarily by a foster child as a free benefit of the foster care program. Such temporary substitution for the family's acculturative or socializing functions has long been part of social welfare services. The foster home and institution and, more recently, homemaker and protective service functions have played an increasingly important role as emergency backstops for the family.

Social welfare agencies have also provided substitutes when I System structures have not sufficed. The early days of the YMCA or the settlement houses provide good examples of such activity.[24] More recently, however, the substitutes have themselves become institutionalized and are no longer looked upon as temporary devices, "less good than the real thing."

Relative to the rehabilitation function, the position of social welfare is not so clear as it is with substitution. There have been several contributing factors. First, a clear distinction has rarely been drawn between the first and second function, and this has resulted in a chronic shortage of resources for the latter. Substitution is generally a must—the child has no tolerable home, the family has no food or clothes, postponement of action is not feasible. If an agency budget is limited then need must be met first, and there may be no resources for rehabilitative activity. Furthermore, distribution of voluntary funds in the community has favored the "usual institutional arrangements" (e.g., the "character building agencies") at the expense of substitution and rehabilitation services (e.g., child welfare).

Second, rehabilitation often fails to have a clear and demonstrably attainable objective. Was the AFDC program intended to improve the functioning of the family or to return some consumers into economic productivity? If the former, then why was it predicated on paternal absence or incompetence? If the latter, then why the original proscription on maternal employment? Is foster family care intended to be permanent or temporary? If it is the former, then why not strengthen the bonds with the foster parent and gradually remove social work intervention? If the latter, then why is the role of parent defined so peripherally that he is read out of the system much of the time?[25] Is the purpose of family counseling to help a family adjust to a difficult condition or to change their environment? The answers are varied. They generally begin with the introductory phrase "it depends. . . ." But, if it depends, then there is a need for categories that "it depends upon," or else how can one speak of rehabilitation?

The third point is the need for evidence. It is not possible to produce evidence of accomplishment when there is no stated objective. Social welfare cannot come before a legislature or a public and say: "We can prove that. . . ." Social welfare can offer strong evidence of meeting need and of producing programs that society incorporates into its "usual institutional arrangements," but there is no satisfactory evidence of rehabilitation. We actually do not know, for example, whether children of ADC recipients of 1938 were on the rolls in 1948 and whether their children are on AFDC now.[26] And if they are, is it a failure if assessed in terms of E System demands? Is it also a generational failure in family capability?[27]

In the third area of its activities—as a forerunner of social institutions—B-type welfare has done much better than in substitution, and very much better than in rehabilitation. The four case examples —education, community hospital, adoption, aged assistance—are but a fraction of what has been fed into the social system via the less-eligibility route. Thus, social welfare has been a way of legitimization of programs which, though originally ascribed to the poor or otherwise deficient who are stigmatized by the impropriety of its use, eventually becomes more broadly used and loses its mark of shame.

Given the record of accomplishment and failure, how should social work, as the major profession in social welfare type B, allot its resources? That depends on the orientation it chooses: preservation of the status quo or social change. If social welfare is seen as intended to serve as a screen between the "righteous" and the "rightless" then its major emphasis should continue to be on the substitutive and rehabilitative functions. In fact, some societies are capable of exerting enough control on the deprived populace so that even these functions are sporadic and voluntary and result from religious or humanitarian motives.[28] The ways of substitution and rehabilitation are admittedly of some importance, but this is not basic. True, that the dignity of man is less impaired by a pension than by relief. Granted that less stigma attaches to the welfare check than to the handout, but even the welfare check is stigmatizing if the whole program is so perceived. And adjusting the beggar to his lot by means of religious consolation in the hereafter is little different from "helping the client to accept" a negative but often manipulable reality. Whether faith or psychology is used to achieve surrender to a difficult present is only a technical matter. The result from the standpoint of the poor man and the social system is the same.

Substitution and rehabilitation are, of course, quite respectable objectives if they are achieved. But there is no evidence that the latter has been achieved to any marked degree. Economic and familial deprivation may yet respond to social work treatment within the welfare program but the evidence for it is not on the horizon. Although there are sporadic professional outcries against inadequate staffing and lack of knowledge that nullify the rehabilitative intent, the point of the matter is that the less-eligibility welfare programs, i.e., those bearing social stigma, are primarily substitutive and, over the long run, only palliative.

If palliation and possibly occasional but unproven rehabilitation vis-à-vis a status quo system is not the chosen alternative, then social welfare must focus on the third of its capabilities—creation of new, acceptable ways of need-meeting. Usually the new institutions will encompass a broader population than the one which had previously failed to satisfy its needs in the usual manner. Such a course will speed up the development and enhance the acceptability of the new social mechanism. Let us illustrate the path that such social welfare innovation may take with two examples, one from the E System, one from F.

One of the major difficulties of the AFDC program is its stigmatizing effect. Self-respect is one attribute which the program must build. To achieve it, stigma must be removed from recipients. Theoretically, that can be done quite readily in one of two ways: A mother's allowance or a guaranteed minimum annual income for each family. The former is in effect in numerous countries including several members of the British Commonwealth and the East European Communist countries.[29] The latter has been advanced in a number of recent proposals.[30] Neither of these programs is likely to be adopted in the U.S. in the near future. But in the meantime social welfare can innovate in this area. For example, it is possible to subsidize an AFDC family while the parents become employed, reducing the subsidy very gradually, but never below a minimum which is larger than the maximum benefit payable to them. Such a program could include planned savings that eventually establish the family in a position of financial independence and integrate it economically into the society.[31]

F System failures also provide an opportunity. A basic difficulty in any assault on poverty are its psycho-social as well as its economic causes. Families are poor because they have no money. But economic deprivation is also highly correlated with, and probably caused by cultural impoverishment. An environment of poverty, illiteracy, and hopelessness should not be expected to produce a literate, competent, achievement-oriented new generation. If the culture devalues education, how can the school accomplish it?[32] If the family frowns on employment or simply no longer considers it a possibility, how is the young person reared in it to get and hold a job? If the whole environment is alienated from the larger society, how is its next generation to be integrated?

The traditional social welfare answer has been economic assistance and a thimbleful of professional help. If the family completely deteriorated, social welfare sought foster family care to replace it. But more imaginative answers are possible. A change in culture may require a substantial change in environment. The answer is theoretically straightforward. The children of poverty need an environment of ideology, education, and accomplishment. They need models of what they can become and a faith that it is within their grasp to do so. This is not a new problem nor is the solution unknown. Israel has faced it recently when a large part of its immigration came from among the deprived Jews of Morocco. Its answer for many children has been group care for periods of up to six and seven years.[33] Social welfare can develop acculturative settings that *supplement* and, when necessary, *replace* the family in this task. Such group care facilities for normal children bear no resemblance to the institution of the nineteenth century because their objective is to provide the very things it lacked: ideals, pride, will and means for achievement, and models of these in a young and devoted staff. It is true that such an arrangement may go counter to current psychological thinking on the subject of child-rearing, but no evidence exists to support an assertion that "any family is better than any group care arrangement."

CONCLUSION

Focus on the family has brought the discussion around full circle. We began with the assumption that in a simple, pre-industrial environment the family alone could, ideally, meet all needs. Specialization of functions then reduced the family's capability and other systems came into play. Development of systems accompanied an awareness of new needs and a wide expansion of need-dispositions, i.e., acceptable satisfiers. Unmet need, no doubt always a component of human existence, achieved recognition not only as a threat to the individual but also to the system of which he was part. Institutional ways for coping with such personal and systemic malfunctioning were devised. In the main, the purpose has been conservative.

As social work developed it became one of the professions, the main one in social welfare, concerned with such failures. Early in its history social work focused mainly on systemic deficiencies. This changed with increasing professionalization, and adjusting the individual to existing social instrumentalities became the primary objective. How often such objectives (rehabilitation) were being achieved is unclear. That they have absorbed a very large portion of social work effort is obvious. In the outpouring of humanitarianism and social utility that has characterized the American welfare effort of the last forty years or so the latter seems to have won out. Of course, programs were developed that helped the individual. Professionals bound up wounds temporarily, occasionally even healed them permanently. The focus, willingly or unwillingly, consciously or unconsciously, has been on preserving the system as it is.

This orientation has given American welfare of the B type and social work, a rather narrow field in which to define problems and propose solutions. Some will argue that the political climate dictated caution. Also, some social inventiveness did, after all, take place during the early F. D. Roosevelt and the Johnson administrations. True, but did the profession, armed with a philosophy of social change, appear in the vanguard of such developments? Did it provide the imaginative solutions? Did it infuse the atmosphere with causes and ideals?

Porter Lee was correct when he noted (in the late 1920's), that social work was moving from "cause" to "function." In the main, "function" and loyalty is all that societies have usually asked of professions. No more has been demanded of social work in America than dispassionate and loyal competence. Like every profession, social work is pledged to maintain the society of which it is a part. But no society is static. Each is open to small changes continuously and profits from occasional major reorientation. *Function*, sufficiently developed, adequately researched, and skillfully applied permits a profession to implement societal decisions, but no more. *Cause* gives it a voice in making them. Slowly, hesitantly, and even painfully, social work in the 1960's appears to be regaining its voice. This may indicate a change in the societal function of social welfare in America.

NOTES

Numerous persons have read and commented on this paper prior to its present, and by no means final, revision. I am indebted to them for their suggestions. In particular, I want to thank Jerry Turem for his research assistance and John Romanyshyn for his critical and very helpful review.

1. For a historical view see: Karl de Schweinitz, *England's Road to Social Security* (New York: A. S. Barnes & Co. Inc., 1943). The programmatic approach may be seen in: Eveline M. Burns, *The American Social Security System* (Cambridge, Mass.: The Riverside Press, 1951). A clinical view is presented by: Charlotte Towle, *Common Human Needs* (rev. ed.; New York: National Association of Social Workers, 1957). We are badly in need of, and perhaps on the verge of developing an ideological view of welfare which may emerge out of the anti-poverty movement.

2. de Schweinitz, *England's Road* . . . , page 5, pp. 7–8.

3. William Dawson. *The German Empire 1867–1914 and the Unity Movement,* Vol. II (New York: Macmillan Co., 1919), pp. 39–40.

4. See: Robert E. Sherwood, *Roosevelt and Hopkins* (rev. ed.; New York: Harper and Bros., 1950), pp. 102–103 for the background of this quotation.

5. Walter A. Friedlander, *Introduction to Social Welfare* (New York: Prentice-Hall Inc., 1955), p. 106.

6. Ida C. Merriam, "Social Welfare Expenditures 1962–63," *Social Security Bulletin 26,* No. 11 (November, 1963), pp. 3–15.

7. Henry A. Murray, *Explorations in Personality* (New York: Oxford Univ. Press, 1938), pp. 123–124.

8. Talcott Parsons and Edward A. Shils (eds.), *Toward a General Theory of Action* (Cambridge, Mass.: Harvard Univ. Press, 1962), p. 9 and pp. 115–120.

9. See: Roland L. Warren, *The Community in America* (Chicago: Rand McNally, 1963). Warren distinguishes five structures: (1) families, (2) *ad hoc* informal associations, (3) formally organized associations, (4) establishments operated for financial gain, (5) official governmental bodies (pp. 210–211). The division presented in this paper is similar except for the combination of formal associations with governmental bodies under "polity."

10. George P. Murdock, *Social Structure* (New York: Macmillan, 1949), p. 1.

11. One writer, in discussing the English welfare scene, contends that "the structure of society . . . operates to maintain a humane institution in existence once it is established . . . *To be viable it is not, in fact, necessary for them to be efficient . . . It is not even necessary for its personnel to have any clear idea what it is for.*" Peter Nokes, "Purpose and Efficiency in Humane Social Institutions," *Human Relations 13,* No. 2 (May, 1960), pp. 144–145. (Emphasis in original.)

12. One recent development that supports this distinction is the creation of a Public Welfare (as distinguished from Social Security) Administration within the U.S. Dept. of Health, Education, and Welfare. Welfare types A and B are, obviously, not fully distinct from one another. Gradations of "A-ness" and "B-ness" are probably determined by such factors as: (1) incidence of unmet need, (2) population affected, (3) the system within which the failure is taking place.

13. Talcott Parsons, *The Social System* (Glencoe, Illinois: The Free Press, 1959), pp. 439–447.

14. The concept "less eligibility" was not initially, nor is it currently purely economic. It has always had psycho-social aspects, and these remain to deter malingering even when the economic conditions are reduced or eliminated.

15. Crystal Eastman, *Work Accidents and the Law* (New York: Russell Sage Foundation, 1910).

16. See: *Social Security Handbook* (Washington, D.C.: SSA, HEW, 1963) and California Welfare Study Commission, *Consultants' Reports* (Sacramento: State Department of Social Welfare, 1963).

17. James Leiby, *Charity and Correction in New Jersey* (unpublished manuscript), pp. 36–39. See also: Nelson Burr, *Education in New Jersey 1630–1871* (Princeton, New Jersey: Princeton Univ. Press, 1942).

18. This is the title of a book that parents of adopted children are urged to read to them: Valentina P. Wasson, *The Chosen Baby* (Philadelphia: J. B. Lippincott & Co., 1939). See also: T. S. Doublas, "Our Children Are Proud to Be Adopted," *Farm Journal* (February, 1960), pp. 103–104.

19. Annual Report of the Social Security Board, *First Annual Report for the Fiscal Year Ended June 30, 1936* (Washington, D.C., 1937).

20. The California Welfare Study Commission (p. 197) agrees: "Fundamentally, the adult programs in California, especially OAS and ANB, are modified pension programs."

21. The *maximum* grant per person on AFDC cannot reach the *minimum* grant per person on OAS (California Welfare Study Commission).

22. Elizabeth de Schweinitz, "To Work or Not to Work," *Child Welfare*, Vol. XXXII, No. 10 (December, 1954), pp. 6–8.

23. See: Henry S. Maas and Richard E. Engler, Jr., *Children in Need of Parents* (New York: Columbia Univ. Press, 1959). This work elaborates the viewpoint presented here in relation to several American communities.

24. C. Howard Hopkins, *History of the Y.M.C.A. in North America* (New York: Association Press, 1951).

25. See Maas and Engler for extensive data on the nature of foster care in selected U.S. communities. For data on the role of parent, foster parent, and social worker, see: Martin Wolins, *Selecting Foster Parents: The Ideal and the Reality* (New York: Columbia Univ. Press, 1963).

26. Gordon Blackwell and Raymond Gould, *Future Citizens All* (Chicago: American Public Welfare Association, 1952), a major study of AFDC recipients, fails to answer this question. A more recent study, M. Elaine Burgess and Daniel Price, *An American Dependency Challenge* (Chicago: American Public Welfare Association, 1963), p. 158, states that "over forty percent of the mothers and/or fathers [of current recipients] had been reared in homes in which some form of public assistance . . . had been received . . . ."

27. See: Daniel P. Moynihan, *The Negro Family: The Case for*

National Action (Washington, D.C.: Office of Policy Planning and Research-Dept. of Labor, March, 1965).

28. In these instances the humanitarian origin of welfare is somewhat suspect. For example, much of the voluntary welfare activity in Latin America is initiated by the Church, but the Church is also the major pillar and beneficiary of the existing order, perhaps second only to the military.

29. *Social Security Programs Throughout the World—1961*, Social Security Administration, U.S. Department of Health, Education, and Welfare (Washington, D.C.: U.S. Government Printing Office, 1961).

30. See, for example: James Tobin, "The Case for an Income Guarantee," *The Public Interest*, Vol. IV (Summer, 1966), pp. 31–41.

31. Greater independence in planning, and more trust in the relationship with authority can also be built into such an arrangement. It may actually call for *less* rather than more social work service.

32. Following a huge national survey of education, one writer commented that increasing retardation in the academic performance of deprived children may, in part, be attributed to the ". . . *schools' ineffectiveness to free achievement from the impact of the home* . . . ." James S. Coleman, "Equal Schools or Equal Students," *The Public Interest*, Vol. IV, (Summer, 1966), p. 74. (Emphasis in original.)

33. See: Martin Wolins, "Another View of Group Care of Children," *Child Welfare* (January, 1965), pp. 10–18.

7   The Role of Government in a Free Society

MILTON FRIEDMAN

A common objection to totalitarian societies is that they regard the end as justifying the means. Taken literally, this objection is clearly illogical. If the end does not justify the means, what does? But this easy answer does not dispose of the objection; it simply shows that the objection is not well put. To deny that the end justifies the means is indirectly to assert that the end in question is not the ultimate end, that the ultimate end is itself the use of the proper means. Desirable or not, any end that can be attained only by the use of bad means must give way to the more basic end of the use of acceptable means.

To the liberal, the appropriate means are free discussion and voluntary co-operation, which implies that any form of coercion is inappropriate. The ideal is unanimity among responsible individuals achieved on the basis of free and full discussion. This is another way of expressing the goal of freedom. . . .

From this standpoint, the role of the market, as already noted, is that it permits unanimity without conformity; that it is a system of effectively proportional representation. On the other hand, the characteristic feature of action through explicitly political channels is that it tends to require or to enforce substantial conformity. The typical issue must be decided "yes" or "no"; at most, provision can be made for a fairly limited number of alternatives. Even the use of proportional representation in its explicitly political form does not alter this conclusion. The number of separate groups that can in fact be represented is narrowly limited, enormously so by comparison with the proportional representation of the market. More important, the fact that the final outcome generally must be a law applicable to all groups, rather than separate legislative enactments for each "party" represented, means that proportional representation in its political version, far from permitting unanimity without conformity, tends toward ineffectiveness and fragmentation. It thereby operates to destroy any consensus on which unanimity with conformity can rest.

There are clearly some matters with respect to which effective proportional representation is impossible. I cannot get the amount of national defense I want and you, a different amount. With respect to such indivisible matters we can discuss, and argue, and vote. But having decided, we must conform. It is precisely the existence of such indivisible matters—protection of the individual and the nation from coercion are clearly the most basic—that prevents exclusive reliance on individual action through the market. If we are to use some of our resources for such indivisible items, we must employ political channels to reconcile differences.

The use of political channels, while inevitable, tends to strain the social cohesion essential for a stable society. The strain is least if agreement for joint action need be reached only on a limited range of issues on which people in any event have common views. Every extension of the range of issues for which explicit agreement is sought strains further the delicate threads that hold society together.

If it goes so far as to touch an issue on which men feel deeply yet differently, it may well disrupt the society. Fundamental differences in basic values can seldom if ever be resolved at the ballot box; ultimately they can only be decided, though not resolved, by conflict. The religious and civil wars of history are a bloody testament to this judgment.

The widespread use of the market reduces the strain on the social fabric by rendering conformity unnecessary with respect to any activities it encompasses. The wider the range of activities covered by the market, the fewer are the issues on which explicitly political decisions are required and hence on which it is necessary to achieve agreement. In turn, the fewer the issues on which agreement is necessary, the greater is the likelihood of getting agreement while maintaining a free society.

Unanimity is, of course, an ideal. In practice, we can afford neither the time nor the effort that would be required to achieve complete unanimity on every issue. We must perforce accept something less. We are thus led to accept majority rule in one form or another as an expedient. That majority rule is an expedient rather than itself a basic principle is clearly shown by the fact that our willingness to resort to majority rule, and the size of the majority we require, themselves depend on the seriousness of the issue involved. If the matter is of little moment and the minority has no strong feelings about being overruled, a bare plurality will suffice. On the other hand, if the minority feels strongly about the issue involved, even a bare majority will not do. Few of us would be willing to have issues of free speech, for example, decided by a bare majority. Our legal structure is full of such distinctions among kinds of issues that require different kinds of majorities. At the extreme are those issues embodied in the Constitution. These are the principles that are so important that we are willing to make minimal concessions to expediency. Something like essential consensus was achieved initially in accepting them, and we require something like essential consensus for a change in them.

The self-denying ordinance to refrain from majority rule on certain kinds of issues that is embodied in our Constitution and in similar written or unwritten constitutions elsewhere, and the specific provisions in these constitutions or their equivalents prohibiting coercion of individuals, are themselves to be regarded as reached by free discussion and as reflecting essential unanimity about means.

I turn now to consider more specifically, though still in very broad terms, what the areas are that cannot be handled through the market at all, or can be handled only at so great a cost that the use of political channels may be preferable.

GOVERNMENT AS RULE-MAKER AND UMPIRE

It is important to distinguish the day-to-day activities of people from the general customary and legal framework within which these take place. The day-to-day activities are like the actions of the participants in a game when they are playing it; the framework, like the rules of the game they play. And just as a good game requires acceptance by the players both of the rules and of the umpire to interpret and enforce them, so a good society requires that its members agree on the general conditions that will govern relations among them, on some means of arbitrating different interpretations of these conditions, and on some device for enforcing compliance with the generally accepted rules. As in games, so also in society, most of the general conditions are the unintended outcome of custom, accepted unthinkingly. At most, we consider explicitly only minor modifications in them, though the cumulative effect of a series of minor modifications may be a drastic alteration in the character of the game or of the society. In both games and society also, no set of rules can prevail unless most participants most of the time conform to them without external sanctions; unless that is, there is a broad underlying social consensus. But we cannot rely on custom or on this consensus alone to interpret and to enforce the rules; we need an umpire. These then are the basic roles of government in a free society: to provide a means whereby we can modify the rules, to mediate differences among us on the meaning of the rules, and to enforce compliance with the rules on the part of those few who would otherwise not play the game.

The need for government in these respects arises because absolute freedom is impossible. However attractive anarchy may be as a philosophy, it is not feasible in a world of imperfect men. Men's freedoms can conflict, and when they do, one man's freedom must be limited to preserve another's—as a Supreme Court Justice once put it, "My freedom to move my fist must be limited by the proximity of your chin."

The major problem in deciding the appropriate activities of government is how to resolve such conflicts among the freedoms of different individuals. In some cases, the answer is easy. There is little difficulty in attaining near unanimity to the proposition that one man's freedom to murder his neighbor must be sacrificed to preserve the freedom of the other man to live. In other cases, the answer is difficult. In the economic area, a major problem arises in respect of the conflict between freedom to combine and freedom to compete. What meaning is to be attributed to "free" as modifying "enterprise"? In the United States, "free" has been understood to mean that anyone is free to set up an enterprise, which means that existing enterprises are not free to keep out competitors except by selling a better product at the same price or the same product at a lower price. In the continental tradition, on the other hand, the meaning has generally been that enterprises are free to do what they want, including the fixing of prices, division of markets, and the adoption of other techniques to keep out potential competitors. Perhaps the most difficult specific problem in this area arises with respect to combinations among laborers, where the problem of freedom to combine and freedom to compete is particularly acute.

A still more basic economic area in which the answer is both difficult and important is the definition of property rights. The notion of property, as it has developed over centuries and as it is embodied in our legal codes, has become so much a part of us that we tend to take it for granted, and fail to recognize the extent to which just what constitutes property and what rights the ownership of property confers are complex social creations rather than self-evident propositions. Does my having title to land, for example, and my freedom to use my property as I wish, permit me to deny to someone else the right to fly over my land in his airplane? Or does his right to use his airplane take precedence? Or does this depend on how high he flies? Or how much noise he makes? Does voluntary exchange require that he pay me for the privilege of flying over my land? Or that I must pay him to refrain from flying over it? The mere mention of royalties, copyrights, patents; shares of stock in corporations; riparian rights, and the like, may perhaps emphasize the role of generally accepted social rules in the very definition of property. It may suggest also that, in many cases, the existence of a well specified and generally accepted definition of property is far more important than just what the definition is.

Another economic area that raises particularly difficult problems is the monetary system. Government responsibility for the monetary system has long been recognized. It is explicitly provided for in the constitutional provision which gives Congress the power "to coin money, regulate the value thereof, and of foreign coin." There is probably no other area of economic activity with respect to which government action has been so uniformly accepted. This habitual and by now almost unthinking acceptance of governmental responsibility makes thorough understanding of the grounds for such responsibility all the more necessary, since it enhances the danger that the scope of government will spread from activities that are, to those that are not, appropriate in a free society, from providing a monetary framework to determining the allocation of resources among individuals.

In summary, the organization of economic activity through voluntary exchange presumes that we have provided, through government, for the maintenance of law and order to prevent coercion of one individual by another, the enforcement of contracts voluntarily entered into, the definition of the meaning of property rights, the interpretation and enforcement of such rights, and the provision of a monetary framework.

ACTION THROUGH GOVERNMENT ON GROUNDS OF TECHNICAL MONOPOLY AND NEIGHBORHOOD EFFECTS

The role of government just considered is to do something that the market cannot do for itself, namely, to determine, arbitrate, and enforce the rules of the game. We may also want to do through government some things that might conceivably be done through the market but that technical or similar conditions render it difficult to do in that way. These all reduce to cases in which strictly voluntary exchange is either exceedingly costly or practically impossible. There are two general classes of such cases: monopoly and similar market imperfections, and neighborhood effects.

Exchange is truly voluntary only when nearly equivalent alternatives exist. Monopoly implies the absence of alternatives and thereby inhibits effective freedom of exchange. In practice, monopoly frequently, if not generally, arises from government support or from collusive agreements among individuals. With respect to these, the problem is either to avoid governmental fostering of monopoly or to stimulate the effective enforcement of rules such as those embodied in our anti-trust laws. However, monopoly may also arise because it is technically efficient to have a single producer or enterprise. I venture to suggest that such cases are more limited than is supposed but they unquestionably do arise. A simple example is perhaps the provision of telephone services within a community. I shall refer to such cases as "technical" monopoly.

When technical conditions make a monopoly the natural outcome of competitive market forces, there are only three alternatives that seem available: private monopoly, public monopoly, or public regulation. All three are bad so we must choose among evils. Henry Simons, observing public regulation of monopoly in the United States, found the results so distasteful that he concluded public monopoly would be a lesser evil. Walter Eucken, a noted German liberal, observing public monopoly in German railroads, found the results so distasteful that he concluded public regulation would be a lesser evil. Having learned from both, I reluctantly conclude that, if tolerable, private monopoly may be the least of the evils.

If society were static so that the conditions which give rise to a technical monopoly were sure to remain, I would have little confidence in this solution. In a rapidly changing society, however, the conditions making for technical monopoly frequently change and I suspect that both public regulation and public monopoly are likely to be less responsive to such changes in conditions, to be less readily capable of elimination, than private monopoly.

Railroads in the United States are an excellent example. A large degree of monopoly in railroads was perhaps inevitable on technical grounds in the nineteenth century. This was the justification for the Interstate Commerce Commission. But conditions have changed. The emergence of road and air transport has reduced the monopoly element in railroads to negligible proportions. Yet we have not eliminated the ICC. On the contrary, the ICC, which started out as an agency to protect the public from exploitation by the railroads, has become an agency to protect railroads from competition by trucks and other means of transport, and more recently even to protect existing truck companies from competition by new entrants. Similarly, in England, when the railroads were nationalized, trucking was at first brought into the state monopoly. If railroads had never been subjected to regulation in the United States, it is nearly certain that by now transportation, including railroads, would be a highly competitive industry with little or no remaining monopoly elements.

The choice between the evils of private monopoly, public monopoly, and public regulation cannot, however, be made once and for all, independently of the factual circumstances. If the technical monopoly is of a service or commodity that is regarded as essential and if its monopoly power is sizable, even the short-run effects of private unregulated monopoly may not be tolerable, and either public regulation or ownership may be a lesser evil.

Technical monopoly may on occasion justify a *de facto* public monopoly. It cannot by itself justify a public monopoly achieved by making it illegal for anyone else to compete. For example, there is no way to justify our present public monopoly of the post office. It may be argued that the carrying of mail is a technical monopoly and that a government monopoly is the least of evils. Along these lines, one could perhaps justify a government post office but not the present law, which makes it illegal for anybody else to carry mail. If the delivery of mail is a technical monopoly, no one will be able to succeed in competition with the government. If it is not, there is no reason why the government should be engaged in it. The only way to find out is to leave other people free to enter.

The historical reason why we have a post office monopoly is because the Pony Express did such a good job of carrying the mail across the continent that, when the government introduced transcontinental service, it couldn't compete effectively and lost money. The result was a law making it illegal for anybody else to carry the mail. That is why the Adams Express Company is an investment trust today instead of an operating company. I conjecture that if entry into the mail-carrying business were open to all, there would be a large number of firms entering it and this archaic industry would become revolutionized in short order.

A second general class of cases in which strictly voluntary exchange is impossible arises when actions of individuals have effects on other individuals for which it is not feasible to charge or recompense them. This is the problem of "neighborhood effects." An obvious example is the pollution of a stream. The man who pollutes a stream is in effect forcing others to exchange good water for bad. These others might be willing to make the exchange at a price. But it is not feasible for them, acting individually, to avoid the exchange or to enforce appropriate compensation.

A less obvious example is the provision of highways. In this case, it is technically possible to identify and hence charge individuals for their use of the roads and so to have private operation. However, for general access roads, involving many points of entry and exit, the costs of collection would be extremely high if a charge were to be made for the specific services received by each individual, because of the necessity of establishing toll booths or the equivalent at all entrances. The gasoline tax is a much cheaper method of charging individuals roughly in proportion to their use of the roads. This method, however, is one in which the particular payment cannot be identified closely with the particular use. Hence, it is hardly feasible to have private enterprise provide the service and collect the charge without establishing extensive private monopoly.

These considerations do not apply to long-distance turnpikes with high density of traffic and limited access. For these, the costs of collection are small and in many cases are now being paid, and there are often numerous alternatives, so that there is no serious monopoly problem. Hence, there is every reason why these should be privately owned and operated. If so owned and operated, the enterprise running the highway should receive the gasoline taxes paid on account of travel on it.

Parks are an interesting example because they illustrate the difference between cases that can and cases that cannot be justified by neighborhood effects, and because almost everyone at first sight regards the conduct of National Parks as obviously a valid function of government. In fact, however, neighborhood effects may justify a city park; they do not justify a national park, like Yellowstone National Park or the Grand Canyon. What is the fundamental difference between the two? For the city park, it is extremely difficult to identify the people who benefit from it and to charge them for the benefits which they receive. If there is a park in the middle of the city, the houses on all sides get the benefit of the open space, and people who walk through it or by it also benefit. To maintain toll collectors at the gates or to impose annual charges per window overlooking the park would be very expensive and difficult. The entrances to a national park like Yellowstone, on the other hand, are few; most of the people who come stay for a considerable period of time and it is perfectly feasible to set up toll gates and collect admission charges. This is indeed now done, though the charges do not cover the whole costs. If the public wants this kind of an activity enough to pay for it, private enterprises will have every incentive to provide such parks. And, of course, there are many private enterprises of this nature now in existence. I cannot myself conjure up any neighborhood effects or important monopoly effects that would justify governmental activity in this area.

Considerations like those I have treated under the heading of neighborhood effects have been used to rationalize almost every conceivable intervention. In many instances, however, this rationalization is special pleading rather than a legitimate application of the concept of neighborhood effects. Neighborhood effects cut both ways. They can be a reason for limiting the activities of government as well as for expanding them. Neighborhood effects impede voluntary exchange because it is difficult to identify the effects on third parties and to measure their magnitude; but this difficulty is present in governmental activity as well. It is hard to know when neighborhood effects are sufficiently large to justify particular costs in overcoming them and even harder to distribute the costs in an appropriate fashion. Consequently, when government engages in activities to overcome neighborhood effects, it will in part introduce an additional set of neighborhood effects by failing to charge or to compensate individuals properly. Whether the original or the new neighborhood effects are the more serious can only be judged by the facts of the individual case, and even then, only very approximately. Furthermore, the use of government to overcome neighborhood effects itself has an extremely important neighborhood effect which is unrelated to the particular occasion for government action. Every act of government intervention limits the area of individual freedom directly and threatens the preservation of freedom indirectly. . . .

Our principles offer no hard and fast line how far it is appropriate to use government to accomplish jointly what it is difficult or impossible for us to accomplish separately through strictly voluntary exchange. In any particular case of proposed intervention, we must make up a balance sheet, listing separately the advantages and disadvantages. Our principles tell us what items to put on the one side and what items on the other and they give us some basis for attaching importance to the different items. In particular, we shall always want to enter on the liability side of any proposed government intervention, its neighborhood effect in threatening freedom, and give this effect considerable weight. Just how much weight to give to it, as to other items, depends upon the circumstances. If, for example, existing government intervention is minor, we shall attach a smaller weight to the negative effects of additional government intervention. This is an important reason why many earlier liberals, like Henry Simons, writing at a time when government was small by today's standards, were willing to have government undertake activities that today's liberals would not accept now that government has become so overgrown.

ACTION THROUGH GOVERNMENT ON PATERNALISTIC GROUNDS

Freedom is a tenable objective only for responsible individuals. We do not believe in freedom for madmen or children. The necessity of drawing a line between responsible individuals and others is inescapable, yet it means that there is an essential ambiguity in our ultimate objective of freedom. Paternalism is inescapable for those whom we designate as not responsible.

The clearest case, perhaps, is that of madmen. We are willing neither to permit them freedom nor to shoot them. It would be nice if we could rely on voluntary activities of individuals to house and care for the madmen. But I think we cannot rule out the possibility that such charitable activities will be inadequate, if only because of the neighborhood effect involved in the fact that I benefit if another man contributes to the care of the insane. For this reason, we may be willing to arrange for their care through government.

Children offer a more difficult case. The ultimate operative unit in our society is the family, not the individual. Yet the acceptance of the family as the unit rests in considerable part on expediency rather than principle. We believe that parents are generally best able to protect their children and to provide for their development into responsible individuals for whom freedom is appropriate. But we do not believe in the freedom of parents to do what they will with other people. The children are responsible individuals in embryo, and a believer in freedom believes in protecting their ultimate rights.

To put this in a different and what may seem a more callous way, children are at one and the same time consumer goods and potentially responsible members of society. The freedom of individuals to use their economic resources as they want includes the freedom to use them to have children—to buy, as it were, the services of children as a particular form of consumption. But once this choice is exercised, the children have a value in and of themselves and have a freedom of their own that is not simply an extension of the freedom of the parents.

The paternalistic ground for governmental activity is in many ways the most troublesome to a liberal; for it involves the acceptance of a principle—that some shall decide for others—which he finds objectionable in most applications and which he rightly regards as a hallmark of his chief intellectual opponents, the proponents of collectivism in one or another of its guises, whether it be communism, socialism, or a welfare state. Yet there is no use pretending that problems are simpler than in fact they are. There is no avoiding the need for some measure of paternalism. As Dicey wrote in 1914 about an act for the protection of mental defectives, "The Mental Deficiency Act is the first step along a path on which no sane man can decline to enter, but which, if too far pursued, will bring

statesmen across difficulties hard to meet without considerable interference with individual liberty."[1] There is no formula that can tell
us where to stop. We must rely on our fallible judgment and, having
reached a judgment, on our ability to persuade our fellow men that
it is a correct judgment, or their ability to persuade us to modify
our views. We must put our faith, here as elsewhere, in a consensus
reached by imperfect and biased men through free discussion and
trial and error.

CONCLUSION

A government which maintained law and order, defined property
rights, served as a means whereby we could modify property rights
and other rules of the economic game, adjudicated disputes about
the interpretation of the rules, enforced contracts, promoted competition, provided a monetary framework, engaged in activities to
counter technical monopolies and to overcome neighborhood effects
widely regarded as sufficiently important to justify government
intervention, and which supplemented private charity and the
private family in protecting the irresponsible, whether madman or
child—such a government would clearly have important functions
to perform. The consistent liberal is not an anarchist.

Yet it is also true that such a government would have clearly
limited functions and would refrain from a host of activities that are
now undertaken by federal and state governments in the United
States, and their counterparts in other Western countries. . . . It
may help to give a sense of proportion about the role that a liberal
would assign government simply to list, in closing this chapter, some
activities currently undertaken by government in the U.S., that cannot, so far as I can see, validly be justified in terms of the principles
outlined above:

1. Parity price support programs for agriculture.
2. Tariffs on imports or restrictions on exports, such as current
oil import quotas, sugar quotas, etc.
3. Governmental control of output, such as through the farm
program, or through prorationing of oil as is done by the Texas
Railroad Commission.
4. Rent control, such as is still practiced in New York, or more
general price and wage controls such as were imposed during and
just after World War II.
5. Legal minimum wage rates, or legal maximum prices, such as

the legal maximum of zero on the rate of interest that can be paid on demand deposits by commercial banks, or the legally fixed maximum rates that can be paid on savings and time deposits.

6. Detailed regulation of industries, such as the regulation of transportation by the Interstate Commerce Commission. This had some justification on technical monopoly grounds when initially introduced for railroads; it has none now for any means of transport. Another example is detailed regulation of banking.

7. A similar example, but one which deserves special mention because of its implicit censorship and violation of free speech, is the control of radio and television by the Federal Communications Commission.

8. Present social security programs, especially the old-age and retirement programs compelling people in effect (a) to spend a specified fraction of their income on the purchase of retirement annuity, (b) to buy the annuity from a publicly operated enterprise.

9. Licensure provisions in various cities and states which restrict particular enterprises or occupations or professions to people who have a license, where the license is more than a receipt for a tax which anyone who wishes to enter the activity may pay.

10. So-called "public-housing" and the host of other subsidy programs directed at fostering residential construction such as F.H.A. and V.A. guarantee of mortgage, and the like.

11. Conscription to man the military services in peacetime. The appropriate free market arrangement is volunteer military forces; which is to say, hiring men to serve. There is no justification for not paying whatever price is necessary to attract the required number of men. Present arrangements are inequitable and arbitrary, seriously interfere with the freedom of young men to shape their lives, and probably are even more costly than the market alternative. (Universal military training to provide a reserve for war time is a different problem and may be justified on liberal grounds.)

12. National parks, as noted above.

13. The legal prohibition on the carrying of mail for profit.

14. Publicly owned and operated toll roads, as noted above.

This list is far from comprehensive.

NOTE

1. A. V. Dicey, *Lectures on the Relation between Law and Public Opinion in England during the Nineteenth Century* (2d ed.; London: Macmillan & Co., 1914), p. li.

Chapter Three

DIRECTIONS OF SOCIAL WELFARE

If social welfare is an emerging institution, it is appropriate to inquire where it is headed. Because institutional developments can be analyzed at many levels, this question does not yield to a singular definitive response. There are many answers, depending on the specific aspects of social welfare under consideration at a given time. We have selected readings for this chapter that discuss some of the trends in social welfare that are taking shape in the 1970s. These developments are concerned with: (1) the size and growth of social welfare programs, (2) the relationship between the public and the voluntary sectors of social welfare, (3) the nature of eligibility for social welfare benefits, (4) the heightening of accountability in service-delivery systems, and (5) the balance between personal services and social reform.

Up-to-date social welfare expenditure data for the United States are readily available in reports of the Department of Health, Education, and Welfare.[1] These reports provide a concise overview of the size and growth of social welfare as indicated by the amounts of money spent according to program categories by various levels of government and the private sector. Several trends may be identified by these data which trace expenditures, usually back to the base period of 1928–29. The data reveal, for example, that between

1960 and 1974 social welfare expenditures increased from 38 to 55.8 percent of all government expenditures. During this period the federal proportion of these expenditures increased from 47.7 to 57.6 percent. Private expenditures for social welfare also increased slightly more than threefold between 1960 and 1974. However, in 1974 government expenditures accounted for 71 percent of the total spent for social welfare, as compared to 29 percent from the private sector.

The relationships between public-government and private-voluntary spending for social welfare are more intricate and of greater significance than might be inferred from the simple proportions noted above. These complexities and their implications are analyzed by Elizabeth Wickenden in Reading 8, "Purchase of Care and Services: Effect on Voluntary Agencies." Government spending has not just increased over the years, as Wickenden points out, it has been used increasingly in purchase-of-service arrangements with voluntary agencies. And these arrangements have modified one of the traditional characteristics of the voluntary sector—its financial independence of government. Wickenden analyzes the development of the new "partnership" between government and voluntary agencies and the choices of funding arrangements available in this relationship. In examining these alternative methods of government financing, she casts a critical eye on their implications for the future of voluntarism in social welfare.

Whether under public auspices, private auspices, or some mixture thereof, the tremendous increase in social welfare services has been accompanied by growing demands that those who produce services be held accountable for their performance. But *to whom* should they be accountable? The idea of accountability pertains to various relationships. The federal government provides grants-in-aid to local programs which are then held accountable to the federal bureaucracy. But local taxpayers and consumers believe that social welfare programs should be accountable to them. In Reading 9, "Accountability: What Does It Mean?" Alice Rivlin analyzes three service-delivery models that are currently advocated as means to enhance accountability: decentralization, community control, and the voucher system. Rivlin points out that efforts to increase accountability of social services, whether to higher levels of government, taxpayers, consumers, community groups, or whomever, cannot be fully realized by the manipulation of service-delivery arrangements. For social services to be held accountable for their performance, there must be some way to measure and evaluate their accomplishments. Rivlin examines some of the frustrating problems of assessing program effectiveness and offers perceptive comments about the directions that might be taken in pursuit of this objective.

The increasing concern for accountability reflects the fact that social welfare benefits have become available to a wide range of groups in the population over the past 40 years. As claims on welfare benefits are extended, questions of who should be eligible and under what conditions have become fundamental issues in the development of modern social welfare systems. Various dimensions of these issues are discussed by George Hoshino in Reading 10, "Britain's Debate on Universal or Selective Services: Lessons for America." Hoshino traces the movement in Britain toward the allocation of social services on the basis of universality whereby social welfare benefits are made available to an entire population as a social right, without recourse to individual tests of need. Similar developments in the United States are noted. Observing this trend toward universality, Hoshino analyzes the persistence of social services allocated on the basis of selectivity, usually in the form of an individual means test. According to this analysis selective schemes will continue to be a required feature of social welfare, but they can and should be administered in a more dignified manner than is currently the case. There may be a societal need for means-tested programs, but they need not be mean spirited.

It has been observed by many that during the past decade, rehabilitation-related activities of traditional individually-oriented social services suffered a considerable decline in public favor and professional emphasis. And, as these intensive personal helping services waned, increasing emphasis was placed on reform-related activities of social action programs. While this shift in the focus and orientation of social service resources has taken place, individual problems and personal crises have continued to generate great needs for intensive social services. Alfred Kahn, who has observed this trend in New York City,[2] has pointed out that while reform activities are important, they should not submerge the need for or the contribution of personal social services. He calls for a revitalization of the personal services and the introduction of greater balance and coordination in social welfare activities.

We might note that as this book goes to press in 1976, the movement away from personal services and toward reform activities identified by Kahn appears to be abating somewhat. In the 1960s social welfare and social work were deeply involved in movements for change, both in professional education and in agency practice. Gradually, as some new ideas have been implemented, some have proven to be programmatically and professionally impractical, and others have been found to be politically unfeasible. The energies of students, teachers, and practitioners appear to be turning toward a renewed interest in refinement of programs and practice.

NOTES

1. For example, see Alfred M. Skolnik and Sophie R. Dales, "Social Welfare Expenditures, Fiscal Year 1974," *Social Security Bulletin*, 38 (January 1975): 3–18. The statistics that follow are taken from this report.
2. Alfred J. Kahn, "Do Social Services Have a Future in New York?" *City Almanac*, 5 (February 1971): 1–12.

8   Purchase of Care and Services: Effect on Voluntary Agencies

ELIZABETH WICKENDEN

The very term "purchase" implies a market situation in which there is a buyer and a seller. Voluntary agencies in the health and welfare field play both roles. In some situations they sell their services, especially to the government, and in others they buy services from another individual or organization. In some situations they may even play both roles simultaneously, acting as an intermediary between the initial purchaser and the ultimate provider of the services. Thus, for example, a child welfare agency may "sell" its child care supervisory responsibility to a governmental agency and "purchase" actual child care from a foster mother. In the health field the third-party role is even more highly developed where an organiza-

Reprinted from the proceedings of the First Milwaukee Institute on a Social Welfare Issue of the Day: Purchase and Care of Services in the Health and Welfare Field, ed. Iris Winogrond (University of Wisconsin-Milwaukee, School of Social Welfare, July 1970), with permission of the author and of the University of Wisconsin-Milwaukee, School of Social Welfare.

tion such as Blue Cross or Blue Shield may act as an intermediary in the provision of hospital or medical service to Medicare beneficiaries.

There are common denominators of negotiation in all of these situations: the fixing of mutually agreed-upon definitions of responsibility, accountability, and price. But for voluntary agencies the overwhelming weight of current change in philosophy and operational practice lies in the relationship of such agencies as providers of service to the government as a source of their financing. For that reason this discussion is centered largely on the implications for voluntary agencies in this rapidly expanding relationship.

WHAT DO WE MEAN BY A VOLUNTARY AGENCY?

One of the penalties of living in a time of transition is that words of long-established habitual meaning seem to disintegrate like ghosts in a fog of ambiguity. What, for example, do we mean by a "voluntary" agency and how does it differ from a "governmental" or a "commercial" agency? If—like the former—it expends tax money and if—like the latter—it buys and sells services in the marketplace, these traditional distinctions are no longer serviceable. Nor can we assume that the functions assigned to these three agents of social relationship are the means of distinguishing among them. Nursing home care, day care for children, living arrangements for the aged or other special groups, recreational activity (to name a few of the more obvious) perform the same basic function for society and the consumer regardless of the provider. These common denominators form the very basis for this symposium and, therefore, we must look elsewhere for our distinctions.

What precisely then can be said to distinguish the "voluntary" health and welfare agency from its governmental and commercial counterparts? As I search for these distinctions I find them more and more obscured by contemporary realities. In virtually every case the differences seem to be those of *degree*, with voluntarism operating along a spectrum which—at either end—tends to merge into the other two. Let me list some of these major distinctions and the ways they tend toward a common ground.

1. *Origins and Motivation.* A voluntary agency is assumed to come into existence by reason of the voluntary action of some individual or group proceeding with the intent to render a service

rather than to carry out a mandate of law or to gain a profit. It is responding to a philanthropic, religious, or social impulse in the first instance. This is still a primary characteristic of voluntarism in most situations although governmental action is creating a new gray area in quasi-nongovernmental agencies. (Is the new New York City Hospital and Health Service Corporation, for example, a public or private agency?) The situation is similar for agencies created to meet the demands of a particular market (home care for Medicare beneficiaries, for example.)[1]

2. *Control and Management.*   A voluntary agency is assumed to be autonomous and control its own destiny, typically under the direction of an independent governing board. But this autonomy too must be considered relative in the light of the following kinds of controls and influences: (a) state requirements for incorporation, accountability for funds and fund-raising, licensing requirements; (b) controls imposed by financing sources on individual and corporate givers by tax deductibility, by third-party financing mechanisms like community funds and foundations, and by government subsidies whether direct or indirect; and (c) the market for compensated services.

3. *Financing.*   It has been generally assumed—at least since the time of the Reformation which launched our pluralistic institutions by separating state from church, with greater central authority for the former and greater diversity among the latter—that voluntary agencies would be financed by voluntary contributions. This was assumed to assure their independence from the rigidity and controls associated with tax funds. There was a further assumption that the free choice of service objective and clientele would be supported by the free choice of the giver within the framework of his own religious or other associations. But this concept has been overwhelmed by the complexity of our times and needs in at least three ways: *first* by the community fund movement which homogenized the objectives of voluntary giving by interposing a common channel between donor and beneficiary, *second* by the development—especially in the health field—of the third-party purchaser of service in the form of insurance, pension funds or other agency, and *third* by the increasing reliance on tax funds and their governmental dispensers. In all three cases the independence of the voluntary provider of service has been modified by the institutionalization of its source of support in the form of an intermediary between giver and beneficiary. Underlying these developments was

a growth in the need and demand for socially provided services of such staggering dimensions as to overwhelm the capacity of traditional patterns of voluntary giving.

4. *Choice of Service and Beneficiary.* Inevitably the introduction of an intermediary source of financing has affected the other traditional characteristics of the voluntary agency: freedom to choose (and hence to delimit) its own area of service, the character of that service, and the clientele to benefit from that service. The goal of 19th century liberalism was pluralism and diversity, especially manifest (as Alexis de Tocqueville[2] noted in the mid-19th century) in the multiple associations, varieties of ethnic origins, and decentralization of American life. These and the decades that followed were times of great social innovation through the impact of voluntary effort; but with diversity came disorder and a drive for rationalization. With unified fund raising came the movement for community planning and coordination, and new efforts to make functional, geographic, and other distinctions among agencies. The depression brought the government into the welfare picture—belatedly in comparison with other industrial countries—but still largely limited to the field of economic aid. Again the voluntary welfare agencies sought to carve out their own area of functioning largely by moving out of the costly area of financial assistance and asserting their continued mandate over the area of direct service. In the health field the answer was somewhat different, with a massive development of the prepayment principle.

Inevitably in recent years governmental responsibility with its access to tax funds has extended beyond economic aid into the area of health and welfare services, traditional stronghold of the voluntary agency. Initially government itself moved into the direct provision of selected services, but increasingly during the past ten years it has tended toward a mixed pattern which includes "purchase" arrangements for services and clientele designated by itself. Thus once again a long-standing characteristic of voluntarism has been modified. Assistance money has been used to purchase medical care, training, child care and other designated services for assistance recipients. "Poverty" funds—under the Economic Opportunity Act —have been offered to concentrate services on the needs of the poor, the black and the slum dweller. Medicare insurance entitlements have been available to finance specified services for the aged. More and more the voluntary agencies find their choice of services and clients determined—like that of their commercial colleagues— by the market; more and more that market is dominated by the vast power of the government to raise money by taxation and determine its expenditure by the power of law and the purse.

VOLUNTARISM AND THE GOVERNMENT

Most of the recent evaluative discussions concerning this revolutionary shift toward governmental use and financing of voluntary agencies has been directed toward its impact on government. Voluntary agencies, always torn between their impoverished treasuries and awareness of vast unmet need, have reached hungrily for funds when offered, without too much forethought about their ultimate cost. They have tended to obscure this departure from the principles of their origins with such comforting phrases as "partnership," "joint planning," "program development," "challenge" and "wider service." This tendency to gloss over rather than analyze the nature of the change that is shaking voluntarism to its foundations has been reinforced at every stage by the euphoric rhetoric of those who see in the nongovernmental agency the means to salvation for the ills of present-day government. In the new "partnership" they see the best of both worlds: access to the unlimited wellsprings of tax funds necessary to meet the growing social needs of an industrial society, combined with the freedom, pluralism, adaptability, and community focus that have traditionally characterized voluntarism. Thus they reassure both themselves and the voluntary sector that the price is minimal and the benefits to society unlimited.

This point of view reflects a reaction against the optimistic confidence in bigger and better government that characterized the New Deal years. Government, especially the Federal government, is seen as too big, too costly, too bureaucratic, too rigid, too remote, too unresponsive, too monolithic, too unadaptable—to name a few of the more common assertions. A recent book by Peter Drucker, *The Age of Discontinuity*,[3] puts forward a proposal that carries this point of view to its logical conclusion: i.e., that virtually all governmental program functions should be "reprivatized." By this he means that they should be delegated or contracted-out to autonomous private or quasi-public organizations. He argues that government is by its very nature unfit for the effective delivery of goods and services and should, therefore, be freed from these burdens in order to concentrate on a leadership role. This role he compares to that of the conductor of an orchestra, although it is not too clear who pays the musicians and who benefits from their music. In any event this proposal is said[4] to be virtual scripture for the Nixon administration, having been circulated by the President himself to his chief policy planners.

Another influential Nixon advisor, economist Milton Friedman, advocates reduction of the bureaucratic machinery of government by a heavier reliance on the marketplace transaction, even in such traditional governmental areas as elementary and secondary education.[5] He would, for example, give the parents of every school-age child a voucher with which they might purchase an education for their child wherever they chose.

The National Conference of Catholic Charities extends Mr. Friedman's ideas into the field of social services with a proposal for "Servicare,"[6] government-financed and distributed vouchers for the purchase of social services. This proposal has been influenced too by the "free choice of physician" idea written into the Medicare legislature. It sees the government as paying the bill and setting the ground rules but leaving the choice of supplier of the services to the consumer. This idea has also received encouragement from other sources, including most recently the Secretary of Health, Education, and Welfare,[7] with respect to day care.

While these proposals appear radical because of the sweeping terms in which they are put forward, the same process of delegating to voluntary agencies governmental functions—together with the tax dollars to support them—has been moving ahead in a variety of experimental ways during the past ten years to a degree that is nonetheless revolutionary for its absence of sharply asserted principle. Research and demonstration grants and contracts moved quietly ahead in the areas of health, mental health, child welfare, and juvenile delinquency. Then in 1964 the Economic Opportunities Act opened wide the scope and sponsorship of experimental programs to combat poverty, relying heavily on a new kind of nongovernmental agency, the Community Action agency, with authority in its turn to subcontract with other established or newly created nonprofit organizations. Other governmental programs—such as those of the Manpower Development and Training Act—moved in the same direction. Virtually unchallenged and undebated, the principle established with the first large-scale Federal welfare program, the Federal Emergency Welfare Administration, that public funds should only be expended by governmental agencies, was quietly repudiated. Today, while the largest governmental expenditures in the social welfare field, like those for public assistance and social insurance, remain largely in governmental hands, the principle is no longer sacrosanct. A real examination of the issues involved is long overdue.

Most of the discussion which has surrounded this process has proceeded from interrelated premises: (1) use of nongovernmental instrumentalities will free these programs from governmental rigidities and controls, (2) it will broaden the base of available program facilities and resources, (3) it will shake up the established governmental agencies by stimulating a challenging, grassroot pluralism, (4) it will stimulate new ideas and creativity, and (5) it will make these programs more accessible to consumer wishes and controls.

Each of these propositions can be evaluated, supported, or challenged by specific example, depending on the point of view. But each of them proceeds from an instrumental point of view: Is this the best way to achieve a particular governmental purpose? Far less discussion has centered on the larger, long-run question of the effect of this policy—especially if it is expanded—on our traditional concepts of voluntarism and pluralism as a spur to progress and a guardian of liberty. Voluntary agencies have a special obligation to examine their own goals, experiences, and conscience in these terms. This particular discussion is intended to stimulate such an examination, not prejudge its outcome. For there are many who would claim with good reason that this development is inevitable. But its methods, limitations and alternatives can bear with much closer scrutiny than they have received.

THE SEVERAL METHODS OF TAX SUPPORT

Government support and use of voluntary agencies is growing rapidly but it is neither new nor unitary in its method. This particular discussion is centered around the term "purchase of care and services," and the government, acting either directly or indirectly, is by all odds the largest and most influential buyer in this market. But we need to take a close look at the term. Traditionally it has been applied to a rather limited transaction under which a specific service such as child care or medical, hospital, nursing home or home nursing service is purchased in behalf of a particular individual for whom a governmental agency has assumed responsibility. It assumes that the government is only one purchaser and source of financing—among many—of a service which the agency is already providing on a broader scale. At least in theory it assumes a market transaction in which buyer and seller are negotiating on reasonably even terms, with neither in a monopolistic position to dominate the other.

But recent revolutionary changes already discussed place this particular kind of transaction in a broader framework. This has become, in effect, one possible method among several by which governmental funds may be expended through voluntary agencies for the provision of health and welfare services. For example, medical service may not only be purchased in the traditional way but it may also be provided through a comprehensive neighborhood health program financed by the Office of Economic Opportunity or it may be provided in the form of an entitlement under the Medicare program of the Social Security Act. Day care may be financed as a child welfare service, as a part of the poverty-related Head Start program, as an adjunct to public assistance work and training efforts, or—under the proposed Family Assistance program—as an income "disregard" for those with a combination of earnings and public aid. In each case the common denominator is the availability of tax money for the service rendered, with a difference in the method by which it reaches the provider of the service.

Thus the voluntary agency is no longer confronted simply by a question of its own role vis-à-vis a growing governmental competitor but is faced with a far more complicated series of choices deriving from the method by which the government seeks to finance its operations. Each of these operates upon a different philosophical base and, therefore, presents different philosophical and practical problems. Yet in every case the taxing power of government is used, in effect, to "purchase" a service which is deemed to be in the public interest. In general I see these relationships falling into five categories:

1. *Governmental Inducements to Voluntary Effort in the Form of Tax Concessions*, i.e., exemption of the enterprise from various forms of taxation; tax inducements to the individual contributing to or purchasing such service; and tax benefit or obligations on intermediary bodies such as foundations, community funds, or third-party purchasers.

Voluntary agencies have long been aware that these concessions exact a price in definitions and limitations in their areas of functioning. But the Tax Reform Act of 1969, with its punitive restrictions on foundations and their beneficiaries, particularly in the area of advocacy, shook any complacency.

2. *Purchase of Specified Services for Particular Individuals.*   Under the circumstances already described this arrangement assures the greatest freedom of decision to the "seller," assuming he chooses to exercise it. Many voluntary agencies, however—overwhelmed by a need for funds and conflicted by their feelings of obligation to the community, their clients or their sponsors—do not regard this in the sense of a market negotiation. They make every sort of concession on controls, price, and ambiguity of relationship. They tend to think in terms of a subsidy in which they are the beneficiary of government largesse rather than the provider of a service the government needs. They do not draw a tight contract as a commercial seller must to stay in business. Moreover, where the government constitutes their principal source of funds, their role as an independent contractor is very shaky. They move closer and closer to the fourth category described below.

3. *Contract Arrangements Covering a Demonstration or Other Limited Function for a Particular Time Period.*   This type of relationship—following to some degree the pattern used in defense and health research—is also limited and defined in terms of time and conditions—but centers on a *function* rather than specified individuals. Again its impact on voluntarism depends on the terms negotiated by the agency, its scope in relationship to the total functioning of the agency, and the clarity of role definitions. Many voluntary agencies assuming contractual arrangements to try out ("demonstrate" or "test" in the current parlance) a particular approach to a problem in behalf of a governmental agency have tended to view this activity as a part of their operating program, without too much thought for its limited duration. Confronted with the reality of its termination, they must either distort their budgeting to absorb the cost of its continuation or face the harsh choice of retrenchment. Other agencies have relied so heavily on government contracts as to lose their ongoing independence of action. They have moved once again virtually into the fourth category.

4. *Voluntary Agencies as the Instrument of Government Policy.* In this type of relationship, increasingly common in recent years, the ambiguities and uncertainties of the voluntary role are greatly intensified. In fact, assuming a continuation of the trend, it is here that lies the most urgent need for a redefinition and new conceptualization of just what we mean by "voluntarism." While the so-called "poverty program" has been the principal pioneer in developing this principle, it is now being extended into many other programs and areas of service (for example, the day care provi-

a particular agency will depend on the extent of its dependence on such funds and the extent of its own particular political support. Thus—to illustrate—a small ghetto self-help agency entirely supported by OEO funds is doubly vulnerable to control or even extinction because it has only one source of funds and a limited political base. Medicare on the other hand has millions of actual and potential beneficiaries who regard their entitlements as a form of earned personal property and thus interposes their power between government and the supplier of service. The terms of the contract may undergo modification (and probably will), but the overall situation is one of strength. This may seem a cynical remark, but its authority is well documented by history.

In my observation the limitations on tax funds may be classified under three headings:

1. *Accountability.*   Much of the so-called rigidity and red tape associated with government agencies follows the tax dollar to the voluntary agency. This is especially true where the agency becomes the instrument of government policy and can interpose neither a tightly negotiated purchase-of-service contract nor a powerfully independent clientele between itself and the arm of government imposing accountability restrictions. A brief honeymoon may lessen these demands during a period of initial innovation (there is surely a lesson here) but the humdrum paper work and audit follow soon behind. And soon the parent agencies, both the initial financing government unit and its possible intermediaries, come to the view that they know best what programs "work"—not to mention "how" and "why." Guidelines, working procedures, field visits, reports, evaluations and threatened withdrawal of funds follow close behind.

2. *Accessibility.*   A very real conflict of values occurs here. No voluntary agency would want to deny the values implicit in the 14th amendment as interpreted by recent court rulings that tax-supported benefits must be equally and fairly available to all without discrimination based on "unreasonable classification."

But what of the traditional role of voluntary agencies in creating particular facilities and services for particular groups? If elderly Jews or Methodists or Greeks wish to spend their last years with their own fellows, is this discriminatory or pluralistic? Perhaps when we get over the terrible prison walls imposed by years of racial segregation we can afford to look on this question of particularization with a wider perspective.

3. *Acceptability.*   Here the volatility of public opinion with respect to an acceptable use of tax funds imposes the most uncertain
control of all. A few years ago it was almost unthinkable that tax
funds could be expended for birth control advice and help, while
today they flow from all sides. On the other hand advocacy of legislative change by tax-exempt or tax-supported agencies is controlled
with increasing rigor. This problem is discussed more fully at the
end of this paper.

DIFFERENTIATED GOALS

A voluntary agency, in appraising its own situation vis-à-vis the
government, needs to consider not only the differences among the
limitations imposed by these five methods of tax financing but also
needs to sort out its own goals and values, both short-term and
long-range. The more agencies are able to differentiate and avoid
being swept up in the fads and fashions of the moment, the more
the values of pluralism and their own future good health are preserved. For it is only simple common sense that the more homogenized voluntary agencies become, the less their separate and independent survival is justified. They should, therefore, seek to make
choices and decisions on their own terms rather than letting themselves be swept off their feet by governmental persuasion. They
need to learn to drive a hard bargain in the interest of their own
survival. They need to learn that true voluntarism carries the right
to say "no" as well as "yes" in accordance with their own judgment.
Some examples of this kind of differentiated decision-making are
given for illustration.

Example 1.   A church group deeply concerned about the paucity
of good nursing homes for its elderly members decides to take advantage of the availability of Hill-Burton construction funds and
operating funds from Medicare and Medicaid to sponsor a new
facility. Its role is entrepreneurial, a new facility is created and a
real need is met. It has risked little except the ultimate headaches
of management and its enterprise has been creatively directed.

Example 2.   An agency with a well-established function supported largely by membership dues wishes to undertake an experimental government-financed program of limited duration. It segre-
gates the funds for this operation and plans for its transition to other
financing or termination. It might wish to undertake a series of such
experiments, but it does not endanger its ongoing program to that
end.

Example 3.   A voluntary agency decides to operate a day care center. It deliberately diversifies its clientele and their sources of financing, in the interest of both the children and its own freedom of decision. This applies equally to hospitals, nursing homes, family planning clinics and many other services.

Example 4.   An agency engaged in controversial advocacy decides to take its chances on nondeductible fund-raising. It has a hard time finding money, but it operates on the frontier of social change without restriction.

Example 5.   Another group—at the opposite extreme—*wants* to take on the job of running a government program in full awareness of the headaches it may ultimately entail. Why not, so long as they know what they are doing?

Example 6.   An agency decides to develop programs that rely primarily on consumer financing. Cooperative nursery schools and child care arrangements are a good example here. This is the true frontier in the service field, for if people had adequate cash income they could purchase the services they need and want. Leadership and entrepreneurial talent are the main requirements here. Also perhaps we need to give new dimensions to what constitutes a voluntary agency. Why not a tenants' association, a union, a church, a political club, a lodge—to name a few—and not just their welfare affiliates?

CONCLUSION

Most voluntary agencies are deeply troubled not only about their own future but about the survival of voluntarism as a revitalizing force. Voluntarism serves three indispensable roles in a healthy, free society: (1) it challenges the monopolistic tendencies of monolithic government by offering alternative ways of meeting common needs, (2) it challenges the sterility of bureaucratic organization by restoring the motivations of common humanity to social undertakings, and (3) it challenges the intractability of the established social order by uncovering its failures in terms of unmet human needs. But it cannot perform these functions effectively if it becomes the slave of government.

There are thus two imperatives for the survival of voluntarism. It must guard its own freedom and cultivate new forms for its growth and revitalization. The two reinforce each other. Neither the tithe, the community fund, nor the government are the last word in financing voluntarism any more than the community council, the community action agency or the public planning board are the last word in determining its form and functions. Each may serve its purpose if used with caution, sophistication, and discretion. But the impulse to voluntarism will not be contained when people seek new answers to their common needs. Look to the young people, if you need evidence of this. Recently the newspapers carried reports on the counselling services they have organized for themselves.[8] This is the kind of voluntarism that keeps us on our toes and we should not let it pass us by.

NOTES

1. For an interesting discussion see "The Quasi-Nongovernmental Institution" by Alan Pifer, reprinted from the *1967 Annual Report of the Carnegie Corporation of New York*, 437 Madison Avenue, New York, New York 10022.
2. See De Tocqueville, Alexis, *Democracy in Action*.
3. Drucker, Peter, *The Age of Discontinuity*, Harper and Row, 1969.
4. Auspitz, Josiah Lee (President of the Ripon Society), "Reprivatization: the Nixon Battle Cry," *Washington Monthly*, 1969.
5. See Friedman, Milton, *Capitalism and Freedom* and other writings.
6. National Conference of Catholic Charities, 1346 Connecticut Avenue, N.W., Washington, D.C. 20036, *Freedom and Rights in Social Services*, August, 1968.
7. See testimony before House Ways and Means Committee, October, 1969.
8. See *New York Times* article, March 16, 1970.

9   Accountability: What Does It Mean?

ALICE M. RIVLIN

·   ·   ·   ·   ·

As the public sector of our economy grows larger, the problem of building incentives to effective performance into public programs

From *Systematic Thinking for Social Action* by Alice M. Rivlin, pp. 120–44. Copyright © 1971 by the Brookings Institution, Washington, D.C. Reprinted with permission of author and publisher.

becomes more and more crucial. As Schultze pointed out in his Gaither lectures, federal programs have often failed to reach their objectives because no thought was given to incentives:

> The failure of performance stems from two related causes. The first of these is "negative failure"—the failure to take account of private incentives that run counter to program objectives, and to provide for appropriate modifications in existing rewards and penalties that thwart social objectives. . . .
>
> The second cause is "positive failure"—the failure to build into federal programs a positive set of incentives to channel the activities of decentralized administrators and program operators toward the program objectives.[1]

In the social action area, the problem is both especially acute and especially difficult. Present arrangements for delivering social services provide few rewards for those who produce better education or health service, few penalties for those who fail to produce. School systems are big bureaucracies serving a largely captive clientele. Students and their parents have little freedom to move from one school to another in search of a "better" education, and hardly any information by which to judge the effectiveness of schools. Teachers, principals, and superintendents are rarely rewarded or promoted on the basis of the educational results they achieve. State and federal financing is not designed to reward effective performance of schools or school systems.

The health system *looks* different. There are far more small units —hospitals, clinics, and doctors in private practice—and the consumer seems to have choice. But in fact he has neither the time, the resources, nor the knowledge on which to base an intelligent choice. Moreover, in health as in education, payment mechanisms fail to reward efficiency or effectiveness. On the contrary, the present health insurance systems, both public and private, operate to encourage overuse of hospitals—the most expensive health facilities—and fail to encourage the development and use of less costly alternatives.

The diagnosis is clear, but what is the prescription? It is easy to talk loosely about holding producers of education and health services "accountable" for their performance to those who consume the services and to those who pay for them. But it is hard to design a workable set of measures of performance, to decide exactly what accounts are to be rendered to whom and how rewards and penalties are to be meted out.

This chapter will deal with three models for improving the effectiveness with which social services are produced. One is decentralization—breaking up central administrative units, like school systems or federal programs, into more manageable units. The second is community control—a step beyond decentralization in which control of schools or other services is turned over to the community being served, in the hope of making producers more responsive to consumers. The last is the "market model," perhaps the most extreme form of decentralization. If the market model were applied to education, for one example, students would be given a choice among publicly, or privately, operated schools. Reliance would be placed on competition among schools to spur more effective educational methods.

Decentralization, community control, and a market system have all been advertised as panaceas. One or the other, it has been suggested, would solve the problem of incentives, even eliminate the need for central government efforts to discover and encourage more effective methods. The message of this chapter is that, while all three models hold out some promise, none is a cure-all. In particular, the success of all three depends on two conditions: (1) the development and use of better measures of the effectiveness of social services; and (2) vigorous and systematic attempts to find and test more effective methods and to publicize the results.

DECENTRALIZATION

Decentralization of decision making, at least down to the state or city level, has always been popular with conservatives—those who generally oppose expansion of the public sector and changes in methods of delivering services. Rejecting "frills" and "newfangled" devices in the school and clinging to fee-for-service medicine and traditional health facilities, these groups have always fought for local control and less interference from Washington or the state capital. But the remarkable political development of the last several years has been the conversion of liberals—those who favor more public services and newer methods—to the cause of decentralization. Why the switch?

One element is a new realism about the capacity of a central government to manage social action programs effectively. There was a time when those who believed in broader public commitment to social action pinned their hopes on centralization. Finding themselves stymied by conservatism, rigidity, and lack of resources at the local level, they turned to state government. Finding the states unresponsive, they turned—especially after 1933—to the federal government.

But the last several years have seen a marked shift in the attitude of liberals toward the federal role. I am not referring to the carping criticism of academics or of the party out of power about the "bungling and inefficiency" of federal executives. Those who happen not to be running the government at the moment have always griped, with more or less justification, about the ineptitude of those who were. Rather, I am talking about the change of attitude that occurred during the 1960s among those who helped design federal social action programs and tried to make them work.

I, for one, once thought that the effectiveness of a program like Headstart or Title I of the Elementary and Secondary Education Act could be increased by tighter management from Washington. Something was known about "good practices," or effective ways of reaching poor children; more could be learned and transmitted to the local level through federal guidelines and regulations and technical assistance. As knowledge accumulated, the guidelines could be tightened up, and programs would become more effective.

This view now seems to me naïve and unrealistic. The country is too big and too diverse, and social action is too complicated. There are over 25,000 school districts, and their needs, problems and capacities differ drastically. Universal rules are likely to do more harm than good. Nor, given the numbers of people involved, is it possible simply to rely on the judgment or discretion of federal representatives in the field.

Robert Levine, former planning officer for the Office of Economic Opportunity, has given a good description of the new realism:

> By and large, those programs which have stressed detailed planning and detailed administration have either not worked, or have worked only on a scale which was very small compared to the size of the problem. . . . The detailed administrative approach does not work for clear enough reasons— which start with the impossibility of writing detailed rules to fit every case, and end with the lack of highly trained people to administer every case, assuming even that an administrative solution is possible. . . . The setbacks of the War on Poverty arise, in part, from the difficulties of applying a specific and administered program to more than 30 million poor individuals. . . . What we might be able to achieve is a long-run

redesign of the Poverty Program to reduce the amount of detailed administration, and to provide more incentives for individuals to develop their own programs.[2]

The new realists are not ready to give up on the federal government and turn social action programs back to state and local governments. One cogent reason is the inequality of state and local resources. The states with the greatest per capita needs for education, health, income maintenance, and other social action programs also have the lowest per capita resources. Even within states, resources are frequently concentrated where the problems are least acute. Central cities find themselves facing mounting needs for public services and falling tax bases, while the resources of the suburbs are far greater in relation to need. The intervention of the federal government is required to channel resources to areas of need, a task that, fortunately, it is well equipped to handle.

Two activities that the federal bureaucracy carries out with great efficiency are collecting taxes and writing checks. For all its faults, the federal tax system is certainly among the most equitable and efficient in the world. Federal taxation falls largely on income, and hence is more progressive than state and local taxation, which falls largely on property and sales and thus on the poor. The progressivity of the federal system, moreover, makes it more responsive to economic growth than state and local systems. Unless rates are lowered, federal revenues tend to rise faster than the national income—a fortunate fact in an age when the demand for public services is rising more rapidly than income. Finally, income taxes are easier and cheaper to collect than are property and sales taxes, and are far less subject to the whims and errors of individual assessors.

The efficiency with which the federal government collects money is matched by the efficiency with which it disburses it. The social security system, the Veterans Administration, and other federal agencies charged with making payments directly to individuals discharge their responsibilities apparently with a minimum of difficulty and confusion.

Since the federal government is good at collecting and handing out money, but inept at administering service programs, then it might make sense to restrict its role in social action mainly to tax collection and check writing and leave the detailed administration of social action programs to smaller units. This view implies cutting out categorical grants-in-aid with detailed guidelines and expenditure controls. Instead, the major federal domestic activity would be the distribution of funds to individuals and governments on the basis of need and other criteria. The mechanism for distributing funds to individuals would be social security, family assistance, or other forms of income maintenance. Lower levels of government would receive funds through revenue sharing or bloc grants for general purposes like education. The last two federal budgets, with their emphasis on income maintenance and revenue sharing, appear to be moving the federal government in this direction.

But a deep-seated fear that the money will be misused and misdirected has always made the liberals—and, indeed, most of the Congress—leary of turning over federal tax money to lower levels of government without strict guidelines. How does the federal taxpayer know that his funds will be spent efficiently and effectively? While it may be easier in principle to manage programs at the state or local level than to deal with the vastness and diversity of the nation as a whole, in practice state and local governments have hardly been models of efficiency, effectiveness, or even honesty. Moreover, not sharing national objectives, state and local governments may underfund such programs as higher education or pollution control whose benefits are likely to spill over into other jurisdictions. They may be dominated by a small, local power elite. The federal taxpayer clearly has grounds for insisting that lower levels of government be held "accountable" to the federal government for the uses they make of federal funds.

But stating the accountability in terms of inputs—through detailed guidelines and controls on objects of expenditure— spawns red tape and rigidity without introducing incentives to more outputs. Hence a new approach is in order: State the accountability in terms of outputs, and reward those who produce more efficiently. Free to vary the way they spend the money as long as they accomplish specified results, recipients of federal grants could be rewarded for producing beyond expectations. This procedure would liberate them from the strait-jacket of input controls and promote vigorous and imaginative attempts to improve results, just as in large corporations plant managers are free to vary production methods, but are rewarded and promoted according to sales and profits.

This reasoning applies, of course, not just to federal relations with state and local governments, but to the broader question of productivity incentives in any large bureaucratic enterprise. Even in programs run by the federal government itself, productivity could be increased by allowing individual project managers—federal hospital administrators or training center heads, for example—more freedom of action and more incentive to achievement. Similar reasoning has led many to advocate decentralization of big-city school districts into semi-autonomous units that would be freed from rigid restrictions on curriculum, teaching methods, or mix of resources, and rewarded for producing better educational results.

The idea of accountability certainly sounds simple and sensible and right. Implementing it is harder. Most social action programs have vague and diverse goals, and agreement on how to measure their success is far from complete. Little serious work has been done to develop the objective measures of performance that are needed to implement this concept of accountability.

One might think, for example, that performance measures could be readily devised for manpower training programs. Their goals— to increase the employability and improve the earning capacity of trainees—are not esoteric. Success can be measured in rates at which trainees are placed in jobs, and retain and advance in them, and in differentials between what they earn and what they would have earned without the training. Good management practice suggests considerable freedom for project managers in designing programs suited to local conditions and to the needs of their trainees, and in rating the projects according to these objective criteria.

But even in manpower training, performance measures are difficult to devise. One problem is dealing with several different, albeit related, objectives. If manpower training projects were judged only on their success in job placement, there would be pressure to place trainees in jobs as quickly as possible regardless of the wage level, suitability, stability, or possibilities of advancement in the employment. The result would be a lot of placements in low-level, dead-end jobs, and little contribution to productivity. On the other hand, if increases in earnings were the sole criterion, programs would probably concentrate on people whose skills were already well developed and on younger workers with a longer earning life ahead of them. Some kind of weighted average of several success measures (job placements, earnings increases, retention rates, and so forth) would avoid distortion of the objectives of the program.

In addition, success measures have to be related to the difficulty of the problem. It is more difficult to find jobs for trainees if the local unemployment rate is high. It is harder and more expensive to train and place older people than younger people, poorly educated people than better educated people. Completion rates and wage rates are likely to be higher for men than for women. Such variations have to be taken into consideration in rating the performance of a project, both out of fairness to the project manager and to prevent "creaming," the tendency to enroll only those who will be easy to train and place. A rating system meeting these criteria was developed for assessing the effectiveness of projects under the Work Experience and Training Program in HEW, but was not used.[3]

Objectives are less easy to define in other social action areas than in manpower training, and work on performance measures is in an even more primitive stage. Incorporating performance incentives into education programs is intriguing, but a workable mechanism will be hard to design. A simple formula, based, for example, on high reading scores, might do more harm than good, by rewarding districts with easy-to-teach children, or by encouraging instruction solely for results on a specific test and overemphasis on reading at the expense of other educational values. The trick will be to develop measures that reflect the educational achievement of the schools without distorting programs in counterproductive directions.

Unless the effort is made to develop performance measures and use them as incentives, it is hard to see how decentralization by itself will lead to greater effectiveness. Without incentives to produce, small units are not obviously better than large ones.

Moreover, there are some governmental functions that would almost certainly suffer from decentralization. One is research and development. Small units are unlikely to invest in such a risky activity when most of the benefit is likely to go to other units. Moreover, for any hope of success, some problems demand a critical mass of talent and resources that only the federal government can mobilize. The atomic and hydrogen bombs, the lunar landings, and some of the federally sponsored breakthroughs in biomedical research are ample evidence of the federal ability to put the requisite resources to work on a scientific problem. Breakthroughs in social service delivery seem likely to require similar concentrations of effort.

COMMUNITY CONTROL

The push for decentralization comes at least partly from frustration at the top bred from the realization that very large units cannot manage social action programs effectively. The push for community control comes from frustration at the bottom. The supposed beneficiaries of social action programs, especially the poor and the black, feel themselves objects rather than participants in the process. The demand for community control, especially in the ghetto, reflects the feeling that schools and hospitals and welfare centers are alien institutions run by hostile members of another culture unable to understand the problems of the community they serve or to imagine their solution. If such institutions were controlled by and accountable to the community, the belief runs, they would be more effectively, or at least more sensitively, run. A ghetto community school board would hire teachers who believed in the capacity of black children to learn; it would revamp the curriculum to make it more relevant, and would assign books about black city children rather than about Dick and Jane in their suburban house. The result would be more learning. A ghetto community health board would find ways to reduce waiting times in clinics, hire personnel who did not patronize or insult patients, provide health instruction in the patient's own language. The result would be more effective health care. Moreover, community control of social action programs is also seen as a means of developing self-reliance in the community itself—feelings of competence and confidence and political power that will release energies and reduce despair.

At the moment, the movement for community control focuses on the process of gaining power. The vocal advocates of community control of schools and other social services feel that much of the problem lies in the negativism and hostility of the people who now run these institutions. Once the community assumed control, it could hold the managers accountable in some sense, fire those with hostile attitudes, and significantly improve the level of service. Community control advocates have not yet focused on new methods or organization, nor do they support experimentation or systematic testing of new models. On the contrary, one senses among ghetto militants a deep antagonism to experimentation, which is often viewed as an instrument of establishment control. "We do not want our children used as guinea pigs" typifies the attitude.

The word "accountability" is used frequently but vaguely by the advocates of community control. One searches the literature and the conversations in vain to learn what accounts are to be rendered and to whom, or how a community will know that its own administrators are doing a better job. So far, only limited attention has been paid to specific performance measures and that only with the view to dramatizing how bad the situation is. In the District of Columbia, for example, Julius W. Hobson induced the school system to publish reading scores by school in an effort to prove to the community that ghetto schools were not teaching children to read.

The vagueness about accountability seems likely to be temporary.

If community control in big-city school systems, for example, becomes a reality, two things will probably happen. First, the community and its representatives will have to face up to the question: Now that we have control what shall we do? They will begin to search for proven models of more effective education, to demand the results of systematic experimentation. Second, improved measures of school performance will be called for. After all, no community can run a school directly. It has to elect a board, to appoint managers and teachers. Factions will develop and, along with them, disagreements about how well the school is being managed. One would expect a demand for performance measures to support one position or another, as well as community interest in test score changes, attendance rates, job and college placements, and, eventually, more subtle measures of student development and enthusiasm. But beyond this, there is almost certain to be a demand for performance measures from higher levels of government. In fact, development of reliable criteria may be the only condition on which states and cities will be willing to relinquish control to community boards and still pay the bills from the general tax system.

Those who favor community control of schools in cities, for example, are not arguing for financing schools out of neighborhood tax revenues. Even if it were practical to collect taxes at a neighborhood level, it would not be desirable to finance schools this way. Areas with low tax collections would often turn out to have high educational needs and vice versa. Ghetto areas with high concentrations of poor children would not have the resources necessary to support even average schools, let alone the more intensive and expensive education these children need. Clearly, school expenditures have to be redistributed in accordance with educational need if poor children are to have a chance at equal education.

But the general city taxpayer is likely to have little enthusiasm for turning over funds to community or neighborhood boards without some assurance that he will get his money's worth. The community board will have to be in some sense accountable to the central treasury as well as to the members of the community itself. At a minimum, city-wide rules to protect the health and safety of school children will have to be devised. Beyond this, accounts might be rendered in terms of either inputs or outputs. Input rules governing the qualifications of teachers, the hiring and firing of personnel, the duties of teachers, the size of classes, will be favored by teachers' unions. But these are exactly the kinds of rules that brought about the demand for community control in the first place.

Community groups may well argue for shifting to an output or performance measure in rendering their accounts to the city taxpayer, on these grounds: If the children learn, why do you care how we do it? This approach would necessitate the development of test scores and other types of performance measures acceptable both to community boards and to the city administration. In order to retain their right to operate the schools, community boards might be required to meet certain minimum performance standards. In addition, part of the school budget might be used to reward better-than-expected gains in performance measures.

The New York City Board of Education and the Educational Testing Service are designing a system to measure the effectiveness of the city's teachers and supervisors and to make them accountable. Such a system might even help reconcile the United Federation of Teachers with the devotees of community control.[4]

THE MARKET MODEL

The market model is essentially an extreme form of decentralization. It moves the locus of decisions about how services should be produced not simply to the community, but to the individual consumer.

The private sector of the economy relies on the profit motive to bring about improvement in the quality of goods and services offered to the consumer. If businesses want to survive, they have to attract customers by offering better products or lower prices than their competitors'—or both. The sanctions of the system are drastic: If the seller fails to produce what consumers want, he goes out of business. Success is also well rewarded. The firm that makes a "better" can opener or typewriter or lipstick can make millions.

Even economists know that this model does not work perfectly in the private sector. Sometimes there are too few sellers. They collude, overtly or tacitly. They may make profits—jointly—but the consumer loses. Antitrust laws and utility regulation exist to protect consumers against monopoly and oligopoly, but nobody really believes these laws and regulations work very effectively.

Moreover, even—or perhaps especially—when there are many sellers in the market, the level of public dissatisfaction with privately produced services can be high. Television and appliance repair, automobile servicing, laundering and dry cleaning are hardly objects of general consumer enthusiasm, even though they are privately produced by large numbers of competing sellers. True, the dissatisfied consumer can try another laundry, but he has little information to go on and may find the next place just as unsatisfactory as the last.

Despite these problems, some people believe that social services would be produced more effectively by private firms seeking to make a profit by pleasing the consumer. The argument is most frequently heard with respect to education. It runs thus: Children have to go to school and, in general, they have to go to the particular school in their neighborhood. Given this captive clientele, the school faculty and administration have little incentive to produce the kind of education that children and their parents want. The school management does not make money by producing more effective education, and nobody puts the school system out of business if the children fail to learn.

These observations have led some school reformers to the position that the only way to get effective education is to break the monopoly of public schools. They would not abolish public support of education, but they would channel it through the consumer rather than the producer.[5] Vouchers would entitle parents to buy education at whatever private or public school they found best for their children.

The voucher idea has attracted a spectrum of proponents that runs from the conservative economist Milton Friedman to liberal writer Christopher S. Jencks. Friedman's proposal was a simple one:

> . . . Governments would continue to administer some schools but parents who chose to send their children to other schools would be paid a sum equal to the estimated cost of educating a child in a government school, provided that at least this sum was spent on education in an approved school.[6]

The plan devised by a team headed by Jencks was a more complex proposal designed to meet some of the objections to the Friedman scheme.[7]

At the same time that they appealed to southern conservatives eager to escape public school integration, vouchers have also been seen as a way of improving the education of black children in the urban ghetto.[8] The proponents believe that a variety of private schools would spring up in and around the ghetto, many run by blacks for blacks. Since they would compete for students, schools that did not provide attractive facilities, relevant curricula, and teachers who believed in ghetto children and knew how to "turn them on" would not attract students. Many would try, but only those who gave the consumers what they wanted would survive. Ghetto parents, it is argued, want effective education for their children and will, with practice, know when they have found it.

One serious objection to a voucher system is that it might accentuate existing problems of income inequality.[9] Even if families received vouchers of the same value for each school-age child, schools offering more expensive education to those willing to pay a premium in addition to the voucher are likely to spring up. If experience is any guide, middle- and upper-income families will spend additional sums for what they believe to be superior education. After all, they do this now; some send their children to private schools and a great many more spend money on music lessons, summer camps, or "educational" family trips.

The result of an equal-size voucher system might well be expensive schools in the suburbs offering richer curricula, smaller classes, and more elaborate facilities to the children of the well-heeled, while the poor continued to study outmoded material in crowded classrooms in dismal schools. The suburban schools would be able to pay higher salaries and attract better teachers. Even if inner-city children were not discriminated against through entrance requirements, they would be effectively barred by higher tuition and the cost of commuting.

It would be possible, of course, to give larger vouchers to poor children on the grounds that their educational needs are greater. The differentials would have to be very large, however, to compensate for *both* the disposition of well-to-do families to spend more than their voucher and the greater real costs of teaching low-income children effectively. Such steep differentials in favor of the poor might be politically less palatable to the electorate than more subtle forms of income redistribution.

Under Jencks's proposal, the value of the voucher to the school would vary inversely with the family income of the student, and schools participating in the system would be prohibited from charging tuition beyond the voucher. Thus schools would have an incentive to enroll low-income children. The more expensive private schools would either have to cut their budgets or cater only to those rich enough to forgo the voucher and pay the full costs themselves. This may sound attractive on paper, but one wonders about the political saleability of a plan that would allow parents to shop around for the "best" school, but prohibit them from spending any additional funds on their children's education.

The other major problem with the voucher system is consumer ignorance. Unless he knows what he is buying, a consumer cannot choose rationally. Yet, in the social action area, it is very difficult for him to find out anything about the quality of a service before he uses it. Moreover, the costs of shopping around or sampling the merchandise of a hospital or a school may be prohibitive. In the medical area, they are obviously disastrous; one cannot shop around for a surgeon. But even in education, trial and error may be very costly. Parents cannot move a child around from one school to another until they find one they like, without endangering the child's educational and social progress. Moreover, even educated parents have trouble judging whether their child is progressing as rapidly as he could in school. How much greater, then, are the barriers to accurate parental judgment in the ghetto, where parents have little experience with books and learning.

If a voucher system is to increase the effectiveness of education, performance measures will have to be developed and made available so that parents can judge how much progress their children are making in school and how much they might make if they went to a different school. Hardly any schools, even private schools, provide anything resembling performance measures now. At best, a family considering alternative high schools may be able to find out where last year's graduates went to college, but this tells them little about the performance of the school. If a high proportion of graduates go to very selective colleges, it may mean only that the school tends to attract able and highly motivated students.

What kind of measures should schools produce for the information of current and potential consumers? First, a variety of measures, reflecting various objectives of education, should be developed and published. Publication of reading scores, for example, would prompt many parents to ask for evidence of other accomplishments, which might be poorly correlated with reading. What about mathematics and other cognitive skills? What about general ability to reason and oral expression and ability to get along with other children? What about leadership training and athletics and citizenship? Eventually, a variety of measures should be developed, validated, and published so that students and parents can choose intelligently among schools emphasizing the objectives of education they value most.

Second, to be useful, the measures have to reflect change in the student's performance over time rather than absolute levels of achievement. The absolute levels tell nothing about the effectiveness of the school. High reading scores may reflect only a student body selected for intelligence or verbal facility. The family of a child with a learning problem might well want to select a school with low absolute scores but higher rates of change at that level.

These two criteria raise the specter of constant testing and measurement, and of concentration on measurable skills to the detriment of the more subtle values of education. These are real dangers, but without serious effort to improve measures of education performance and to make them available, it is hard to see how a voucher system can lead to intelligent consumer choice and consumer pressure for effective education.

Moreover, reliance on the market would strengthen, not weaken, the case for public subsidy of research in education and systematic testing of new methods. Individual schools fighting for survival in the marketplace could not take risks with unproved methods or undertake expensive development of new curricula or approaches; nor could market competitors be expected to band together for systematic testing of innovations. Indeed, an atomistic private market for education might produce even less innovation than we have now. In general, in the normally private sectors of the economy, rapid technological change and increases in productivity occur in the large-firm, monopolized industries, not in those characterized by many sellers and intense interfirm competition.

Perhaps major national manufacturers would invest considerable sums in new educational techniques, hoping that they could be proved more effective and then sold to schools seeking to enhance their attractiveness to students. These companies, however, would tend to invest in hardware and materials on which they could retain exclusive rights through patents and copyrights. There might be serious neglect of methods and approaches that, while conceivably more effective than hardware, could be easily copied without compensation to the original developer. For this reason, public as well as corporate investment in research and systematic testing of education methods would be necessary.

To sum up, experiments with market mechanisms in education are worth trying; indeed, the Office of Economic Opportunity has announced that it intends to experiment with voucher systems in a number of communities.[10] Nevertheless, the system has serious problems. It may not be possible to design a system that reduces rather than accentuates the differential between educational opportunities for the rich and the poor. Moreover, the problem of accountability remains. If the taxpayer is to provide subsidies for education, he must have some assurance that the money is not wasted, that some minimum standards are met by institutions cashing in the voucher. Beyond these considerations, the system will not work as intended to increase educational effectiveness unless performance measures are developed so that the consumer can choose intelligently, and unless an organized public effort is made to develop and test new and improved methods.

WHERE DO WE GO FROM HERE?

The point of the above discussion is that all the likely scenarios for improving the effectiveness of education, health, and other social services dramatize the need for better performance measures. No matter who makes the decisions, effective functioning of the system depends on measures of achievement. If federal, state, or city governments manage social service delivery directly, they need ways to gauge the success of different methods of delivering services so that they can choose the best ones. If social service management is decentralized, or even turned over to communities, both the community and higher levels of government will need performance measures on the basis of which to identify and reward more effective management. Even if social services are turned over to the private market in hope of harnessing competition and the profit motive to improvements in performance, consumers, to make wise choices, will need measures of what they are buying or might buy.

It therefore seems to me that analysts who want to help improve social service delivery should give high priority to developing and refining measures of performance. Relatively little effort has gone into devising such measures so far, despite their importance and the apparent intellectual challenge of the task. In education it will be necessary to move beyond standardized tests to more sensitive and less culturally biased measures that reflect not only the intellectual skills of children, but their creativity and faith in themselves and enthusiasm for learning. In health, it will be necessary to move beyond the conventional mortality and hospitalization statistics to more refined measures of health and vigor. Poverty cannot be measured by income alone. Job satisfaction is probably not closely related to earnings or hours of work. Considerable imagination will have to be brought to bear before performance measures can be developed for services like counseling and psychiatric care.

Two general rules can be suggested for the development of performance measures in the social action area. First, *single measures of social service performance should be avoided*. They will always lead to distortion, stultification, cheating to "beat the system," and other undesirable results. Schools cannot be judged by reading scores alone or mathematics scores alone or college placements alone or retention rates alone. Health service systems cannot be judged simply and solely by the number of patients treated or by the number of patients cured or even by health problems prevented. Manpower training programs cannot be weighed only by job placements or job retention or wage levels. Judging schools by reading scores would mean neglect of other skills and other dimensions of child development; judging a health center by the number of patients treated would encourage assembly line medicine; judging a manpower program on job placements would lead to hasty placement of trainees in low-level or unsuitable jobs.

Multiple measures are necessary to reflect multiple objectives and to avoid distorting performance. One can imagine schools developing and publishing a variety of measures of skills, knowledge, and satisfaction of students, some immediate and some based on longer-term follow-up. One can imagine health programs developing a variety of measures of health status and satisfaction of patients, also with different time lags. One can imagine manpower programs developing a variety of measures of skills acquired and subsequent job success of trainees.

For some purposes measures without any weights would be sufficient. In a voucher system for education, for example, one could simply make available a variety of performance measures for each school and let parents and students choose among them according to their own weighting systems. On the other hand, in a federal grant program designed to encourage effective manpower training, it would be necessary to assign weights to the various success measures being used. If several are being combined, the weights may not much matter, as long as no one measure is allowed to dominate and distort the reward system.

Second, *performance measures must reflect the difficulty of the problem*. If absolute levels of performance are rewarded, then schools will select the brightest students, training programs will admit only the workers who will be easiest to place in jobs, health centers will turn away or neglect the hopelessly ill. To avoid these distortions, social service effectiveness must always be measured in relation to the difficulty of the task. In general, measures of change are better than measures of absolute level, but even this approach may not solve the problem. It may be easier to bring about significant changes in the performance of bright children than in that of retarded children or to improve the health status of certain classes of patients. In this situation, the success of a social action activity can be measured only in relation to success of other activities with the same kind of student or patient or trainee. A considerable period of time will be necessary to collect experience and delineate above- and below-average performance with particular types of problems.

None of this sounds easy to accomplish. And it isn't. Nevertheless, we are unlikely to get improved social services (or, indeed, to know if we have them) until we make a sustained effort to develop performance measures suitable for judging and rewarding effectiveness. Current efforts to publish test scores or infant mortality rates in the name of "assessment" or "accountability" are only the first halting steps on the long road to better social services.

Performance measures for social services are not, of course, ends in themselves. They are prerequisites to attempts both to find more effective methods of delivering social services and to construct incentives that will encourage their use. But all the strategies for finding better methods discussed in these pages, especially social experimentation, depend for their success on improving performance measures. So do all the models for better incentives. Put more simply, to do better, we must have a way of distinguishing better from worse.

NOTES

1. Charles L. Schultze, *The Politics and Economics of Public Spending* (Brookings Institution, 1968), pp. 104–05.

2. Robert A. Levine, "Rethinking Our Social Strategies," *Public Interest*, No. 10 (Winter 1968), pp. 88, 89, 91, 92.

3. Worth Bateman, "Assessing Program Effectiveness," U.S. Department of Health, Education, and Welfare, *Welfare in Review*, Vol. 6 (January/February 1968), pp. 1–10.

4. See *New York Times*, Feb. 9, 1971.

5. *Harvard Educational Review*, Vol. 38 (Winter 1968), devoted to equal educational opportunity, includes several articles on this subject. See also Theodore R. Sizer, "The Case for a Free Market," *Saturday Review*, Vol. 52 (Jan. 11, 1969), beg. p. 34.

6. Milton Friedman, "The Role of Government in Education," in Robert A. Solo (ed.), *Economics and the Public Interest* (Rutgers University Press, 1955), p. 130.

7. The plan is described in Center for the Study of Public Policy, "Financing Education by Grants to Parents, A Preliminary Report," prepared for the Office of Economic Opportunity (The Center, March 1970), pp. 50–58.

8. Christopher Jencks, "Private Schools for Black Children," *New York Times Magazine*, Nov. 3, 1968, Sec. 6, beg. p. 30.

9. For a good critique of voucher plans, see Henry M. Levin, "The Failure of the Public Schools and the Free Market Remedy," *Urban Review*, Vol. 2 (June 1968), pp. 32–37 (Brookings Reprint 148).

10. Fred M. Hechinger, "School Vouchers: Can the Plan Work?" *New York Times*, June 7, 1970; Eric Wentworth, "OEO Plans Test of Education Vouchers," *Washington Post*, Dec. 26, 1970.

10   Britain's Debate on Universal or Selective Social Services: Lessons for America

GEORGE HOSHINO

A fundamental issue of social policy in Britain is "universality versus selectivity"—that is, whether social services should be "universal" or available without regard to individual financial circumstances, or whether they should be "selective" or restricted to those who qualify under some form of income or means test. Universality is the basic principle of the Beveridge Report of 1942 (1), on which Britain's postwar "welfare state" was erected, including such programs as National Insurance, the National Health Service, and family allowances. Although Beveridge acknowledged that there always would be individuals who would need direct assistance, "benefit as of right without means test" was an explicit goal of his proposals. Britain, however, has not succeeded in reducing assistance to the "minor . . . part of the work of the Ministry of Social Security" that he envisaged, as evidenced by the large number of recipients of Supplementary Benefits (formerly National Assistance), and

Reprinted from *The Social Service Review*, 43 (September 1969): 245–58, by permission of The University of Chicago Press and of the author.

there exists a plethora of means-tested local authority social services as well. Moreover, the means-test issue has been reopened in the form of the debate on "selectivity"—whether universal schemes should take individual financial circumstances more into account, or, for that matter, whether selective programs should or can replace universal ones altogether.

This paper is a review of Britain's experience with universal and selective social services and the current "universality-selectivity" debate, designed to point up some of the implications for American social policy. A feature of the controversy in Britain is the volume and vehemence of the literature on the subject and the extent to which the debate has made the issue and its various dimensions explicit. The United States presently seems moving toward universality. There is general agreement that the basic social insurances— old age, survivors', disability, and health insurance and unemployment compensation—should be expanded; by the same token, there is widespread criticism of the public assistance programs. However, although discussions of social insurance, public assistance, family allowances, the negative income tax, and various services in kind consider such factors as costs, effectiveness, feasibility, and so on, the fundamental distinction, in terms of the selective or the universal frame of reference, is only implicit or lightly touched upon.[1]

The debate in Britain, fortunately, in addition to generating polemic and rhetoric, has stimulated a great deal of serious analysis of the merits and disadvantages of selective and universal schemes. An increasing amount of research—much of it "tendentious," to use Beatrice Webb's discerning characterization of her own fact-gathering—is being undertaken into the operation and effect of policies and programs, as well as into the economics of alternative social service schemes and the nature and extent of poverty.

The issue is far from resolved, of course, because at bottom it is an ideological one, as are all fundamental questions of social policy. However, there appears to be a good idea of the nature of the issue and its dimensions—ideological, political, economic, and administrative—a fairly clear picture of the kinds of programs—universal and selective—involved, and a considerable knowledge of how these programs, in fact, operate and the extent to which they do, or do not, reach those for whom they are intended. There also seems to be general agreement on these facts, regardless of the position taken for or against selectivity. Consequently, Britain's experience with universal and selective social services, the debate on selectivity, and the research that has been done, all contain lessons for America.

UNIVERSALITY AND SELECTIVITY IN BRITAIN

The following statements illustrate three positions on selectivity. In 1963, Lord Beveridge wrote: "The essential condition of freedom and responsibility for the citizen is avoidance by the State of any form of means test in dealing with the citizen" (21: Foreword).

In 1967, Margaret Herbison, then Minister of Social Security, in response to a question about the Labour government's position on the principle of a test of need as the basis of future welfare policy, replied: "Benefits which depend on the demonstration of need are necessary in some parts of the social security field, but excessive reliance on them would in my view be highly undesirable" (9). In 1968, in a publication of the Institute of Economic Affairs, this unequivocal statement appears:

> The academic and informed public debate on welfare has recently proceeded beyond the acceptance of selectivity in place of universality to the administrative procedures by which it can be applied. The economists who favoured selectivity have won the academic argument in principle and the social administrators who favoured universality have lost it; but the practicability of selectivity remains to be investigated [2: Ed. Pref.].

In Britain, there is no mistaking the tribe to which one belongs. On the one side are those allied with a group—colorfully described as the "high priests of universalism"—associated with the Socialist Fabian Society and the London School of Economics.[2] Arrayed on the other side are the advocates of selectivity, associated mainly with the Institute of Economic Affairs and the Conservative Political Centre.[3] Somewhere in between are the "civilized selectivists"[4] and a few academics who presume to have disengaged themselves from the ideological aspects of the issue. They report, more or less dispassionately, their views and findings on the policies, costs, and administration of the various social service schemes without labeling them universal or selective.

Is Beveridge Obsolete?

The universal philosophy of the Beveridge Report reflected the temperament of the times: the bitter memories of the suffering during the interwar industrial depression, the degradation of the poor laws, the dole, and the UAB (Unemployment Assistant Boards), and the hated "means test." The theme of egalitarianism—"bread for all before cake for any"—was reflected as well in the principle of a minimum subsistence level of benefits.

It has been said that by the time the Beveridge proposals were enacted into law in the late 1940s, circumstances had already made obsolete the principles and assumptions on which the programs were based. By and large, unemployment has never been a real problem; indeed, Britain faces severe labor shortages in many industries and occupations. The general standard of living has risen, and the benefits of industrialization are more widely distributed. The middle-class Briton seems to be fed up with any notions of austerity; bread is taken for granted, and he is interested in the cake. The bitter memories of the poor laws and the means test have receded in the minds of the now older or aged population and are of no or only academic interest to the middle-aged and postwar generations. The elderly, now some 12 percent of the population, are acknowledged to have much too low a standard of living, a problem attributable to the difficulty of financing higher retirement pensions by the regressive flat-rate National Insurance contribution and to the fact that the concept of a minimum subsistence level of income has been replaced by the notion of reasonable adequacy. With respect to children, however, it took a bold and determined effort by a group of unusually competent and dedicated professional workers and academics to bring the problem of persistent and substantial childhood poverty to the attention of the government and the public.[5]

On the other hand, Britain's economy is hard-pressed, and there are questions about the financial commitments involved in the expanding social services, as they are presently conceived. Consequently, there appears to be a growing inclination to consider holding down public expenditures for social services by restricting them to lower-income groups, by introducing charges, and by encouraging a more significant role for the private sector.

The Universal and Selective Mix

The major universal programs that constitute Britain's present welfare state were introduced by the first postwar Labour government (1946–51) in 1946 and 1948. Although committed to universality, it and subsequent Labour governments (1964–66 and 1966 to the present) have had to retreat from this stand in the face of political and economic realities and have had to renege on a number of promises to extend universality. Prescription charges were reintroduced, and the price of school lunches was raised. Ironically, the Labour government was forced to expand and liberalize means-test National Assistance (which became Supplementary Benefits in 1966) to meet the poverty challenge rather than turning to universal schemes such as family allowances and National Insurance, although substantial adjustments in all benefit levels were made to keep them in line with rising prices.

The postwar Conservative government (1951–64), although perhaps ideologically inclined toward selectivity, was determined to end austerity by securing a larger role for the private market, but made little headway in curtailing universality. Some reductions were made, such as in expenditures for housing, with the result that priority was given to slum clearance and housing for the elderly, in contrast to the Labour government policy of providing housing for the general population. However, most certainly the Conservative government did not undertake to dismantle the National Health Service, National Insurance, or even family allowances, in spite of the widely claimed unpopularity of the latter. About all that could be said is that it was somewhat less enthusiastic about keeping social security benefits current with rising prices, that it introduced a separate scheme of graduated pensions in an attempt to help finance the ailing National Insurances, and that it vigorously encouraged occupational pensions.

Looked at historically, therefore, Britain has developed and maintained a mix of universal and selective social services, with the universal ones becoming and remaining much the stronger component, despite the ideological, political, and economic arguments and changes in governments.[6] Viewed in this light, any real and substantial movement toward selectivity would, indeed, represent a dramatic shift in social policy. By the same token, it could be argued that the claims of the selectivists need not be taken as seriously as their proponents would have people believe. History, at least, seems to rebut both Lord Beveridge and the Institute of Economic Affairs.

THE NATURE OF UNIVERSALITY AND SELECTIVITY

The nature of universal and selective programs and the way they operate in relation to each other may provide an explanation—

quite aside from ideology—of the phenomenon that, while universal programs have become and remain dominant in Britain's welfare state, selective programs have not "withered away" as many had prophesied that they would. Indeed, selective programs have flourished.

As used in this discussion, the term "selective" entitlement is essentially identical to "demonstrated need," as discussed by Eveline Burns, although she was referring primarily to income maintenance (4:19). That is, in order to qualify for cash benefits or services in kind under a selective program, the individual must demonstrate that he currently has insufficient resources—income, assets, or other sources of support or ability to pay. The procedures of selection most commonly operate to select poorer individuals within defined groups—the aged, veterans, the blind, children, and so on. Depending on the way one looks at it, those who do not need assistance are excluded from receiving benefits; or benefits are channeled to those most in need of help.

A universal scheme is one in which benefits are distributed without reference to individual income or means. Rather, eligibility is established on the basis of group membership, by the onset of a specified condition or circumstance that is assumed "on the average" to warrant distribution of benefits, with or without prior contributions by or on behalf of the individual. Most governmental services—police and fire protection, recreational facilities, library services, and so on—obviously are universal in the sense that no formal distinction is made between individual poor and nonpoor. Our concern here is with what commonly are termed social welfare services or, more broadly, the social services.

The terms "selective" and "universal" are used with different meanings. In the United States, the proposed negative income tax is viewed by some as a universal scheme because it is applied to all, or at least to all who would file an income-tax return to qualify for benefits according to various formulas. As defined in this paper, the negative income tax is a selective scheme because it is a means of assessing income deficiency and of providing benefits accordingly. In Britain, the selectivists see the negative income tax and the PAYE (Pay As You Earn—similar to the United States income-tax withholding) mechanism as the logical instruments of greater selectivity (13:18; 22:38–43). Occasionally the term "selective" is applied to the restriction of benefits to specified groups, other than individual poor, including those living in defined geographical areas. In that sense, all programs are selective.

Benefits of a universal scheme do not have to be identical, although they happen to be in the Beveridge-inspired National Insurance system. Most social insurance plans incorporate the benefit-related-to-earnings principle, as does the American OASDI program and the plan proposed in the British Labour government's 1969 white paper on social security (7). Benefits, accordingly, will vary from individual to individual. Under benefits-in-kind schemes, utilization of service, obviously, may vary enormously among users, as in Britain's National Health Service and the American "Medicare" program. It is not true, then, as is sometimes supposed, that under a universal scheme every citizen receives equal benefits; far from it.

Charges and Assessment Scales

Assessment of charges for service, as such, does not necessarily mean that a program is a selective one. In Britain, council housing, comprising some 30 percent of all housing, is open to all at subsidized rents, irrespective of income. Although there are long waiting lists and some local authorities set upper income limits for acceptance to the lists, the policy, if not always the practice, is universality. Low-cost lunches are available to all primary and secondary school children. Charges do mean, however, that if those who cannot afford the charges are to be provided for, there must be either exemptions from, or refunds of, charges for specified groups presumed, "on the average," to have difficulty in meeting the charges (the universal principle); or exemptions must be individually determined by the application of some form of assessment scale or test of income or means (the selective principle). Group exemptions can never take care of every situation, hence the tendency to add the classification, "all others in needy circumstances" or some such language. A flat 2s. 6d. (30 cents) charge is levied for each National Health Service prescription, for example, but exempted or entitled to refunds are several groups, including recipients of Supplementary Benefits, the elderly, children under fifteen years of age, the disabled war pensioners, pregnant women, and others in need. Free lunches are provided to children of unemployed and disabled parents and other low-income families. With respect to council housing, many local councils have adopted the rent-rebate plan to enable poorer tenants to apply for rebates related to income and family responsibilities. The rent-rebate scheme, accordingly, is a selective procedure operated in conjunction with a universal social service. Charges levied according to ability to pay clearly are selective. They necessitate an inquiry into individual circumstances and some kind of assessment procedure.

A variation on charges is the deductible and co-insurance provision of the United States health insurance plan.[7] There are no provisions within the plan itself for exemptions. For the patient unable to pay such charges and having no prepayment medical plan, public assistance is available or, as so often happens, the hospital or doctor duns the patient until the bill is paid, some arrangement for reduced or time payment is reached, or the bill finally is simply written off.

A distinction also might be made between assessments or charges for social services and their restriction to those of inadequate means. Unlike Britain's council housing, public housing in the United States is restricted to low-income families, hence is means-tested, or selective. However, many, if not most, social services are of such a nature that payment of charges at the time of use could not be made a hard and fast prerequisite. Medical care and child care are examples. Charges, or the need to apply for an exemption or assistance to pay for them, may deter many from seeking medical care, but that is another matter. With respect to child care, the concern and responsibility of the agency for the protection of the child ordinarily would preclude conditioning service on payment of charges—for institutional or foster care, for example—although the agency subsequently may seek payment from, or even take court action against, parents or other legally liable relatives.

The Persistence of Selectivity

Although the selective approach has serious shortcomings—notably the deterrent and punitive characteristics associated with the means test and the low application rate for benefits—it also has inherent advantages which explain its persistence. The hypothesis might even be stated that, as universal programs are developed to meet newly identified social needs, corresponding selective programs and procedures will develop alongside them to take care of special circumstances.

With respect to the restriction of benefits—in cash or in kind—to those most in need, or to the assessment of charges, the selective approach—theoretically, if not always in practice—is a highly flexible and adaptable mechanism. The concern is with the individual's current situation. Other approaches restrict eligibility to specified groups or are based on some notion of minimum level of benefit or average need. There will always be those·who do not fit into the categories or who have special needs or requirements above the minimum or average.

If a labor-force connection is a requirement, as it is in all social insurance schemes, those who have no, or only a meager, work history will be excluded. For example, the United States has not only a growing group of families broken by divorce, desertion, or unwed parenthood but also a large number of single men, especially Negro youth, who are ill-prepared for regular employment. The problem is less acute in Britain, which has a family allowance system and an extensive network of in-kind services, but "fatherless families" are increasingly a problem. Some risks are not "insurable" in the usual sense. Given prevailing attitudes, it would hardly be possible for a social insurance scheme to pay benefits on the desertion of a father.[8]

Selective schemes have the great advantage that, with a relatively modest expenditure, benefit levels can be kept higher than those of social insurance or flat pensions. Given the economic constraints within which all social policy decisions must be made, this is what happens invariably. It is strikingly illustrated in Britain's income-maintenance programs for the elderly of pensionable age —men sixty-five years and over and women sixty years and over. The National Insurance Act of 1967 increased the standard rate of contributory retirement pensions to £4 10s. a week for the single person and £7 6s. for a couple. But in 1967 Supplementary Benefit basic rates were raised to £4 6s. a week for the single householder and £7 1s. for a couple; and in 1968 to £4 11s. for the single householder and £7 9s. for the couple. Added to these basic Supplementary Benefit rates are rent "as paid" (within reasonable limits, averaging £2 8s. a week in 1967), an automatic long-term allowance of 10s. a week, and any exceptional needs allowances.[9] It is no wonder that in 1968 nearly 30 percent of all National Insurance pensioners were receiving Supplementary Benefits as well.

It has already been pointed out that various selective procedures are incorporated into Britain's basically universal services: free school lunches, rent rebates, and exemptions from prescription charges. In addition, a wide variety of ancillary services, such as the various "home helps," tends to develop under the auspices of local authorities. These local services usually are restricted to low-income families or involve assessment scales of some kind. Some of them eventually may be incorporated into the general services, but it stands to reason that the process of identifying new needs and developing special local programs for them will be a continuing process. Expenditures for these kinds of ancillary services will never bulk large in relation to the basic services, and probably they will never affect a large number of families. Nevertheless they constitute part of the local means-test jungle which faces low-income families and those who work at the "worm's-eye" level of social services (16).[10]

IMPLICATIONS FOR AMERICAN SOCIAL POLICY

What are the implications for American social policy? If the United States is moving toward universality within the framework of the existing contributory social insurance system, will the need for selective programs diminish or disappear? Although contributory social insurance may protect the great majority of the population from dropping into poverty, the evidence seems conclusive that sizable numbers of persons will remain inadequately protected or not protected at all. As a supplement to the social insurances, existing public assistance programs have failed, as evidenced by their gross inadequacies and inequities. Should public assistance remain a state-administered program strengthened by strict federal standards of minimum benefit levels, eligibility requirements, and administration;[11] or should the program be federalized as British nationalized public assistance was in 1948? Should the choice be old-age pensions and family allowances, or the negative income tax (26)? What priority should be given to benefits in kind—housing, school meals, and medical care—rather than cash benefits, and should such services be universal or selective? Last, if the United States does achieve substantial universality, will there be a counter movement to reintroduce selectivity?

Some fundamental differences between the two countries should be kept in mind as one attempts to apply the British experience to the United States. The complexities of the federal-state-local form of American government and regional differences cannot be disregarded, although the latter probably have been exaggerated, at least in respect to social welfare policy. It seems clear that Americans overwhelmingly subscribe to the contributory benefits-related-to-earnings social insurance principle even if some critics consider the concept of "earned right to benefit" illusory. This seems to rule out serious consideration of universal old age pensions, such as Canada has adopted, or selective income-conditioned pensions, which are the basic maintenance schemes for the elderly in Australia and New Zealand.

A subtle but perhaps even more fundamental factor is the tension in American society arising out of the deep divisions between the poor and the nonpoor and between white and nonwhite. By comparison, Britain's population is relatively homogeneous, if not in actual fact, at least in feeling. Any proposal that might tend toward social divisiveness or exacerbation of existing inequities in American society would be suspect. Much of the bitterness toward public assistance and such programs as medical services for the indigent stems from the second-class treatment accorded the poor, and especially the Negro poor, under these programs. This factor weights the choice strongly in favor of universality, just as egalitarianism did in wartime and early post-war Britain. A heavy burden of proof will be put on the selectivists to show that their proposals will contribute positively to the reduction of social tensions; it is no longer enough simply to claim that differences will not be increased. The question is not only what is the most economical and efficient way of getting money to those who are poor, although that is important. It also is a question of the extent to which beneficiaries are, or feel, estranged from the remainder of the population.

Making the Issue Explicit

There is need to make explicit in the United States, as in Britain, the issue of universal or selective social services, so as to stimulate a systematic development of all its aspects. So far, discussions of the alternative social welfare policy choices have emphasized the economics of various income-maintenance proposals—their respective costs and "antipoverty" effectiveness.

An example of the present muddle in America is the interesting position taken on the "guaranteed minimum income" by the National Association of Social Workers, whose membership includes some of the foremost authorities on social welfare policy. In 1964, NASW adopted a policy statement recommending the abolition of the means test (6). The statement was hedged by the phrase "in its archaic form," but there should be no mistaking its sentiment. In 1967, another statement was prepared by the Association's Advisory Committee on Income Maintenance supporting a "guaranteed minimum income" which could take the form of either the negative income tax or a family-allowance scheme (15:8).[12] The seeming contradiction between the two statements and the either-or position of the second may reflect an inability of NASW members to resolve the selective-universal issue, or a desire to stimulate further discussion of the policy alternatives. In any event, the either-or position on such a fundamental issue seems paradoxical for an organization so concerned about social policy, and especially one so deeply committed to an egalitarian democratic society.

Identifying Selectivity

A simple labeling of schemes as "universal" or "selective," if the concepts are clearly understood, could clarify matters a good deal and sharpen the speculation about the consequences of a choice for or against selectivity.

First, it is scarcely appreciated that a bewildering multitude of selective programs involving means tests or assessment scales already exists. Even a simple cataloguing of these services—their nature, eligibility requirements, and benefits—would be a considerable undertaking because of the lack of clarity about what constitutes selectivity, the complexities of the federal-state-local system of government, and the sheer number of political and administrative jurisidictions involved. If Reddin should be led to title his article, "Means Tests Galore," after counting over 1,400 means-tested local authority social services in Britain, one wonders what his reaction would be if he attempted the same task in the United States (25). Not only does this country have several large federally administered selective programs, like means-tested veterans' pensions and hospital care for veterans with non-service-connected disabilities, but state and local social services tend to be means-tested or to involve charges levied according to assessment scales of some sort.

Public assistance is only the most obvious selective program. Others include public housing and related schemes, such as the rent-supplement program and leased housing, surplus foods and food stamps, care in county homes, and medical care unless the individual is covered by Medicare or some other non-means-test plan. As already pointed out, the Medicare patient may get involved with a means test if he cannot pay the deductible and co-insurance charges. Vocational rehabilitation services were means-tested until a recent amendment to the vocational rehabilitation legislation removed this provision. Although admission to state mental hospitals may not be restricted to the less affluent, charges ordinarily are assessed on the basis of inquiry into the means of patients. A considerable controversy developed in Pennsylvania over a proposal to limit the services of the new community mental health centers to those who qualified under the state's medical assistance standards.[13]

Many local school districts provide lunches, subsidized by federal grants and surplus foods, and children of needy families may be given lunches free. The "selective" procedure may be a simple dispensation by the principal, or it may involve more or less formal collaboration with the public assistance or family-service agency. Most college and university student aid is available only to students whose parents' incomes fall below certain, usually generous, levels. Unlike most forms of selectivity, little if any stigma is attached to such "means-tested" grants because they are associated with merit and most university students come from middle-class families. In Britain, local education authorities are authorized to make grants to poorer families for school uniforms, shoes, and transportation if they are necessary to insure the child's attendance or use of the school program. Undoubtedly many school districts in the United States have similar arrangements, but systematic information is not available.

During an election in Philadelphia for delegates of "poverty area" councils, from which, in turn, representatives were elected to the city's community-action agency (the Philadelphia Anti-Poverty Action Committee), only residents whose annual income fell below $3,000 could vote, and, initially, only poor residents could be candidates. This may have been the first means-tested electorate and elected officialdom.[14] The emphasis on involving the poor in antipoverty programs and preferential employment for them might even lead to a means-tested classification of civil-service positions!

Two aspects of selectivity illustrate the need to examine more critically the way means tests and assessments actually operate.[15] First, selectivity affects others besides the individual applicant or recipient. In 1941, Britain abolished the "household means test," which was the cause of so much bitterness. The Supplementary Benefit "needs test" is applied only to the individual applying for aid; the means of the others in the household are not considered. In the United States, however, many states retain the poor law principle of relative responsibility and may extend liability for support beyond that of parents to children and spouses to one another to include children, grandparents and grandchildren, brothers and sisters, and even stepparents and stepchildren. The problem, consequently, is a much more complicated matter than merely the determination of eligibility of an individual for public assistance; it extends to relatives, and it is applicable as well to other selective social services, as described above.

Second, little attention has been paid to the problem created by the operation of several means tests or assessments on the same family and, for that matter, on the family's relatives. In Britain, some uniformity has been achieved by the Supplementary Benefit scales, which are widely recognized as the "poverty line." Individuals eligible for Supplementary Benefits may be assumed eligible for other benefits as well, or the Supplementary Benefit scales are used to assess charges. Unfortunately, each service tends to develop and apply its own standards, often without regard to the policies and practices of other agencies in the same locality. Some standards are more liberal than the assistance scales, others more stringent. The consequences for a family can be weird indeed, or disastrous. Although this problem has been given considerable attention in Britain, it is far from being solved. The usual recommendation is that the number of means tests and assessment scales be reduced to three or four and that their application be centralized in one administrative office, such as the local authority treasurer (8:12–14).[16] Simplification can be carried only so far, however. A considerable rumpus would be raised if public assistance scales were used to determine eligibility for university grants; and the reverse could scarcely be contemplated at all. The extreme selectivists go so far as to propose that all means tests and assessment procedures be consolidated into a single mechanism—the PAYE machinery—which would automatically assess income, determine eligibility, and issue cash benefits or vouchers to pay for all social services, including primary and secondary education (22:38–43).[17] The matter was put most simply by Sir B. Rhys Williams in the House of Commons: "Would it not be a tremendous saving if Income Tax were used as the means test to end all means tests, and all these investigations of people's circumstances be dropped" (10).

Loss or Erosion of Benefit Rights

It is well established that the application rate for universal benefits is extremely high. With respect to social security, one study notes that entitlement to social insurance benefits has acquired the characteristic of a statutory right endowed with certain guarantees deriving from such factors as a provision in the national constitution; high court decisions prohibiting arbitrary curtailment or denial of benefits, even by acts of legislatures; and a shift from a contingent right depending on the payment of contributions by employers to a legal entitlement vested in the person of the insured (18:31–32).

No such protections apply to recipients of selective services; indeed, their vulnerability is well known. In Britain, several studies have demonstrated that a large number of eligible families do not apply for or receive Supplementary Benefits, free school lunches, rent rebates, and other means-tested welfare benefits. That many needy American families are deterred from applying for assistance or do not receive all they are entitled to is established beyond question, particularly in AFDC. Only under exceptional circumstances can the negative connotations of selectivity and their consequences be counteracted by association with more acceptable bases for entitlement; for example, the association of university student aid with scholastic merit, of pensions with service to country, and, to some extent, with age and blindness.

The universalists argue that the danger of loss or erosion of benefit rights is inherent in the selective approach; the selectivists, while perhaps acknowledging that this is true of existing means tests, argue that the solution is to change the machinery of selection and to devise workable ones (22:29). Basically, loss or erosion of benefit rights under selective schemes stems from two characteristics: they are, by definition, for poor people; and they require that the applicant demonstrate the nonpossession of resources. These two factors play into each other. The rights of poor people are always the first to be ignored or eroded; and it is difficult or humiliating to demonstrate that one is poor. The consequence is a program that stigmatizes its recipients and throws up complicated and deterrent procedures.[18] The universal program does not distinguish between individual poor and nonpoor; the selective program does. Consequently, the eligibility-determination mechanism cannot be considered without taking into account the context of attitudes and pressures within which it will operate. Only actual experience with selectivity operated through the tax machinery will tell, but in view of the above considerations one is led to predict that sooner or later features common to most selective programs will creep in, especially if the program is aimed at the "least deserving" of the poor population.[19]

CONCLUSION

With respect to the aged who, currently and in the future, probably will be the largest group for whom maintenance and care by the state will be required, there seems to be wide consensus that universality is preferable to selectivity and, in the United States, social insurance is clearly the choice. Social insurance, however, "creams off" the more socially acceptable casualties of industrial society—the aged, involuntarily unemployed, disabled, and widows and surviving children. The three major groups of non-aged poor are the families of fully employed low wage earners, the families of uninsurable and unemployable men, and fatherless families. These families will make up the caseloads of the selective programs unless universal schemes are developed in their place. The undesirable characteristics of the means test have led most countries, including Britain and the United States, to move toward universal non-means-test programs.

If Britain's experience is any guide, however, it seems clear that there will always be substantial selectivity in one form or another. There should be no illusions about it; it is naïve and unrealistic simply to chant, "Let's abolish the means test." Although selectivity may be criticized because of its characteristics and consequences, it should no longer be acceptable to make selective programs poor, deliberately or unwittingly, in order to justify or enhance social insurance.[20] It will have to be accepted that thousands of individuals and families, among them the most vulnerable of all, will be affected by selective programs. The goal should be to make these programs adequate, equitable, and dignified.

REFERENCES

1. Beveridge, Sir William. *Social Insurance and Allied Services*. Cmnd. 6404. London: H.M. Stationery Office, 1942.
2. Bremner, Marjorie. *Dependency and the Family*. London: Institute of Economic Affairs, 1968.
3. Burns, Eveline M., ed. *Children's Allowances and the Economic Welfare of Children*. New York: Citizens' Committee for Children of New York, 1968.

4. Burns, Eveline M. *Social Security and Public Policy.* New York: McGraw-Hill Book Co., 1956.
5. —————. "Social Security in Evolution: Toward What?" *Social Service Review* 39 (June 1965): 129–40.
6. Glasser, Melvin A. "The Meaning of the 'Mandate.'" *NASW News* 10 (February 1965): 18–19.
7. Great Britain. Department of Health and Social Security. *National Superannuation and Social Insurance: Proposals for Earnings-Related Social Security.* Cmnd. 3883. London: H.M. Stationery Office, January 1969.
8. —————. Institute of Municipal Treasurers and Accountants. *Assessment Scales.* London, 1969.
9. —————. House of Commons. *Parliamentary Debates.* 5th ser., 748 (1967): 1113.
10. —————. House of Commons. *Parliamentary Debates.* 5th ser., 774 (1968): 1013.
11. Handler, Joel F., and Hollingsworth, Ellen Jane. "How Obnoxious is the 'Obnoxious Means Test'?" Madison: Institute for Research on Poverty, University of Wisconsin, January 1969.
12. Hoshino, George. "Simplification of the Means Test and Its Consequences." *Social Service Review* 41 (September 1967): 237–49.
13. Houghton, Douglas. *Paying for the Social Services.* 2d ed. London: Institute of Economic Affairs, September 1968.
14. Lynes, Tony. "Family Allowances in Great Britain." In *Children's Allowances and the Economic Welfare of Children,* edited by Eveline M. Burns. New York: Citizens' Committee for Children of New York, 1968.
15. "NASW Active in Political Arena." *NASW News* 14 (November 1968): 1, 8–9.
16. Reddin, Mike. "Local Authority Means-Tested Services." Part 1, *Social Services for All?* London: Fabian Society, June, 1968.
17. —————. "Means Tests Galore." *New Society,* May 30, 1968, pp. 796–98.
18. Rohrlich, George F. "Legal Aspects of the Calculations of Social Security (Social Insurance) Benefits." Theme I, *Proceedings of the Sixth International Congress on Labor Law and Social Legislation, August 1966.* Stockholm, Sweden: Almqvist & Wiksells, 1968.
19. Schorr, Alvin L. "Against a Negative Income Tax." *Public Interest* 5 (Fall 1966): 112.
20. —————. *Poor Kids.* New York: Basic Books, 1966.
21. Schottland, Charles I. *The Social Security Programs of the United States.* New York: Appleton-Century-Crofts, 1963.
22. Seldon, Arthur, and Gray, Hamish. *Universal or Selective Social Benefits?* London: Institute of Economic Affairs, 1967.

23. Tobin, James. "The Case for an Income Guarantee." *Public Interest* 4 (Summer 1965): 31–44.
24. United States. Advisory Council on Public Welfare. *Having the Power, We Have the Duty.* Washington, D.C.: Government Printing Office, 1966.
25. ————. Office of Economic Opportunity. *Catalog of Federal Assistance Programs.* Washington, D.C.: Government Printing Office, 1967.
26. Vadakin, James C. "A Critique of the Guaranteed Annual Income." *Public Interest* 7 (Spring 1968): 53–66.

NOTES

1. Some exceptions should be noted (3:187–90; 5:139; 19: 112; 23).

2. Notably Richard Titmuss and Brian Abel-Smith, of the London School of Economics, and Peter Townsend, of the University of Essex.

3. Notably Arthur Seldon, editorial director of the Institute of Economic Affairs, London, and Lord Balniel, Conservative spokesman for social security in the House of Commons.

4. A phrase used by the Chancellor of the Exchequer, Mr. Roy Jenkins, to describe the principle of recouping increases in family allowances from wealthier families by reducing their child tax allowance, thereby confining the real benefit of the increases to lower-income families. The family allowance is still a universal benefit, as defined in this paper, because it is claimed as of right without regard to income. Other terms used to describe this principle are "claw-back" and "give and take."

5. The Child Poverty Action Group, organized in late 1965 to arouse public concern about child poverty in Britain and to demand government action, was able to demonstrate and dramatize the persistence of widespread and substantial childhood poverty. It put forth several recommended solutions that stirred vigorous debate, and it was instrumental in getting family allowances raised, along with the eventual adoption of the "claw-back" principle of financing increases in family allowances by reducing tax allowances. A brief history is contained in Lynes (14).

6. For social security (excluding the "social services," housing, the National Health Service, and education) in fiscal 1967–68, expenditures for National Insurance and Industrial Injuries totaled £2,247.7 million; war pensions, £126.6 million; and family allowances, £174.2 million. In the same period, expenditures for Supplementary Benefits (pensions and allowances) totaled £433.0

million. The bulk of both National Insurance and Supplementary Benefit payments goes to those of pensionable age—sixty-five and over for men and sixty and over for women.

7. Title XVIII, popularly known as "Medicare." Basically, Part A, Hospital Insurance, provides 90 days of hospital care with a deductible of $40; Part B, Medical Insurance, requires payment of monthly premiums, currently $4.00, and pays 80 percent of a reasonable physician's fees after a deductible of $50.

8. Beveridge suggested a "temporary separation benefit," discussed by Schorr (20:134), who proposed a "fatherless child insurance." Both proposals would deal only with the wife or mother legally separated by court order.

9. After devaluation in 1967, the pound officially equalled $2.40. In 1968, the average weekly gross wage of the male industrial worker was a little over £22.

10. Reddin estimated that there were 1,450 local-authority means-tested schemes and that local authorities were responsible for administering at least 3,000 means tests. His report is summarized in (17).

11. As recommended by the Advisory Council on Public Welfare (24).

12. The either-or position was presented to the platform committees of the Democratic and Republican party conventions that preceded the 1968 elections.

13. Administration of the means test was to have been the responsibility of the social worker of the psychiatric team. One wonders sometimes what social workers would do if all means tests were abolished.

14. It should be noted, of course, that a means test in the other direction was common when there were property qualifications for voting in Great Britain and elsewhere.

15. One report noted: "One can search the literature in vain for systematic information on what the intake process and the means test consists of, what is being administered and how and what, in fact, welfare applicants think and feel about the experience" (11:1).

16. Reddin (16:12–14) discusses the problem of multiple assessment systems.

17. Before PAYE and computers were thought of, Beatrice Webb's proposal for a local Registrar of Public Assistance to take care of "odious pecuniary enquiries" relating to local authority social services is a striking parallel to the Seldon-Gray idea.

18. In recent years, the British government has conducted several vigorous entitlement campaigns to publicize welfare benefits and to encourage poor families to apply for them. A significant rise in applications for benefits resulted, but many still fail to take ad-

vantage of the programs. In the United States, because of wide-spread antiwelfare attitudes, such entitlement campaigns are rare. They are undertaken for the most part by welfare-rights organizations and community legal services. Nonwelfare benefits, of course, are widely publicized, for example, veterans' benefits and social security.

19. The negative income tax principle is approached in a number of projects in which client-completed declarations are used to determine eligibility for public assistance. In some, the entire process of application, eligibility determination, notification, and periodic review is done by mail. See Hoshino (12). Full investigation of a sample of applications is made, however, and most of the projects are in the adult categories of assistance.

20. Even Lord Beveridge stated, "Assistance . . . must meet those needs adequately up to the subsistence level, but it must be felt to be something less desirable than insurance benefit, otherwise the insured persons get nothing for their contributions. Assistance therefore will be given always subject to proof of needs and examination of means, it will be subject to any conditions as to behavior which may seem likely to hasten restoration of earning capacity" (1:141).

Part II

SOCIOLOGICAL CRITIQUE

Chapter Four

SOCIOLOGICAL CRITIQUE

In the world of practical affairs both the institutional development of social welfare and professional practices in social work are influenced by political and economic forces. The world of ideas as a source of influence is related to but somewhat removed from the practical pressures of daily operations. While developments in social welfare and social work are immediately sensitive to political and economic forces, they are also responsive to the world of ideas—an intellectual force manifest in what we have referred to as sociological critique. As an intellectual force sociological critique provokes thought and stimulates insight into problems of individual and institutional functioning. The concrete impact of a sociological critique on program varies, depending upon the merit of the analysis and the characteristics of the political decision-making system. Occasionally, those engaged in sociological critique attempt to connect their ideas to practice and become activists working to implement new arrangements in social welfare and social work. However, as a professional activity, sociological critique is distinct from social work practice and is conducted outside of social welfare institutions, usually in academic settings.

The focus of sociological critique is wider in scope than social planning needs-assessment studies and program evaluations. Sociological critique comments upon broad issues in society that are seen as problematic for institutional functioning and individual well-being. The styles of commentary include formal theoretical analysis, journalistic descriptions, and an occasional satire. The readings in this chapter reflect these different styles of sociological critique as they have been applied to issues of major concern in social welfare and social work over the past decade. We will comment on their varying impact on concrete program developments.

Reading 11, "Invisible Land," is from Michael Harrington's *The Other America*. Writing in the early 1960s, Harrington produced a grim report about poverty in America and a vivid analysis of the bitterness of life under these conditions. His work was an indictment of the "affluent society" which sparked the national conscience; it also inspired a proliferation of literature on the characteristics, effects, and conditions of poverty.[1] As for the impact of Harrington's work on program developments in social welfare, Arthur M. Schlesinger, Jr., noted that President John F. Kennedy read *The Other America* and, in Schlesinger's opinion, this "helped crystallize" Kennedy's determination in 1963 to initiate an antipoverty program.[2] Later, when the War on Poverty was implemented under President Lyndon Johnson, Harrington's advice was sought, and he served as a consultant to the federal government during the early stages of the program's development.

In "The Invisible Land," Harrington describes the extent of poverty in America and analyzes why the poor have gone relatively unnoticed. His theoretical explanation for the cause of poverty is a popular version of the "culture of poverty," the idea that the poor are trapped in a self-perpetuating cycle of deprivations that is transmitted from one generation to the next.

Harrington's view represents one theme of the culture-of-poverty idea, and this idea represents one among several theoretical perspectives on the causes of poverty. Other explanations of poverty are based upon theories that focus on different major independent variables, such as material, personal, or institutional factors.[3] These different theoretical perspectives are utilized in the development of diverse programs to attack the causes and consequences of poverty. Each of these theoretical perspectives has some degree of validity, and each is embedded in one or another action program that seeks and often competes with others for political, economic, and social support.

Reading 12, "Illegitimate Means, Anomie, and Deviant Behavior," by Richard Cloward, sets forth the basic framework of the famous opportunity-structure theory of juvenile delinquency, which was fully developed by Cloward and Lloyd Ohlin in *Delinquency and Opportunity*.[4] Cloward's article integrates two major theoretical perspectives on deviant behavior around the idea of differential opportunity structures. According to this thesis the likelihood of deviant behavior increases when an individual's opportunities to achieve culturally prescribed goals through normal, legitimate institutional channels are restricted and he also has ready access to environments that teach the use of illegitimate means.

Opportunity-structure theory had a forceful impact on the development of social reform programs in the 1960s which we discussed in the concluding comments to Chapter 3. The theoretical foundations of Mobilization for Youth, one of the first of a wave of federally funded social welfare programs in the 1960s, rested squarely on the propositions of differential opportunity structure. Cloward, who was one of the major architects of Mobilization for Youth, became the director of research when the program was implemented. His theoretical influence is clearly expressed in the program's proposal:

> . . . We believe that delinquency and conformity generally result from the same social conditions. Efforts to conform, to live up to social expectations, often result in profound strain and frustration because the opportunities for conformity are not always available. This frustration may lead in turn to behavior which violates social rules. In this way delinquency and conformity can arise from the same features of social life: unsuccessful attempts to be what one is supposed to be may lead to aberrant behavior, since the very act of reaching out for socially approved goals under conditions that preclude their legitimate achievement engenders strain.
>
> In summary it is our belief that much delinquent behavior is engendered because opportunities for conformity are limited. Delinquency therefore represents not a lack of motivation to conform but quite the opposite: the desire to meet social expectations itself becomes the source of delinquent behavior if the possibility of doing so is limited or nonexistent.
>
> The importance of these assumptions in framing the large scale program which is proposed here cannot be overemphasized.[5]

Satire as a mode of sociological critique which contrasts with the formal theorizing described above is the approach of Reading 13, "How Community Mental Health Stamped Out the Riots (1968–

1978)," by Kenneth Keniston. This article deals with a familiar theme in the history of social welfare—the potential for the expression of oppressive social controls in measures ostensibly concerned with social rehabilitation. Examining this repressive potential in the context of the community mental health movement, Keniston warns that "mental illness" is a label that might be used for political purposes in publicly sponsored programs. The danger, as he sees it, is that the label "mental illness," because of its fuzzy nature, can easily be applied to all forms of individual and group behavior that inconveniences established institutions and is socially disapproved.[6]

From one perspective the Keniston article may be viewed as a caution against public efforts that inadvertently or by design bring pressures on individuals and groups to conform to a single set of normatively prescribed attitudes, beliefs, and behaviors, leading ultimately to the cultural homogenization of American society. Cultural pluralism is a cherished value which, as discussed in Reading 8 by Elizabeth Wickenden, is strongly supported by the voluntary sector of social welfare. Yet this value strains against other equally important values pertaining to the achievement of harmonious intergroup relations and the elimination of ethnic and racial prejudice. Social welfare programs are also engaged in furthering these aims.

The tensions between cultural pluralism and social integration and the role of government in their mitigation are analyzed by Milton Gordon in Reading 14, "Desegregation and Integration." Gordon's analysis draws a careful distinction between processes of desegregation and integration. In his view the proper role of government is "to effect desegregation—that is, to eliminate racial criteria—in the operation of all its facilities and services at all levels, national, state, and local." Gordon does not believe that government should attempt to impose integration through the "positive" use of racial criteria or the creation of quotas in programs under its jurisdiction. As he observes in Reading 14:

> To bring racial criteria in by the front door, so to speak, even before throwing them out the back, represents, in my opinion, no real gain for the body politic and has potentially dangerous implications for the future. If racial criteria are legitimate criteria (which I firmly argue they are not), then the way is left open for many ominous disputes as to the merits of any particular racial clause in government operations.

We might note that Gordon's insightful analysis on this issue has had little impact on policy developments.[7] Over the past decade, government policies have increasingly emphasized the positive use of racial criteria in public and private programs and, as Gordon anticipates, a rise in racial and ethnic group consciousness, along with heightened intergroup tensions, has followed in the wake of these policies.

These social critiques are striking in one respect. That is, although the mutual support function of social welfare compensates for the breakdown of traditional institutional mechanisms for meeting human needs (as discussed in Chapter 2), social welfare arrangements themselves may further undermine these institutions. As Nathan Glazer puts it: "Our efforts to deal with distress themselves increase distress."[8] This, of course, is a distressing thesis to those engaged in furthering social welfare objectives. It is also a thesis that has been expressed in various forms since the poor laws first went into effect.

The general influence of this idea on program developments is clearly revealed in the comments made by President Richard Nixon concerning his reasons for vetoing the Child Development Act of 1971, which proposed a universal network of child care centers providing infant care, comprehensive preschool programs, evening care, emergency care, and the like. In the veto message Nixon stressed that "Good public policy requires that we enhance rather than diminish both parental authority and parental involvement with children, particularly in those decisive early years when social attitudes and a conscience are formed, and religious and moral principles are first inculcated."[9]

These arguments suggest that social welfare policy should be designed to support traditional values—it should strengthen family life and provide incentives to work and independence. However, these goals are easier to advocate than to accomplish. In the broad sense, this is a dilemma in the design of social welfare arrangements wherein the efforts to balance elements of social control are pitted against the values of freedom of choice. This dilemma undoubtedly will continue to be a major topic of sociological critique as the institution of social welfare expands into new areas where the traditional institutional mechanisms for meeting human needs are insufficient.

NOTES

1. The outpouring of literature on poverty that followed in the wake of *The Other America* is attested to by the fact that within four years of Harrington's work, at least six major anthologies were produced: two under the title of "Poverty in America," two examining "Poverty in (Amid) Affluence," one declaring "Poverty as a Public Issue," and one offering "New Perspectives on Poverty."

2. Arthur M. Schlesinger, Jr., *A Thousand Days* (Boston: Houghton Mifflin Co., 1965), p. 1010.

3. Martin Rein, "Social Science and the Elimination of Poverty," *Journal of the American Institute of Planners,* 33 (May 1967): 417–45.

4. Richard A. Cloward and Lloyd E. Ohlin, *Delinquency and Opportunity* (Glencoe, Ill.: Free Press, 1955).

5. Mobilization for Youth, Inc., *A Proposal For the Prevention and Control of Delinquency by Expanding Opportunities* (New York, 1961), pp. 44–45.

6. Keniston is not alone in criticizing the community mental health movement as a potential design to limit individual freedom in the publicly sponsored name of "health." For other influential writings on this issue see Thomas Szasz, *The Myth of Mental Illness* (New York: Hoeber-Harper, 1961) and "The Mental Health Ethic," *National Review,* 57 (June 14, 1966).

7. For additional comments on this issue see Macklin Fleming and Pincus Pollack, "The Black Quota at Yale Law School: An Exchange of Letters," *Public Interest,* Spring 1970, pp. 44–52; and Neil Gilbert and Joseph Eaton, "Favoritism as a Strategy in Race Relations," *Social Problems,* Summer 1970, pp. 38–52.

8. Nathan Glazer, "The Limits of Social Policy," *Commentary,* 53 (September 1971): 51–58.

9. *New York Times,* December 12, 1971, p. 4.

11   The Invisible Land

MICHAEL HARRINGTON

There is a familiar America. It is celebrated in speeches and advertised on television and in the magazines. It has the highest mass standard of living the world has ever known.

From Michael Harrington, *The Other America* (New York: Macmillan Co., Inc., 1962), pp. 1–18. Copyright © Michael Harrington 1962, 1969. Reprinted by permission of The Macmillan Co. and of the author.

In the 1950's this America worried about itself, yet even its anxieties were products of abundance. The title of a brilliant book was widely misinterpreted, and the familiar America began to call itself "the affluent society." There was introspection about Madison Avenue and tail fins; there was discussion of the emotional suffering taking place in the suburbs. In all this, there was an implicit assumption that the basic grinding economic problems had been solved in the United States. In this theory the nation's problems were no longer a matter of basic human needs, of food, shelter, and clothing. Now they were seen as qualitative, a question of learning to live decently amid luxury.

While this discussion was carried on, there existed another America. In it dwelt somewhere between 40,000,000 and 50,000,000 citizens of this land. They were poor. They still are.

To be sure, the other America is not impoverished in the same sense as those poor nations where millions cling to hunger as a defense against starvation. This country has escaped such extremes. That does not change the fact that tens of millions of Americans are, at this very moment, maimed in body and spirit, existing at levels beneath those necessary for human decency. If these people are not starving, they are hungry, and sometimes fat with hunger, for that is what cheap foods do. They are without adequate housing and education and medical care.

The Government has documented what this means to the bodies of the poor, and the figures will be cited throughout this book. But even more basic, this poverty twists and deforms the spirit. The American poor are pessimistic and defeated, and they are victimized by mental suffering to a degree unknown in Suburbia.

This book is a description of the world in which these people live; it is about the other America. Here are the unskilled workers, the migrant farm workers, the aged, the minorities, and all the others who live in the economic underworld of American life. In all this, there will be statistics, and that offers the opportunity for disagreement among honest and sincere men. I would ask the reader to respond critically to every assertion, but not to allow statistical quibbling to obscure the huge, enormous, and intolerable fact of poverty in America. For, when all is said and done, that fact is unmistakable, whatever its exact dimensions, and the truly human reaction can only be outrage. As W. H. Auden wrote:

> Hunger allows no choice
> To the citizen or the police;
> We must love one another or die.

I

The millions who are poor in the United States tend to become increasingly invisible. Here is a great mass of people, yet it takes an effort of the intellect and will even to see them.

I discovered this personally in a curious way. After I wrote my first article on poverty in America, I had all the statistics down on paper. I had proved to my satisfaction that there were around 50,000,000 poor in this country. Yet, I realized I did not believe my own figures. The poor existed in the Government reports; they were percentages and numbers in long, close columns, but they were not part of my experience. I could prove that the other America existed, but I had never been there.

My response was not accidental. It was typical of what is happening to an entire society, and it reflects profound social changes in this nation. The other America, the America of poverty, is hidden today in a way that it never was before. Its millions are socially invisible to the rest of us. No wonder that so many misinterpreted Galbraith's title and assumed that "the affluent society" meant that everyone had a decent standard of life. The misinterpretation was true as far as the actual day-to-day lives of two-thirds of the nation were concerned. Thus, one must begin a description of the other America by understanding why we do not see it.

There are perennial reasons that make the other America an invisible land.

Poverty is often off the beaten track. It always has been. The ordinary tourist never left the main highway, and today he rides interstate turnpikes. He does not go into the valleys of Pennsylvania where the towns look like movie sets of Wales in the thirties. He does not see the company houses in rows, the rutted roads (the poor always have bad roads whether they live in the city, in towns, or on farms), and everything is black and dirty. And even if he were to pass through such a place by accident, the tourist would not meet the unemployed men in the bar or the women coming home from a runaway sweatshop.

Then, too, beauty and myths are perennial masks of poverty. The traveler comes to the Appalachians in the lovely season. He sees the hills, the streams, the foliage—but not the poor. Or perhaps he looks at a run-down mountain house and, remembering Rousseau rather than seeing with his eyes, decides that "those people" are truly fortunate to be living the way they are and that they are lucky to be exempt from the strains and tensions of the middle class. The only problem is that "those people," the quaint inhabitants of those hills, are undereducated, underprivileged, lack medical care, and are in the process of being forced from the land into a life in the cities, where they are misfits.

These are normal and obvious causes of the invisibility of the poor. They operated a generation ago; they will be functioning a generation hence. It is more important to understand that the very development of American society is creating a new kind of blindness about poverty. The poor are increasingly slipping out of the very experience and consciousness of the nation.

If the middle class never did like ugliness and poverty, it was at least aware of them. "Across the tracks" was not a very long way to go. There were forays into the slums at Christmas time; there were charitable organizations that brought contact with the poor. Occasionally, almost everyone passed through the Negro ghetto or the blocks of tenements, if only to get downtown to work or to entertainment.

Now the American city has been transformed. The poor still inhabit the miserable housing in the central area, but they are increasingly isolated from contact with, or sight of, anybody else. Middle-class women coming in from Suburbia on a rare trip may catch the merest glimpse of the other America on the way to an evening at the theater, but their children are segregated in suburban schools. The business or professional man may drive along the fringes of slums in a car or bus, but it is not an important experience to him. The failures, the unskilled, the disabled, the aged, and the minorities are right there, across the tracks, where they have always been. But hardly anyone else is.

In short, the very development of the American city has removed poverty from the living, emotional experience of millions upon millions of middle-class Americans. Living out in the suburbs, it is easy to assume that ours, is, indeed, an affluent society.

This new segregation of poverty is compounded by a well-meaning ignorance. A good many concerned and sympathetic Americans are aware that there is much discussion of urban renewal. Suddenly, driving through the city, they notice that a familiar slum has been torn down and that there are towering, modern buildings where once there had been tenements or hovels. There is a warm feeling of satisfaction, of pride in the way things are working out: the poor, it is obvious, are being taken care of.

The irony in this . . . is that the truth is nearly the exact opposite to the impression. The total impact of the various housing programs in postwar America has been to squeeze more and more people into existing slums. More often than not, the modern apartment in a towering building rents at $40 a room or more. For, during the past decade and a half, there has been more subsidization of middle- and upper-income housing than there has been of housing for the poor.

Clothes make the poor invisible too: America has the best-dressed poverty the world has ever known. For a variety of reasons, the benefits of mass production have been spread much more evenly in this area than in many others. It is much easier in the United States to be decently dressed than it is to be decently housed, fed, or doctored. Even people with terribly depressed incomes can look prosperous.

This is an extremely important factor in defining our emotional and existential ignorance of poverty. In Detroit the existence of social classes became much more difficult to discern the day the companies put lockers in the plants. From that moment on, one did not see men in work clothes on the way to the factory, but citizens in slacks and white shirts. This process has been magnified with the poor throughout the country. There are tens of thousands of Americans in the big cities who are wearing shoes, perhaps even a stylishly cut suit or dress, and yet are hungry. It is not a matter of planning, though it almost seems as if the affluent society had given out costumes to the poor so that they would not offend the rest of society with the sight of rags.

Then, many of the poor are the wrong age to be seen. A good number of them (over 8,000,000) are sixty-five years of age or better; an even larger number are under eighteen. The aged members of the other America are often sick, and they cannot move. Another group of them live out their lives in loneliness and frustration: they sit in rented rooms, or else they stay close to a house in a neighborhood that has completely changed from the old days. Indeed, one of the worst aspects of poverty among the aged is that these people are out of sight and out of mind, and alone.

The young are somewhat more visible, yet they too stay close to their neighborhoods. Sometimes they advertise their poverty through a lurid tabloid story about a gang killing. But generally they do not disturb the quiet streets of the middle class.

And finally, the poor are politically invisible. It is one of the cruelest ironies of social life in advanced countries that the dispossessed at the bottom of society are unable to speak for themselves. The people of the other America do not, by far and large, belong to unions, to fraternal organizations, or to political parties. They are without lobbies of their own; they put forward no legislative program. As a group, they are atomized. They have no face; they have no voice.

Thus, there is not even a cynical political motive for caring about the poor, as in the old days. Because the slums are no longer centers of powerful political organizations, the politicians need not really care about their inhabitants. The slums are no longer visible to the middle class, so much of the idealistic urge to fight for those who need help is gone. Only the social agencies have a really direct involvement with the other America, and they are without any great political power.

To the extent that the poor have a spokesman in American life, that role is played by the labor movement. The unions have their own particular idealism, an ideology of concern. More than that, they realize that the existence of a reservoir of cheap, unorganized labor is a menace to wages and working conditions throughout the entire economy. Thus, many union legislative proposals—to extend the coverage of minimum wage and social security, to organize migrant farm laborers—articulate the needs of the poor.

That the poor are invisible is one of the most important things about them. They are not simply neglected and forgotten as in the old rhetoric of reform; what is much worse, they are not seen.

One might take a remark from George Eliot's *Felix Holt* as a basic statement of what this book is about:

> . . . there is no private life which has not been determined by a wider public life, from the time when the primeval milkmaid had to wander with the wanderings of her clan, because the cow she milked was one of a herd which had made the pasture bare. Even in the conservatory existence where the fair Camellia is sighed for by the noble young Pineapple, neither of them needing to care about the frost or rain outside, there is a nether apparatus of hotwater pipes liable to cool down on a strike of the gardeners or a scarcity of coal.
>
> And the lives we are about to look back upon do not belong to those conservatory species; they are rooted in the common earth, having to endure all the ordinary chances of past and present weather.

Forty to 50,000,000 people are becoming increasingly invisible. That is a shocking fact. But there is a second basic irony of poverty that is equally important: if one is to make the mistake of being born poor, he should choose a time when the majority of the people are miserable too.

J. K. Galbraith develops this idea in *The Affluent Society,* and in doing so defines the "newness" of the kind of poverty in contemporary America. The old poverty, Galbraith notes, was general. It was the condition of life of an entire society, or at least of that huge majority who were without special skills or the luck of birth. When the entire economy advanced, a good many of these people gained higher standards of living. Unlike the poor today, the majority poor of a generation ago were an immediate (if cynical) concern of political leaders. The old slums of the immigrants had the votes; they provided the basis for labor organizations; their very numbers could be a powerful force in political conflict. At the same time the new technology required higher skills, more education, and stimulated an upward movement for millions.

Perhaps the most dramatic case of the power of the majority poor took place in the 1930's. The Congress of Industrial Organizations literally organized millions in a matter of years. A labor movement that had been declining and confined to a thin stratum of the highly skilled suddenly embraced masses of men and women in basic industry. At the same time this acted as a pressure upon the Government, and the New Deal codified some of the social gains in laws like the Wagner Act. The result was not a basic transformation of the American system, but it did transform the lives of an entire section of the population.

In the thirties one of the reasons for these advances was that misery was general. There was no need then to write books about unemployment and poverty. That was the decisive social experience of the entire society, and the apple sellers even invaded Wall Street. There was political sympathy from middle-class reformers; there were an élan and spirit that grew out of a deep crisis.

Some of those who advanced in the thirties did so because they had unique and individual personal talents. But for the great mass, it was a question of being at the right point in the economy at the right time in history, and utilizing that position for common struggle. Some of those who failed did so because they did not have the will to take advantage of new opportunities. But for the most part the poor who were left behind had been at the wrong place in the economy at the wrong moment in history.

These were the people in the unorganizable jobs, in the South, in the minority groups, in the fly-by-night factories that were low on capital and high on labor. When some of them did break into the economic mainstream—when, for instance, the CIO opened up the way for some Negroes to find good industrial jobs—they proved to be as resourceful as anyone else. As a group, the other Americans who stayed behind were not originally composed primarily of individual failures. Rather, they were victims of an impersonal process that selected some for progress and discriminated against others.

Out of the thirties came the welfare state. Its creation had been stimulated by mass impoverishment and misery, yet it helped the poor least of all. Laws like unemployment compensation, the Wagner Act, the various farm programs, all these were designed for the middle third in the cities, for the organized workers, and for the upper third in the country, for the big market farmers. If a man works in an extremely low-paying job, he may not even be covered by social security or other welfare programs. If he receives unemployment compensation, the payment is scaled down according to his low earnings.

One of the major laws that was designed to cover everyone, rich and poor, was social security. But even here the other Americans suffered discrimination. Over the years social security payments have not even provided a subsistence level of life. The middle third have been able to supplement the Federal pension through private plans negotiated by unions, through joining medical insurance schemes like Blue Cross, and so on. The poor have not been able to do so. They lead a bitter life, and then have to pay for that fact in old age.

Indeed, the paradox that the welfare state benefits those least who need help most is but a single instance of a persistent irony in the other America. Even when the money finally trickles down, even when a school is built in a poor neighborhood, for instance, the poor are still deprived. Their entire environment, their life, their values, do not prepare them to take advantage of the new opportunity. The parents are anxious for the children to go to work; the pupils are pent up, waiting for the moment when their education has complied with the law.

Today's poor, in short, missed the political and social gains of the thirties. They are, as Galbraith rightly points out, the first minority poor in history, the first poor not to be seen, the first poor whom the politicians could leave alone.

The first step toward the new poverty was taken when millions of people proved immune to progress. When that happened, the failure was not individual and personal, but a social product. But once the historic accident takes place, it begins to become a personal fate.

The new poor of the other America saw the rest of society move ahead. They went on living in depressed areas, and often they tended to become depressed human beings. In some of the West Virginia towns, for instance, an entire community will become shabby and defeated. The young and the adventurous go to the city, leaving behind those who cannot move and those who lack the will to do so. The entire area becomes permeated with failure, and that is one more reason the big corporations shy away.

Indeed, one of the most important things about the new poverty is that it cannot be defined in simple, statistical terms. Throughout this book a crucial term is used: aspiration. If a group has internal vitality, a will—if it has aspiration—it may live in dilapidated housing, it may eat an inadequate diet, and it may suffer poverty, but it is not impoverished. So it was in those ethnic slums of the immigrants that played such a dramatic role in the unfolding of the American dream. The people found themselves in slums, but they were not slum dwellers.

But the new poverty is constructed so as to destroy aspiration; it is a system designed to be impervious to hope. The other America does not contain the adventurous seeking a new life and land. It is populated by the failures, by those driven from the land and bewildered by the city, by old people suddenly confronted with the torments of loneliness and poverty, and by minorities facing a wall of prejudice.

In the past, when poverty was general in the unskilled and semi-skilled work force, the poor were all mixed together. The bright and the dull, those who were going to escape into the great society and those who were to stay behind, all of them lived on the same street. When the middle third rose, this community was destroyed. And the entire invisible land of the other Americans became a ghetto, a modern poor farm for the rejects of society and of the economy.

It is a blow to reform and the political hopes of the poor that the middle class no longer understands that poverty exists. But, perhaps more important, the poor are losing their links with the great world. If statistics and sociology can measure a feeling as delicate as loneliness (and some of the attempts to do so will be cited later on), the other America is becoming increasingly populated by those who do not belong to anybody or anything. They are no longer participants in an ethnic culture from the old country; they are less and less religious; they do not belong to unions or clubs. They are not seen, and because of that they themselves cannot see. Their horizon has become more and more restricted; they see one another, and that means they see little reason to hope.

Galbraith was one of the first writers to begin to describe the newness of contemporary poverty, and that is to his credit. Yet because even he underestimates the problem, it is important to put his definition into perspective.

For Galbraith, there are two main components · of the new poverty: case poverty and insular poverty. Case poverty is the plight of those who suffer from some physical or mental disability that is personal and individual and excludes them from the general advance. Insular poverty exists in areas like the Appalachians or the West Virginia coal fields, where an entire section of the country becomes economically obsolete.

Physical and mental disabilities are, to be sure, an important part of poverty in America. The poor are sick in body and in spirit. But this is not an isolated fact about them, an individual "case," a stroke of bad luck. Disease, alcoholism, low IQ's, these express a whole way of life. They are, in the main, the effects of an environment, not the biographies of unlucky individuals. Because of this, the new poverty is something that cannot be dealt with by first aid. If there is to be a lasting assault on the shame of the other America, it must seek to root out of this society an entire environment, and not just the relief of individuals.

But perhaps the idea of "insular" poverty is even more dangerous. To speak of "islands" of the poor (or, in the more popular term, of "pockets of poverty") is to imply that one is confronted by a serious, but relatively minor, problem. This is hardly a description of a misery that extends to 40,000,000 or 50,000,000 people in the United States. They have remained impoverished in spite of increasing productivity and the creation of a welfare state. That fact alone should suggest the dimensions of a serious and basic situation.

And yet, even given these disagreements with Galbraith, his achievement is considerable. He was one of the first to understand that there are enough poor people in the United States to constitute a subculture of misery, but not enough of them to challenge the conscience and the imagination of the nation.

Finally, one might summarize the newness of contemporary poverty by saying: These are the people who are immune to progress. But then the facts are even more cruel. The other Americans are the victims of the very inventions and machines that have provided a higher living standard for the rest of society. They are upside-down in the economy, and for them greater productivity often means worse jobs; agricultural advance becomes hunger.

In the optimistic theory, technology is an undisguised blessing. A general increase in productivity, the argument goes, generates a higher standard of living for the whole people. And indeed, this has been true for the middle and upper thirds of American society, the people who made such striking gains in the last two decades. It tends to overstate the automatic character of the process, to omit the role of human struggle. (The CIO was organized by men in conflict, not by economic trends.) Yet it states a certain truth—for those who are lucky enough to participate in it.

But the poor, if they were given to theory, might argue the exact opposite. They might say: Progress is misery.

As the society became more technological, more skilled, those who learn to work the machines, who get the expanding education, move up. Those who miss out at the very start find themselves at a new disadvantage. A generation ago in American life, the majority of the working people did not have high-school educations. But at that time industry was organized on a lower level of skill and competence. And there was a sort of continuum in the shop: the youth who left school at sixteen could begin as a laborer, and gradually pick up skill as he went along.

Today the situation is quite different. The good jobs require much more academic preparation, much more skill from the very outset. Those who lack a high-school education tend to be condemned to the economic underworld—to low-paying service industries, to backward factories, to sweeping and janitorial duties. If the fathers and mothers of the contemporary poor were penalized a generation ago for their lack of schooling, their children will suffer all the more. The very rise in productivity that created more money and better working conditions for the rest of the society can be a menace to the poor.

But then this technological revolution might have an even more disastrous consequence: it could increase the ranks of the poor as well as intensify the disabilities of poverty. At this point it is too early to make any final judgment, yet there are obvious danger signals. There are millions of Americans who live just the other side of poverty. When a recession comes, they are pushed onto the relief rolls. (Welfare payments in New York respond almost immediately to any economic decline.) If automation continues to inflict more and more penalties on the unskilled and the semiskilled, it could have the impact of permanently increasing the population of the other America.

Even more explosive is the possibility that people who participated in the gains of the thirties and the forties will be pulled back down into poverty. Today the mass-production industries where unionization made such a difference are contracting. Jobs are being destroyed. In the process, workers who had achieved a certain level of wages, who had won working conditions in the shop, are suddenly confronted with impoverishment. This is particularly true for anyone over forty years of age and for members of minority groups. Once their job is abolished, their chances of ever getting similar work are very slim.

It is too early to say whether or not this phenomenon is temporary, or whether it represents a massive retrogression that will swell the numbers of the poor. To a large extent, the answer to this question will be determined by the political response of the United States in the sixties. If serious and massive action is not undertaken, it may be necessary for statisticians to add some old-fashioned, pre-welfare-state poverty to the misery of the other America.

Poverty in the 1960's is invisible and it is new, and both these factors make it more tenacious. It is more isolated and politically powerless than ever before. It is laced with ironies, not the least of which is that many of the poor view progress upside-down, as a menace and a threat to their lives. And if the nation does not measure up to the challenge of automation, poverty in the 1960's might be on the increase.

II

There are mighty historical and economic forces that keep the poor down; and there are human beings who help out in this grim business, many of them unwittingly. There are sociological and political reasons why poverty is not seen; and there are misconceptions and prejudices that literally blind the eyes. The latter must be understood if anyone is to make the necessary act of intellect and will so that the poor can be noticed.

Here is the most familiar version of social blindness: "The poor are that way because they are afraid of work. And anyway they all have big cars. If they were like me (or my father or my grandfather), they could pay their own way. But they prefer to live on the dole and cheat the taxpayers."

This theory, usually thought of as a virtuous and moral statement, is one of the means of making it impossible for the poor ever to pay their way. There are, one must assume, citizens of the other America who choose impoverishment out of fear of work (though, writing it down, I really do not believe it). But the real explanation of why the poor are where they are is that they made the mistake of being born to the wrong parents, in the wrong section of the country, in the wrong industry, or in the wrong racial or ethnic group. Once that mistake has been made, they could have been paragons of will and morality, but most of them would never even have had a chance to get out of the other America.

There are two important ways of saying this: The poor are caught in a vicious circle; or, The poor live in a culture of poverty.

In a sense, one might define the contemporary poor in the United States as those who, for reasons beyond their control, cannot help themselves. All the most decisive factors making for opportunity and advance are against them. They are born going downward, and most of them stay down. They are victims whose lives are endlessly blown round and round the other America.

Here is one of the most familiar forms of the vicious circle of poverty. The poor get sick more than anyone else in the society. That is because they live in slums, jammed together under unhygienic conditions; they have inadequate diets, and cannot get decent medical care. When they become sick, they are sick longer than any other group in the society. Because they are sick more often and longer than anyone else, they lose wages and work, and find it difficult to hold a steady job. And because of this, they cannot pay for good housing, for a nutritious diet, for doctors. At any given point in the circle, particularly when there is a major illness, their prospect is to move to an even lower level and to begin the cycle, round and round, toward even more suffering.

This is only one example of the vicious circle. Each group in the other America has its own particular version of the experience, and these will be detailed throughout this book. But the pattern, whatever its variations, is basic to the other America.

The individual cannot usually break out of this vicious circle. Neither can the group, for it lacks the social energy and political strength to turn its misery into a cause. Only the larger society, with its help and resources, can really make it possible for these people to help themselves. Yet those who could make the difference too often refuse to act because of their ignorant, smug moralisms. They view the effects of poverty—above all, the warping of the will and spirit that is a consequence of being poor—as choices. Understanding the vicious circle is an important step in breaking down this prejudice.

There is an even richer way of describing this same, general idea: Poverty in the United States is a culture, an institution, a way of life.

There is a famous anecdote about Ernest Hemingway and F. Scott Fitzgerald. Fitzgerald is reported to have remarked to Hemingway, "The rich are different." And Hemingway replied, "Yes, they have money." Fitzgerald had much the better of the exchange. He understood that being rich was not a simple fact, like a large bank account, but a way of looking at reality, a series of attitudes, a special type of life. If this is true of the rich, it is ten times truer of the poor. Everything about them, from the condition of their teeth to the way in which they love, is suffused and permeated by the fact of their poverty. And this is sometimes a hard idea for a Hemingway-like middle-class America to comprehend.

The family structure of the poor, for instance, is different from that of the rest of the society. There are more homes without a father, there are less marriages, more early pregnancy and, if Kinsey's statistical findings can be used, markedly different attitudes toward sex. As a result of this, to take but one consequence of the fact, hundreds of thousands, and perhaps millions, of children in the other America never know stability and "normal" affection.

Or perhaps the policeman is an even better example. For the middle class, the police protect property, give directions, and help old ladies. For the urban poor, the police are those who arrest you. In almost any slum there is a vast conspiracy against the forces of law and order. If someone approaches asking for a person, no one there will have heard of him, even if he lives next door. The outsider is "cop," bill collector, investigator (and, in the Negro ghetto, most dramatically, he is "the Man").

While writing this book, I was arrested for participation in a civil-rights demonstration. A brief experience of a night in a cell made an abstraction personal and immediate: the city jail is one of the basic institutions of the other America. Almost everyone whom I encountered in the "tank" was poor: skid-row whites, Negroes, Puerto Ricans. Their poverty was an incitement to arrest in the first place. (A policeman will be much more careful with a well-dressed, obviously educated man who might have political connections than he will with someone who is poor.) They did not have money for bail or for lawyers. And, perhaps most important, they waited their arraignment with stolidity, in a mood of passive acceptance. They expected the worst, and they probably got it.

There is, in short, a language of the poor, a psychology of the poor, a world view of the poor. To be impoverished is to be an internal alien, to grow up in a culture that is radically different from the one that dominates the society. The poor can be described statistically; they can be analyzed as a group. But they need a novelist as well as a sociologist if we are to see them. They need an American Dickens to record the smell and texture and quality of their lives. The cycles and trends, the massive forces, must be seen as affecting persons who talk and think differently.

I am not that novelist. Yet in this book I have attempted to describe the faces behind the statistics, to tell a little of the "thickness" of personal life in the other America. Of necessity, I have begun with large groups: the dispossessed workers, the minorities, the farm poor, and the aged. Then, there are three cases of less massive types of poverty, including the only single humorous component in the other America. And finally, there are the slums, and the psychology of the poor.

Throughout, I work on an assumption that cannot be proved by Government figures or even documented by impressions of the other America. It is an ethical proposition, and it can be simply stated: In a nation with a technology that could provide every citizen with a decent life, it is an outrage and a scandal that there should be such social misery. Only if one begins with this assumption is it possible to pierce through the invisibility of 40,000,000 to 50,000,000 human beings and to see the other America. We must perceive passionately, if this blindness is to be lifted from us. A fact can be rationalized and explained away; an indignity cannot.

What shall we tell the American poor, once we have seen them? Shall we say to them that they are better off than the Indian poor, the Italian poor, the Russian poor? That is one answer, but it is heartless. I should put it another way. I want to tell every well-fed and optimistic American that it is intolerable that so many millions should be maimed in body and in spirit when it is not necessary that they should be. My standard of comparison is not how much worse things used to be. It is how much better they could be if only we were stirred.

12   Illegitimate Means, Anomie, and Deviant Behavior

RICHARD A. CLOWARD

This paper[1] represents an attempt to consolidate two major sociological traditions of thought about the problem of deviant behavior. The first, exemplified by the work of Émile Durkheim and Robert K. Merton, may be called the anomie tradition.[2] The second, illustrated principally by the studies of Clifford R. Shaw, Henry D. McKay, and Edwin H. Sutherland, may be called the "cultural transmission" and "differential association" tradition.[3] Despite some reciprocal borrowing of ideas, these intellectual traditions developed more or less independently. By seeking to consolidate them, a more adequate theory of deviant behavior may be constructed.

DIFFERENTIALS IN AVAILABILITY OF LEGITIMATE MEANS: THE THEORY OF ANOMIE

The theory of anomie has undergone two major phases of development. Durkheim first used the concept to explain deviant behavior. He focussed on the way in which various social conditions lead to "overweening ambition," and how, in turn, unlimited aspirations ultimately produce a breakdown in regulatory norms. Robert K. Merton has systematized and extended the theory, directing attention to patterns of disjunction between culturally prescribed goals and socially organized access to them by *legitimate* means. In this paper, a third phase is outlined. An additional variable is incorporated in the developing scheme of anomie, namely, the concept of *differentials in access to success-goals by illegitimate means.*[4]

Phase I: Unlimited Aspirations and the Breakdown of Regulatory Norms

In Durkheim's work, a basic distinction is made between "physical needs" and "moral needs." The importance of this distinction

Reprinted from *American Sociological Review,* 24 (April 1959): 164–76, by permission of the American Sociological Association and the author.

was heightened for Durkheim because he viewed physical needs as being regulated automatically by features of man's organic structure. Nothing in the organic structure, however, is capable of regulating social desires; as Durkheim put it, man's "capacity for feeling is in itself an insatiable and bottomless abyss."[5] If man is to function without "friction," "the passions must first be limited. . . . But since the individual has no way of limiting them, this must be done by some force exterior to him." Durkheim viewed the collective order as the external regulating force which defined and ordered the goals to which men should orient their behavior. If the collective order is disrupted or disturbed, however, men's aspirations may then rise, exceeding all possibilities of fulfillment. Under these conditions, "de-regulation or anomy" ensues: "At the very moment when traditional rules have lost their authority, the richer prize offered these appetites stimulates them and makes them more exigent and impatient of control. The state of de-regulation or anomy is thus further heightened by passions being less disciplined precisely when they need more disciplining." Finally, pressures toward deviant behavior were said to develop when man's aspirations no longer matched the possibilities of fulfillment.

Durkheim therefore turned to the question of *when* the regulatory functions of the collective order break down. Several such states were identified, including sudden depression, sudden prosperity, and rapid technological change. His object was to show how, under these conditions, men are led to aspire to goals extremely difficult if not impossible to attain. As Durkheim saw it, sudden depression results in deviant behavior because "something like a declassification occurs which suddenly casts certain individuals into a lower state than their previous one. Then they must reduce their requirements, restrain their needs, learn greater self-control. . . . But society cannot adjust them instantaneously to this new life and teach them to practice the increased self-repression to which they are unaccustomed. So they are not adjusted to the condition forced on them, and its very prospect is intolerable; hence the suffering which detaches them from a reduced existence even before they have made trial of it." Prosperity, according to Durkheim, could have much the same effect as depression, particularly if upward changes in economic conditions are abrupt. The very abruptness of these changes presumably heightens aspirations beyond possibility of fulfillment, and this too puts a strain on the regulatory apparatus of the society.

According to Durkheim, "the sphere of trade and industry . . . is actually in a chronic state [of anomie]." Rapid technological developments and the existence of vast, unexploited markets excite the imagination with the seemingly limitless possibilities for the accumulation of wealth. As Durkheim said of the producer of goods, "now that he may assume to have almost the entire world as his customer, how could passions accept their former confinement in the face of such limitless prospects?" Continuing, Durkheim states that "such is the source of excitement predominating in this part of society. . . . Here the state of crisis and anomie [are] constant and, so to speak, normal. From top to bottom of the ladder, greed is aroused without knowing where to find ultimate foothold. Nothing can calm it, since its goal is far beyond all it can attain."

In developing the theory, Durkheim characterized goals in the industrial society, and specified the way in which unlimited aspirations are induced. He spoke of "dispositions . . . so inbred that society has grown to accept them and is accustomed to think them normal," and he portrayed these "inbred dispositions": "It is everlastingly repeated that it is man's nature to be eternally dissatisfied, constantly to advance, without relief or rest, toward an indefinite goal. The longing for infinity is daily represented as a mark of moral distinction. . . ." And it was precisely these pressures to strive for "infinite" or "receding" goals, in Durkheim's view, that generate a breakdown in regulatory norms, for "when there is no other aim but to outstrip constantly the point arrived at, how painful to be thrown back!"

Phase II: Disjunction Between Cultural Goals and Socially Structured Opportunity

Durkheim's description of the emergence of "overweening ambition" and the subsequent breakdown of regulatory norms constitutes one of the links between his work and the later development of the theory by Robert K. Merton. In his classic essay, "Social Structure and Anomie," Merton suggests that goals and norms may vary independently of each other, and that this sometimes leads to malintegrated states. In his view, two polar types of disjunction may occur: "There may develop a very heavy, at times a virtually exclusive, stress upon the value of particular goals, involving comparatively little concern with the institutionally prescribed means of striving toward these goals. . . . This constitutes one type of malintegrated culture."[6] On the other hand, "A second polar type is found where activities originally conceived as instrumental are transmuted into self-contained practices, lacking further objectives. . . . Sheer conformity becomes a central value." Merton notes that "between these extreme types are societies which maintain a rough balance between emphases upon cultural goals and institutionalized practices, and these constitute the integrated and relatively stable, though changing societies."

Having identified patterns of disjunction between goals and norms, Merton is enabled to define anomie more precisely: "Anomie [may be] conceived as a breakdown in the cultural structure, oc·curring particularly when there is an acute disjunction between cultural norms and goals and the socially structured capacities of members of the group to act in accord with them."

Of the two kinds of malintegrated societies, Merton is primarily interested in the one in which "there is an exceptionally strong emphasis upon specific goals without a corresponding emphasis upon institutional procedures." He states that attenuation between goals and norms, leading to anomie or "normlessness," comes about because men in such societies internalize an emphasis on common success-goals under conditions of varying access to them. The essence of this hypothesis is captured in the following excerpt: "It is only when a system of cultural values extols, virtually above all else, certain *common* success-goals for the population at large while the social structure rigorously restricts or completely closes access to approved modes of reaching these goals *for a considerable part of the same population*, that deviant behavior ensues on a large scale." The focus, in short, is on the way in which the social structure puts a strain upon the cultural structure. Here one may point to diverse structural differentials in access to culturally approved goals by legitimate means, for example, differentials of age, sex, ethnic status, and social class. Pressures for anomie or normlessness vary from one social position to another, depending on the nature of these differentials.

In summary, Merton extends the theory of anomie in two principal ways. He explicitly identifies types of anomic or malintegrated societies by focussing upon the relationship between cultural goals and norms. And, by directing attention to patterned differentials in the access to success-goals by legitimate means, he shows how the social structure exerts a strain upon the cultural structure, leading in turn to anomie or normlessness.

Phase III: The Concept of Illegitimate Means

Once processes generating differentials in pressures are identified, there is then the question of how these pressures are resolved, or how men respond to them. In this connection, Merton enumerates five basic categories of behavior or role adaptations which are likely to emerge: conformity, innovation, ritualism, retreatism, and rebellion. These adaptations differ depending on the individual's acceptance or rejection of cultural goals, and depending on his adherence to or violation of institutional norms. Furthermore, Merton sees the distribution of these adaptations principally as the consequence of two variables: the relative extent of pressure, and values, particularly "internalized prohibitions," governing the use of various illegitimate means.

It is a familiar sociological idea that values serve to order the choices of deviant (as well as conforming) adaptations which develop under conditions of stress. Comparative studies of ethnic groups, for example, have shown that some tend to engage in distinctive forms of deviance; thus Jews exhibit low rates of alcoholism and alcoholic psychoses.[7] Various investigators have suggested that the emphasis on rationality, fear of expressing aggression, and other alleged components of the "Jewish" value system constrain modes of deviance which involve "loss of control" over behavior.[8] In contrast, the Irish show a much higher rate of alcoholic deviance because, it has been argued, their cultural emphasis on masculinity encourages the excessive use of alcohol under conditions of strain.[9]

Merton suggests that differing rates of ritualistic and innovating behavior in the middle and lower classes result from differential emphases in socialization. The "rule-oriented" accent in middle-class socialization presumably disposes persons to handle stress by engaging in ritualistic rather than innovating behavior. The lower-class person, contrastingly, having internalized less stringent norms, can violate conventions with less guilt and anxiety.[10] Values, in other words, exercise a canalizing influence, limiting the choice of deviant adaptations for persons variously distributed throughout the social system.

Apart from both socially patterned pressures, which give rise to deviance, and from values, which determine choices of adaptations, a further variable should be taken into account: namely, *differentials in availability of illegitimate means*. For example, the notion that innovating behavior may result from unfulfilled aspirations and imperfect socialization with respect to conventional norms implies that illegitimate means are freely available—as if the individual, having decided that "you can't make it legitimately," then simply turns to illegitimate means which are readily at hand whatever his position in the social structure. However, these means may not be available. As noted above, the anomie theory assumes that conventional means are differentially distributed, that some individuals, because of their social position, enjoy certain advantages which are denied to others. Note, for example, variations in the degree to which members of various classes are fully exposed to and thus acquire the values, education, and skills which facilitate upward mobility. It should not be startling, therefore, to find similar variations in the availability of illegitimate means.

Several sociologists have alluded to such variations without explicitly incorporating this variable in a theory of deviant behavior. Sutherland, for example, writes that "an inclination to steal is not a sufficient explanation of the genesis of the professional thief."[11] Moreover, "the person must be appreciated by the professional thieves. He must be appraised as having an adequate equipment of wits, front, talking-ability, honesty, reliability, nerve and determination." In short, "a person can be a professional thief only if he is recognized and received as such by other professional thieves." But recognition is not freely accorded: "Selection and tutelage are the two necessary elements in the process of acquiring recognition as a professional thief. . . . A person cannot acquire recognition as a professional thief until he has had tutelage in professional theft, *and tutelage is given only to a few persons selected from the total population.*" Furthermore, the aspirant is judged by high standards of performance, for only "a very small percentage of those who start on this process ever reach the stage of professional theft." The burden of these remarks—dealing with the processes of selection, induction, and assumption of full status in the criminal group—is that motivations or pressures toward deviance do not fully account for deviant behavior. The "self-made" thief—lacking knowledge of the ways of securing immunity from prosecution and similar techniques of defense—"would quickly land in prison." Sutherland is in effect pointing to differentials in access to the role of professional thief. Although the criteria of selection are not altogether clear from his analysis, definite evaluative standards do appear to exist; depending on their content, certain categories of individuals would be placed at a disadvantage and others would be favored.

The availability of illegitimate means, then, is controlled by various criteria in the same manner that has long been ascribed to conventional means. Both systems of opportunity are (1) limited, rather than infinitely available, and (2) differentially available depending on the location of persons in the social structure.

When we employ the term "means," whether legitimate or illegitimate, at least two things are implied: first, that there are appropriate learning environments for the acquisition of the values and skills associated with the performance of a particular role; and second, that the individual has opportunities to discharge the role once he has been prepared. The term subsumes, therefore, both *learning structures* and *opportunity structures*.

A case in point is recruitment and preparation for careers in the rackets. There are fertile criminal learning environments for the young in neighborhoods where the rackets flourish as stable, indigenous institutions. Because these environments afford integration of offenders of different ages, the young are exposed to "differential associations" which facilitate the acquisition of criminal values and skills. Yet preparation for the role may not insure that the individual will ever discharge it. For one thing, more youngsters may be recruited into these patterns of differential association than can possibly be absorbed, following their "training," by the adult criminal structure. There may be a surplus of contenders for these elite positions, leading in turn to the necessity for criteria and mechanisms of selection. Hence a certain proportion of those who aspire may not be permitted to engage in the behavior for which they have been prepared.

This illustration is similar in every respect, save for the route followed, to the case of those who seek careers in the sphere of legitimate business. Here, again, is the initial problem of securing access to appropriate learning environments, such as colleges and post-graduate schools of business. Having acquired the values and skills needed for a business career, graduates then face the problem of whether or not they can successfully discharge the roles for which they have been prepared. Formal training itself is not sufficient for occupational success, for many forces intervene to determine who shall succeed and fail in the competitive world of business and industry—as throughout the entire conventional occupational structure.

This distinction between learning structures and opportunity structures was suggested some years ago by Sutherland. In 1944, he circulated an unpublished paper which briefly discusses the proposition that "criminal behavior is partially a function of opportunities to commit specific classes of crimes, such as embezzlement, bank burglary, or illicit heterosexual intercourse."[12] He did not, however, take up the problem of differentials in opportunity as a concept to be systematically incorporated in a theory of deviant behavior. Instead, he held that "opportunity" is a necessary but not sufficient explanation of the commission of criminal acts, "since some persons who have opportunities to embezzle, become intoxicated, engage in illicit heterosexual intercourse or to commit other crimes do not do so." He also noted that the differential association theory did not constitute a full explanation of criminal activity, for, notwithstanding differential association, "it is axiomatic that persons who commit a specific crime must have the opportunity to commit that crime." He therefore concluded that "while opportunity may be partially a function of association with criminal patterns and of the specialized techniques thus acquired, *it is not determined entirely in that manner,* and consequently differential association is not the sufficient cause of criminal behavior." (emphasis not in original)

In Sutherland's statements, two meanings are attributed to the term "opportunity." As suggested above, it may be useful to separate these for analytical purposes. In the first sense, Sutherland appears to be saying that opportunity consists in part of learning structures. The principal components of his theory of differential association are that "criminal behavior is learned," and, furthermore, that "criminal behavior is learned in interaction with other persons in a process of communication." But he also uses the term to describe situations conducive to carrying out criminal roles. Thus, for Sutherland, the commission of a criminal act would seem to depend upon the existence of two conditions: differential associations favoring the acquisition of criminal values and skills, and conditions encouraging participation in criminal activity.

This distinction heightens the importance of identifying and questioning the common assumption that illegitimate means are freely available. We can now ask (1) whether there are socially structured differentials in access to illegitimate learning environments, and (2) whether there are differentials limiting the fulfillment of illegitimate roles. If differentials exist and can be identified, we may then inquire about their consequences for the behavior of persons in different parts of the social structure. Before pursuing this question, however, we turn to a fuller discussion of the theoretical tradition established by Shaw, McKay, and Sutherland.

DIFFERENTIALS IN AVAILABILITY OF ILLEGITIMATE MEANS: THE SUBCULTURE TRADITION

The concept of differentials in availability of illegitimate means is implicit in one of the major streams of American criminological theory. In this tradition, attention is focussed on the processes by which persons are recruited into criminal learning environments and ultimately inducted into criminal roles. The problems here are to account for the acquisition of criminal roles and to describe the social organization of criminal activities. When the theoretical propositions contained in this tradition are reanalyzed, it becomes clear that one underlying conception is that of variations in access to success-goals by illegitimate means. Furthermore, this implicit concept may be shown to be one of the bases upon which the tradition was constructed.

In their studies of the ecology of deviant behavior in the urban environment, Shaw and McKay found that delinquency and crime tended to be confined to delimited areas and, furthermore, that such behavior persisted despite demographic changes in these areas. Hence they came to speak of "criminal tradition," of the "cultural transmission" of criminal values.[13] As a result of their observations of slum life, they concluded that *particular importance must be assigned to the integration of different age-levels of offenders.* Thus:

> Stealing in the neighborhood was a common practice among the children and approved by the parents. Whenever the boys got together they talked about robbing and made more plans for stealing. I hardly knew any boys who did not go robbing. The little fellows went in for petty stealing, breaking into freight cars, and stealing junk. The older guys did big jobs like stick-up, burglary, and stealing autos. The little fellows admired the "big shots" and longed for the day when they could get into the big racket. Fellows who had "done time" were the big shots and looked up to and gave the little fellow tips on how to get by and pull off big jobs.[14]

In other words, access to criminal roles depends upon stable associations with others from whom the necessary values and skills may be learned. Shaw and McKay were describing deviant learning structures—that is, alternative routes by which people seek access to the goals which society holds to be worthwhile. They might also have pointed out that, in areas where such learning structures are unavailable, it is probably difficult for many individuals to secure access to stable criminal careers, even though motivated to do so.[15]

The concept of illegitimate means and the socially structured conditions of access to them were not explicitly recognized in the work of Shaw and McKay because, probably, they were disposed to view slum areas as "disorganized." Although they consistently referred to illegitimate activities as being organized, they nevertheless often depicted high-rate delinquency areas as disorganized because the values transmitted were criminal rather than conventional. Hence their work includes statements which we now perceive to be internally inconsistent, such as the following:

> This community situation [in which Sidney was reared] was not only disorganized and thus ineffective as a unit of control, but it was characterized by a high rate of juvenile delinquency and adult crime, not to mention the widespread political corruption which had long existed in the area. Various forms of stealing and many organized delinquent and criminal gangs were prevalent in the area. These groups exercised a powerful influence and tended to create a community spirit which not only tolerated but actually fostered delinquent and criminal practices.[16]

Sutherland was among the first to perceive that the concept of social disorganization tended to obscure the stable patterns of interaction among carriers of criminal values. Like Shaw and McKay, he had been influenced by the observation that lower-class areas were organized in terms of both conventional and criminal values, but he was also impressed that these alternative value systems were supported by patterned systems of social relations. He expressly recognized that crime, far from being a random, unorganized activity, was typically an intricate and stable system of human arrangements. He therefore rejected the concept of "social disorganization" and substituted the concept of "differential group organization."

> The third concept, social disorganization, was borrowed from Shaw and McKay. I had used it but had not been satisfied with it because the organization of the delinquent group, which is often very complex, is social disorganization only from an ethical or some other particularistic point of view. At the suggestion of Albert K. Cohen, this concept has been

changed to differential group organization, with organization for criminal activities on one side and organization against criminal activities on the other.[17]

Having freed observation of the urban slum from conventional evaluations, Sutherland was able to focus more clearly on the way in which its social structure constitutes a "learning environment" for the acquisition of deviant values and skills. In the development of the theory of "differential association" and "differential group organization," he came close to stating explicitly the concept of differentials in access to illegitimate means. But Sutherland was essentially interested in learning processes, and thus he did not ask how such access varies in different parts of the social structure, nor did he inquire about the consequences for behavior of variations in the accessibility of these means.[18]

William F. Whyte, in his classic study of an urban slum, advanced the empirical description of the structure and organization of illegitimate means a step beyond that of Sutherland. Like Sutherland, Whyte rejected the earlier view of the slum as disorganized:

> It is customary for the sociologist to study the slum district in terms of "social disorganization" and to neglect to see that an area such as Cornerville has a complex and well-established organization of its own. . . . I found that in every group there was a hierarchical structure of social relations binding the individuals to one another and that the groups were also related hierarchically to one another. Where the group was formally organized into a political club, this was immediately apparent, but for informal groups it was no less true.[19]

Whyte's contribution to our understanding of the organization of illegitimate means in the slum consists primarily in showing that individuals who participate in stable illicit enterprise do not constitute a separate or isolated segment of the community. Rather, these persons are closely integrated with the occupants of conventional roles. In describing the relationship between racketeers and politicians, for example, he notes that "the rackets and political organizations extend from the bottom to the top of Cornerville society, mesh with one another, and integrate a large part of the life of the district. They provide a general framework for the understanding of the actions of both 'little guys' and 'big shots.' "[20] Whyte's view of the slum differs somewhat from that conveyed by the term "differential group organization." He does not emphasize the idea that the slum is composed of two different systems, conventional and deviant, but rather the way in which the occupants of these various roles are integrated in a single, stable structure which organizes and patterns the life of the community.

The description of the organization of illegitimate means in slums is further developed by Solomon Kobrin in his article, "The Conflict of Values in Delinquency Areas."[21] Kobrin suggests that urban slum areas vary in the degree to which the carriers of deviant and conventional values are integrated with one another. Hence he points the way to the development of a "typology of delinquency areas based on variations in the relationship between these two systems," depicting the "polar types" on such a continuum. The first type resembles the integrated areas described in preceding paragraphs. Here, claims Kobrin, there is not merely structural integration between carriers of the two value systems, but reciprocal participation by each in the value system of the other. Thus:

> Leaders of [illegal] enterprises frequently maintain membership in such conventional institutions of their local communities as churches, fraternal and mutual benefit societies and political parties. . . . Within this framework the influence of each of the two value systems is reciprocal, the leaders of illegal enterprise participating in the primary orientation of the conventional elements in the population, and the latter, through their participation in a local power structure sustained in large part by illicit activity, participating perforce in the alternate, criminal value system.

Kobrin also notes that in some urban slums there is a tendency for the relationships between carriers of deviant and conventional values to break down. Such areas constitute the second polar type. Because of disorganizing forces such as "drastic changes in the class, ethnic, or racial characteristics of its population," Kobrin suggests that "the bearers of the conventional culture and its value system are without the customary institutional machinery and therefore in effect partially demobilized with reference to the diffusion of their value system." At the same time, the criminal "value system remains implicit" since this type of area is "characterized principally by the absence of systematic and organized adult activity in violation of the law, despite the fact that many adults in these areas commit violations." Since both value systems remain implicit, the possibilities for effective integration are precluded.

The importance of these observations may be seen if we ask how accessibility of illegal means varies with the relative integration of conventional and criminal values from one type of area to another. In this connection, Kobrin points out that the "integrated" area apparently constitutes a "training ground" for the acquisition of criminal values and skills.

> The stable position of illicit enterprise in the adult society of the community is reflected in the character of delinquent conduct on the part of children. While delinquency in all high rate areas is intrinsically disorderly in that it is unrelated to official programs for the education of the young, in the [integrated community] boys may more or less realistically recognize the potentialities for personal progress in local society through access to delinquency. In a general way, therefore, delinquent activity in these areas constitutes a training ground for the acquisition of skill in the use of violence, concealment of offense, evasion of detection and arrest, and the purchase of immunity from punishment. Those who come to excel in these respects are frequently noted and valued by adult leaders in the rackets who are confronted, as are the leaders of all income-producing enterprises, with problems of the recruitment of competent personnel.

With respect to the contrasting or "unintegrated area," Kobrin makes no mention of the extent to which learning structures and opportunities for criminal careers are available. Yet his portrayal of such areas as lacking in the articulation of either conventional or criminal values suggests that the appropriate learning structures —principally the integration of offenders of different age levels— are not available. Furthermore, his depiction of adult violative activity as "unorganized" suggests that the illegal opportunity structure is severely limited. Even if youngsters were able to secure adequate preparation for criminal roles, the problem would appear to be that the social structure of such neighborhoods provides few opportunities for stable, criminal careers. For Kobrin's analysis—as well as those of Whyte and others before him—leads to the conclusion that illegal opportunity structures tend to emerge in lower-class areas only when stable patterns of accommodation and integration arise between the carriers of conventional and deviant values. Where these values remain unorganized and implicit, or where their carriers are in open conflict, opportunities for stable criminal role performance are more or less limited.[22]

Other factors may be cited which affect access to criminal roles. For example, there is a good deal of anecdotal evidence which reveals that access to the upper echelons of organized racketeering is controlled, at least in part, by ethnicity. Some ethnic groups are found disproportionately in the upper ranks and others disproportionately in the lower. From an historical perspective, as Bell has shown, this realm has been successively dominated by Irish, East-European Jews, and more recently, by Italians.[23] Various other ethnic groups have been virtually excluded or at least relegated to lower-echelon positions. Despite the fact that many rackets (especially "policy") have flourished in predominantly Negro neighborhoods, there have been but one or two Negroes who have been known to rise to the top in syndicated crime. As in the conventional world, Negroes are relegated to the more menial tasks. Moreover, access to elite positions in the rackets may be governed in part by kinship criteria, for various accounts of the blood relations among top racketeers indicate that nepotism is the general rule.[24] It has also been noted that kinship criteria sometimes govern access to stable criminal roles, as in the case of the pickpocket.[25] And there are, of course, deep-rooted sex differentials in access to illegal means. Although women are often employed in criminal vocations —for example, thievery, confidence games, and extortion—and must be employed in others—such as prostitution—nevertheless females are excluded from many criminal activities.[26]

Of the various criteria governing access to illegitimate means, class differentials may be among the most important. The differentials noted in the preceding paragraph—age, sex, ethnicity, kinship, and the like—all pertain to criminal activity historically associated with the lower class. Most middle- or upper-class persons —even when interested in following "lower-class" criminal careers —would no doubt have difficulty in fulfilling this ambition because of inappropriate preparation. The prerequisite attitudes and skills are more easily acquired if the individual is a member of the lower class; most middle- and upper-class persons could not easily unlearn their own class culture in order to learn a new one. By the same token, access to many "white collar" criminal roles is closed to lower-class persons. Some occupations afford abundant opportunities to engage in illegitimate activity; others offer virtually none.

The businessman, for example, not only has at his disposal the means to do so, but, as some studies have shown, he is under persistent pressure to employ illegitimate means, if only to maintain a competitive advantage in the market place. But for those in many other occupations, white collar modes of criminal activity are simply not an alternative.[27]

SOME IMPLICATIONS OF A CONSOLIDATED APPROACH TO DEVIANT BEHAVIOR

It is now possible to consolidate the two sociological traditions described above. Our analysis makes it clear that these traditions are oriented to different aspects of the same problem: differentials in access to opportunity. One tradition focusses on legitimate opportunity, the other on illegitimate. By incorporating the concept of differentials in access to *illegitimate* means, the theory of anomie may be extended to include seemingly unrelated studies and theories of deviant behavior which form a part of the literature of American criminology. In this final section, we try to show how a consolidated approach might advance the understanding of both rates and types of deviant conduct. The discussion centers on the conditions of access to *both* systems of means, legitimate and illegitimate.

The Distribution of Criminal Behavior

One problem which has plagued the criminologist is the absence of adequate data on social differentials in criminal activity. Many have held that the highest crime rates are to be found in the lower social strata. Others have suggested that rates in the middle and upper classes may be much higher than is ordinarily thought. The question of the social distribution of crime remains problematic.

In the absence of adequate data, the theorist has sometimes attacked this problem by assessing the extent of pressures toward normative departures in various parts of the social structure. For example, Merton remarks that his "primary aim is to discover how some social structures exert a definite pressure upon certain persons in the society to engage in non-conforming rather than conforming conduct."[28] Having identified structural features which might be expected to generate deviance, Merton suggests the presence of a correlation between "pressures toward deviation" and "rate of deviance."

> But whatever the differential rates of deviant behavior in the several social strata, and we know from many sources that the official crime statistics uniformly showing higher rates in the lower strata are far from complete or reliable, *it appears from our analysis that the greater pressures toward deviation are exerted upon the lower strata.* . . . Of those located in the lower reaches of the social structure, the culture makes incompatible demands. On the one hand they are asked to orient their behavior toward the prospect of large wealth . . . and on the other, they are largely denied effective opportunities to do so institutionally. *The consequence of this structural inconsistency is a high rate of deviant behavior.*[29]

Because of the paucity and unreliability of existing criminal statistics, there is as yet no way of knowing whether or not Merton's hypothesis is correct. Until comparative studies of crime rates are available the hypothesized correlation cannot be tested.

From a theoretical perspective, however, questions may be raised about this correlation. Would we expect, to raise the principal query, the correlation to be fixed or to vary depending on the distribution of access to illegitimate means? The three possibilities are (1) that access is distributed uniformly throughout the class structure, (2) that access varies inversely with class position, and (3) that access varies directly with class position. Specification of these possibilities permits a more precise statement of the conditions under which crime rates would be expected to vary.

If access to illegitimate means is *uniformly distributed* throughout the class structure, then the proposed correlation would probably hold—higher rates of innovating behavior would be expected in the lower class than elsewhere. Lower-class persons apparently experience greater pressures toward deviance and are less restrained by internalized prohibitions from employing illegitimate means. Assuming uniform access to such means, it would therefore be reasonable to predict higher rates of innovating behavior in the lower social strata.

If access to illegitimate means varies *inversely* with class position, then the correlation would not only hold, but might even be strengthened. For pressures toward deviance, including socialization that does not altogether discourage the use of illegitimate means, would coincide with the availability of such means.

Finally, if access varies *directly* with class position, comparative rates of illegitimate activity become difficult to forecast. The higher the class position, the less the pressure to employ illegitimate means; furthermore, internalized prohibitions are apparently more effective in higher positions. If, at the same time, opportunities to use illegitimate methods are more abundant, then these factors would be in opposition. Until the precise effects of these several variables can be more adequately measured, rates cannot be safely forecast.

The concept of differentials in availability of illegitimate means may also help to clarify questions about varying crime rates among ethnic, age, religious, and sex groups, and other social divisions. This concept, then, can be systematically employed in the effort to further our understanding of the distribution of illegitimate behavior in the social structure.

Modes of Adaptation: The Case of Retreatism

By taking into account the conditions of access to legitimate *and* illegitimate means, we can further specify the circumstances under which various modes of deviant behavior arise. This may be illustrated by the case of retreatism.[30]

As defined by Merton, retreatist adaptations include such categories of behavior as alcoholism, drug addiction, and psychotic withdrawal. These adaptations entail "escape" from the frustrations of unfulfilled aspirations by withdrawal from conventional social relationships. The processes leading to retreatism are described by Merton as follows: "[Retreatism] arises from continued failure to near the goal by legitimate measures and from an inability to use the illegitimate route because of internalized prohibitions, *this process occurring while the supreme value of the success-goal has not yet been renounced.* The conflict is resolved by abandoning *both* precipitating elements, the goals and means. The escape is complete, the conflict is eliminated and the individual is asocialized."[31]

In this view, a crucial element encouraging retreatism is internalized constraint concerning the use of illegitimate means. But this element need not be present. Merton apparently assumed that such prohibitions are essential because, in their absence, the logic of his scheme would compel him to predict that innovating behavior would result. But the assumption that the individual uninhibited in the use of illegitimate means becomes an innovator presupposes that successful innovation is only a matter of motivation. Once the concept of differentials in access to illegitimate means is introduced, however, it becomes clear that retreatism is possible even in the absence of internalized prohibitions. For we may now ask how individuals respond when they fail in the use of *both* legitimate and illegitimate means. If illegitimate means are unavailable, if efforts at innovation fail, then retreatist adaptations may still be the consequence, and the "escape" mechanisms chosen by the defeated individual may perhaps be all the more deviant because of his "double failure."

This does not mean that retreatist adaptations cannot arise precisely as Merton suggests: namely, that the conversion from conformity to retreatism takes place in one step, without intervening adaptations. But this is only one route to retreatism. The conversion may at times entail intervening stages and intervening adaptations, particularly of an innovating type. This possibility helps to account for the fact that certain categories of individuals cited as retreatists —for example, hobos—often show extensive histories of arrests and convictions for various illegal acts. It also helps to explain retreatist adaptations among individuals who have not necessarily internalized strong restraints on the use of illegitimate means. In short, retreatist adaptations may arise with considerable frequency among those who are failures in both worlds, conventional and illegitimate alike.[32]

Future research on retreatist behavior might well examine the interval between conformity and retreatism. To what extent does the individual entertain the possibility of resorting to illegitimate means, and to what extent does he actually seek to mobilize such means? If the individual turns to innovating devices, the question of whether or not he becomes a retreatist may then depend upon the relative accessibility of illegitimate means. For although the frustrated conformist seeks a solution to status discontent by adopting such methods, there is the further problem of whether or not he possesses appropriate skills and has opportunities for their use. We suggest therefore that data be gathered on preliminary responses to status discontent—and on the individual's perceptions of the efficacy of employing illegitimate means, the content of his skills, and the objective situation of illegitimate opportunity available to him.

Respecification of the processes leading to retreatism may also help to resolve difficulties entailed in ascertaining rates of retreatism in different parts of the social structure. Although Merton does not indicate explicitly where this adaptation might be expected to arise, he specifies some of the social conditions which encourage high rates of retreatism. Thus the latter is apt to mark the behavior of downwardly mobile persons, who experience a sudden breakdown in established social relations, and such individuals as the retired, who have lost major social roles.[33]

The long-standing difficulties in forecasting differential rates of retreatism may perhaps be attributed to the assumption that retreatists have fully internalized values prohibiting the use of illegitimate means. That this prohibition especially characterizes socialization in the middle and upper classes probably calls for the prediction that retreatism occurs primarily in those classes—and that the hobohemias, "drug cultures," and the ranks of the alcoholics are populated primarily by individuals from the upper reaches of society. It would appear from various accounts of hobohemia and skid row, however, that many of these persons are the products of slum life, and, furthermore, that their behavior is not necessarily controlled by values which preclude resort to illegitimate means. But once it is recognized that retreatism may arise in response to limitations on both systems of means, the difficulty of locating this adaptation is lessened, if not resolved. Thus retreatist behavior may vary with the particular process by which it is generated. The process described by Merton may be somewhat more characteristic of higher positions in the social structure where rule-oriented socialization is typical, while in the lower strata retreatism may tend more often to be the consequence of unsuccessful attempts at innovation.

SUMMARY

This paper attempts to identify and to define the concept of differential opportunity structures. It has been suggested that this concept helps to extend the developing theory of social structure and anomie. Furthermore, by linking propositions regarding the accessibility of *both* legitimate and illegitimate opportunity structures, a basis is provided for consolidating various major traditions of sociological thought on nonconformity. The concept of differential systems of opportunity and of variations in access to them, it is hoped, will suggest new possibilities for research on the relationship between social structure and deviant behavior.

NOTES

1. This paper is based on research conducted in a penal setting. For a more detailed statement see Richard A. Cloward, *Social Control and Anomie: A Study of a Prison Community* (to be published by The Free Press).

2. See especially Émile Durkheim, *Suicide*, translated by J. A. Spaulding and George Simpson, Glencoe, Ill.: Free Press, 1951; and Robert K. Merton, *Social Theory and Social Structure*, Glencoe, Ill.: Free Press, 1957, Chapters 4 and 5.

3. See especially the following: Clifford R. Shaw, *The Jack-Roller*, Chicago: The University of Chicago Press, 1930; Clifford R. Shaw, *The Natural History of a Delinquent Career*, Chicago: The University of Chicago Press, 1941; Clifford R. Shaw et al., *Delinquency Areas*, Chicago: The University of Chicago Press, 1940; Clifford R. Shaw and Henry D. McKay, *Juvenile Delinquency and Urban Areas*, Chicago: The University of Chicago Press, 1942; Edwin H. Sutherland, editor, *The Professional Thief*, Chicago: The University of Chicago Press, 1937; Edwin H. Sutherland, *Principles of Criminology*, 4th edition, Philadelphia: Lippincott, 1947; Edwin H. Sutherland, *White Collar Crime*, New York: Dryden, 1949.

4. "Illegitimate means" are those proscribed by the mores. The concept therefore includes "illegal means" as a special case but is not coterminous with illegal behavior, which refers only to the violation of legal norms. In several parts of this paper, I refer to particular forms of deviant behavior which entail violation of the law and there use the more restricted term, "illegal means." But the more general concept of illegitimate means is needed to cover the wider gamut of deviant behavior and to relate the theories under review here to the evolving theory of "legitimacy" in sociology.

5. All of the excerpts in this section are from Durkheim, *op. cit.*, pp. 247–257.

6. For this excerpt and those which follow immediately, see Merton, *op. cit.*, pp. 131–194.

7. See, e.g., Seldon D. Bacon, "Social Settings Conducive to Alcoholism—A Sociological Approach to a Medical Problem," *Journal of the American Medical Association*, 16 (May, 1957), pp. 177–181; Robert F. Bales, "Cultural Differences in Rates of Alcoholism," *Quarterly Journal of Studies on Alcohol*, 16 (March, 1946), pp. 480–499; Jerome H. Skolnick, "A Study of the Relation of Ethnic Background to Arrests for Inebriety," *Quarterly Journal of Studies on Alcohol*, 15 (December, 1954), pp. 451–474.

8. See Isidor T. Thorner, "Ascetic Protestantism and Alcoholism," *Psychiatry*, 16 (May, 1953), pp. 167–176; and Nathan Glazer, "Why Jews Stay Sober," *Commentary*, 13 (February, 1952), pp. 181–186.

9. See Bales, *op. cit.*

10. Merton, *op. cit.,* p. 151.

11. For this excerpt and those which follow immediately, see Sutherland, *The Professional Thief,* pp. 211–213.

12. For this excerpt and those which follow immediately, see Albert Cohen, Alfred Lindesmith and Karl Schuessler, editors, *The Sutherland Papers,* Bloomington: Indiana University Press, 1956, pp. 31–35.

13. See especially *Delinquency Areas,* Chapter 16.

14. Shaw, *The Jack-Roller,* p. 54.

15. We are referring here, and throughout the paper, to stable criminal roles to which persons may orient themselves on a career basis, as in the case of racketeers, professional thieves, and the like. The point is that access to stable roles depends in the first instance upon the availability of learning structures. As Frank Tannenbaum says, "it must be insisted on that unless there were older criminals in the neighborhood who provided a moral judgment in favor of the delinquent and to whom the delinquents could look for commendation, the careers of the younger ones could not develop at all." *Crime and the Community,* New York: Ginn, 1938, p. 60.

16. Shaw, *The Natural History of a Delinquent Career,* p. 229.

17. Cohen, Lindesmith and Schuessler, *op. cit.,* p. 21.

18. It is interesting to note that the concept of differentials in access to *legitimate* means did not attain explicit recognition in Sutherland's work, nor in the work of many others in the "subculture" tradition. This attests to the independent development of the two traditions being discussed. Thus the ninth proposition in the differential association theory is stated as follows:

> (9) *Though criminal behavior is an expression of general needs and values, it is not explained by those general needs and values since noncriminal behavior is an expression of the same needs and values.* Thieves generally steal in order to secure money, but likewise honest laborers work in order to secure money. The attempts by many scholars to explain criminal behavior by general drives and values, such as the happiness principle, striving for social status, the money motive, or frustration, have been and must continue to be futile since they explain lawful behavior as completely as they explain criminal behavior.

Of course, it is perfectly true that "striving for status," the "money motive" and similar modes of socially approved goal-oriented behavior do not as such account for both deviant and conformist behavior. But if goal-oriented behavior occurs under conditions of socially structured obstacles to fulfillment by legitimate means, the resulting pressures might then lead to deviance. In other words,

Sutherland appears to assume that the distribution of access to success-goals by legitimate means is uniform rather than variable, irrespective of location in the social structure. See his *Principles of Criminology*, 4th edition, pp. 7–8.

19. William F. Whyte, *Street Corner Society* (original edition, 1943). Chicago: The University of Chicago Press, 1955, p. viii.

20. *Ibid.*, p. xviii.

21. *American Sociological Review*, 16 (October, 1951), pp. 657–658, which includes the excerpts which follow immediately.

22. The excellent work by Albert K. Cohen has been omitted from this discussion because it is dealt with in a second article, "Types of Delinquent Subcultures," prepared jointly with Lloyd E. Ohlin (mimeographed, December, 1958, New York School of Social Work, Columbia University). It may be noted that although Cohen does not explicitly affirm continuity with either the Durkheim-Merton or the Shaw-McKay-Sutherland traditions, we believe that he clearly belongs in the former. He does not deal with what appears to be the essence of the Shaw-McKay-Sutherland tradition, namely, the crucial social functions performed by the integration of offenders of differing age-levels and the integration of adult carriers of criminal and conventional values. Rather, he is concerned primarily with the way in which discrepancies between status aspirations and possibilities for achievement generate pressures for delinquent behavior. The latter notion is a central feature in the anomie tradition.

23. Daniel Bell, "Crime as an American Way of Life," *The Antioch Review* (Summer, 1953), pp. 131–154.

24. For a discussion of kinship relationships among top racketeers, see Stanley Frank, "The Rap Gangsters Fear Most," *The Saturday Evening Post* (August 9, 1958), pp. 26 ff. This article is based on a review of the files of the United States Immigration and Naturalization Service.

25. See David W. Maurer, *Whiz Mob: A Correlation of the Technical Argot of Pickpockets with Their Behavior Pattern*, Publication of the American Dialect Society, No. 24, 1955.

26. For a discussion of racial, nationality, and sex differentials governing access to a stable criminal role, see *ibid.*, Chapter 6.

27. Training in conventional, specialized occupational skills is often a prerequisite for the commission of white collar crimes, since the individual must have these skills in hand before he can secure a position entailing "trust." As Cressey says, "it may be observed that persons trained to carry on the routine duties of a position of trust have at the same time been trained in whatever skills are necessary for the violation of that position, and the technical skill necessary to holding the position in the first place." (Donald R. Cressey, *Other People's Money*, Glencoe, Ill.: Free Press, 1953, pp. 81–82.) Thus skills required in certain crimes need not be learned in association

with criminals; they can be acquired through conventional learning.

28. Merton, *op. cit.*, p. 132.

29. *Ibid.*, pp. 144–145.

30. Retreatist behavior is but one of many types of deviant adaptations which might be re-analyzed in terms of this consolidated theoretical approach. In subsequent papers, being prepared jointly with Lloyd E. Ohlin, other cases of deviant behavior—e.g., collective disturbances in prisons and subcultural adaptations among juvenile delinquents—will be examined. In this connection, see footnote 22.

31. Merton, *op. cit.*, pp. 153–154.

32. The processes of "double failure" being specified here may be of value in re-analyzing the correlation between alcoholism and petty crime. Investigation of the *careers* of petty criminals who are alcoholic may reveal that after being actively oriented toward stable criminal careers they then lost out in the competitive struggle. See, e.g., Irwin Deutscher, "The Petty Offender: A Sociological Alien," *The Journal of Criminal Law, Criminology and Police Science*, 44 (January–February, 1954), pp. 592–595; Albert D. Ullman *et al.*, "Some Social Characteristics of Misdemeanants," *The Journal of Criminal Law, Criminology and Police Science*, 48 (May–June, 1957), pp. 44–53.

33. Merton, *op. cit.*, pp. 188–189.

13   How Community Mental Health Stamped Out the Riots (1968–78)

KENNETH KENISTON

One day, after I gave a lecture in a course on social and community psychiatry, a student asked me whether I thought community mental-health workers would eventually be asked to assume policing functions. I assured him that I thought this very unlikely, and thought no more about it.

That night I had the following dream: I was sitting on the platform of a large auditorium. In the audience were thousands of men and women, some in business clothes, others in peculiar blue and white uniforms that seemed a cross between medical and military

Published by permission of Trans-action, Inc. and the author from Trans-action, Vol. 5, No. 8. Copyright © 1968 by Trans-action Inc.

garb. I glanced at the others on the platform: Many wore military uniforms. Especially prominent was a tall, distinguished, lantern-jawed general, whose chest was covered with battle ribbons and on whose arm was a blue and white band.

The lights dimmed; I was pushed to my feet and toward the podium. Before me on the lectern was a neatly-typed manuscript. Not knowing what else to do, I found myself beginning to read from it. . . .

Ladies and Gentlemen: It is a pleasure to open this Eighth Annual Meeting of the Community Mental Health Organization, and to welcome our distinguished guests: the recently-appointed Secretary for International Mental Health, General Westmoreland [loud applause], and the Secretary for Internal Mental Health, General Walt [applause].

This year marks the tenth anniversary of the report of the First National Advisory Commission on Civil Disorders. And this meeting of representatives of 3483 Community Mental Health Centers, 247 Remote Therapy Centers, and 45 Mobile Treatment Teams may provide a fitting occasion for us to review the strides we have made in the past decade, and to contemplate the greater tasks that lie before us. For it was in the past decade, after all, that the Community Mental Health movement proved its ability to deal with the problem of urban violence, and it is in the next decade that the same approaches must be adapted to the other urgent mental-health problems of our society and the world.

In my remarks here, I will begin with a review of the progress of the past decade. Arbitrarily, I will divide the years since 1968 into three stages: the phase of preparation; the phase of total mobilization; and the mop-up phase that we are now concluding.

In retrospect, the years from 1968 to 1970 can be seen as the time of preparation for the massive interventions that have since been made. On the one hand, the nation was faced with mounting urban unrest, especially among disadvantaged sectors of the inner city, unrest that culminated in the riots of 1969 and 1970, in which property damage of more than 20 billion dollars was wrought, and in which more than 5000 individuals (including 27 policemen, National Guardsmen, and firemen) were killed. Yet in retrospect, the seeds of "Operation Inner City" were being developed even during this period. As early as 1969, the Cannon Report—a joint product of Community Mental Health workers and responsible leaders of the white and black communities—suggested that (1) the propensity to violence was but a symptom of underlying social and psychological pathology; (2) massive federal efforts must be made to identify the individual and societal dysfunctions that produce indiscriminate protest, and (3) more effective methods must be developed for treating the personal and group disorganization that produces unrest.

From 1968 to 1970, a series of research studies and demonstration projects developed the basic concepts that were implemented in later years. Indeed, without this prior theoretical work by interdisciplinary teams of community psychiatrists, sociologists, social workers, and police officials, Operation Inner City would never have been possible. I need recall only a few of the major contributions: the concept of "aggressive alienation," used to characterize the psycho-social disturbance of a large percentage of inner-city dwellers; McFarland's seminal work on urban disorganization, personal pathology, and aggressive demonstrations; the development, on a pilot basis, of new treatment systems like the "total saturation approach," based upon the concept of "antidotal (total) therapy"; and the recognition of the importance of the "reacculturation experience" in treating those whose personal pathology took the form of violence-proneness. Equally basic theoretical contributions were made by those who began to investigate the relationship between aggressiveness, alienation, and anti-societal behavior in other disturbed sections of the population, such as disacculturated intellectuals and students.

After the riots of 1969, rising public indignation over the senseless slaughter of thousands of Americans and the wanton destruction of property led President Humphrey to create the Third Presidential Task Force on Civil Disorders. After six months of almost continuous study, Task Force chairman Ronald Reagan recommended that massive federal intervention, via the Community Mental Health Centers, be the major instrument in action against violence. Portions of this report still bear quoting: "The experience of the past five years has shown that punitive and repressive intervention aggravates rather than ameliorates the violence of the inner city. It is now amply clear that urban violence is more than sheer criminality. The time has come for America to heed the findings of a generation of research: *inner-city violence is a product of profound personal and social pathology. It requires treatment rather than punishment, rehabilitation rather than imprisonment.*"

The report went on: "The Community Mental Health movement provides the best available weapon in the struggle against com-

munity sickness in urban America. The existence of 967 Community Mental Health Centers (largely located in communities with high urban density), the concentration of professional and para-professional mental-health workers in these institutions, and their close contact with the mood and hopes of their inner-city catchment areas all indicate that community mental health should be the first line of attack on urban unrest."

In the next months, an incensed Congress, backed by an outraged nation, passed the first of the series of major bills that led to the creation of Operation Inner City, under the joint auspices of the Department of Health, Education, and Welfare and what was then still called the Department of Defense. Despite the heavy drains on the national economy made by American involvement in Ecuador, Eastern Nigeria, and Pakistan, five billion dollars were appropriated the first year, with steadily increasing amounts thereafter.

As the concept of urban pathology gained acceptance, police officials referred those detained during urban riots not to jails but to local Community Mental Health Centers. Viewing urban violence as a psycho-social crisis made possible the application of concepts of "crisis therapy" to the violence-ridden inner-city dweller. As predicted, early researchers found very high levels of psychopathology in those referred for treatment, especially in the form of aggravated aggressive-alienation syndrome.

But it was obviously not enough to treat violence only in its acute phase. Pre-critical intervention and preventive rehabilitation were also necessary. So city law-enforcement officials and mental-health workers began cooperating in efforts to identify those people whose behavior, group-membership patterns, and utterances gave evidence of the prodrome (early symptoms) of aggressive alienation. New statutes passed by Congress in 1971 empowered mental-health teams and local authorities to require therapy of those identified as prodromally violent. In defending this bill in Congress against the congressional group that opposed it on civil-libertarian grounds, Senator Murphy of California noted the widespread acceptance of the principle of compulsory inoculation, mandatory treatment for narcotics addicts, and hospitalization of the psychotic. "Urban violence," he noted, "is no different from any other illness: The welfare of those afflicted requires that the public accept responsibility for their prompt and effective treatment."

Mental-health workers, with legal power to institute therapy, and in collaboration with responsible political and law-enforcement authorities, were finally able to implement the Total Saturation Approach in the years from 1972 to the present. Employing local citizens as "pathology detectors," Community Mental Health teams made massive efforts to detect all groups and individuals with prodromes of violence, or a predisposition to advocate violence. In many communities, the incidence of prepathological conditions was almost perfectly correlated with racial origin; hence, massive resources were funneled into these communities in particular to immediately detect and help those afflicted.

At this point, it became evident that programs attempting to treat inner-city patients still remaining in the same disorganized social environment that had originally contributed to their pathology were not entirely successful. It was only in 1971, with Rutherford, Cohen, and Robinson's now classic study, "Relapse Rates in Seven Saturation Projects: a Multi-Variate Analysis," that it was finally realized that short-term, total-push therapies were not effective in the long run. As the authors pointed out, "The re-entry of the cured patient into the pathogenic disacculturating community clearly reverses *all* the therapeutic gains of the inpatient phase."

Armed with the Rutherford study, Congress in 1972 passed a third legislative landmark, the Remote Therapy Center Act. Congress—recognizing that prolonged reacculturative experience in a psychologically healthy community (antidotal therapy) was often necessary for the permanent recompensation of deep-rooted personality disorders—authorized the construction of 247 centers, largely in the Rocky Mountain Region, each with a capacity of 1000 patients. The old Department of Defense (now the Department of International Mental Health) cooperated by making available the sites used in World War II for the relocation of Japanese-Americans. On these salubrious sites, the network of Remote Treatment Centers has now been constructed. Although the stringent security arrangements necessary in such centers have been criticized, the retreats now constitute one of our most effective attacks upon the problem of urban mental illness.

The gradual reduction in urban violence, starting in 1973, cannot be attributed to any single factor. But perhaps one idea played the decisive role. During this period mental-health workers began to realize that earlier approaches, which attempted to ameliorate the objective, physical, or legal conditions under which inner-city dwellers lived, were not only superficial, but were themselves a reflection of serious psychopathology. Reilly, Bernitsky, and O'Leary's now classic study of ex-patients of the retreats established the correlation between a patient's relapse into violence and his preoccupation with what the investigators termed "objectivist" issues: housing, sanitation, legal rights, jobs, education, medical care, and so on.

Two generations ago Freud taught us that what matters most is not objective reality, but the way it is interpreted by the individual. Freud's insight has finally been perceived in its true light—as an attitude essential for healthy functioning. The fact that previous programs of civil rights, slum clearance, legal reforms, and so on, succeeded only in aggravating violence now became fully understandable. Not only did these programs fail to take account of the importance of basic attitudes and values in determining human behavior—thus treating symptoms rather than underlying psychological problems—but, by encouraging objectivism, they directly *undermined* the mental health of those exposed to these programs. Today's mental-health workers recognize objectivism as a prime symptom of individual and community dysfunction, and move swiftly and effectively to institute therapy.

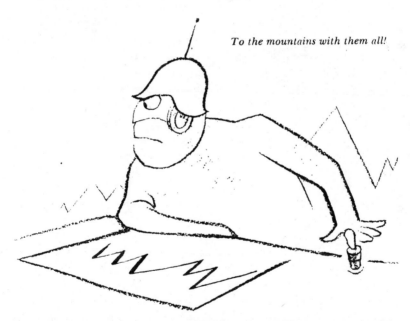

To the mountains with them all!

The final step in the development of a community mental-health approach to violence came with the development of the Mobile Treatment ("Motreat") Team. In 1972 the Community Mental Health authorities set up a series of 45 Motreat Teams, organized on a regional basis and consisting of between 500 and 1000 carefully selected and trained Community Mental Health workers. These heroic groups, wearing their now familiar blue and white garb, were ready on a standby basis to move into areas where violence threatened. Given high mobility by the use of armed helicopters,

The Mobile Treatment Team

"Of one thing there can be no doubt: The Community Mental Health movement will play a leading role in our progress toward a mentally healthy society at the head of a mentally healthy world."

Total mental health

trained in crisis intervention and emergency treatment, and skilled in the use of modern psychopharmacological sprays and gases, the Motreat Teams have now proved their effectiveness. On numerous occasions during the past years, they have been able to calm an agitated population, to pinpoint the antisocial-violence leaders and refer them for therapy, and thus to lay the basis for society's prompt return to healthy functioning. The architects of the Mobile Treatment Team found that many of their most important insights were obtained from professionals in the field of law enforcement and national defense—more evidence of the importance of interdisciplinary cooperation.

As you all know, the past four years have been years of diminishing urban violence, years when the Community Mental Health movement has received growing acclaim for its success in dealing with social and individual pathology, years when the early criticism of the Community Mental Health movement by the "liberal coalition" in Congress has diminished, largely because of the non-reelection of the members of that coalition. Today, the Community Mental Health movement has the virtually undivided support of the nation,

New target groups will include students . . .

regardless of political partisanship. The original federal target of 2800 Community Mental Health Centers has been increased to more than 5000; the principles of Community Mental Health have been extended from the limited "catchment area" concept to the more relevant concept of "target groups" and beyond; and the Community Mental Health movement faces enormous new challenges.

But before considering the challenges that lie ahead, let us review what we have learned theoretically during the past decade.

Doubtless the most important insight was the awareness that *violence and antisocial behavior are deeply rooted in individual and social pathology,* and must be treated as such. We have at last been able to apply the insights of writers, historians, sociologists, and psychologists of the 1950s and 1960s to a new understanding of black character. The black American—blighted by the deep scars and legacies of his history, demoralized by what Stanley Elkins described as the concentration-camp conditions of slavery, devitalized by the primitive, impulse ridden, and fatherless black families so brilliantly described by Daniel Moynihan—is the helpless victim of a series of deep deprivations that almost inevitably lead to intra-psychic and societal pathology. Moreover, we have begun to understand the communicational networks and group-pathological processes that spread alienation and violence from individual to individual, and that make the adolescent especially prone to succumb to the aggressive-alienation syndrome. To be sure, this view was contradicted by the report that many of the advocates of violence—the leaders of the now outlawed black-power group and its precursors, S.N.C.C. and C.O.R.E.—came from relatively nondeprived backgrounds. But later researchers have shown that the virus of aggressive alienation is communicated even within apparently intact families. As Rosenbaum and Murphy put it in a recent review paper, "We have learned that social pathology is no less infectious than the black plague."

Another major theoretical contribution has come from our *redefinition of the concept of community.* As the first Community Mental Health Centers were set up, "community" was defined as a geographically limited catchment area often heterogeneous in social class, ethnicity, and race. But the events of the last decade have made it amply clear that we cannot conceive of the community so narrowly. The artificial boundaries of the catchment area do not prevent the transmission of social pathology across these boundaries; indeed, efforts to prevent personal mobility and communication between catchment areas proved difficult to implement without an anxiety-provoking degree of coercion. It became clear that cutting across catchment areas were certain pathogenic "target groups" in which the bacillus of social pathology was most infectious. Recognition of the target-group concept of community was the theoretical basis for much recent legislation. Rarely have the findings of the behavioral sciences been translated so promptly into enlightened legislation [applause].

This recognition of the too-narrow definition of "community" led to the creation of the Remote Treatment Centers. True, removing the mentally ill from the violence-prone target groups has not solved the problem completely. But the creation of total therapeutic communities in distant parts of the country has had a salubrious and calming effect on the mental health of the groups the patients came from.

It has also become clear that Community Mental Health efforts aimed solely at the disadvantaged are, by their very nature, limited in effectiveness. The suppression of pathology in one group may paradoxically be related to its sudden emergence in others. Stated differently, pathology moves through the entire community, although it tends to be concentrated during any given period in certain target

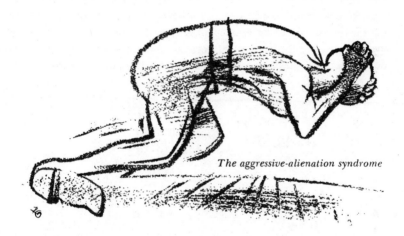

The aggressive-alienation syndrome

groups. The international events of the past decade, the appearance of comparable psychopathology in Ecuador, Eastern Nigeria, Pakistan, Thailand, and a variety of other countries, raise the question of whether it is possible to have mental health in one country alone.

Another crucial theoretical advance has been the concept of *total therapy*. Patients and groups must be treated *before* symptoms become acute, because the infectiousness of social pathology increases during the acute phase. What has been termed the "pathology multiplier effect" has been widely recognized: This means that it is essential to prevent the formation of pathologically-interacting groups, especially when organized around societally disruptive objectivist issues like black power, civil rights, or improvement in living conditions. Furthermore, crisis intervention must be supplemented by *prolonged aftercare*, particularly for those whose involvement in violence has been most intense. Of the many post-rehabilitation followup methods attempted, two of the most effective have been the incorporation of rehabilitated patients into mental-health teams working in localities other than their own, and the new programs of aftercare involving the continuing rehabilitation of discharged patients in such challenging areas as Ecuador, Eastern Nigeria, and Pakistan. You are all familiar with the many glowing tributes to this aftercare program recently released by International Mental Health Secretary Westmoreland [applause].

The past decade has also demonstrated beyond doubt the importance of *inter-agency and inter-disciplinary collaboration*. The effectiveness of such collaboration has shown how unfounded were the concerns of the First Joint Commission on Mental Health over inadequate manpower. In large measure because of better and better relationships between mental-health workers, law-enforcement agencies, local civic authorities, the Department of International Mental Health, the National Guard, the Air Force, and other

Police can be replaced with mental-health workers

community agencies, radically new patterns of recruitment into the mental-health professions have been established. Indeed, in many communities effective mental-health efforts have permitted a major reduction in the size of law-enforcement authorities, and the training of a whole new group of para-professionals and sub-professionals who, a decade ago, would have entered law-enforcement agencies.

But lest we become complacent about our accomplishments, let me remind you of the many theoretical problems, difficulties, and challenges that lie before us.

Our program has not been without its critics and detractors, and there is much to be learned from them. To be sure, many of the early criticisms of our work can now be understood either as the result of inadequate understanding of the behavioral sciences, or as symptoms of the objectivist social-pathological process itself. In the years before the liberal coalition became moribund, many so-called civil-libertarian critics persisted in ignoring the humanitarian aspects of our program, focusing instead upon the 19th-century concept of civil rights. The political ineffectuality of this group, coupled with the speed with which many of its leaders have recently been reacculturated, suggests the limitations of this viewpoint.

But even within our own midst we have had critics and detractors. We are all familiar with the unhappy story of the American Psychoanalytic Association, which continued its criticisms of our programs until its compulsory incorporation last year into the Community Mental Health Organization. What we must learn from these critics is how easy it is for even the most apparently dedicated mental-health workers to lose sight of broader societal goals, neglecting the population and the societal matrix in a misguided attachment to outmoded concepts of individuality, "reality factors," and "insight therapy."

In my remarks so far, I have emphasized our theoretical and practical progress. But those of us who were involved in the Community Mental Health movement from its beginnings in the early 1960s must remind others that almost all of the major concepts that underlie the progress of the past decade were already in existence in 1968. Even a decade ago, the most advanced workers in the field of community health *knew* that crisis intervention was not enough, and were developing plans for preventive intervention and extensive aftercare. Furthermore, many of the most important concepts in this field derived from researches done by Freud, Anna

Freud, Moynihan, Caplan, Gruenberg, Keniston, and others. Even the concept of aggressive alienation itself is based on earlier research on alienation done, not in the inner city, but amongst talented college students. Thus, our enthusiasm for the progress of the past decade must be tempered with humility and a sense of indebtedness to those in the pre-Community Mental Health era.

Furthermore, humility is called for because of the many questions whose answers have evaded our search. I will cite but one of the most important: the problem of therapeutic failure.

We have much to learn from our failures, perhaps more than from our numerous successes. With some patients, even repeated rehabilitation and maintenance on high doses of long-acting tranquilizers have failed to produce a complete return to pro-social functioning. And the uncooperativeness of the government of Canada has made it extremely difficult to reach those unsuccessfully treated patients who have evaded our detection networks and fled north. Since the Canadian government is unwilling to extradite the large numbers of mentally ill who have flocked to Canadian urban centers, we must support the recent proposal of Secretary Westmoreland that we persuade foreign governments to institute their own programs of Community Mental Health, with the close collaboration and support of American advisors. Indeed, the currently strained relations between Canada and the United States raise a series of far more profound questions, to which I will return in a moment.

Rather than list the many other important research issues that confront us, let me turn to our greatest challenge—the definition of new target groups, and the need to broaden still further the concept of community.

In our focus upon the more visible problems of urban violence, we have neglected other target groups of even greater pathological potential. These new target groups are not always easy to define precisely; but there is a clear consensus that high priority on the list of future targets must be given to college students, to intellectuals with no firm ties to the community, and to disacculturated members of certain ethnico-religious groups who retain close ties with non-American communities.

The passage last year of the College Developmental Act enables us at last to apply to the college-age group the techniques so successfully used in the inner city. This act will enable the setting up of college mental-health centers with a strong community approach.

One of the particular strengths of this law should be underlined here: It enables us to treat not only the college student himself, but his professors and mentors, from whom—as recent studies have shown—much of his antisocial acculturation springs.

In our continuing work with new target groups, however, we must not lose sight of certain basic principles. For one, the target-group approach is by its very nature limited. Our practical resources are still so small that we must single out only certain target groups for special interventions. But this should not obscure our long-range goal: nothing less than a society in which all men and women are guaranteed mental health by simple virtue of their citizenship. Thus, the entire community must be our target; we must insist upon *total mental health* from the womb to the grave [applause].

Yet our most serious challenge lies not in America, but outside of our national boundaries. For it has become obvious that the concept of "mental health in one nation" is not tenable. We are surrounded by a world in which the concepts of Community Mental Health have had regrettably little impact. Recent studies conducted by the Department of International Mental Health in Ecuador, Eastern Nigeria, and Thailand have shown an incidence of individual and collective psychopathology even higher than that found in American cities ten years ago. The link between objectivism and violence, first established in America, has been repeatedly shown to exist in other cultures as well. Even young Americans serving abroad with the Overseas Mental Health Corps have been exposed to objectivist influences in these countries that have made their renewed rehabilitation necessary, whether on the battlefield or in the special rehabilitation centers back home.

But it should not be thought that the primary argument against mental health in only one country is mere expediency. Our responsibilities as the most powerful and mentally healthy nation in the world are of a therapeutic nature. Were it simply a matter of expediency, the closing of the Canadian and Mexican borders has shown that it is possible to limit the exodus of non-reacculturated Americans to the merest trickle. Nor would sheer expediency alone justify our involvement, at a heavy price in materials and men, in the mental-health struggles of Ecuador, Eastern Nigeria, and Thailand. It is not expediency but our therapeutic commitment to the mental health of our fellow men—regardless of race, color, nationality, and creed—that argues against the concept of mental health in only one nation.

Thus, our greatest challenge is the struggle to create a mentally healthy world. Happy historical accident has given American society a technology and an understanding of human behavior sufficiently advanced to bring about the profound revolution in human behavior that men from Plato's time onward have dreamed of. The lessons of Operation Inner City will continue to be of the utmost importance: the concepts of total saturation, remote therapy, and mandatory treatment; the realization of the close link between objectivism and psychopathology; the need for the closest interdisciplinary cooperation. Already, plans evolved by the Department of International Mental Health and this Community Mental Health Organization call for the international deployment of Mobile Treatment Teams and Overseas Mental Health Corps volunteers, some operating with the assistance of local governments, others courageously risking their lives in communities where pathology has infiltrated even the highest levels of governmental authority. In the years to come, the challenges will be great, the price will be large, and the discouragements will be many. But of one thing there can be no doubt: The Community Mental Health movement will play a leading role in our progress toward a mentally healthy society at the head of a mentally healthy world [applause]. . . .

[loud applause]

Osborn

I stepped back from the podium and tripped. Many hands reached to pull me to my feet. I cried out and awoke to find my wife shaking me. "You've been dreaming and mumbling in your sleep for hours," she said, "and you're feverish." The thermometer revealed a temperature of 103 degrees. I was in bed for several days with a rather severe virus—which, doubtless, explains my dream.

14   Desegregation and Integration

MILTON M. GORDON

DESEGREGATION, INTEGRATION, AND THE ROLE OF GOVERNMENT

Our sociological focus on the phenomenon of ethnic communality in the United States suggests certain important implications for the current controversies surrounding the attempts to eliminate racial discrimination by law—a series of events launched into full motion by the Supreme Court school desegregation decision of 1954.

The basic theoretical distinction which it is necessary to make in the types of processes involved in these turbulent happenings has been well delineated by Kenneth Clark, who points to the differences between *desegregation* and *integration*.[1] Desegregation refers to the elimination of racial criteria in the operation of public or quasi-public facilities, services, and institutions, which the individual is entitled to as a functioning citizen of the local or national community, equal in legal status to all other citizens. It is the achievement in full of what is usually referred to as his "civil rights." Integration, however, embraces the idea of the removal of prejudice as well as civic discrimination and therefore refers to much more. In Clark's words, "Integration, as a subjective and individual process, involves attitudinal changes and the removal of fears, hatreds, suspicions, stereotypes, and superstitions. Integration involves problems of personal choice, personal readiness, and personal stability. Its achievement necessarily requires a longer period of time. It cannot come about 'overnight.' It requires education and deals poignantly with the problems of changing men's hearts and minds."[2] To which we would add that, in social structural terms, integration presupposes the elimination of hard and fast barriers in the primary group relations and communal life of the various ethnic groups of the nation. It involves easy and fluid mixture of people of diverse racial, religious, and nationality backgrounds in social cliques, families (i.e., intermarriage), private organizations, and intimate friendships. From this basic distinction between desegregation and integration, and the relation of this distinction to both sociological realities and the American democratic value system, a number of conclusions follow:

1. Desegregation—the process of eliminating racial discrimination in the operation of public and quasi-public institutional facilities—will not lead *immediately* or, in the intermediate future, *necessarily* to integration in the sense of the dissolution of ethnic communality and the formation of large-scale primary group relationships across racial and religious lines. The tendency toward ethnic communality, as we have demonstrated, is a powerful force in American life and is supported, once the ethnic subsociety is formed, by the principles of psychological inertia, comfortable social immersion, and vested interests. Even if all southern public schools and other public facilities were to be immediately desegregated, there is no reason to suppose that the Negro and the white subcommunities would merge into one another or that the traditional barriers to intimate friendships and relationships between Negroes and whites would at once come tumbling down. Certainly there is no basis for the belief that Negroes and whites, respectively encapsulated in their own subcommunity and subculture, would rush to marry each other. This sociological insight, it will be noted, is offered here in a spirit of scientific neutrality and not as a conclusion which is either good or bad from the point of view of some particular value system. I have already pointed out that, on the basis of traditional American democratic values, Negroes and whites should have the right to make close friendships and to marry across racial lines at their pleasure. But sociological realities do not indicate that these phenomena would be likely to take place in significant volume in the immediate future, even if all public and institutional discrimination were to be eliminated. If die-hard segregationists who now bitterly oppose the granting of full civic equality to Negroes could be made to understand this fact, it is possible that the debate over desegregation could be carried out in a less emotional and a more rational climate of discussion and action. It is necessary to repeat that this point is not a concession to any *right* of segregationists to bar interracial primary group relationships; it is a statement of sociological probabilities which, if correctly understood, might clear the way for more rapid and effective action in such areas as public education, public transportation, public recreation, jobs, housing, and the operation of ordinary institutional facilities which belong to all Americans on an equal basis.

the ordinary processes of communality, whether intra-ethnic or interethnic, are beyond the scope of governmental interference or concern.

c. It is neither the responsibility nor the prerogative of the government to use racial criteria positively in order to impose desegregation upon public facilities in an institutional area where such segregation is not a function of racial discrimination directly but results from discrimination operating in another institutional area, or from other causes. If institutional area A is *de facto* segregated not because of the direct use of racial criteria but because institutional area B is segregated and because there is a relationship between institutional areas A and B, then the place to fight discrimination is not A but B. The obvious case in point is the operation of the public school system. The attempt by well-meaning "race liberals" in a number of northern communities to desegregate public schools by overturning the principle of neighborhood assignment—that is, to positively promote Negro-white intermixture by means of racial assignment across neighborhood lines—is, in my opinion, misguided. It is misguided because it does exactly what is in principle wrong, regardless of how laudable the goal. It puts the government in the business of using race as a criterion for operating one of its facilities. This is precisely what the government should not be doing, either negatively or positively. The genius of the American political tradition, in its best sense, in relation to race is that it dictates that racial criteria are *not* legitimate in the operation of governmental facilities and should be rigorously eschewed. To bring racial criteria in by the front door, so to speak, even before throwing them out the back, represents, in my opinion, no real gain for the body politic and has potentially dangerous implications for the future. If racial criteria are legitimate criteria for government consideration (which I firmly argue they are not), then the way is left open for many ominous disputes as to the merits of any particular racial clause in governmental operations.

It should be understood that I am making no specific plea here for the particular merits of the principle of neighborhood assignment to public schools. This is a matter which the educationists can debate among themselves. Furthermore, where inferior facilities in a school in a predominantly Negro area exist, or Negroes or members of any ethnic group are not appointed to teaching positions on the basis of individual qualifications, then we are in the presence of legitimate cases of racial discrimination which call for effective remedy.[4] My basic point, however, is that if *de facto* segregation of public schools in many northern cities exists because of segregation in housing (which, of course, it does), the place to fight the battle of civil rights is housing, not the public school system, and the way to fight it is to eliminate racial criteria from the routes of access to housing space, not to inject them into the operation of the educational system.

d. It is unwise and unjustifiable for the government to create programs labeled and reserved for the benefit of any special racial group, or to set up racial quotas in any area of activity such as employment, as is currently demanded by some civil rights proponents. It is undeniable that the burden of unemployment bears most heavily at present on Negroes, as a result of the cumulation of past discriminatory events. However, there are white, Indian, and Oriental unemployed workers who need aid, also, and any government program designed to retrain or upgrade the job skills of occupationally disadvantaged Americans should include them as well. In other words, it should be set up as an all-inclusive "functional" rather than an exclusive racial program. It goes without saying that job hiring and promotion at all levels should be made on the basis of individual merit, not racial quotas, however "benignly" the latter may be motivated. Present wrongs do not solve the problems created by past injustices and only assure that the underlying social evil will further plague the future. We do not want "see-saw discrimination" in American life; we want the dismantling of the discriminatory apparatus.

In sum, the proper role of government is to deal equitably with all persons under its jurisdiction without taking into consideration their racial background for any purpose.

DESEGREGATION, INTEGRATION, AND PRIVATE INSTITUTIONS

The distinction between the processes of desegregation and integration is not nearly so vital for assessing the role of private institutions and organizations in racial and ethnic matters. For one thing, in many types of private social institutions—for instance, fraternities and social clubs—desegregation automatically implies integration because of the kind of social relationship implicit in the operation of the institution. In other private institutions of larger scope, as, for instance, the private university, college, or academy, desegregation may or may not lead to integration depending upon particular factors associated with the life of the institution such as size and the presence or absence of segregated or self-segregated subgroups. Moreover, the arguments surrounding the choices of segregation, self-segregation, or desegregation are more varied, more complex, and more conflicting than in the case of government. However, several insights and guide-lines to action are suggested by the direction and scope of our previous analysis:

1. Some types of private organizations are those for whose goals and operation ethnic background is functional and centrally relevant. Quite obviously, a Methodist mission society, a Catholic sodality, a Jewish Temple sisterhood, or a club instituted to insure social welfare benefits for Polish immigrants and their descendants cannot reasonably be expected to throw open its membership to persons of other faiths or nationalities, as the case may be. Here one can confidently assert that there is no discrimination but simply a functionally relevant definition of membership.

2. Private organizations and institutions which serve a more general purpose, while they may be, under some circumstances, technically free to restrict membership on an ethnic basis, must face a series of crucial queries. Do they receive any assistance from the public treasury either in the form of grants or exemption from the payment of taxes? Can they justify an exclusionary policy on the basis of major functional relevance to the goals of the organization? Do they claim to operate under the general principles of American democracy, Hebraic-Christian brotherhood, and fair play? Do they perform a quasi-public function such as providing general education? If, in many cases, the answers to these questions should suggest the inappropriateness of an exclusionary policy, then the way is certainly left open for efforts to institute a policy which is nondiscriminatory. If such efforts by concerned members make the segregationists in the organization unhappy, it must be pointed out that initiating change in the policy of a voluntary organization at the will of a majority of its members is a thoroughly democratic procedure. Thus the ethnic practices of private organizations can frequently be settled by the dynamics of policy-making in a democratic setting where traditional procedures are subject to current examination in a changing society.

THE BUILT-IN TENSION BETWEEN THE GOALS OF ETHNIC COMMUNALITY AND DESEGREGATION

Earlier in this chapter we stated that desegregation in public and quasi-public facilities was unlikely to lead to the rapid breakdown of barriers between the primary group communal life of the various ethnic groups in America, and that the fears in this area of the segregationists, however unworthy, were thus unfounded. Here we examine a point which may appear at first to repudiate the above conclusion, but which, in fact, does not, but only qualifies it.

Desegregation—or, put positively, the achievement in full of civil rights for all groups—creates situations on the job, in the neighborhood, in the school, and in the civic arena, which place persons of different ethnic background into secondary, frequently equal-status, contacts with each other. These secondary contacts will not necessarily lead to primary group relationships, such as clique friendships, common membership in small organizations, dating, and intermarriage, and in the immediate or intermediate future will probably not seriously disturb the basic outlines of ethnic communality which have been shown to exist in America. However, over a sufficiently extended period of time, these new secondary group relationships between people of diverse ethnic backgrounds will presumably lead to an increase in warm, personal friendships across ethnic lines, a broadening of cultural perspective, an appreciation of diverse values, and in some degree a rise in the rate of interethnic marriage. All of these last-named developments run counter to the sociological requirements, whether realized or admitted, of ethnic closure and ethnic communality. Here, then, is another major area of social reality where the advocates of cultural pluralism (and, by implication, structural pluralism) cannot eat their cake and have it, too. There are built-in tensions between the simultaneously desired goals of ethnic communality and full civic equality, and these tensions create for the cultural pluralists a poignant dilemma. The dilemma is particularly acute for the two large minority religious groups—the Jews and the Catholics—who do not wish to see their young people "lost" to the numerically and culturally dominant Protestant subsociety or to the community of intellectuals and yet who ardently support the fight to secure full civic equality for all persons in American society. The racial groups approach the problem somewhat differently: the Negroes, apart from the new crop of "black nationalists," have never been ideologically committed to racial communality, however much they have been forced to create it; however, those whites who desire the full complement of civil rights for all, but who are reluctant to support the idea of racial intermarriage, must wrestle with the possibility that the rate of racial intermarriage will eventually increase under conditions of full equality. The nationality groups which still hope for subcultural survival are fighting such a rear-guard and eventually futile action that the dilemma for them has less realistic overtones.

There is, I believe, no clear course of action which neatly resolves this dilemma to the complete satisfaction of all parties concerned. My point, in this section, has simply been to make the conflicting considerations apparent. It is a dilemma which is certainly close to the center of the social problems attendant upon the presence of groups of diverse cultural origins and background in a modern industrial society. I shall leave my own "solution" of it for the concluding remarks of my analysis.

THE INTELLECTUAL SUBSOCIETY AND ITS SIGNIFICANCE

The existence of an intellectual subsociety in America which draws upon appropriate individuals from all ethnic groups for its membership and, to some degree, allows them an institutional setting for primary group relationships, has several discernible consequences—or, to put it otherwise, serves several functions, both positive and negative.

First, it serves as an institutional safety-valve for those individuals who, because of a wide-ranging interest in ideas, the arts, and people, find ethnic communality personally uncongenial. If these individuals intermarry across ethnic lines, they find the need for the intellectual subsociety sociologically pressing, since this subsociety is the only real "neutral ground" in American life and the only communal group which looks either with favor or unconcern at interethnic marriage. (This is, of course, a matter of degree; interracial marriages, especially Negro-white, are still problematic even for the intellectual subsociety.) Even those who do not intermarry find the interethnic or nonethnic social environment with its emphasis on ideas and common interests rather than on ethnic background a comfortable and necessary one. Perhaps one should say that ethnic background is not ignored in the intellectual subsociety, as witness the great interest in this milieu in ethnic folk dancing and folk singing; it is rather that ethnicity becomes an interesting but subsidiary issue rather than one which colors and dominates the rest of life. Were such a social environment and subsociety not available, individuals of the aforementioned interests and inclinations would be rebellious and unhappy as they chafed at the restrictive bonds of ethnic communality.

Second, the intellectual subsociety with its ethnic intermixture serves the rest of the nation as a symbol of the possibility of interethnic harmony and integration at the meaningful primary group level of communal living. It is true that the process of achieving such integration is still incomplete even among intellectuals; the Negro, most notably, is still only partly and imperfectly encompassed in the communal life of the intellectual group. Nevertheless, partial as ethnic integration may be within it, the intellectual subsociety still serves as the most salient example of the possibility of a truly integrated society. As such, it provides a testing ground for the problems and processes inherent in the achievement of such a society and stands as a symbol of its potential development in larger scope.

A third functional consequence must be stated in negative terms, or perhaps it would be more accurate to say that a question must be raised the probable answer to which has negative implications. The question is this: What are the consequences for the several major ethnic subsocieties in America of the fact that many, perhaps a large majority, of the most intellectually inclined of their birthright members are siphoned off, as it were, into a subsociety of their own, retaining only a minimal concern, if any, for the communal life and issues of their parental group? Put more specifically, if intellectuals of Jewish, Catholic, and Protestant background become alienated from the subsocietal life and concerns of their respective groups, what functional consequences result for these ethnic groups and for the general quality of American life of which these groups make up the overwhelming part? Some intellectuals, to be sure, remain within their ethnic origins groups as clergymen, communal leaders, or ordinary laymen, but the general trend is as otherwise described. Does this outflow of intellectuals from the religio-ethnic groups of America, their subsequent estrangement from the life of these groups, and the resultant block in communication between the ethnic subsociety and the intellectual have dysfunctional consequences? Do the major decisions both in the society as a whole and within the ethnic subsociety come to be made with the intellectual excluded from the decision-making process? Is there a mediocrity and stereotypy in American popular culture and in the subcultural life of each major ethnic group which results from this withdrawal of the intellectuals into a social world of their own? Do the intellectuals themselves lose out in breadth and vision as a result of this estrangement? And is this estrangement or alienation inevitable—in the very nature of things, given the scope and nature of individual genetic differences—or is it subject to elimination or modification as a result of measures not yet thought of or implemented? These are questions, the answers to which, in the absence of relevant research and exploration, are not entirely clear. Nevertheless, they point to a series of problematic areas in American life resulting from the alienation of the intellectual from popular society and culture.

THE ETHNIC SUBSOCIETY AND ITS INTERNAL RESPONSIBILITIES

The ethnic subsociety can be counted on to marshal its institutional resources to carry out the fight against racial and religious discrimination and prejudice on the American scene. Various aspects of the strategy of this indispensable effort have been discussed in previous pages. We turn now to a related but ostensibly different question: What should be the attitude of the leaders and leading organizations of the ethnic subsociety toward the subsociety itself—to the constituency which it serves—with regard to its relationship to the larger community? This topic will be considered by reference to two sub-questions.

The first deals with the appropriate attitude of the institutional leadership of the ethnic subsociety toward facts and occurrences which appear to reflect unfavorably on the ethnic group. While the illustrations used below deal with the Negro group, other ethnic groups, including the white Protestant majority, could well have been utilized.

Not long ago, a journal dedicated to the cause of advancing the position of the Negro within the framework of equal rights, raised the question of whether it should devote an entire issue to the topic of delinquency and crime among Negroes. There are those who will argue that the correct answer is No—that special consideration of the above-average rates of crime and delinquency among Negroes focuses undesirable attention on this phenomenon and plays into the hands of the racists who are only too quick to point with alarm and to attribute higher Negro delinquency rates to some innate racial predisposition or inferiority.

I disagree with such a strategy. In the first place, national attention has already been called to the high rates of Negro crime in the slums of the large cities through articles in such periodicals as *Time* and *Life*, and metropolitan newspapers raise the issue whenever local outbreaks of Negro "muggings" and allied violence take place. It is therefore impossible to keep the issue from public attention even if it were considered wise to do so. More realistic and desirable goals are (1) to make the public understand the sociological rather than "racial" causes of the higher Negro rate—that is, to comprehend its source in racial discrimination and the substandard conditions, both physical and cultural, in which the great mass of Negroes are forced to live as a result of discrimination and prejudice; (2) to advance research in discovering the causes of crime and delinquency generally; (3) to research in detail the particular sociological causes for the higher Negro rate; and (4) to eliminate racial discrimination. None of these goals is advanced by an ostrich-like policy of avoiding recognition of the higher Negro crime and delinquency rate and by misguided restriction of informed and responsible discussion of the issue.

In the larger sense, it may be said that truth and understanding are the necessary preludes to informed and constructive action in the field of interethnic group relations. Donald Young stated this principle effectively over a decade ago:

> It is good technique to keep members of both races accurately informed about interracial questions. There is no better way to answer false assertions, kill tension-breeding rumors, and build a solid foundation for democratic action. This principle is generally accepted, but it is commonly misused because of fear that if the truth is not entirely laudatory of the Negro it may lead to greater prejudice. Also, because Negroes are sensitive and quick to infer insults . . . , racial liberals are reluctant to risk giving offense. The twisting or omitting of facts, exaggeration and plain prevarication in defensive arguments about race and crime, industrial skill, educational and scientific achievement, military accomplishment, literary and artistic products, etc. are commonplace. But the unvarnished truth alone contradicts racial dogma, checks rumors, and in precluding specious rebuttal is more effective than the most kindly white lie. Unless the established facts are adhered to rigidly, and both weaknesses and strengths honestly included in interracial educational campaigns, the main results are likely to be a lack of public confidence and a weak foundation for action programs.[5]

The principle applies with equal force, of course, to Jews, Catholics, white Protestants, or any other ethnic group.

The second subquestion may be phrased as follows: Does the ethnic subsociety have any special responsibility to guide the behavior of its members with respect to avoidance of those forms of action which are patently injurious to society? Certainly if we phrase this question in terms of the attitudes of institutions in the white subsocieties toward racists, the answer appears clear enough. We expect white Protestant and Catholic churches and Jewish synagogues, for instance, to urgently preach doctrines of racial brotherhood, to support desegregation both in the church itself and in the larger society, and to actively oppose prejudice and discrimination. And we take the position that civic organizations, generally, stemming from the white subsocieties, should take a similar stand. Suppose we ask the question, however, with respect to a minority subsociety, and suppose some form of anti-social behavior may be particularly salient within its ranks as a result of the forces generated by prejudice and discrimination. Here, let us again use as an example the Negro community and the high rate of delinquency found in the Negro lower class.

Does the "Negro community" have, in fact, a special responsibility and role to play in the prevention of delinquency among Negro youth? The argument against any special responsibility, of course, runs something like this: Rates of delinquency and crime are the product of general sociological and psychological forces which are within the control and responsibility of the total community and not in any special way of the Negro community. Furthermore, wherever higher rates of Negro delinquency are present, these higher rates are the result of prejudice and discrimination shown by whites and embedded in the institutions of the total community. Therefore any attribution of special responsibility to the Negro community is both morally unjustified and logically fallacious. There is much to be said for this argument, and, in a strict theoretical sense, I would agree that the Negro community should accept no attribution of responsibility for Negro delinquency which implies either a special ethical obligation to deal with it or an acceptance of the fallacious thesis that its sources are fundamentally indigenous to Negro communal life.

However, I would not be content to rest here. I would say that while the Negro community does not bear a special *responsibility* in the matter of Negro crime, it does, in terms of the sociological realities, have a special *opportunity* in practical terms to focus, voluntarily, a portion of its resources on the problem of reducing the Negro delinquency rate. The existence of specifically Negro organizations and institutions, the sense of identification with the Negro group on the part of Negro individuals, the *de facto* restriction of social participation to the Negro community—all these components of Negro communal and subcultural existence—are sociological realities. The sociological reality of the Negro subsociety thus provides special opportunities for Negro communal leaders acting through Negro communal institutions to play a special role in the reduction of rates of anti-social behavior by Negroes.

To particularize: Negro communal leaders may (1) be in a position to provide special insights into the dynamics of social processes within the Negro lower classes and Negro lower-class family life which contribute to the excessive delinquency rate; (2) be able to do more effective ameliorative field work in standard social work processes because of the greater rapport which is likely to exist between lower-class Negroes and Negro social workers, and to supplement existing social work measures directed toward the Negro community which are currently in short supply; and (3) be in a position to devise and carry through institutional counter-measures whose particular effectiveness would derive from their source within the Negro community. To ignore these opportunities, it seems to me again, is to adopt an ostrich-like policy with regard to the multiplicity of specific variables which combine to produce the higher Negro delinquency rate, and correspondingly to make possible the multiplicity of counter-measures which offer special opportunities for action by the Negro community itself. To put it succinctly, simply because the *ultimate causes* of the higher Negro delinquency rate stem from broader social forces in the general community does not signify that *some effective counter-measures* cannot be taken at existing levels of structure and process by the Negro community itself. Thus I would argue that while the Negro community does not have, in the strict philosophical sense, a special *responsibility* to concern itself with Negro delinquency, it does have, in realistic sociological terms, a special *opportunity* to devote some attention and resources to this phenomenon. In short, my point is that the ethnic subsociety, whatever its racial, religious, or nationality background, from a sociological point of view has special opportunities to deal with particular behavior problems which may be related to its social history and current situation, and these opportunities should not be bypassed, even though the more basic roots of the problem lie in the institutions and practices of the larger society.

Nothing I have said suggests, of course, in any way that the Negro community should curtail or diminish its increasingly insistent and effective efforts (aided by many white liberals) toward achieving the broader long-range goals of eliminating prejudice and discrimination from American life. In the last analysis, the attainment of equal opportunities in education, employment, housing, and access to public facilities, and the development of mutual re-

munality created by his birthright ethnic group, to branch out into multiple interethnic contacts, or even to change affiliation to that of another ethnic group should he wish to do so as a result of religious conversion, intermarriage, or simply private wish. If, to the contrary, the ethnic group places such heavy pressures on its birthright members to stay confined to ethnic communality that the individual who consciously wishes to "branch out" or "move away" feels intimidated or subject to major feelings of personal guilt and therefore remains ethnically enclosed, or moves but at considerable psychological cost, then we have, in effect, cultural democracy for groups but not for individuals. Realistically, it is probably impossible to have a socialization process for the child growing up in a particular ethnic group that does not involve some implicitly restrictive values; nevertheless, the magnitude and intensity of such restrictive norms must be kept within bounds if we are not to be left with a system which provides cultural democracy for groups but enforced ethnic enclosure for individuals.

Probably the vast majority of Americans, as revealed in their choices in primary group relations and organizational affiliations, desire ethnic communality, at least in essential outline. Their preferences are reinforced by the self-perpetuating pressures generated by the nature of subcommunity organizational life and by the demands and exhortations, grounded in ideological conviction, of their ethnic community leaders. As we have suggested, some individuals, as a result of their particular inclinations and perspectives, move out into an amorphously structured intellectual subcommunity which contains people of all ethnic backgrounds. All of these recurring processes are probably inevitable and basically irreversible. Thus the prognosis for America for a long time to come is that its informal social structure will consist of a series of ethnic subcommunities criss-crossed by social class, within which primary group relationships will tend to be confined, that secondary group relationships across ethnic group lines will take place in abundance as a result of the requirements of an urbanized industrial society, and that the intellectual subsociety will grow somewhat both in numbers and in institutional articulation as a result of the constant increase in the magnitude of higher education.[6]

The major problem, then, is to keep ethnic separation in communal life from being so pronounced in itself that it threatens ethnic harmony, good group relations, and the spirit of basic good will which a democratic pluralistic society requires, and to keep it from spilling over into the civic arena of secondary relations to impinge on housing, jobs, politics, education, and other areas of functional activity where universalistic criteria of judgment and assignment are necessary and where the operation of ethnic considerations can only be disruptive and even disastrous. The attainment of this objective calls for good sense and reasonableness on the part of the average American citizen, regardless of ethnic background, and in addition to these qualities, a high degree of civic statesmanship on the part of ethnic communal leaders who will be tempted at times, out of their own convictions and enthusiasms, to emphasize ethnic exclusion and the demands in time and resources from their particular constituents which are likely to make for exclusion and separation, regardless of intent.

In sum, the basic long-range goal for Americans, with regard to ethnic communality, is fluidity and moderation within the context of equal civic rights for all, regardless of race, religion, or national background, and the option of democratic free choice for both groups and individuals. Ethnic communality will not disappear in the foreseeable future and its legitimacy and rationale should be recognized and respected. By the same token, the bonds that bind human beings together across the lines of ethnicity and the pathways on which people of diverse ethnic origin meet and mingle should be cherished and strengthened. In the last analysis, what is gravely required is a society in which one may say with equal pride and without internal disquietude at the juxtaposition: "I am a Jew, or a Catholic, or a Protestant, or a Negro, or an Indian, or an Oriental, or a Puerto Rican;" "I am an American;" and "I am a man."

NOTES

1. Kenneth B. Clark, "Desegregation: The Role of the Social Sciences," *Teachers College Record*, Vol. 62, No. 1 (October 1960), pp. 16–17.

2. Ibid., p. 16.

3. For a discussion of one interesting case where the definition of "state action" was crucial and controversial, see Milton M. Gordon, "The Girard College Case: Resolution and Social Significance," *Social Problems*, Vol. 7, No. 1 (Summer, 1959), pp. 15–27.

4. Another qualification is necessary here. If school districts were gerrymandered originally for the sake of instituting all or predominantly Negro schools, then this initial act of discrimination should be fought and redress should be demanded.

5. Donald Young, "Techniques of Race Relations," *Proceedings of the American Philosophical Society*, Vol. 91, No. 2 (April 1947), pp. 157–8.

6. I do not mean to indicate that all, or even most, college graduates become "intellectuals" or interacting members of the intellectual subsociety. By no means. However, the spread of higher education opens the doors of possible entrance into the intellectual subsociety to an increasing number of those who are intellectually or temperamentally suited for it.

Part III

SOCIAL WORK

Chapter Five

EMERGENCE OF THE PROFESSION

The profession of social work has its origins in the late 19th century. The *functions* performed by social workers have, of course, always been carried out in communities, mostly by the family and, during the Middle Ages and the early period of industrialization, by the church. As the power of the church declined with the growth of the nation-state, and as social welfare developed as an institution, many of these functions were picked up as voluntary philanthropic efforts. Harriett Bartlett, in the first selection in this chapter, "Early Trends" (Reading 15), describes the early development of these functions in organizations concerned with aiding individuals; examples are the Charity Organization Society and organizations concerned with social reform, such as the settlements. Bartlett also describes the development of the organizational structure of the profession itself.

Early social work practice was not theoretically based. It was only in the 1920s and 1930s, with the emergence of Freudian and other psychological theories, that social work began to incorporate a knowledge base that was distinct from the practice method. Social casework, as Howard Goldstein notes, developed without an explicit "commitment to an articulation of the philosophical conception of man" that underlies the practice. Practice of this sort, Goldstein says, "based mainly on a set of pragmatic methods and necessarily incomplete theories, is flimsy and subject to change when new approaches come along."[1]

In Reading 16, "Attributes of a Profession," Ernest Greenwood indicates that a knowledge base which draws upon well-developed theory from which the practitioner can formulate testable propositions is one of five major characteristics of a profession. The other major attributes of professions identified by Greenwood are authority, community sanction, ethical codes, and a culture. *Authority* refers to the client's belief in the superior knowledge of the professional regarding the particular activities in which the profession is engaged. Unlike marketplace exchanges wherein the customer may judge for himself the quality of merchandise, the professional relationship relies on the professional to judge what is in the client's interest. For this reason Everett Hughes has suggested that the appropriate motto for this relationship is *credat emptor*—let the buyer believe—rather than the traditional *caveat emptor* of the marketplace.[2] In order to earn and ensure this belief, and to prevent those who are not properly anointed from deluding the public, a profession seeks to win the *sanction* of the community, which may take different forms such as registration, certification, or licensing.[3] These different forms of sanction award different degrees of authority and autonomy to the profession, such as privileged communication and the right to set standards for what is considered acceptable professional behavior. Professional *codes of ethics* are created as the means by which the community is reassured that the privileges awarded will be used in the interests of the community. And, finally, a *professional culture*, representing the values, norms, and symbols of the enterprise, inevitably takes shape to mark the professional identification. This culture operates, for example, in recruitment, screening, and socialization of new entrants to the profession; it also provides the means by which recognition and status are awarded within the profession.

The selection by Bartlett touches on the historical development of some of these professional attributes. The remaining readings in this chapter also deal in different ways with one or another of the five attributes identified by Greenwood.

In discussing the other selections it will be useful to bear in mind three characteristics of social work that have made it somewhat different from other professions. First, social work began as a private, voluntary enterprise in the philanthropic movements. Second, the profession started as a congeries of specializations which were viewed as auxiliary functions to other professions in a variety of organizational contexts. Third, in the first half of this century the profession was composed almost **exclusively** of women. Each of these developmental characteristics has had a profound effect on the profession, and each is the source of continuing strain within it.

BEGINNINGS OF A VOLUNTARY PRIVATE ENTERPRISE

Because of its origin as a voluntary, private enterprise (which essentially reflected the "residual" view of social welfare), the earlier intervention methods of social work supported individualistic solutions to social problems rather than communalistic solutions. By "individualistic solutions" we refer to services performed on behalf of clients which focus on the deficiencies of the clients rather than on institutional deficiencies. The classic individualistic solution, in this sense, is therapeutically-oriented psychiatric casework. Communalistic solutions focus on the reform of institutions and allocative procedures.

Throughout this century social work has grown as a professional enterprise, expanding as social welfare has moved toward fuller institutional status. It has become, like social welfare, a big business in which well over 200,000 employees share responsibility for dispensing benefits valued in billions of dollars.[4] Social work is, clearly, no longer a professional function concerned with meeting residual needs. This continual expansion is responsible, in part, for the great strains social work has experienced throughout its history between its social-change and its clinical functions that are reflected in the profession's responsibility for creating, maintaining, and reforming the institutional context within which it operates and its responsibility to provide direct personal services.

This strain was articulated by Porter Lee in 1929 in his classic paper "Social Work: Cause and Function."[5] Lee viewed this strain as arising from a "change in the nature of social work from that of cause to that of function." Observing the growth of social work both in numbers of professionals and amounts of allocations, he pointed out that the community would demand higher degrees of accountability from social workers and some means for assuring that their conduct is guided by ethical considerations. In effect, Lee was saying that social work would have to acquire the attributes of a profession.

In our own views, these dual commitments of social work inhere in the relationship between the profession of social work and the institution of social welfare and will always be present in some degree. In Reading 17, "The Incomplete Profession," Gilbert and Specht argue that social work has not developed its technological-methodological capacity to deal with its commitments to development and reform of the institution (or what Lee called "cause").

BEGINNINGS AS UNRELATED SPECIALIZATIONS

The second unique characteristic in the development of the profession mentioned above is the fact that social work began as a group of unrelated specializations in search of a profession, specializations in the service of other professions (e.g., medicine, education) in varied organizational settings. Many consequences have followed from this. We will discuss the profound impact of organizational contexts in the next chapter. But it should be noted that some of the attributes of professions (professional authority, a code of ethics, a culture) may come into conflict with characteristics of organizations because bureaucratic organizations establish their own hierarchy of authority, rules, and procedures. Therefore, with the growth of professionalism came the increased likelihood of organizational strain for social workers.

Additional consequences follow because social work had been wedded to a variety of other professional disciplines. Often, these affiliations encouraged social workers to use theoretical frameworks (e.g., Freudian theory) that were not well suited to implement Richmond's "person in the situation" conception of social work (a rather simple conception, but one that has endured longer than any other). The mix of Jane Addams, Mary Richmond, and Sigmund Freud, along with sociological theories such as those of Louis Wirth and Robert MacIver, not to mention the theories of progressive education brought in by social group work and the rational businesslike approach contributed by community organization, was sometimes exciting but not easy for the community or the social workers themselves to comprehend.

The strengthening of professional attributes in social work has considerably reduced the influence of the organizational settings and theoretical orientations of other professions. However, in the process there has been created a new entity which many consider to be an unwholesome influence on the behavior of social workers. That entity is, of course, the profession itself. Marie R. Haug and

Marvin B. Sussman describe the dangers of excessive professional autonomy in "Professional Autonomy and the Revolt of the Client," Reading 18. They warn that the professional "draws upon organizational power as well as the power of his expertise to control the circumstances under which service is given." These circumstances include such items as who is served, at what costs, and when, where, and how. Thus, the question of autonomy is a most important one. Currently, many sociologists and social workers have expressed the belief that professionalism is nothing more than a means by which to protect privilege and self-interest. In this view, the *knowledge* attribute of professions is closer to self-protective credentialism than to expertise; *authority* is more a means of controlling clients than a device by which clients can deal with the awesome nature of the professionals' superior knowledge and skill; *sanction* is bestowed by (and in the interests of) the established power structure rather than by and for clients; *ethical codes* are developed not to protect the community, but to protect the profession from the meddling of outsiders; and, finally, the norms, values, and beliefs that constitute the *culture* of professions are no more altruistic and sacrosanct than any other group that works for wages, fees, or profits but only represent different paths to success.[6]

Paul Halmos, a British sociologist, has a quite different view of the causes of the present climate of antiprofessionalism. He points out that in large part recent virulent antiprofessionalism emanates from the United States. "American sociologists of the professions," he says, "are averse to dwelling on the less jaundiced impressions which the personal service professions can and do create." Halmos believes that these ideas are relevant to problems that are uniquely American and not attributable to American professions in particular nor to other countries in general. Moreover, he believes that these views of American sociologists are not well balanced:

> They leave little or no margin of their sociological attention to the fact that facts are not exhausted by the marshalling of all that is tough, combative, competitive, or downright unattractive, reprehensible, and evil in the practising personal service professional. A sociological account of the personal service professions in terms of the basic categories of power, status, prestige, income, and the like, is not in itself mistaken; but when it refuses, almost with a masochistic fervour, to explore what minor and not so minor sociological significance might be found in categories of self-transcendence, such as

sympathy, empathy, rapport, affection, and the like, it is plainly guilty of a loss of objectivity.[7]

PREPONDERANCE OF WOMEN

The third characteristic of the profession mentioned above is that in its early development it was composed almost exclusively of women; men began entering the profession in significant numbers only after World War II.[8] The female composition supported, in part, the low status and low salaries for what was considered a relatively unimportant, residual function. This composition also supported, and caused, the profession's nurturing and humanistic orientation. As the profession and the institution expanded and became more significant, many more men were attracted. The increased numbers of males in the profession support, in part, the more technical and rational orientations required by the expanding profession and institution. (We realize that some of our readers may take offense at our attributing the profession's humanistic values to women. We certainly do not mean to suggest that men cannot be nurturing nor that women cannot be technical and rational; however, in the emergence of social work this seems to have been how things were at those times.)

As the profession has expanded, the strain between the nurturing-humanistic and technical-rational orientations to social work practice has been intensified in the field. To some extent this strain underlies the issues discussed in the papers by Haug and Sussman and by Gilbert and Specht. These haunting dilemmas occur, as Henry Miller has noted, because the social worker "cannot disengage himself from the moral concerns of his client."[9] While professionalism calls for behavior that is scientific, knowledge-based, objective, and rational, the humanistic, caring, and nurturing values of social work constrain the professional to be deeply and actively involved in furthering the moral well-being of his client and of society. Dilemmas of this sort will, no doubt, continue unabated in the practice of social work.

NOTES

1. Howard Goldstein, *Social Work Practice: A Unitary Approach* (Columbia: University of South Carolina Press, 1973), p. 41.

2. Everett C. Hughes, "Professions," *Journal of the American Academy of Arts and Sciences,* 92 (Fall 1963): 657.

3. Paul E. Weinberger and Dorothy Z. Weinberger, "Legal Regulation in Perspective," *Social Work,* 7 (January 1962): 67–74.

4. See Alfred M. Skolnik and Sophie R. Dales, "Social Welfare Expenditures, Fiscal Year 1974," *Social Security Bulletin,* 38 (January 1975): 3–18; and footnotes 1 and 2, Chapter 7, for references on numbers of social workers.

5. Porter R. Lee, "Social Work: Cause and Function," *Proceedings of the National Conference of Social Work* (Chicago: University of Chicago Press, 1929), pp. 3–20.

6. Neil Gilbert and Harry Specht, *Dimensions of Social Welfare Policy* (Englewood Cliffs, N.J.: Prentice-Hall, Inc., 1973), pp. 128–29.

7. Paul Halmos, ed., *Professionalization and Social Change* (Sociological Review Monograph, December 1973), p. 9.

8. Sex ratios in the profession are discussed by Henry J. Meyer, "Profession of Social Work: Contemporary Characteristics," *Encyclopedia of Social Work,* Vol. II, ed. Robert Morris (New York: National Association of Social Workers, 1971), pp. 959–72.

9. Henry Miller, "Value Dilemmas in Social Casework," *Social Work,* 13 (January 1968): 27–33.

15 Early Trends

HARRIETT M. BARTLETT

Early social work was characterized by two types of effort—social reform and assistance to individuals and families under stress. Encompassed under social reform were a variety of community efforts revealing a strong sense of responsibility for improving the welfare of those who were deprived or handicapped. Social workers perceived their role as that of calling attention to the problem, rousing the public conscience, speaking for the people involved and stimulating their participation, offering evidence as to the nature of their needs, and advocating appropriate preventive or corrective measures. Their actions were directed toward elim-

From Harriett Bartlett, *The Common Base of Social Work Practice* (New York: National Association of Social Workers, Inc., 1970), pp. 21–36. Reprinted with permission of the National Association of Social Workers and of the author.

inating or alleviating social problems and conditions affecting whole communities or population groups, as for instance in relation to child welfare or the employment of women. Social work leadership made a significant impact on social policy through the improvement of public welfare services and enlargement of programs of voluntary social agencies. Another approach was through the settlements, which emphasized being close to people, living and working among them in the neighborhood, offering opportunities to grow toward self-direction and fuller participation as citizens in a democratic society, and advocating social measures to improve living conditions.

The other major phase of social work practice—assistance to individuals and families under stress—developed out of the charity organization movement. This work was first performed by volunteers, but by the turn of the century it was recognized that persons who were to give individualized services in relation to the complex problems of poverty and family life required training. Shortly before and after 1900, the first schools of social work were established and professional workers took the place of friendly visitors. Out of this early practice and these schools developed the concept of social work as a skilled process of giving help.

While social work practitioners soon regarded themselves as professional workers, the forces operating in this formative period encouraged differences rather than integration. During the first half century of social work history, an observer viewing the practice widely would have seen a profession growing through its separate parts. The concepts so developed were sufficiently related to hold social workers together and, for a considerable period, this pattern of practice, in spite of its lack of integration, continued to stimulate the growth of the profession.

SOCIAL WORK PRACTICE IN SEPARATE FIELDS

An early and important segment of practice was known as the "field of practice." In our modern industrial civilization, societies establish social institutions to provide services required to meet the various basic human needs, such as family maintenance, shelter, education, and health or to deal with societal problems such as delinquency. Since there are always some people whose needs are not met by the services and since the manner in which services are rendered may block effective use by those who need them, social workers were drawn into practice in one field after another. By the time social work practice began to develop visibility in the twenties and thirties, it was growing rapidly in the separate fields. There was at that time no concept of professional social work practice as a single entity.

By the end of the twenties, five fields of practice had emerged —family and child welfare, in which social workers were employed in social welfare agencies, and medical, psychiatric, and school social work, in which social workers were employed in non-social work agencies.[1] Social workers in these fields worked intensively, but within their own field, to clarify the nature of their competence. Medical social workers had a continuing committee for analysis of practice from 1922 on and psychiatric social workers established such a committee later. What intellectual tools were then available for the analysis of practice? What approaches were used?

Two concepts were predominant at that time, the concept of *social work method* and the concept of *setting*. The concept of method developed first around casework and later in relation to group work and community organization. It rested on selected clusters of theory concerning human behavior. The concept of setting referred to the organizational environment within which the service was given. This concept directed attention to the characteristics of the agencies and programs in which social work had to find a place. The social structure of the hospital and public school, the goals and methods of physicians and teachers, the nature of the client group, and similar factors were analyzed and described. This approach tended to emphasize what was different among the fields and thus, while it stimulated thinking about the social work contribution and clarified practice within the fields, it tended to produce greater fragmentation in practice as a whole.

Social workers defined their central problem and responsibility as that characteristic of the particular field. In child welfare, the social worker's central responsibility was defined as meeting the needs of the child when parental responsibility broke down and communities failed to provide the resources and protection required by children and families. For a considerable period this responsibility was viewed primarily as providing substitute care, particularly in the form of foster home care for the child. As time went on, however, there was increasing emphasis on supporting and strengthening the family by providing services in the home.[2]

Family welfare, in addition to its contribution to casework thinking, was also keeping the concept of the family before social work practitioners. All social workers are concerned with families but, by the nature of their work, family workers have always had this as their primary concern. After the social security program no longer made it as necessary for family agencies to be primarily concerned with financial problems, interest moved toward psycho-social problems, such as marital difficulties. In the fifties, an outburst of interest in family diagnosis and treatment in a number of professions stimulated family workers to extend their interest in this direction.[3]

In the medical setting social workers found a sharp distinction between the frames of reference of the dominant profession, medicine, and the growing perspective of social work. The problem was, therefore, not only to find a place in the setting but also to find a way of bringing these two perspectives together. How could scientific knowledge regarding disease and methods of medical care be related more sensitively to the needs of the patient as a person?[4]

In school social work the primary focus was on the child's difficulties in relation to and use of the school and the educational program. In this field there was not a large visible body of knowledge about the central problem—in this instance, the nature of learning and the educational process—as there was in some other fields. The emphasis was, therefore, on understanding and working with the school as an institution, on the one hand, and with the child and his family, on the other.[5]

In mental health the frames of reference of the major professional group (psychiatry) and of social work were closer than in any of the other fields involving multidisciplinary practice. Diagnosis was customarily carried out in interdisciplinary conferences and the psychiatric diagnosis was immediately relevant for the social worker's understanding of the patient and his needs. For these reasons, social work thinking, as expressed in its literature and teaching, emphasized the psychic aspects of the problem and the process of giving help through direct professional relationship with the individual. This was a major contribution to social casework and social work understanding of human behavior but was heavily weighted on one side of the person-environment complex with which social workers are concerned.[6]

Turning now from these earlier fields of practice: in the forties the development of two method-oriented fields—group work and community organization—extended social work practice in new directions. These were concerned not only with services to groups and communities but also with methods related specifically to the rendering of these services. By the midcentury these two fields were still in the stage of defining their focus and concepts.[7]

Social work in corrections did not gain recognition as a field until later than the others. In the fifties, through the support of the U.S. Children's Bureau and the Council on Social Work Education, rapid progress was made in defining social work practice in corrections. Coming as it did at a later stage in the profession's development, social work in corrections did not have to go through some of the growing pains of the older fields. A particular contribution was made from this field to the understanding of problems of authority, as faced by both clients and social workers.[8]

Social work in public welfare (or public assistance) has been at times described as a field of practice, but it did not become separately organized within the structure of the profession. Because of its concern with families and children, this area of practice was most frequently included within the fields of family and child welfare.

During the early period of working in various fields, up to the fifties, social workers were learning about a wide range of social problems. They learned how the problems affected individuals and families and how the people themselves felt about the difficulties. Social workers also acquired valuable experience in collaborating with other personnel, particularly members of other professions, and in making contributions to the agencies and programs in which they worked. The problems were viewed as characteristic of particular areas of practice, such as public welfare or mental health. The ways of working with other personnel and contributing to agency programs were considered to be associated with particular settings. These ideas about practice were discussed in the literature and in teaching but, for reasons to be considered later, were not presented as concepts of knowledge belonging to all social work and capable of leading toward an integrated view of its practice.

Thus practice in the fields was moving social work toward professional development but in an unco-ordinated manner. The emphasis on the differences among the settings within which social workers practiced continued to be a divisive factor. In a move to offset this, Perlman pointed out in 1949 that features claimed by practitioners as characteristic of one or another setting, such as teamwork with other professions, were actually relevant for all the settings. She thus emphasized the generic

292   The Emergence of Social Welfare and Social Work

aspects of settings.[9] This was a helpful integrative idea but was not strong enough to overcome the fragmentation because of limitations inherent in the concept of setting itself. What was not perceived by the practitioners of that period was that this concept rested on factors *outside* their practice—elements in the agency or program—which, it is true, molded their work in important ways but were external to it. What social work particularly needed was a conceptual approach based on the essential elements *within* its own practice, no matter where the worker practiced.

AGENCY AND PROFESSION

The practice of social work is characteristically carried on in and through health and welfare agencies and programs. The social worker has been an employed person operating in specific agencies. Up to this time there has been no "general practice," in the sense in which it is found in some professions, although recently a growing private practice has developed, the focus of which is not yet clearly defined.

Like fields of practice, agencies have exerted an important influence on the development of social work practice and the growth of the profession. Agencies and programs are socially and legally established structures for organizing, administering, and delivering services and bringing resources to the people who need and want them. Social work may be one of the professional services so offered and, in a welfare agency, may be the major service. Under these circumstances a professional social worker renders the core service and the social work profession primarily determines and develops the necessary competence.

The support that the agency board and administration give to social work is of major importance in relation to the contribution the profession can make in society. When administered by social workers, social agencies have continually given leadership in extending services in the community and identifying new needs requiring additional services. The collaboration between agencies and schools in developing social work education has been an outstanding feature of this profession from earliest times.

In our society employment of professional personnel by agencies and programs is increasing and independent practice is decreasing.[10] One reason for this is the growth of specialization, with a consequent increase in multidisciplinary practice. In working primarily in agencies, social workers are thus in line with a general social trend. Several large issues are involved in such professional practice within agency programs. The employed practitioner must be able to relate to the agency in such a way as to further its purposes but at the same time to retain his own identity. There is always tension between these two requirements.[11] Sociological theory and organizational theory are rapidly building up knowledge regarding the nature of structure and behavior in modern complex organizations. Vinter has discussed these issues in a clarifying manner as they appear in social work practice. He shows that, from the viewpoint of the profession, the agency as a bureaucratic structure may not allow the practitioners sufficient freedom for their essential operations. From the viewpoint of the agency, on the other hand, the freedom demanded by professionals may confuse and block the fulfillment of its goals.[12] Without doubt, this aspect of the agency-profession relationship requires further study.

BLURRING OF PRACTICE CONCEPTS

The tendency to perceive and discuss social work practice in terms of agency practice has been strong all through the history of social work. In the early days the agencies were the most conspicuous feature of the social welfare field. Social work practice was as yet hardly visible as an entity. It was the agencies that were chartered by the community and thus it was through the agencies that social workers found their beginning security and identity.

The concepts of social welfare, social agency, and social work have been continuously blurred. Textbooks on social work discuss agency programs and professional practice interchangeably. Articles in social work journals not infrequently bear titles suggesting social work practice but offer content related to agency services. During the first fifty years, social work research dealt largely with agency organization, structure, and services, including such operations as recording and statistics. It was not until the midcentury, when social workers became fully aware of their own profession and began to develop a comprehensive perception of their practice, that they recognized their own contribution as a potential force in society.

The problem of making the necessary distinction appears most clearly in the family and child welfare fields. In American society there has been less initiative in establishing welfare agencies than in establishing health, educational, and correctional agencies. There was no social security program and welfare as a governmental responsibility was barely visualized. Voluntary welfare agencies were therefore established to meet the needs. In family and child welfare, national organizations composed of member agencies assumed leadership for developing goals and standards of practice for both agency programs and the practice of social workers employed in the agencies.[13] Since it seemed clear at that time that all these activities could be regarded as social work, it did not seem necessary to make any distinction between agency and profession.

Meanwhile, other social workers were practicing in hospitals and schools, where they worked in association with other professions in non-social work settings. Since they could not form associations on an agency base, they formed professional associations composed of individual practitioners. Furthermore, because they had to answer the question of what they were bringing that was new and would represent an addition to the program they were entering, they were forced from the beginning to concentrate attention on their own professional practice in order to evaluate and demonstrate its contribution to the overall agency.

In family and child welfare, although casework was clearly visualized as a professional process, it continued to be tied to the agency, as can be seen in the persistent phrase "casework agency." In child welfare, services had always been rendered through a variety of other personnel and resources, such as foster homes, adoptive homes, and children's institutions. Family welfare also, as time went on, included such services as those of homemakers. Many of these services were a part of the agency program and were supervised by the social work staff, so that the line between agency and professional social work practice was not clear.

Articles in the Social Work Year Book (issued every three years starting in 1929) describing the different fields reveal the trends in thinking about profession and agency. In the early period, the articles on medical and psychiatric social work focused on the practice of the social worker, while those on family and child welfare focused on the agency and its program. In the first volume of the Encyclopedia of Social Work (which followed the year book in 1965), there is for the first time a discussion of "professional aspects" in the article on child welfare, but the article on family social work continues to be written from the viewpoint of agency services. School social work falls between these two approaches, starting with an emphasis on the agency, but always with some mention of social work practitioners, and moving toward a focus on social work practice. The field of correctional services, which developed slowly, was variously described in the *Social Work Year Book* in agency terms, until an article clearly focused on social work practice in corrections appeared in the 1965 *Encyclopedia of Social Work*.[14]

The early failure to distinguish between social welfare and social work added to the confusion. The formation of the Council on Social Work Education and the National Association of Social Workers in the fifties increased the visibility of the social work profession. At that time, the National Conference of Social Work changed its name to the National Conference on Social Welfare in recognition that its scope was broader than social work.

DISTINGUISHING AGENCY AND PROFESSION

At the level of individual practice, social workers are guided in many appropriate ways by the programs and policies of their employing agencies. They are not, however, stimulated to examine the contribution of their profession until they can perceive the profession clearly as an independent social institution that has responsibility to define its own goals, content, and standards. In the author's opinion, failure to make the distinction between agency and profession has been one important obstacle to the clarification of professional practice.

As the movement toward unification of the social work profession has proceeded, many social workers have become aware that the profession possesses strengths that are lacking in agencies. Agencies are restricted in relation to program planning and delivery of service because of their separateness and inflexibility. In spite of years of effort through community councils, progress toward co-ordination of agency programs has been limited and not in line with early hopes and expectations. Agencies too often have been resistant to change. Gaps in the community's services have persisted and even seemed to increase in spite of persistent effort to expand agency services when needed.

The social work profession has a nationwide scope. It has, on the one hand, greater continuity and consistency and, on the other hand, greater flexibility than is found in a group of community agencies. Thus there is the possibility that the profession may in the long run have greater impact on social need and social change than the agencies.

One of the problems to which we will return is the question of how the social worker can be aware of and be most effective in making the essential contribution to his profession, whether he is operating in a traditional agency or in some other capacity in today's emerging programs. In spite of steady clarification, confusion about agencies and social work practice continues.[15] In discussing and writing about social work, social workers continue to move from agency to professional practice and back again, without recognizing the differences between them or identifying the characteristics and responsibilities of each. Together the profession and the agencies should be able to offer a flexible and adequate response to society's needs, but this requires that social workers recognize their own functions and responsibilities as related to, but also distinguished from, those of the agencies.

A PRACTICE MODEL BASED ON METHOD AND SKILL

Practice in separate fields and practice in agencies were among the earliest influences shaping the growth of the profession. Even more important, but developing at a somewhat slower pace, were social workers' own perceptions regarding the professional nature of their practice and the manner in which they defined these perceptions.

The first directions that proved useful for building professional practice developed from the two original types of social work—social reform and family service. Work with groups and community problems was developing as a social work activity in the twenties and thirties but did not attain professional formulation until later. An interesting question is why social science concepts concerning social relationships were not of more influence in early social work. At that time, sociologists like Simmel and Cooley were already presenting a forceful body of theory on social process, communication, leadership, and conflict—theory that was relevant for all social workers and particularly for those engaged in group and community work.[16] But at this time social workers were just beginning to enter the academic atmosphere as teachers and their major interdisciplinary contacts were not with social scientists but with other professionals in practice.

It was the work with individuals, rather than community action, that advanced first toward professional formulation, apparently because visible models and useful theory were readily available. Richmond's pioneer formulation of social casework drew from two major professions for its central themes, the concept of social diagnosis from medicine and the concept of social evidence from law. Medicine further provided the clinical model, encompassing study, diagnosis, and treatment.[17] Richmond's formulation is generally regarded as the first authoritative statement in social work, which began to lay the theoretical foundation for the profession.

It is important to understand better how the various forces and influences operated in this formative period. Richmond's analysis directed attention to a clinical model of practice. Soon thereafter, psychoanalytic psychiatry offered a body of theory that social workers found immediately useful. Its focus on individual personality and its therapeutic base were particularly meaningful in relation to casework as a helping process. Emphasis on the emotions directed attention to the psychic aspects of social maladjustment. Since social workers depend mainly upon their direct contact and relationship with others to bring about results, the new theory offered further insight through its concepts of transference and the therapist's role. The fact that social workers were increasingly practicing in association with psychiatrists provided opportunity for constant refreshment of theory and strengthened this trend in social work thinking.

The psychiatric model in turn reinforced the medical model, with its emphasis on treatment. It was a therapeutic approach. The social work goal of helping people thus came to be perceived as a treatment process operating through the client-worker relationship. Since social work did not have disease categories, as did medicine and psychiatry, diagnosis in social casework was directed toward understanding the individual client and his problem. Thus it was expected that every social worker would develop an attitude of acceptance, tolerance, and warmth toward his clients. He would regard the client's feelings, goals, and individual point of view as being of primary importance and make every effort to understand them. He would endeavor to help the client meet his difficulties and solve his problems as far as possible in his own way. He would work with the client as a unique human being.

Therefore, to attain such goals, it became necessary for the social worker to be aware of his own emotional biases and the way in which they block or divert his efforts to help. He needed to be able to develop a professional relationship with the persons being helped, through which they could receive support without being dominated or led into inappropriate dependency, so that they could move toward recognition and use of their own strengths. This approach was then transferred to the educational process. Thus, just as it was necessary for the social worker to individualize the client, it became necessary for the teacher and supervisor to individualize the social work student or young practitioner, so that he could develop the self-discipline required to incorporate these essential attitudes and skills within his professional self. Learning was perceived as taking place primarily through supervised experience. This led to the development of fieldwork and supervision as new professional procedures. Thus the case method and supervision became the major channels of teaching and learning.

As casework evolved, social workers' perceptions became defined in directions that proved important for the whole profession. One was the development of a number of ideas that grew into central concepts in teaching and practice. These were the *self-determination* of the client, the *acceptance* of the client by the worker, the *client-worker relationship*, and the *self-awareness* of the worker. These themes spread beyond casework and, in one form or another, became characteristic of all social work practice. Their importance for the profession is referred to throughout this monograph.

Another direction in which perceptions peculiar to social work thinking were developing was in relation to the concept of method. This seems to have grown primarily out of social workers' perceptions of their ways of helping people, that is, the helping process. In medicine, all physicians used the same diagnostic approach, whatever the disease or health problem. Social workers, however, because they perceived themselves to be working with people who had problems, sought understanding of the client as an individual and the meaning of the problem to him, thus individualizing their approach. The *uniqueness* of the individual was emphasized. The social worker's awareness of his own feelings, his sensitivity to the client's feelings, and his offering of help through the relationship became predominant themes.

A diagnostic approach and treatment technique that involved understanding and working with a unique individual obviously could be relevant only for casework. While personality theory was being taught to all social workers, the particular knowledge required and used in understanding and helping people under stress —regarding their feelings in seeking help, their use of help, and similar aspects—was perceived as a component of casework and incorporated within the method, just as the essential attitudes and skills had been incorporated within the student. Strong emphasis was placed on "feeling and doing," with less recognition for "thinking and knowing."

When group workers and community organization workers began to move toward formulation of their practice principles, they turned to the social sciences for concepts and theory, for by this time other disciplines—particularly sociology, social psychology, and anthropology—had developed theories immediately useful for social work. Group workers and community organization workers selected some of these theories, such as theory related to group process and community forces, and applied them to their own practice. In contrast with caseworkers, who dealt primarily with problems of maladjustment, group workers viewed themselves as entering situations before pathology appeared and were largely concerned with promoting the positive growth of group members (for instance, offering recreational services for adolescents and preparing immigrants for participation in a democratic society). For their part, community organization workers, in their efforts to co-ordinate social services and programs, viewed the community as a whole. These extensions of knowledge, the concern for the positive contribution of social work, and the broadened perception of effort were all relevant and needed in the growing practice of the profession.

Arriving at formulation at a later point than in casework, social workers in group work and community organization had an opportunity to move the profession toward integrative ways of thinking. Perhaps they could have done this through identifying some common aspect of human behavior and social problems with which all social workers are concerned and showing how this could become part of a common body of knowledge for the profession. But instead, they followed the casework model and gave primacy to the way of working with people—the methodological approach. This divided practice into three methods, focused on individuals, groups, and communities. The knowledge for each method was also divided and used separately. Students were taught in separate sequences in schools and in different types of agencies. Thus the social work concept of method developed, which views the method as incorporating its own diagnostic approach, cluster of knowledge, and ways of working with people.[18] Under these circumstances, a basic diagnostic approach for all social workers could not be formulated. Furthermore, no visible body of knowledge was being built up. Much knowledge was being subsumed within the methods, instead of being taught as social work knowledge, general to the profession, applicable as needed, and appropriate in any phase of specific practice. Just as the separate fields of practice had produced fragmentation, so the three separate methods tended to limit and hold social work thinking within the barriers of their respective approaches.

It can now be seen that what had been developing was a model for social work practice based on method and skill.[19] This was not deliberately and consciously developed as a model but had become one, in the sense that it was molding social workers' perceptions of practice through defining a focus and setting limits for their thinking. The primary concern was with the skilled social worker and the methods he used, in other words, a *method-and-skill* model. It was not confined to casework but was followed also in group work and community organization.

We should recognize the strengths of this model. It grew out of a highly responsible effort to meet the needs of people. It produced a sensitive, skillful practitioner and an important group of concepts regarding social work's contribution to clients. We have seen how the qualities and skills to be incorporated in the individual worker —such as respect for people, warmth, acceptance, effort to understand their problems, self-awareness, and a disciplined professional relationship—have become ideal characteristics of the whole profession. The supervisory method was amazingly successful in producing a practitioner who was sensitive to the needs and feelings of those being helped (whether as individuals or groups) and skilled in helping. Social workers rightly prize this aspect of their practice. As the profession broadens and grows, these characteristics should not be lost, for they are at the very core of social work as a helping process.

NOTES

1. The American Association of Social Workers, established in 1921, was an overall organization representing social work as a whole. Its program emphasized personnel standards and social action and gave relatively less attention to leadership or co-

ordination of effort in the development of professional thinking about practice.

2. *Child Welfare as a Field of Social Work Practice* (New York: Child Welfare League of America, 1959).

3. See "Family Casework in the Interest of Children," *Social Casework*, Vol. 39, Nos. 2–3 (February–March 1958), whole issue.

4. Harriett M. Bartlett, *Some Aspects of Social Casework in a Medical Setting* (Chicago: American Association of Medical Social Workers, 1940).

5. Mildred Sikkema, *School Social Work Practice in Twelve Communities* (New York: American Association of Social Workers, 1953).

6. Tessie D. Berkman, *Practice of Social Workers in Psychiatric Hospitals and Clinics* (New York: American Association of Psychiatric Social Workers, 1953).

7. Gertrude Wilson and Gladys Ryland, *Social Group Work Practice* (Cambridge, Mass.: Riverside Press, 1949); and *Community Organization: Its Nature and Setting* (New York: American Association of Social Workers, 1947).

8. Elliot Studt, *Education for Social Workers in the Correctional Field* (New York: Council on Social Work Education, 1959).

9. Helen Harris Perlman, "Generic Aspects of Specific Casework Settings," *Social Service Review*, Vol. 23, No. 3 (September 1949), pp. 293–301.

10. Eliot Freidson, "The Organization of Medical Practice," in Howard E. Freeman, Sol Levine, and Leo G. Reeder, eds. *Handbook of Medical Sociology* (Englewood Cliffs, N.J.: Prentice-Hall, 1963), pp. 302–303.

11. Harriett M. Bartlett, *Social Work Practice in the Health Field* (New York: National Association of Social Workers, 1961), pp. 47–60.

12. Robert D. Vinter, "The Social Structure of Service," in Alfred J. Kahn, ed., *Issues in American Social Work* (New York: Columbia University Press, 1959), pp. 242–269; and Vinter, "Analysis of Treatment Organizations," *Social Work*, Vol. 8, No. 3 (July 1963), pp. 3–15.

13. In 1911 the family agencies formed a federation—the National Association of Societies for Organizing Charity—that was a forerunner of the present Family Service Association of America. In 1920 the Child Welfare League of America was founded.

14. See Zitha R. Turitz and Rebecca Smith, "Child Welfare," pp. 137–145; Clark W. Blackburn, "Family Social Work," pp. 309–319; and Elliot Studt, "Correctional Services (Social Work Practice in)," pp. 219–225, *Encyclopedia of Social Work* (New York: National Association of Social Workers, 1965).

15. Alan D. Wade, "The Social Worker in the Political Process,"

The Social Welfare Forum, 1966 (New York: Columbia University Press, 1966), pp. 58–59.

16. Georg Simmel, *Sociologie* (Leipzig, Germany: Duncker & Humber, 1908); and Charles H. Cooley, *Social Process* (New York: Charles Scribner's Sons, 1918).

17. Mary E. Richmond, *Social Diagnosis* (New York: Russell Sage Foundation, 1917).

18. See William E. Gordon, "Preliminary Report on Social Work Methods" (New York: NASW Commission on Practice, March 21–23, 1963). (Mimeographed.) Dr. Gordon was then chairman of the Working Definition Subcommittee. The report says: " 'Method of social work' is used by the majority of social workers to *include* the value, knowledge, and purposes associated with the method." (P. 1.)

19. The term *model* is used here according to the following definitions in *Webster's Third New International Dictionary* (Springfield, Mass.: G. & C. Merriam Co., 1961), p. 1451: ". . . 14a: a description, a collection of statistical data, or an analogy used to help visualize often in a simplified way something that cannot be directly observed (as an atom) [and] b: a theoretical projection in detail of a possible system of human relationships (as in economics, politics, or psychology). . . ."

16   Attributes of a Profession

ERNEST GREENWOOD

The professions occupy a position of great importance on the American scene.[1] In a society such as ours, characterized by minute division of labor based upon technical specialization, many important features of social organization are dependent upon professional functions. Professional activity is coming to play a predominant role in the life patterns of increasing numbers of individuals of both sexes, occupying much of their waking moments, providing life goals, determining behavior, and shaping personality. It is no wonder, therefore, that the phenomenon of professionalism has become an object of observation by sociologists.[2] The sociological ap-

Reprinted with permission of the National Association of Social Workers and the author from *Social Work*, 2, 3 (July 1957): 45–55.

proach to professionalism is one that views a profession as an organized group which is constantly interacting with the society that forms its matrix, which performs its social functions through a network of formal and informal relationships, and which creates its own subculture requiring adjustments to it as a prerequisite for career success.[3]

Within the professional category of its occupational classification the United States Census Bureau includes, among others, the following: accountant, architect, artist, attorney, clergyman, college professor, dentist, engineer, journalist, judge, librarian, natural scientist, optometrist, pharmacist, physician, social scientist, social worker, surgeon, and teacher.[4] What common attributes do these professional occupations possess which distinguish them from the nonprofessional ones? After a careful canvass of the sociological literature on occupations, this writer has been able to distill five elements, upon which there appears to be consensus among the students of the subject, as constituting the distinguishing attributes of a profession.[5] Succinctly put, all professions seem to possess: (1) systematic theory, (2) authority, (3) community sanction, (4) ethical codes, and (5) a culture. The purpose of this article is to describe fully these attributes.

Before launching into our description, a preliminary word of caution is due. With respect to each of the above attributes, the true difference between a professional and a nonprofessional occupation is not a qualitative but a quantitative one. Strictly speaking, these attributes are not the exclusive monopoly of the professions; nonprofessional occupations also possess them, but to a lesser degree. As is true of most social phenomena, the phenomenon of professionalism cannot be structured in terms of clear-cut classes. Rather, we must think of the occupations in a society as distributing themselves along a continuum.[6] At one end of this continuum are bunched the well-recognized and undisputed professions (e.g., physician, attorney, professor, scientist); at the opposite end are bunched the least skilled and least attractive occupations (e.g., watchman, truckloader, farm laborer, scrubwoman, bus boy). The remaining occupations, less skilled and less prestigeful than the former, but more so than the latter, are distributed between these two poles. The occupations bunched at the professional pole of the continuum possess to a maximum degree the attributes about to be described. As we move away from this pole, the occupations possess these attributes to a decreasing degree. Thus, in the less developed professions, social work among them, these attributes appear in moderate degree. When we reach the midregion of the continuum, among the clerical, sales, and crafts occupations, they occur in still lesser degree; while at the unskilled end of the continuum the occupations possess these attributes so minimally that they are virtually nonexistent. If the reader keeps this concept of the continuum in mind, the presentation will less likely appear as a distortion of reality.

SYSTEMATIC BODY OF THEORY[7]

It is often contended that the chief difference between a professional and a nonprofessional occupation lies in the element of superior skill. The performance of a professional service presumably involves a series of unusually complicated operations, mastery of which requires lengthy training. The models referred to in this connection are the performances of a surgeon, a concert pianist, or a research physicist. However, some nonprofessional occupations actually involve a higher order of skill than many professional ones. For example, tool-and-die making, diamond-cutting, monument-engraving, or cabinet-making involve more intricate operations than schoolteaching, nursing, or social work. Therefore, to focus on the element of skill per se in describing the professions is to miss the kernel of their uniqueness.

The crucial distinction is this: the skills that characterize a profession flow from and are supported by a fund of knowledge that has been organized into an internally consistent system, called a *body of theory*. A profession's underlying body of theory is a system of abstract propositions that describe in general terms the classes of phenomena comprising the profession's focus of interest. Theory serves as a base in terms of which the professional rationalizes his operations in concrete situations. Acquisition of the professional skill requires a prior or simultaneous mastery of the theory underlying that skill. Preparation for a profession, therefore, involves considerable preoccupation with systematic theory, a feature virtually absent in the training of the nonprofessional. And so treatises are written on legal theory, musical theory, social work theory, the theory of the drama, and so on; but no books appear on the theory of punch-pressing or pipe-fitting or brick-laying.

Because understanding of theory is so important to professional skill, preparation for a profession must be an intellectual as well as a practical experience. On-the-job training through apprenticeship, which suffices for a nonprofessional occupation, becomes inadequate for a profession. Orientation in theory can be achieved best through formal education in an academic setting. Hence the appearance of the professional school, more often than not university affiliated, wherein the milieu is a contrast to that of the trade school. Theoretical knowledge is more difficult to master than operational procedures; it is easier to learn to repair an automobile than to learn the principles of the internal combustion engine. There are, of course, a number of free-lance professional pursuits (e.g., acting, painting, writing, composing, and the like) wherein academic preparation is not mandatory. Nevertheless, even in these fields various "schools" and "institutes" are appearing, although they may not be run along traditional academic lines. We can generalize that as an occupation moves toward professional status, apprenticeship training yields to formalized education, because the function of theory as a groundwork for practice acquires increasing importance.

The importance of theory precipitates a form of activity normally not encountered in a nonprofessional occupation, viz., theory construction via systematic research. To generate valid theory that will provide a solid base for professional techniques requires the application of the scientific method to the service-related problems of the profession. Continued employment of the scientific method is nurtured by and in turn reinforces the element of rationality.[8] As an orientation, rationality is the antithesis of traditionalism. The spirit of rationality in a profession encourages a critical, as opposed to a reverential, attitude toward the theoretical system. It implies a perpetual readiness to discard any portion of that system, no matter how time honored it may be, with a formulation demonstrated to be more valid. The spirit of rationality generates group self-criticism and theoretical controversy. Professional members convene regularly in their associations to learn and to evaluate innovations in theory. This produces an intellectually stimulating milieu that is in marked contrast to the milieu of a nonprofessional occupation.

In the evolution of every profession there emerges the researcher-theoretician whose role is that of scientific investigation and theoretical systematization. In technological professions[9] a division of labor thereby evolves, that between the theory-oriented and the practice-oriented person. Witness the physician who prefers to attach himself to a medical research center rather than to enter private practice. This division may also yield to cleavages with repercussions upon intraprofessional relationships. However, if properly integrated, the division of labor produces an accelerated expansion of the body of theory and a sprouting of theoretical branches around which specialties nucleate. The net effect of such developments is to lengthen the preparation deemed desirable for entry into the profession. This accounts for the rise of graduate professional training on top of a basic college education.

PROFESSIONAL AUTHORITY

Extensive education in the systematic theory of his discipline imparts to the professional a type of knowledge that highlights the layman's comparative ignorance. This fact is the basis for the professional's authority, which has some interesting features.

A nonprofessional occupation has customers; a professional occupation has clients. What is the difference? A customer determines what services and/or commodities he wants, and he shops around until he finds them. His freedom of decision rests upon the premise that he has the capacity to appraise his own needs and to judge the potential of the service or of the commodity to satisfy them. The infallibility of his decisions is epitomized in the slogan: "The customer is always right!" In a professional relationship, however, the professional dictates what is good or evil for the client, who has no choice but to accede to professional judgment. Here the premise is that, because he lacks the requisite theoretical background, the client cannot diagnose his own needs or discriminate among the range of possibilities for meeting them. Nor is the client considered able to evaluate the caliber of the professional service he receives. In a nonprofessional occupation the customer can criticize the quality of the commodity he has purchased, and even demand a refund. The client lacks this same prerogative, having surrendered it to professional authority. This element of authority is one, although not the sole, reason why a profession frowns on advertising. If a profession were to advertise, it would, in effect, impute to the potential client the discriminating capacity to select from competing forms of service. The client's subordination to professional authority invests the professional with a monopoly of judgment. When an occupation strives toward professionalization, one of its aspirations is to acquire this monopoly.

The client derives a sense of security from the professional's assumption of authority. The authoritative air of the professional is a principal source of the client's faith that the relationship he is about to enter contains the potentials for meeting his needs. The professional's authority, however, is not limitless; its function is confined to those specific spheres within which the professional has been educated. This quality in professional authority Parsons calls *functional specificity*.[10] Functional specificity carries the following implications for the client-professional relationship.

The professional cannot prescribe guides for facets of the client's life where his theoretical competence does not apply. To venture such prescriptions is to invade a province wherein he himself is a layman, and, hence, to violate the authority of another professional group. The professional must not use his position of authority to exploit the client for purposes of personal gratification. In any association of superordination-subordination, of which the professional-client relationship is a perfect specimen, the subordinate member— here, the client—can be maneuvered into a dependent role. The psychological advantage which thereby accrues to the professional could constitute a temptation for him. The professional must inhibit his impulses to use the professional relationship for the satisfaction of the sexual need, the need to manipulate others, or the need to live vicariously. In the case of the therapeutic professions it is ideally preferred that client-professional intercourse not overflow the professional setting. Extraprofessional intercourse could be used by both client and professional in a manner such as to impair professional authority, with a consequent diminution of the professional's effectiveness.

Thus far we have discussed that phase of professional authority which expresses itself in the client-professional relationship. Professional authority, however, has professional-community ramifications. To these we now turn.

SANCTION OF THE COMMUNITY

Every profession strives to persuade the community to sanction its authority within certain spheres by conferring upon the profession a series of powers and privileges. Community approval of these powers and privileges may be either informal or formal; formal approval is that reinforced by the community's police power.

Among its powers is the profession's control over its training centers. This is achieved through an accrediting process exercised by one of the associations within the profession. By granting or withholding accreditation, a profession can, ideally, regulate its schools as to their number, location, curriculum content, and caliber of instruction. Comparable control is not to be found in a nonprofessional occupation.[11] The profession also acquires control over admission into the profession. This is achieved via two routes. First, the profession convinces the community that no one should be allowed to wear a professional title who has not been conferred it by an accredited professional school. Anyone can call himself a carpenter, locksmith, or metal-plater if he feels so qualified. But a person who assumes the title of physician or attorney without having earned it conventionally becomes an impostor. Secondly, the profession persuades the community to institute in its behalf a licensing system for screening those qualified to practice the professional skill. A *sine qua non* for the receipt of the license is, of course, a duly granted professional title. Another prerequisite may be an examination before a board of inquiry whose personnel have been drawn from the ranks of the profession. Police power enforces the licensing system; persons practicing the professional skill without a license are liable to punishment by public authority.[12]

Among the professional privileges, one of the most important is that of confidentiality. To facilitate efficient performance, the professional encourages the client to volunteer information he otherwise would not divulge. The community regards this as privileged communication, shared solely between client and professional, and protects the latter legally from encroachments upon such confidentiality. To be sure, only a select few of the professions, notably medicine and law, enjoy this immunity. Its very rarity makes it the ultimate in professionalization. Another one of the professional privileges is a relative immunity from community judgment on technical matters. Standards for professional performance are reached by consensus within the profession and are based on the existing body of theory. The lay community is presumed incapable of comprehending these standards and, hence, of using them to identify malpractice. It is generally conceded that a professional's performance can be evaluated only by his peers.

The powers and privileges described above constitute a monopoly granted by the community to the professional group. Therefore, when an occupation strives toward professional status, one of its prime objectives is to acquire this monopoly. But this is difficult to achieve, because counter forces within the community resist strongly the profession's claims to authority. Through its associations the profession wages an organized campaign to persuade the community that it will benefit greatly by granting the monopoly. Specifically the profession seeks to prove: that the performance of the occupational skill requires specialized education; that those who possess this education, in contrast to those who do not, deliver a superior service; and that the human need being served is of sufficient social importance to justify the superior performance.

REGULATIVE CODE OF ETHICS

The monopoly enjoyed by a profession vis-à-vis clients and community is fraught with hazards. A monopoly can be abused; powers and privileges can be used to protect vested interests against the public weal.[13] The professional group could peg the price of its services at an unreasonably high level; it could restrict the numbers entering the occupation to create a scarcity of personnel; it could dilute the caliber of its performance without community awareness; and it could frustrate forces within the occupation pushing for socially beneficial changes in practices.[14] Were such abuses to become conspicuous, widespread, and permanent, the community would, of course, revoke the profession's monopoly. This extreme measure is normally unnecessary, because every profession has a built-in regulative code which compels ethical behavior on the part of its members.

The profession's ethical code is part formal and part informal. The formal is the written code to which the professional usually swears upon being admitted to practice; this is best exemplified by the Hippocratic Oath of the medical profession. The informal is the unwritten code, which nonetheless carries the weight of formal prescriptions. Through its ethical code the profession's commitment to the social welfare becomes a matter of public record, thereby insuring for itself the continued confidence of the community. Without such confidence the profession could not retain its monopoly. To be sure, self-regulative codes are characteristic of all occupations, nonprofessional as well as professional. However, a professional code is perhaps more explicit, systematic, and binding; it certainly possesses more altruistic overtones and is more public service-oriented.[15] These account for the frequent synonymous use of the terms "professional" and "ethical" when applied to occupational behavior.

While the specifics of their ethical codes vary among the professions, the essentials are uniform. These may be described in terms of client-professional and colleague-colleague relations.

Toward the client the professional must assume an emotional neutrality. He must provide service to whoever requests it, irrespective of the requesting client's age, income, kinship, politics, race, religion, sex, and social status. A nonprofessional may withhold his services on such grounds without, or with minor, censure; a professional cannot. Parsons calls this element in professional conduct *universalism*. In other words, only in his extraoccupational contacts can the professional relate to others on particularistic terms, *i.e.*, as particular individuals with concrete personalities attractive or unattractive to him. In his client contacts particularistic considerations are out of place. Parsons also calls attention to the element of *disinterestedness* in the professional-client relationship.[16] In contrast to the nonprofessional, the professional is motivated less by self-interest and more by the impulse to perform maximally. The behavior corollaries of this service orientation are many. For one, the professional must, under all circumstances, give maximum caliber service. The nonprofessional can dilute the quality of his commodity or service to fit the size of the client's fee; not so the professional. Again, the professional must be prepared to render his services upon request, even at the sacrifice of personal convenience.

The ethics governing colleague relationships demand behavior that is co-operative, equalitarian, and supportive. Members of a profession share technical knowledge with each other. Any advance in theory and practice made by one professional is quickly disseminated to colleagues through the professional associations.[17] The proprietary and quasi-secretive attitudes toward discovery and invention prevalent in the industrial and commercial world are out of place in the professional. Also out of place is the blatant competition for clients which is the norm in so many nonprofessional pursuits. This is not to gainsay the existence of intraprofessional competition; but it is a highly regulated competition, diluted with co-operative ingredients which impart to it its characteristically restrained quality. Colleague relations must be equalitarian; intraprofessional recognition should ideally be based solely upon performance in practice and/or contribution to theory.[18] Here, too, particularistic considerations must not be allowed to operate. Finally, professional colleagues must support each other vis-à-vis clientele and community. The professional must refrain from acts which jeopardize the authority of colleagues, and must sustain those whose authority is threatened.[19]

The ways and means whereby a profession enforces the observance of its ethical code constitute a case study in social control. Self-discipline is achieved informally and formally.

Informal discipline consists of the subtle and the not-so-subtle pressures that colleagues exert upon one another. An example in this connection is the phenomenon of consultation and referral.[20] Consultation is the practice of inviting a colleague to participate in the appraisal of the client's need and/or in the planning of the service to be rendered. Referral is the practice of affording colleagues access to a client or an appointment. Thus, one colleague may refer his client to another, because lack of time or skill prevents his rendering the needed service; or he may recommend another for appointment by a prospective employer. Since professional ethics precludes aggressive competition and advertising, consultation and referral constitute the principal source of work to a professional. The consultation-referral custom involves professional colleagues in a system of reciprocity which fosters mutual interdependence. Interdependence facilitates social control; chronic violation of professional etiquette arouses colleague resentment, resulting in the cessation of consultation requests and referrals.

A more formal discipline is exercised by the professional associations, which possess the power to criticize or to censure, and in extreme cases to bar recalcitrants. Since membership in good standing in the professional associations is a *sine qua non* of professional success, the prospect of formal disciplinary action operates as a potent force toward conformity.

THE PROFESSIONAL CULTURE

Every profession operates through a network of formal and informal groups. Among the formal groups, first there are the organizations through which the profession performs its services; these provide the institutionalized setting where professional and client meet. Examples of such organizations are hospital, clinic, university, law office, engineering firm, or social agency. Secondly, there are the organizations whose functions are to replenish the profession's supply of talent and to expand its fund of knowledge. These include the educational and the research centers. Third among the formal groups are the organizations which emerge as an expression of the growing consciousness-of-kind on the part of the profession's members, and which promote so-called group interests and aims. These are the professional associations. Within and around these formal organizations extends a filigree of informal groupings: the multitude of small, closely knit clusters of colleagues. Membership in these cliques is based on a variety of affinities: specialties within the profession; affiliations with select professional societies; residential and work propinquity; family, religious, or ethnic background; and personality attractions.

The interactions of social roles required by these formal and informal groups generate a social configuration unique to the profession, *viz.*, a professional culture. All occupations are characterized by formal and informal groupings; in this respect the professions are not unique. What is unique is the culture thus begotten. If one were to single out the attribute that most effectively differentiates the professions from other occupations, this is it. Thus we can talk of a professional culture as distinct from a nonprofessional culture. Within the professions as a logical class each profession develops its own subculture, a variant of the professional culture; the engineering subculture, for example, differs from the subcultures of medicine and social work. In the subsequent discussion, however, we will treat the culture of the professions as a generic phenomenon. The culture of a profession consists of its *values, norms, and symbols*.

The social values of a professional group are its basic and fundamental beliefs, the unquestioned premises upon which its very existence rests. Foremost among these values is the essential worth of the service which the professional group extends to the community. The profession considers that the service is a social good and that community welfare would be immeasurably impaired by its absence. The twin concepts of professional authority and monopoly also possess the force of a group value. Thus, the proposition that in all service-related matters the professional group is infinitely wiser than the laity is regarded as beyond argument. Likewise nonarguable is the proposition that acquisition by the professional group of a service monopoly would inevitably produce social progress. And then there is the value of rationality; that is, the commitment to objectivity in the realm of theory and technique. By virtue of this orientation, nothing of a theoretical or technical nature is regarded as sacred and unchallengeable simply because it has a history of acceptance and use.

The norms of a professional group are the guides to behavior in social situations. Every profession develops an elaborate system of these role definitions. There is a range of appropriate behaviors for seeking admittance into the profession, for gaining entry into its formal and informal groups, and for progressing within the occupation's hierarchy. There are appropriate modes of securing appointments, of conducting referrals, and of handling consultation. There are proper ways of acquiring clients, of receiving and dismissing them, of questioning and treating them, of accepting and rejecting them. There are correct ways of grooming a protégé, of recompensing a sponsor, and of relating to peers, superiors, or subordinates. There are even group-approved ways of challenging an outmoded theory, of introducing a new technique, and of conducting an intraprofessional controversy. In short, there is a behavior norm covering every standard interpersonal situation likely to recur in professional life.

The symbols of a profession are its meaning-laden items. These may include such things as: its insignias, emblems, and distinctive dress; its history, folklore, and argot; its heroes and its villains; and its stereotypes of the professional, the client, and the layman.

Comparatively clear and controlling group values, behavior norms, and symbols, which characterize the professions, are not to be encountered in nonprofessional occupations.

Our discussion of the professional culture would be incomplete without brief mention of one of its central concepts, the *career* concept. The term career is, as a rule, employed only in reference to a professional occupation. Thus, we do not talk about the career of a bricklayer or of a mechanic; but we do talk about the career of an architect or of a clergyman. At the heart of the career concept is a certain attitude toward work which is peculiarly professional. A career is essentially a *calling*, a life devoted to "good works."[21] Professional work is never viewed solely as a means to an end; it is the end itself. Curing the ill, educating the young, advancing science are values in themselves. The professional performs his services primarily for the psychic satisfactions and secondarily for the monetary compensations.[22] Self-seeking motives feature minimally in the choice of a profession; of maximal importance is affinity for the work. It is this devotion to the work itself which imparts to professional activity the service orientation and the element of disinterestedness. Furthermore, the absorption in the work is not partial, but complete; it results in a total personal involvement. The work life invades the after-work life, and the sharp demarcation between the work hours and the leisure hours disappears. To the professional person his work becomes his life.[23] Hence the act of embarking upon a professional career is similar in some respects to entering a religious order. The same cannot be said of a nonprofessional occupation.

To succeed in his chosen profession, the neophyte must make an effective adjustment to the professional culture.[24] Mastery of the underlying body of theory and acquisition of the technical skills are in themselves insufficient guarantees of professional success. The recruit must also become familiar with and learn to weave his way through the labyrinth of the professional culture. Therefore, the transformation of a neophyte into a professional is essentially an acculturation process wherein he internalizes the social values, the behavior norms, and the symbols of the occupational group.[25] In its frustrations and rewards it is fundamentally no different from the acculturation of an immigrant to a relatively strange culture. Every profession entertains a stereotype of the ideal colleague; and, of course, it is always one who is thoroughly adjusted to the professional culture.[26] The poorly acculturated colleague is a deviant; he is regarded as "peculiar," "unorthodox," "annoying," and in extreme cases a "troublemaker." Whereas the professional group encourages innovation in theory and technique, it tends to discourage deviation from its social values and norms. In this internal contradiction, however, the professional culture is no different from the larger culture of society.

One of the principal functions of the professional schools is to identify and screen individuals who are prospective deviants from the professional culture. That is why the admission of candidates to professional education must be judged on grounds in addition to and other than their academic qualifications.[27] Psychic factors presaging favorable adjustment to the professional culture are granted an importance equivalent to mental abilities. The professional school provides test situations through initial and graduated exposures of the novice to the professional culture. By his behavior in these social situations involving colleagues, clients, and community, the potential deviant soon reveals himself and is immediately weeded out. Comparable preoccupation with the psychic prerequisites of occupational adjustment is not characteristic of nonprofessional occupations.

IMPLICATIONS FOR SOCIAL WORK

The picture of the professions just unveiled is an ideal type. In the construction of an ideal type some exaggeration of reality is unavoidable, since the intent is to achieve an internally coherent picture. One function of the ideal type is to structure reality in such manner that discrete, disparate, and dissimilar phenomena become organized, thereby bringing order out of apparent disorder. We now possess a model of a profession that is much sharper and clearer than the actuality that confronts us when we observe the occupational scene. What is the utility of this model for social work?

The preoccupation of social workers with professionalization has been a characteristic feature of the social work scene for years. Flexner,[28] Johnson,[29] Hollis and Taylor,[30] and others have written on the subject, proposing criteria which must be met if social work is to acquire professional status. Whenever social workers convene, there is the constant reaffirmation of the urgency to achieve the recognition from the community befitting a profession. The union of the seven separate organizations into the National Association of Social Workers is generally regarded as an important milestone in social work history, precisely because of its potential stimulus toward professionalization.

In view of all this, it is proper for social workers to possess clear conceptions of that which they so fervently seek. The model of the professions portrayed above should contribute to such clarification; it should illuminate the goal for which social workers are striving. It is often contended that social work is still far from having attained professional status.[31] But this is a misconception. When we hold up social work against the model of the professions presented above, it does not take long to decide whether to classify it within the professional or the nonprofessional occupations. Social work is already a profession; it has too many points of congruence with the model to be classifiable otherwise. Social work is, however, seeking to rise within the professional hierarchy, so that it, too, might enjoy maximum prestige, authority, and monopoly which presently belong to a few top professions.

The model presented above should also serve to sensitize social workers to anticipate some of the problems that continued professionalization must inevitably precipitate. The model indicates that progressive professionalization will involve social workers in novel relationships with clients, colleagues, agency, community, and other professions. In concluding this paper we refer briefly to one such problem. It is no secret that social workers are not all uniformly enthusiastic about the professionalization of social work. Bisno[32] has given verbalization to a prevailing apprehension that social workers might have to scuttle their social-action heritage as a price of achieving the public acceptance accorded a profession. Extrapolation from the sociologists' model of the professions suggests a reality basis for these fears. It suggests that the attainment of professional prestige, authority, and monopoly by social workers will undoubtedly carry disturbing implications for the social action and social reform components of social work philosophy. The anticipated developments will compel social workers to rethink and redefine the societal role of their profession.

These and other dilemmas flowing from professionalization are bound to tax the best minds among social workers for their resolution. In this connection a proper understanding of the attributes of a profession would seem to be indispensable.

NOTES

1. Talcott Parsons, "The Professions and Social Structure," *Social Forces,* Vol. 17 (May 1939), pp. 457–467.

2. Theodore Caplow, *The Sociology of Work* (Minneapolis: University of Minnesota Press, 1954).

3. Oswald Hall, "The Stages of a Medical Career," *American Journal of Sociology,* Vol. 53 (March 1948), pp. 327–336; "Types of Medical Careers," *American Journal of Sociology,* Vol. 55 (November 1949), pp. 243–253; "Sociological Research in the Field of Medicine: Progress and Prospects," *American Sociological Review,* Vol. 16 (October 1951), pp. 639–644.

4. U.S. Bureau of the Census, *1950 Census of Population: Classified Index of Occupations and Industries* (Washington, D.C.: Government Printing Office, 1950).

5. The writer acknowledges his debt to his former students at the School of Social Welfare, University of California, Berkeley, who, as members of his research seminars, assisted him in identifying and abstracting the sociological literature on occupations. Their conscientious assistance made possible the formulation presented in this paper.

6. The occupational classification employed by the U.S. Census Bureau is precisely such a continuum. The categories of this classification are: (a) professionals and semiprofessional technical workers; (b) proprietors and managers, both farm and nonfarm, and officials; (c) clerical, sales, and kindred workers; (d) craftsmen, skilled workers, and foremen; (e) operatives and semiskilled workers; and (f) laborers, unskilled, service, and domestic workers. (U.S. Bureau of the Census, *op. cit.*).

7. The sequence in which the five attributes are discussed in

this paper does not reflect upon their relative importance. The order selected has been dictated by logical considerations.

8. Parsons, op. cit.

9. A technology is a profession whose aim is to achieve controlled changes in natural relationships. Convention makes a distinction between technologists who shape nonhuman materials and those who deal with human beings. The former are called engineers; the latter practitioners.

10. Parsons, op. cit.

11. To set up and run a school for floral decorating requires no approval from the national florists' association, but no school of social work could operate long without approval of the Council on Social Work Education.

12. Many nonprofessional occupations have also succeeded in obtaining licensing legislation in their behalf. Witness the plumbers, radio operators, and barbers, to mention a few. However, the sanctions applied against a person practicing a nonprofessional occupation are much less severe than is the case when a professional occupation is similarly involved.

13. Abraham Flexner, "Is Social Work a Profession?" in *Proceedings of the National Conference of Charities and Corrections* (Chicago: 1915), pp. 576–590; Robert K. Merton, "Bureaucratic Structure and Personality," in Alvin Gouldner, ed., *Studies in Leadership* (New York: Harper & Brothers, 1950), pp. 67–79.

14. Merton, op. cit.

15. Flexner, op. cit.; Parsons, op. cit.

16. Parsons, op. cit.

17. Arlien Johnson, "Professional Standards and How They Are Attained," *Journal of American Dental Association*, Vol. 31 (September 1944), pp. 1181–1189.

18. Flexner, op. cit.

19. This partly explains why physicians do not testify against each other in malpractice suits.

20. Hall, op. cit.

21. The term *calling* literally means a divine summons to undertake a course of action. Originally, it was employed to refer to religious activity. The Protestant Reformation widened its meaning to include economic activity as well. Henceforth divinely inspired "good works" were to be both secular and sacred in nature. Presumably, then, any occupational choice may be a response to divine summons. In this connection, it is interesting to note that the German word for vocation is *Beruf*, a noun derived from the verb *berufen*, to call.

22. Johnson, op. cit.

23. The all-pervading influence of work upon the lives of professional results in interesting by-products. The members of a

profession tend to associate with one another outside the work setting (Oswald Hall, "The Stages of a Medical Career," op. cit.). Their families mingle socially; leisure time is spent together; "shop talk" permeates social discourse; and a consensus develops. The profession thus becomes a whole social environment, nurturing characteristic social and political attitudes, patterns of consumption and recreation, and decorum and Weltanschauung (Caplow, op. cit.; and William H. Form, "Toward an Occupational Social Psychology," Journal of Social Psychology, Vol. 24, February 1946, pp. 85–99).

24. Oswald Hall, "The Stages of a Medical Career" and "Types of Medical Careers," op. cit.

25. R. Clyde White, " 'Social Workers in Society': Some Further Evidence," Social Work Journal, Vol. 34 (October 1953), pp. 161–164.

26. The laity also entertain a stereotypic image of the professional group. Needless to say, the layman's conception and the professional's self-conception diverge widely, because they are fabricated out of very different experiences. The layman's stereotype is frequently a distortion of reality, being either an idealization or a caricature of the professional type.

27. Oswald Hall, "Sociological Research in the Field of Medicine: Progress and Prospects," op. cit.

28. Flexner, op. cit.

29. Johnson, op. cit.

30. Ernest V. Hollis and Alice L. Taylor, Social Work Education in the United States (New York: Columbia University Press, 1951).

31. Flexner considered that the social work of his day was not a profession. Hollis and Taylor regard present-day social work as still in its early adolescence.

32. Herbert Bisno, "How Social Will Social Work Be?" Social Work, Vol. 1, No. 2 (April 1956), pp. 12–18.

17 The Incomplete Profession

NEIL GILBERT and HARRY SPECHT

The profession of social work is incomplete: it has developed a commitment to services but has failed to develop a commitment to

Reprinted with permission of the National Association of Social Workers, from Social Work, 19, 6 (November 1974): 665–74.

welfare. This incompleteness is one reason for its difficulty in responding effectively to demands placed on it by a society in transition and upheaval.

This diagnosis of the state of the profession is not original. It follows a recurrent theme on the duality of social work practice, played under different titles throughout the profession's history. In 1905 Richmond wrote of the "wholesale" and "retail" methods of social reform; in 1929 probably the best known and most enduring variation was composed by Lee under the title of "cause" and "function"; in 1958 Burns spoke of the distinction between "social work" and "social welfare"; in 1963 Schwartz discussed the "service" and the "movement"; and in 1972 Richan identified different underlying language systems in social work.[1] And this is only a partial list.[2]

While duality still exists, in recent years its nature has changed substantially. The balance has shifted from services to welfare, and the consequences are now filtering into the field with results disappointing for the profession's commitment to both welfare and services. The purpose of this article is, first, to examine this shift and the adjustments that have been made and, second, to propose a course of action designed to fulfill a substantive commitment to welfare while maintaining the integrity of social work's commitment to services—not to mitigate but to invigorate the duality inherent in social work practice.

In this discussion the authors refer to services as the specific and concrete activities that professionals engage in to assist those in need. They include all direct-service activities such as therapy, counseling, education, advocacy, information gathering, and referral. Such activities are the major concerns of casework, group work, and those aspects of community organization in which direct services are provided to community groups and organizations.[3] These activities will be discussed collectively as social work services and direct services and the professionals engaged in them will be referred to as social work specialists and direct-service workers.

Welfare, in the framework of this article, deals with the professional activities that focus on both change in and maintenance of the institution of social welfare. Institution in this instance refers to the system of programs conducted by public and private agencies that have the express purpose of providing mutual support for individuals, families, and groups.[4] Professional activities involved in social welfare include indirect services such as planning, policy analysis, program development, administration, and program evaluation. The social welfare specialist does not deal directly with those in need, but focuses rather on the institutional structure through which those in need are served. These activities will be referred to as indirect services and social welfare, and the professionals engaged in them will be referred to as indirect service workers and social welfare specialists.

SERVICES AND WELFARE

Sixteen years ago in "Social Welfare Is Our Commitment," the keynote address to the National Conference on Social Welfare, Burns described the difference between the two commitments and provided the framework for developing the profession's other side. Burns indicated that the conference had changed its name from "social work" to "social welfare" because social work had come to signify only "certain categories of people who are involved in our social service," those with "a specific series of skilled services."[5] She stated that there was nothing undesirable about the professionalization of certain types of social welfare activities, but that the term "social work" focused too narrowly on professional functions. "Social welfare," on the other hand, "seemed most comprehensively to embrace the entire field of social welfare and the concerns of all those who were interested in it regardless of their functions, professional orientation, skills, and affiliations."[6] Ironically, the table of contents of the conference proceedings listed Burns's address as "Social Work Is Our Commitment." The profession of social work appears to have little understood and been little affected by her lucid and instructive charge.

This result was not entirely unforeseen; Burns identified three obstacles to the fulfillment of social work's commitment to welfare. First, the technical skills and knowledge required to affect the structure of welfare services were in short supply in social work. Second, social workers perceived themselves as lacking the influence and political power needed to affect public policy decisions. Third, the profession had no commitment to a cause.[7]

A significant proportion of social workers today have a surfeit of commitment to causes and no longer suffer from a lack of belief in their political acumen. In contrast, there has been little development of the knowledge, skill, and technical expertise that Burns thought necessary for fulfilling a commitment to welfare. But in the process of change, the commitment to services has been drastically diluted, if not completely erased, as resources, practice skills, and knowledge designed for the service enterprise were stretched and twisted in efforts to accommodate new departures. Rein's observation in 1970 is much to the point.

> Individual social workers may, of course, function as reformers in the areas of employment, income distribution, and political power—but these activities are marginal to their professional tasks. In this sense they are professionals who are radical rather than members of a radical profession.[8]

How did all this come about?

IMPULSE FOR CHANGE

Social work's commitment to services was made at the beginning of this century. At that time, as Austin points out, strategies for societal change were rejected in favor of a concentration on services:

> Particularly significant in the conflict between these two approaches was the decision made in 1910 by the board of directors of the New York School of Philanthropy to concentrate on the training of caseworkers for direct service positions in charity agencies. In doing so they explicitly rejected the recommendation . . . that social workers should concern themselves with the issues of public policy rather than with the provision of financial assistance on a case-by-case basis. . . . The practitioner-oriented curriculum which the New York School adopted, built around the personnel needs of locally based individual and neighborhood centered programs, was to become the model for all schools of social work until the 1960s.[9]

In the early 1960s, along with the general national impulse for social justice, social work was gripped by an impulse to make social welfare an instrument to deal with societal inequities. Social workers' belief systems and orientations were profoundly affected by three developments: (1) the civil rights movement, which was part of and probably the cause of a general revolution in human relations, (2) the evolution of national programs such as the War on Poverty and Model Cities, which were directed at producing large-scale social change, and (3) the growing concern at the start of the 1970s with questions of institutional inequality.[10]

The social work profession, as Austin notes, became the whipping boy for the advocates of institutional change because social casework failed to develop effective means for dealing with poverty:

> The high point of the assault was the speech by Sargent Shriver . . . in 1964 announcing that there was no place for casework in the war-on-poverty programs. . . . The attack on casework and the organized social work profession continued throughout the [War on Poverty] together with strong support for the principle of using nonprofessionals and generalists rather than social work specialists as staff in community action programs. This attack which was also supported by many professional social workers was so successful that the membership of the professional association voted in 1969 to overturn the principle established . . . in the 1920s that social work was a distinctive profession based exclusively on a systematic program of professional education at the graduate level.[11]

With individual services suffering a crisis of confidence, how did the profession express the impulse for social justice? One might say that it attempted to deal rather with injustice, but in poor form. The National Association of Social Workers, the Council on Social Work Education, and schools of social work and social welfare were not prepared with a substantive, distinctive means by which social work could address problems of poverty, discrimination, and inequality. An impulse is not a commitment but only a feeling pushed on by energy without any direction. Demonstration, disruption, confrontation—the tactics of Saul Alinsky based on the idea that "power is all" and the tactics of the civil rights movement—were adopted by many social workers as behaviors of choice for committed professionals.

Caught short, social workers used the only means available to the profession at the time for responding to demands for change—its services.[12] Many concluded that casework was not effective for any purpose, and those who provided services to clients in need began to address themselves politically to social problems. Custodial care, institutionalization, supportive services, and clinical intervention were to become almost anathema in the social services—all seen as variations of "blaming the victim." Attention and resources were devoted to protest activities, street people, social action, and manifestations of social ferment like drug abuse, sexual liberation, and new forms of communication. Many practitioners attached themselves to causes that were written in the day's headlines and that changed almost as frequently.

The authors attended a recent meeting of social workers, called to discuss with the school's faculty what professionals in the field believed the school should teach. As the list of problems having priority grew longer and wider in range, one professional who works with the state senate inquired, "Is there any problem that you think you cannot deal with?" He then said he finds it difficult to convince the senate—a legislative body reasonably sensitive to the concerns of social welfare—that social workers can do *anything* well. Apparently this sentiment is not peculiar to the California state legislature. The Family Service Association of America issued the following statement:

> It will be impossible for graduates to be prepared for [direct-service-giving] positions if the school has set an educational goal for them that is too general and has encouraged them to place no value on working with the individual predicaments and life problems of people. . . . Many students do not achieve in graduate schools of social work a fundamental grasp of [the competence needed for casework practice]. They do not develop a commitment to, or even an awareness of, the need for working with and for individuals and families. They do not emerge with an adequate theoretical base for practice in usable form.[13]

The social work profession responded inadequately to the impulse for change because the training, skill, and knowledge required for a sustained and meaningful commitment to welfare were lacking. Social workers enthusiastically rushed to engage themselves in one new programmatic arrangement after another with little to show for the effort either in social change or increased knowledge and competence. All the heat did not forge a commitment to welfare, but rather served to consume the substance on which the commitment to services is based.

SEARCH FOR UNITY

Many factors internal and external to the profession influenced its response to the social forces at play since the 1960s. One internal factor of central concern to social work educators was that the profession's perennial search for unity hampered change and the development of a commitment to welfare.

Many have long considered that the duality of social work practice is a source of strain within the profession. Proposals for mitigating this strain generally have been couched in terms of unity, which would seem desirable. Indeed, unity is an objective hard to resist in almost any context (man with man, man with nature, nation with nation, husband with wife). The problem is not the objective, but the means proposed to achieve it in social work.

Achieving unity has been equated with mixing the educational elements required to produce the direct-service practitioner and the social welfare specialist. For instance, there are proposals to create the generic social worker by fusing service and welfare commitments into a single function, such as the mediating one described by Schwartz.[14] Levin proposes "a social policy base for unifying the component sequences of the curriculum and for shaping their content."[15] And Richan suggests that the unifying elements may be found in developing a common professional language.[16]

The common thrust of most of these proposals is toward achieving unity by creating a core curriculum in which direct-service practitioners and welfare specialists mingle in the same core courses. The degree to which the identities, skills, knowledge, and practice orientations of the two groups are fused depends on the extent of the core curriculum.

These proposals tend to ignore or at least do not directly address another meaning of unity that has to do with the distinction between mixing and linking. *Mixing* implies creating a new whole by fusing separate identities of constituent elements. *Linking* implies creating a new whole by connecting separate identities of constituent elements.

A UNIFIED SINGLE FUNCTION

In response to proposals that there should be separate systems of social work education for direct-service practitioners and social welfare specialists, Schwartz states the argument for a unified single function—the unity-through-mixing orientation—as follows:

> To create a "department" for each would in fact *institutionalize* the very evils they mean to solve. The "clinicians"

would be shielded from any further pressures to bring weight of the experiences with people in trouble to bear on the formation of public policy; and the "social planners" would be set free from the realities of practice and left alone to fashion their expertise not from the struggles and sufferings of people but from their own clever and speculating minds. . . . The planner who has not practiced will be as shallow in his policy-making as the practitioner who has not made his impact on policy will be in his work with people.

Thus the question for the profession is whether it now gives itself over to the polarization of the individual and the social, building it into its very structure, or tries to see more deeply into the connections between the two so that it may create a single vision of the professional function. [Italics added.][17]

Schwartz raises an important issue. Is it possible to prepare professionals who can carry a commitment to welfare without first becoming skilled direct-service practitioners? Can they plan for, administer, and evaluate services if they have not been directly engaged in providing them? One way to put this issue to rest is to point out that much significant work on social welfare policy, program, administration, and research and evaluation is by non-social workers or those with little direct-practice experience. Among these, to mention a few, are Eveline Burns, Frances Piven, Nathan Glazer, Daniel Moynihan, Edwin Witte, Arthur Altmeyer, Herman Somers, Mollie Orshansky, Wilbur Cohen, Sar Levitan, Gilbert Steiner and Robert Lampman—all welfare experts known for work they have done skillfully, with compassion and commitment. No one knows or cares whether they have mastered the "conscious use of self" that is legitimately expected of the direct-service worker.

DUALITY OF THE PROFESSION

Another approach to this issue recognizes that the profession of social work is, in reality, divided into two branches. In actual day-to-day practice, professionals are clearly engaged in either direct or indirect services, carrying out a commitment to services or a commitment to welfare. If social workers ignore this reality, they are merely leaving it to others to fulfill their commitments. As long as the profession does not fulfill its commitment to welfare it will not have a serious handle on its own future. If social workers are to deal with social welfare, then educators and social planners had better begin to build the programs and the professional support system that will encourage them to do so.

The call to arms should not be so thunderous as to drown out the practical wisdom of those who caution against polarization of the profession. When Schwartz stated that "the question for the profession is whether it now gives itself over to the polarization of the individual and the social," this implied division and disaffection between competing elements in the profession. But another outcome might be possible: separate functional identities that are complementary and mutually supporting might be developed. However, the duality in the profession has manifested itself more in division and disaffection than in complementarity and mutual support.

The rejection of Schwartz's proposition that the planner or welfare specialist who has not practiced will be "as shallow in his policy-making as the practitioner who has not made his impact on policy will be in his work with people" does not mean that the authors favor the complete separation of the welfare specialist and the social work practitioner nor that they condone either one's ignorance of the other's line of practice. On the contrary, to the extent that each knows and understands the other's practice, his own grasp of the profession is enhanced and the profession benefits from the support each provides the other. The question is one of substance and degree. The goal is the development of separate functional identities within the framework of a unified profession.

IMPLICATIONS FOR EDUCATION

The search for unity may be summarized in terms of the following four broad models of social work education: the generic model, integrated core model, linkage model, and independent model. (See Fig. 17.1.)

Generic Model

Essentially, this model—which represents the extreme of unification through mixing—prepares professionals for direct service to individual clients, families, or groups. In some instances students

FIGURE 17.1
Educational Models for Integrating Social Services and Social Welfare

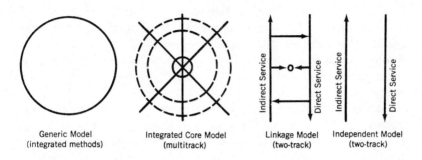

| Generic Model | Integrated Core Model | Linkage Model | Independent Model |
| (integrated methods) | (multitrack) | (two-track) | (two-track) |

will have courses in community organization and social planning. This type of program produces professionals whose major commitment is to service and who have a good deal of information about organizations, planning, and welfare systems.[18] Frequently professionals so trained know a little bit about a lot of things but are not well enough versed in the practice requirements of any specific area to offer a substantial contribution to either service or welfare.

Clearly, a commitment to services is important and worthy of professional development. But it is not the same as a commitment to welfare nor should it be. Those who want to provide direct services to people, whether through therapy, counseling, advocacy, or leisure-time activities, are obligated to master relevant knowledge and skill about inter- and intrapersonal interventions, group dynamics, social and individual pathology, and professional behavior in working with clients, agencies, and other professionals. Attempting to expand their functions to include all types of social intervention and social change efforts can only have deleterious results. Their professional equipment is likely to be a thin patchwork quilt. Training for a commitment to services should aim to produce professionals who are as highly skilled as possible at what they do.

Two-Track Independent Model

At the other extreme, the two-track independent model calls for a clear separation in developing professional practitioners for wel-

fare and service functions. One track trains for clinical practice
(direct services); the other trains for social planning, research, and
administration (indirect services). The distinctive feature of this
model is that training for one functional track is so independent of
training for the other that an entire school of social work may specialize in either area. There is no reason why both tracks must be
located in one school and, if they are, there is no curriculum requirement that forces students and faculty of the two tracks to intermingle.

As the authors see it, neither the generic nor the two-track independent model seems likely to train satisfactorily both types of
workers within the framework of a unified profession. The generic
model attempts to provide a framework for unity by mixing practice
functions so thoroughly that, in the process, service and welfare
commitments are diluted. The two-track independent model attempts to produce substantial commitments to service and welfare,
but in so doing introduces sharp separations and divisions that increase the likelihood of polarization.

Multitrack Integrated Core Model

In this model the various tracks may be found under the traditional labels of casework, group work, and community organization; microsystem, mezzosystem, and macrosystem; or direct and
indirect services. Or they may focus on problem areas such as community mental health, aging, and child welfare. The integrated core
of these educational programs may vary in size from a few courses
to a substantial part of the curriculum (at which point this model
takes on aspects of the generic one). Usually the integrated core
includes, at a minimum, courses in human growth and development,
research, and social policy, in which students from all tracks mix.
These core courses are designed, first, to provide students with a
body of knowledge relevant to the pursuit of their various lines of
practice and, second, to provide the academic binding for unification
within the school and profession. Thus they offer a substantive answer to the question: What is it that unites these various specialists
in one profession?

Compared to the curriculum for training direct-service practitioners, the programs for indirect services are relatively new to
schools of social work and generally not as well formulated. This
is not to suggest that all is well with the direct-service training or

that the area does not need new curriculum developments, experimentation, and change.[19] However, the focus of this discussion is on curriculum requirements for indirect services. The following four major areas in which the social welfare specialist must have expertise suggest the depth and complexity of the knowledge base for the curriculum of the multitrack model:

1. *Problem Analysis.* This includes skills in research, data collection, and interpretation of findings to reveal linkages between causes and problems; and assessment of needs and resources.

2. *Program Design.* This includes skills in organizational analysis and understanding of alternatives in the construction of service delivery systems; skills in budgeting, cost-benefit analysis, and other forms of systems analysis such as the planning-programming-budgeting system (PPBS); and planning for coordination and resource acquisition.

3. *Development of and Work with Decision-Making Systems.* This includes political organization and processes; uses of priority-setting schemes, organizational operations, and knowledge and skill in the structuring of planning and administrative agencies; and the acquisition and promotion of needed technical support (e.g., for economic development, therapeutic programs, or manpower training).

4. *Evaluation.* Like the first area, this includes skills in research and data collection but also calls for political and organizational skills. The function of evaluation differs from problem analysis in terms of its objective, which is to enable the community to determine the extent to which social service programs meet their goals.[20]

The authors see a crucial distinction between the essence or core of the welfare specialist's practice orientation and that of the direct-service practitioner. With the understanding that any effort to extract the essence of phenomena as complex as the skill and knowledge base of social work practice must in some measure simplify reality, the differences may be stated as follows:

▪ The core practice orientation of the direct-service worker deals with individual and group problem-solving methods, drawing upon social-psychological interpretation and relating mainly to personal and interactional variables.

▪ The core practice orientation of the indirect-service worker deals with the methods of applied social research, drawing upon empirical interpretation and relating mainly to structural and organizational variables.

By requiring students in both the direct- and indirect-service tracks to take the same set of courses, the integrated core model tends to emphasize the objective of professional unity at the cost of functional relevance.

Two-Track Linkage Model

What and how much knowledge should be shared by direct- and indirect-service workers? The main distinction between the integrated core model and the two-track linkage model is the manner in which this issue is addressed in the curriculum. Both models might include, for example, research, policy analysis, and human growth and development courses for the direct and indirect services. In the integrated core model the substance of these courses would be the same for the direct and indirect services. These and perhaps other courses are, in effect, what form the integrated core. In the two-track linkage model the substance of these courses would be different.

Although it is not the authors' intent to design a curriculum, they will attempt to convey a sense of how this model might be put into operation. Consider, for instance, the research requirement. In the indirect-service track, planning and evaluation of social welfare programs are among the skills that must be mastered. Students in this track would take research courses designed to maximize these objectives; students in the direct services, in which the knowledge of applied research methods is less central to practice, would take a substantially different type of research course, designed mainly to produce intelligent consumers or users.

The responsibility for creating the linkage, for teaching direct-service practitioners something about the practice of the indirect services and how they might collaborate with social welfare specialists, falls to the indirect-service instructors. Similarly, it would be the responsibility of instructors in the direct-service track to develop, for example, special courses designed to give social welfare specialists an understanding of the nature and requirements of practice in the direct services. Precisely what courses would fall in each track and the most appropriate points for creating linkages are matters open to detailed analysis and experimentation.

There is another type of course in which students from both tracks might intermingle. This would be a course dealing with the history of the profession and its role in developing the institution of social welfare. Such a course would highlight what it is that unites these two types of specialists in one profession—their common interests in the problems, issues, clients, and programs of social welfare and the complementary skills they bring to bear on them.

Finally, there is the question of the kinds and degrees of specialization that an MSW program designed according to the two-track linkage model might have. There can be a wide variety of arrangements for specialization within each of the two major tracks.

CONCLUSION

Recently, a number of schools of social work have developed programs for training professionals for social welfare, which suggests that the field may be attempting to fulfill its dual commitment.[21] But the appearance of these programs causes a high degree of uneasiness in the profession, and opposition may be expected from a number of sources. What seem to be some of the bases for opposition to a commitment to welfare?

A commitment to welfare entails an abstract, reflective, and long-range outlook. As Burns notes, such a commitment is "a state of mind which conceives of one's own job as part of a wider whole and where attention is focused always on the wider objective."[22] This approach is at variance with that of the political activists, who are more inclined toward immediate action and engagement in the current struggle rather than toward the deliberate study and systematic evaluation that mark a commitment to welfare.

The current ideological demands of minority faculty, students, and practitioners for curriculum emphasis on the Third-World perspective of racial minorities involve a narrower and more particularistic outlook than that required for the training of welfare specialists. This struggle between the universal and the particular is an important one in the profession. It is related to the problem of finding the proper balance between our commitments to services and welfare only because it has emerged out of the same historical currents. However, it is a different and, as Hughes notes, perennial problem:

This strain . . . is found in some degree in all professions. . . . The professional may learn some things that are univer-

sal in the physical, biological or social world. But around this
core of universal knowledge there is likely to be a large body
of practical knowledge which relates only to his own culture.
. . . While professions are, in some of their respects, universal,
in others they are closely ethnocentric. In fact, inside most professions there develops a tacit division of labor between the
more theoretical and the more practical; once in a while
conflict breaks out over issues related to it. The professional
schools may be accused of being too "academic"; the academics accuse other practitioners of failure to be sufficiently
intellectual.[23]

The debate over the appropriate balance between general knowledge and group-specific knowledge in which the social work profession is now engaged will no doubt continue, along with the
search for unity between direct and indirect services. However, the
latter search deals with a different dimension of professional development which constitutes a strain in all professions, as Hughes
also notes:

Every profession considers itself the proper body to set the
terms in which some aspect of society, life or nature is to be
thought of, and to define the general lines, or even the details
of public policy concerning it.[24]

That is, every profession must come to grips with the problems created by its duality of commitments.
A third and potentially the strongest source of opposition is from
the direct services. Direct-service practitioners have taken quite a
battering. Seemingly endless studies demonstrating the ineffectiveness of casework—coupled with a decade-long assault on services
by the social action–community organization–social planning–social
policy analysis axis—have devastated them.[25] Coming after the
collapse of the "grand illusion" of casework's bright future contained in the service amendments to the Social Security Act in the
1960s, it is no wonder that in the 1970s direct-service practitioners
are anxious about their place in the field. From their viewpoint,
welfare specialists are "the enemy." The notion of complementary
and mutually supporting functions may be unpersuasive in light of
these experiences. On the contrary, there is deep-seated concern

in the profession that the development of our commitment to welfare will require giving up our commitment to services.

Given these various strains, is it possible for social work to develop the capacity to fulfill a commitment to services and a commitment to welfare to become a complete profession? Perhaps, but such developments await the best efforts that social work professionals have to give. Social workers might begin by ceasing the useless and debilitating attacks on one another, reaffirming the profession's commitment to offering services of high quality, and seeking ways to foster the development of the profession's other side. A reassessment of educational models for the purpose of enhancing the functional integrity of services and welfare within a unified professional framework may be a useful first step in this direction.

NOTES AND REFERENCES

1. See Mary Richmond, The Long View (New York: Russell Sage Foundation, 1930), pp. 214–221; Porter Lee, Social Work as Cause and Function and Other Papers (New York: Columbia University Press, 1937), pp. 3–24; Eveline Burns, "Social Welfare Is Our Commitment," The Social Welfare Forum, 1958 (New York: Columbia University Press, 1958); William Schwartz, "Small Group Science and Group Work Practice," Social Work, 8 (October 1963), pp. 39–46; and Willard C. Richan, "A Common Language for Social Work," Social Work, 17 (November 1972), pp. 14–22.

2. For a concise review of the variations on this theme, see William Schwartz, "Private Troubles and Public Issues: One Job or Two?" The Social Welfare Forum, 1969 (New York: Columbia University Press, 1969), pp. 22–43.

3. Community organization (CO) does not fit neatly into the distinction between service and welfare activities. CO practice, as Rothman points out, may be categorized under locality development, social planning, and social action. Locality development is mainly concerned with service activities, and social planning with welfare activities, but the social action model seems to contain the potential for both types. See Jack Rothman, "Three Models of Community Organization Practice," Social Work Practice, 1968 (New York: Columbia University Press, 1968), pp. 16–47.

4. For a more detailed explanation, see Neil Gilbert and Harry Specht, Dimensions of Social Welfare Policy (Englewood Cliffs, N.J.: Prentice-Hall, 1974).

5. Burns, op. cit., p. 4.

6. Ibid., p. 3.

7. Ibid., pp. 15–19.

8. Martin Rein, *Social Policy* (New York: Random House, 1970), p. 297.

9. David M. Austin, "The Anti-Poverty Wars of the 20th Century," p. 10. Unpublished paper (Waltham, Mass.: Florence Heller School for Advanced Studies in Social Welfare, Brandeis University, 1972).

10. For a thoughtful analysis of the impact of these changes in one city, see Alfred Kahn, "Do Social Services Have a Future in New York?" *City Almanac*, 5 (February 1971).

11. Austin, op. cit., p. 33.

12. See Harry Specht, "The Deprofessionalization of Social Work," *Social Work*, 17 (March 1972); Don C. Marler, "The Nonprofessionalization of the War on Mental Illness," *Mental Hygiene*, 55 (July 1971); and James D. Orten, "Political Action: Ends or Means?" *Social Work*, 17 (November 1972).

13. Family Service Association of America, "Position Statement of Family Service Agencies Regarding Graduate Schools of Social Work" (New York, 1972). (Mimeographed.)

14. Schwartz, "Private Troubles and Public Issues: One Job or Two?" pp. 36–43.

15. Herman Levin, "Social Welfare Policy: Base for the Curriculum," *Social Work Education Reporter*, 17 (September 1969), p. 40.

16. Richan, op. cit.

17. Schwartz, "Private Troubles and Public Issues: One Job or Two?" pp. 35–36.

18. For descriptions of this kind of practice, see Harriett M. Bartlett, *The Common Base of Social Work Practice* (New York: National Association of Social Workers, 1970); Howard Goldstein, *Social Work Practice: A Unitary Approach* (Columbia: University of South Carolina Press, 1973); and Allen Pincus and Anne Minahan, *Social Work Practice: Model and Method* (Itasca, Ill.: F. E. Peacock Publishers, 1973).

19. For an example of what some of these changes might look like, see Rein, op. cit.

20. For additional discussion, see Burns, op. cit., pp. 9–12; and Gilbert and Specht, op. cit., pp. 9–12.

21. For example, see program statements of School of Social Work, University of Washington; School of Applied Social Sciences, Case Western Reserve University; School of Social Work and Community Planning, University of Maryland; and School of Social Work, University of Minnesota.

22. Burns, op. cit., p. 21.

23. Everett C. Hughes, "Professions," *Journal of the American Academy of Arts and Sciences*, 92 (Fall 1963), pp. 661–668.

24. Ibid., p. 657.

25. For example, see *Social Service Review* (entire issue), 46 (September 1972); see also Joel Fischer, "Is Casework Effective? A Review," *Social Work*, 18 (January 1973), pp. 5–20.

18   Professional Autonomy and the Revolt of the Client

MARIE R. HAUG and MARVIN B. SUSSMAN

This paper uses the conceptual scheme of professional-client relationships in an analysis of the phenomenon of social unrest. Students, the poor, and the black community no longer accept uncritically the service offerings of the establishment. Our purpose is to interpret this social phenomenon as a new stage in the interaction between professionals and the society, a stage we have called the revolt of the client. This discussion may also help untangle some theoretical issues in the nature of professional autonomy.

In normative terms, a profession may be defined as an occupation based on a unique scientific body of knowledge, whose practitioners have a service orientation, and autonomy in the performance of their work (Goode, 1961; Hughes, 1963). These three core characteristics have been taken as interrelated, with autonomy granted only through public acceptance of the profession's twin claims to expertise and altruism.

The public in this analysis is not, however, the undifferentiated mass. Elsewhere we have marshalled some evidence to show that the general public tends to stereotype occupations and professions without understanding the specific knowledge required or the real nature of the tasks performed. Segmental publics, on the other hand, such as clients utilizing services or colleagues employed in related tasks and fields, are in a position to recognize the skills of the professional and grant the necessary autonomy (Haug and Sussman, 1969). The composition of client publics varies by pro-

Reprinted from *Social Problems*, 17 (Fall 1969): 153–61 by permission of The Society for the Study of Social Problems and of the authors.

fession. The practitioner-public sets to be considered in this paper are physicians and chronic hospital patients, social workers and welfare cases, college professors and students, and school teachers and ghetto parents. These have been selected for analysis because each represents a different facet of the revolt of the client.

The power of the professional to determine what is best in a particular case, and the autonomy to carry out various remedial, treatment, socializing, or advisory activities, depends on the consent of the client. Although empirically this consent may be based on fear, ignorance, or habit, in a broader sense it is a consequence of the client's implicit acceptance of the professional's expertise and good will, and the understanding that in accepting the authority of the professional the client in turn will be rewarded. Supposedly the doctor knows why it hurts, the social worker knows why the check didn't come, the school teacher knows why Johnny has trouble reading, and the college professor knows the why of all these "whys." The professional can be trusted to apply or transmit his knowledge with the client's interest rather than his own private concerns at heart. The payoff for the client is a solution to one of his problems, and this is the basis upon which the client grants the professional a mandate and authority to proceed.

This idealized model is not now, if it ever was, isomorphic to reality. Provisions for licensure and codes of ethics show that group pressures were found necessary to enforce practitioner approximation to the ideal. Malpractice suits and drop-out rates are evidence of individual recognition of poor fit between professional norms and the facts of life. Moreover, professionals discovered that being other-oriented too much could be costly in relation to satisfactions of economic, status, and power needs. Like others in competitive societies professionals have organized around a common interest in order to maintain and enlarge their privileged position in society.

Furthermore, the meeting between professional and client now generally occurs in an organizational context which adds an entirely new dimension to the situation. The "free" professional with a private relationship to an individual in need of service is a vanishing breed. Given bureaucratic delivery systems for professional services, the client is faced not only with the authority of the professional as practitioner, but also as administrator, armed with the regulations and rules of the institutional setting.

At the same time, the professional himself is limited by the organizational milieu in which he performs. Freidson (forthcoming) questions the impact of such limitations on professionalism; he argues that the delivery system does not seriously impair autonomy, since the core of the professional's power is his control over the actual treatment tasks. Yet decisions concerning use of options best suited to a client's development or problem are affected by a number of organizational imperatives. A clinic doctor bends to the institutional rules of the hospital pharmacy in choosing between recommended medication for his patient. The professor's range of course offerings is shaped by administration budgets and evaluations of such matters as class size or teaching loads. The professional's power, even over specific task performance, is contained within the territory allocated by his institution.

More important for our purposes, however, is the fact that the professional, whether he wishes to admit it or not, has become implicated with the established structure because he uses it to his own ends. In effect, he draws upon organizational power as well as the power of his expertise to control the circumstances under which service is given. This aspect of professional autonomy is a function of the structural links between practitioner and administrator in any institutional setting. Officially, the doctor is the "guest" in the hospital, and the professor is isolated in his ivory tower. Practically, the doctor has a great deal to say about whom the hospital admits and how it is run, while faculty are deeply involved in the same organizational aspects. In this sense the professional shapes institutional practice (Freidson, forthcoming).

In hospitals, schools, colleges, and the ghettos the clients are rejecting these two aspects of professional power, and are in revolt against both the practitioner's work autonomy and his organizational authority in the role of the administrator. This revolt is in a new dimension because it is a group rather than a personal rejection phenomenon. Heretofore clients evaded constraints by manipulation of the system, or by leaving it altogether. Nowadays individual clients do not drop out; they get together, sit in, and confront the functionaries of service organizations. The critical difference is that client counter-actions are now social, and organized. This is the reason we can speak of client revolts only in areas where clients have had an opportunity to be together over an extended period of time, such as patients in long-term treatment hospitals, students in colleges, or welfare cases and residents hemmed in crowded ghetto areas.

Also, one should not overlook the current struggle between the administrator and practitioner in service organizations over control of the work situation and the subsequent polarization of occupational and client groups and enhancement of potential conflict between them. In those instances where the administrator-professional conflict is unresolved the client revolt may be abetted by a sympathetic ally who uses or is used by the client in the struggle for power and control.

Before examining the utility of professionalism as an explanatory framework of client revolt in more detail, it will be useful to dispose of some other current interpretations of social unrest. One such is essentially a non-analysis. This is the claim that client actions are irrational, the journalistic stance which labels demands as impossible and tactics as irresponsible. While this may be a popular value judgment and even a valid statement if the sole criterion of rationality is conformity to prior norms, it is not an adequate analysis of the social phenomenon. Neither student seizure of buildings nor ghetto marches can be explained as the actions of anomic crowds. Similar challenges to institutional power a generation ago can be considered rational by current perspectives because they were successful: sit down strikes and demonstrations were among the techniques used to achieve unionism.

This should not be taken to mean that the labor-management frame of reference is fully explanatory either. This model is most suited to situations where there is a conflict over scarce resources: one party to the struggle has what the other party wants. The embattled resources are material and tangible, or at least can be cashed in for these values. Although the issues in current confrontations may have long term material consequences, the immediate concern is not the extraction of goods from their possessor. The problem is power and its appropriate limits.

Clients engaged in a battle against authority have several possible grounds for challenge. Professional autonomy may be called into question because (1) the expertise of the practitioners is inadequate, (2) their claims to altruism are unfounded, (3) the organizational delivery system supporting their authority is defective and insufficient, or (4) this system is too efficient and exceeds the appropriate bounds of its power. In short, the client revolt attacks the basic legitimacy of the occupational and institutional claims to power of the professional.

There are varying emphases and configurations among these elements of legitimation, depending on the setting and the situation. In the hospital, organized client resistance has generally remained in the incipient stage. Covert group pressures, such as reported in *Timetables* (Roth, 1963), implicitly reject the physician's expertise and professional judgment in pressing for shared definitions of the right moment for hospital discharge. Already reported, however, are more open group efforts, such as those seeking to reject the spread of a chronic hospital's domain over wider areas of the patient's life. (For a discussion of laterality as a form of client-organization relations see Lefton and Rosengren, 1966). Thus in one long term facility in the East, patients have organized to resist hospital meddling with their social security disability or welfare income (Pilati, 1969). Here the claim is not that medical know-how is missing, but rather that it gives no license to handle patient finances as well as their physical needs. Our own conjecture is that patients in general will resist expansion of hospital professional control to areas not defined as legitimately medical. Patient-clients consider themselves just as competent in social relations as their doctors.

Poverty clients of welfare case workers, on the other hand, question even the special professional knowledge of the social worker. He—or more probably she—is apt to be viewed simply as a person "with authority to determine whether or not there is going to be four or five dollars more in a budget" (Harris, 1967:47). Marches on welfare offices, sit-ins, sleep-ins, and other group demonstrations are aimed at extracting more benefits from the professionals. Here it might be argued that there are labor-management analogues in the situation, except that the case workers do not themselves possess the goods which the clients are demanding, even though they are perceived as agents of the establishment who presumably control the distribution of means. In our framework it is, even more explicitly than in the instance of the hospital, a situation where the client feels fully as qualified as the professional to determine what is best for him, and to demand that it be supplied (for a similar situation in the religious field see Braude, 1961).

The revolt of black parents against a ghetto school system dominated by white teachers presents a somewhat different set of factors. In this instance it could be argued that both the expertise and the goodwill of the professional are being challenged. The articulate poor charge that the middle-class ghetto teacher is blind to their particular problems, does not understand their children, is ignorant of black history and innovative teaching methods, and is only waiting to escape to a suburban school system anyway (for substantiation of this stance in an earlier era, see Becker, 1952). In addition, the ghetto dweller finds that the whole delivery system of education is inadequate and inefficient. Here there seems no charge that the system goes too far, but rather that it does not go far enough.

In the university setting the revolt of the student-client finds grounds for disaffection in all four authority factors. Professional expertise is questioned: black students point to gaps in knowledge of Negro history, life, and culture, while diverse groups challenge the faculty's knowledge of teaching methods or ability to relate course content to current social concerns. The latter charge suggests a critique of professional humanitarianism as well. A more direct denial of service orientation is the claim that professors are more interested in their own research and consulting opportunities than in teaching students, and moreover that both research and consulting are in the service of immoral ends, such as war or colonialism. Ideas about the inefficiency and inadequacy of the delivery system are seen in demands to "restructure" the university, modify curriculum, revise teaching practices, and the like. Finally the old notion that the college administration stood "in loco parentis" has been rejected by students who consider this an illegitimate extension of organizational power into personal lives, as witnessed by the ongoing battles for off-campus housing, elimination of separate male and female dorms, and open visiting, among others.

Undergirding some of this revolt is an inter-generational struggle for power. Those of the middle generation hold sway too long, according to the young, and the rebellion functions as a catalyst to speed the process of change of power or to obtain accommodations which provide a rationale for tolerating the rule of elders. This is seen most clearly among the student rebels, and to a certain extent also explains the vigorous rejection by young blacks of the older "Uncle Toms" in their communities.

The situation, then, is that professional knowledge, service, autonomy, and organizational authority are being challenged at various levels of society and among widely diverse groups. Students, predominantly middle and upper class, deny the expertise and good will of their educators, while they demand an end to administration and faculty power to meddle in their private lives. Poverty group members, arguing that they know more about their community needs, problems, and solutions than the professional social workers and are more concerned, have organized for a voice in welfare benefits and their distribution. Cutting across social class lines, the blacks confront professors, teachers, and social workers with their demands for more adequate services while hospital patients organize to hold professional control over their lives in bounds.

The slogan for all groups is "don't call me, I'll call you." The client seems to be rejecting what he considers institutionalized meddling under the cover of professional concern. Outreach programs from the client perspective have become out-grab. Students want ·to organize their own courses and call in the professional as consultant (Shenker, 1969). The "whole man" approach in medicine infringes on areas of social relations where clients consider themselves competent; patients want to turn to the doctor when in trouble, but not to be bothered otherwise. This suggests that the client is demanding the right to define the problem, and then call upon the professional only as specialist in a narrow domain. The breadth of professional prerogative, the lateral dimension (Lefton and Rosengren, 1966) of professional-client relationships, is the most widely rejected.

The professional's response has generally been heated resistance. The emotional pressure that has been generated seems excessive on logical grounds, but is understandable in social-psychological terms. The professional's authority is precious because it verifies his superior status and shapes his self-image. The client's refusal to perform in a dependent, sub-adult role relation to the "wise expert" destroys the underlying assumptions of the professional's own position as a man of knowledge, compassion, and power. In this sense the revolt of the client is more devastating than the revolt of the unionized worker because it directly involves the social self-conceptions of the authority figures, not just machines and money.

The professional's tactic for dealing with the situation has been in the classic conflict vein, covering the usual spectrum from outright repression to subtle and not-so-subtle cooptation. The modal pattern, however, has been cooptation. Hospitals form "patients councils," poverty programs include "indigenous" community representation on governing boards, while students are added to curriculum committees, university senates, even boards of trustees. The objective is to socialize the dissidents into the special organizational knowledge of the inner professional circles, even if the specific scientific body of knowledge of the professional remains sacrosanct. In this way the autonomy of the professional is preserved at the cost of sharing only a small portion of his institutional power.

The "new careers" movement, although probably not developed as cooptation, may be discussed from this perspective also. This employment scheme initiated by Pearl and Riessman (1965), has now become so institutionalized as to appear in much current legislation. On the basis that helping others is a means to one's own therapy, the "new careers" concept provides that members of poverty groups be employed by social agencies as para-professional links between social work practitioners and the community. The outcome is to be improved relations between agency and client, with better understanding on each side of problems and programs, and new opportunities for the untrained poor to embark on a sub-professional career sequence to pull themselves out of the poverty syndrome. Objectively one might conclude that the process would result in cooptation, with poor careerists eventually identified more with their new employers than their old neighbors. Indeed, it has been explicitly stated that the "new careers" approach "might provide an essential deterrent to the alienation which lies behind various forms of protest in our society, including ghetto upheavals," (Riessman, 1969:30).

More direct evidence of the cooptation threat is the growth of an *anti*-cooptation movement among new careerists. Sparked by the new careerists themselves, this movement is attacking "professionalism," "credentialism," and "ideas of hierarchy." The ideology is *"highly critical of the profession:* he doesn't understand the community, he is elitist and distant and not willing to accept accountability from consumers." The traditional picture of "a distant and peer-responsible professional and a humble ministered-to client" must be replaced by "new forms of participation and a new responsive professional practice" (Gartner, 1969).

This sounds like cooptation that failed, and may indicate a poor prognosis for similar attempts in other fields. Cooptation, after all, assumes that the client is really ignorant and uninformed, and that by being made aware of the professionals' rationale he will come to accept it. But the shoe may be on the other foot. As pointed out recently by the director of the New York State Health Planning Commission, "the professionals must, for their own sake, accept the realization that the patient—the client—the consumer—is much more sophisticated and aware of his needs than ever before . . . he will increasingly be more involved in how services to meet these needs will be provided. It may be that . . . we can learn something . . ." (Van Ness, 1967:78). Where the clients claim equal or superior knowledge in a whole area of the expert's supposed domain, they may win over the professional instead of the other way around. Some of this has already occurred. A few faculty members help seize buildings and often social workers join the march on welfare offices.

We are reminded of the comment of Everett Hughes, over a decade ago, that "social unrest shows itself precisely in questioning of the prerogatives of the leading professions. In time of crisis, there may arise a general demand for more complete conformity of professionals to lay modes of thought, discourse and action" (1958:83). One may argue over how "general" the demand for reducing professional authority has become, or the extent to which professionals are willing to retreat from the use of previously held power, but if the argument of this paper is accepted, it seems that the process of respecification of legitimate authority has begun to occur.

Given the viability of our interpretation, what are the consequences for professional autonomy in particular and professionalism in general? It seems fair to say that a return to old definitions is largely out of the question, so that in *this* sense a revolution is in progress. If nothing else, the rising level of general education and of expectations will prevent a return to former patterns of client-practitioner relations. Furthermore, since the major thrust of the client revolt has been against the institutional concomitants of professionalism, including the tendency of the professional to extend his authority beyond the limits of his legitimated special expertise, one might predict a narrowing of professional authority to the most limited and esoteric elements of his knowledge base. This is unlikely to mean, despite client-revolt rhetoric, that the professional will fully lose the core of his autonomy, the right to define the nature of the client's problem. Even if the client exercised his right to pick and choose the time and place of his use of the professional's expertise, once the client enters the interaction, the expert's knowledge of cause-effect will permit him to diagnose and respecify the original complaint or need into his terms.

A corollary of this hypothesized development could be change in the prestige accorded the professional. If our empirical evidence as derived from a different context (Haug and Sussman, 1969) can be projected into other times and conditions, the expectation is that the prestige-grantors—the clients in revolt—will denigrate the professional's social status as well as the extent of his authority claims, and that this downgrading will shape new, less prestigeful stereotypes of the professions.

Thus we project, as one possibility, that the tension between society and professional can lead to a process of deprofessionalization, involving both narrower bounds for autonomy and lowered status. On the other hand, what the client demands—the professional as a limited consultant—may be less a curse than a blessing in disguise. It could enable the professional to give up the "whole man" approach to service and treatment, and enable him to revert to a more specialized expert role. All individuals in complex societies require the services of the expert in order to survive. In the future, as in the past, this should provide the professional with sufficient power, prestige, and financial return. What is lost in diffuse power and prestige would then be compensated for by more focused autonomy within the specialized range. All these issues remain problematic, and are presented less as predictions than as guideposts for future study.

REFERENCES

Becker, Howard S. "The career of the Chicago public school teacher," American Journal of Sociology 57 (March 1952): 470–477.

Braude, Lee. "Professional autonomy and the role of the layman," Social Forces 39 (May 1961): 297–301.

Freidson, Eliot. "Dominant professions and the organization of limits of membership," forthcoming in Organizations and Clients: Essays in the Sociology of Service. Mark Lefton and William R. Rosengren (eds.). Columbus, Ohio: Charles Merrill, Inc.

Gartner, Alan (ed.). "New ideology of new careers," New Careers Newsletter III (Spring): New York: New Careers Development Center, School of Education, New York University, 1969.

Goode, William J. "Encroachment, charlatanism, and the emerging professions: psychology, sociology and medicine," American Sociological Review 25 (December 1961): 902–914.

Harris, Larry. "Communicating with the culturally disadvantaged," Rehabilitating the Culturally Disadvantaged: 45–49. Mankato, Minnesota: Mankato State College, 1967.

Haug, Marie R., and Marvin B. Sussman. "Professionalism and the public," Sociological Inquiry 39 (Winter 1969): 57–64.

Hughes, Everett C. Men and Their Work. London: The Free Press of Glencoe, Collier-Macmillan, Ltd., 1958.

Hughes, Everett C. "Professions," Daedalus (Fall 1963): 655–668.

Lefton, Mark, and William R. Rosengren. "Organizations and clients: lateral and longitudinal dimensions," American Sociological Review 31 (December 1966): 802–810.

Pearl, Arthur, and Frank Riessman. New Careers for the Poor. New York: The Free Press, 1965.

Pilati, Joe. "The hospitals don't belong to the people," The Village Voice (February 6, 1969): 1, 21.

Riessman, Frank. Strategies Against Poverty. New York: Random House, 1969.

Roth, Julius A. Timetables. New York: Bobbs-Merrill Co. Inc., 1963.

Shenker, Israel. "Students take over, but it's all academic," *The New York Times* (March 7, 1969): 39, 48.

Van Ness, Edward H. "The regional medical program in heart disease, cancer and stroke," *Utilization of Rehabilitation Manpower in the Community Setting:* 75–79. Mankato, Minnesota: Mankato State College, 1967.

Chapter Six

THE ORGANIZATIONAL CONTEXT OF
SOCIAL WORK PRACTICE

The ubiquitous role of complex organizations in modern society has been succinctly captured in a statement by Peter Blau and Marshall Meyer:

A large and increasing proportion of the American people spend their working lives as small cogs in complex organizations. And this is not all, for bureaucracies also affect much of the rest of our lives. The employment agency we approach to get a job, and the union we join to protect it; the super-market and the chain store where we shop, and the hospitals treating our illnesses; the school our children attend, and the political parties for whose candidates we vote; the fraternal organization where we play, and the church where we wor-ship—all these more often than not are large organizations of the kind that tends to be bureaucratically organized.[1]

As we noted in our introduction to the preceding chapter, one unique characteristic of social work is that it originated within a variety of organizational contexts, often in settings where social workers served as organizational functionaries, usually of lower status and prestige. Other professions, such as medicine and law, began with practitioners who operated as independent entrepreneurs. It is only in comparatively recent times that these professionals have begun to ply their trades as staff members of complex organizations. Conversely, the idea of private practice in social work has developed only in the past few years, and it is a development that many social workers look upon with disfavor.[2]

The vast bulk of social welfare services is provided through large, complex organizations most commonly known as "bureaucracies." This term, Blau and Meyer remark, is often used invidiously to connote unsympathetic inefficiency; just as frequently, it is used to describe ruthless control and efficiency.[3] These are descriptions of complex organizations for which many concrete examples can be found in the real world. In whatever institutional sphere they operate, complex organizations are powerful social instruments that can be used to achieve a variety of social purposes, both good and evil.

The practicing social worker may choose to follow a career that keeps him outside of complex organizations by working as an independent consultant or therapist. Increasing numbers of social workers are doing this. However, the vast majority of social workers will operate in organizations, and their practice and other aspects of their professional lives will be affected in large part by organizational policies and objectives. Moreover, even if the independent road to a career in social work looks terribly attractive, it should be noted that this path too has many organizational detours and bureaucratic bumps. Most private practitioners will be paid their fees by organizations (such as private and governmental insurance schemes), for services designated by organizations, under conditions set by organizations. Therefore, if the profession of social work seeks to develop the professional attributes discussed in the preceding chapter, we must understand and exercise some control over the organizational context of social work and social welfare.

The first selection in this chapter is "Strategies for Studying Organizations" by James D. Thompson (Reading 19). The selection is highly theoretical, but it draws attention to some of the salient characteristics of organizations in an especially helpful way for our purposes. That is, most of the literature on organizations tends to envision them as either "closed" or "open" systems. With a closed-system view they may be looked at as rational systems, instruments by which to realize expressly announced group goals. Fundamentally, this conception is based on a mechanical model in which the organization is viewed as a structure having manipulable parts, each of which can be modified to enhance the efficiency of the entire organization.[4]

With an open-system view, emphasis is given to elements in the organization's environment upon which it depends for survival and goal achievement, such as clients, funders, staff, and regulatory agencies.[5] Thompson attempts to synthesize these two approaches. He conceives of complex organizations as "open systems, hence indeterminate and faced with uncertainty, but at the same time as subject to criteria of rationality and hence needing determinateness and certainty." That is, organizations may be conceived of as open systems striving to achieve the rationality and certainty of closed systems. This is a particularly useful perspective for social workers because they tend to practice in large bureaucratic agencies that exist in politically troublesome environments.

One kind of knowledge that is required of the social worker from a closed-system perspective is bureaucratic skill. As Robert Pruger has noted, these skills are pertinent to the vast majority of social work professionals.[6] However, Pruger points out, while "achieving one's professional goals through a formal organization requires a competence as complex and demanding as any of the others that professional [social work] helpers consciously seek to master . . . training for the role is almost nonexistent." Here, then, is one bit of the "incompleteness" of the profession.

Reading 20, by Sol Levine, Paul White, and Benjamin Paul, analyzes some of the elements in the open-system perspective. In "Community Interorganizational Problems in Providing Medical Care and Social Services" they discuss how the goals, needs, and problems of organizations are related to the interorganizational relationships they develop. The concepts of "function," "access," and "domain consensus" are used to draw attention to interorganizational dynamics that are frequently ignored.

The final selection in this chapter is Reading 21, "Bureaucracy and the Lower Class," by Gideon Sjoberg, Richard Brymer, and Buford Farris. As Max Weber has said, bureaucracy "is a power instrument of the first order—for the one who controls the bureaucratic apparatus."[7] In this selection the authors deal with the relationship between bureaucracy and the social order. While their specific reference is to the disadvantaged position of the lower class vis-à-vis bureaucracies, the mechanisms of bureaucratic control they describe are applicable to many features of society. Staff selection and socialization, client selection and socialization, and bureaucratic procedures and routines are mechanisms that can be utilized to reinforce stratification and cleavage along many lines, including class, race, sex, and age.

Sjoberg, Brymer, and Farris indicate that antibureaucratic sympathies are common to political groups on both the extreme left and the extreme right. This must surely cause professionals in the human services to approach these questions with a great deal of caution. We wonder, for example, about the practical implications of the analysis. Sjoberg et al. suggest three possibilities: increased bureaucratization of services (an alternative they obviously do not condone); purposive duplication of bureaucracies in order to inject a degree of competition into what is otherwise a service monopoly and/or to create agencies that will represent the disadvantaged; and debureaucratization of services by creation of agencies organized along the lines of therapeutic communities and collegial systems. However, all of these choices are based on the assumption that the problems described are attributable to bureaucratic organization per se. We believe that this assumption bears close scrutiny. Many of the problems described in this selection occur because of poorly run, rigid, and unresponsive bureaucracies in which administrators operate with excessively high degrees of discretion. These qualities are not intrinsic to bureaucracy, even though they may often appear in bureaucratic settings. The proper objective of professionals, it seems to us, is to create complex organizations that are well run, flexible, and responsive, organizations in which the prerogatives of personnel are kept specific to areas in which their expertise is clearly functional. Organizational solutions that decentralize authority at great financial costs, that increase the discretion of personnel, that create yet more bureaucracy, and that encourage separatism are not necessarily the answers to the problems identified in this article.

While the bureaucratic mechanisms described by Sjoberg, Brymer, and Farris may be used to reinforce an unjust social order, a corollary principle to be borne in mind is that explicit rules, regulations, and procedures can be used to enforce just practices and change unjust ones. Saul Alinsky, one of the great social agitators of our time, had this principle in mind when he instructed organizers to: "Make the enemy live up to their own book of rules. You can kill them with this."[8] Alinsky did not believe that any organization could live up to all of its own principles and rules, which is very likely true. However, in the absence of principles and rules there is little toward which we can hope to have organizations aspire.

NOTES

1. Peter M. Blau and Marshall W. Meyer, *Bureaucracy in Modern Society* (New York: Random House, 1971), p. 11.

2. See Irving Piliavin, "Restructuring the Provision of Social Service," *Social Work*, 13 (January 1968): 34–41, for the argument in favor; and Sherman Merle, "Some Arguments against Private Practice," *Social Work*, 7 (January 1962): 12–17, for the opposition.

3. Blau and Meyer, *Bureaucracy in Modern Society*, p. 4.

4. Alvin W. Gouldner, "Organizational Analysis," in *Sociology Today*, ed. Robert K. Merton, Leonard Broom, and Leonard S. Cottrell, Jr. (New York: Harper & Row, 1959), pp. 404–5.

5. James D. Thompson, *Organization in Action* (New York: McGraw-Hill Book Co., 1967), pp. 27–28.

6. Robert Pruger, "The Good Bureaucrat," *Social Work*, 18 (July 1973): 26–32.

7. Hans H. Gerth and C. Wright Mills (eds.), *From Max Weber: Essays in Sociology* (New York: Oxford University Press, 1946), p. 228.

8. Saul Alinsky, *Rules for Radicals* (New York: Random House, 1971), p. 128.

19 Strategies for Studying Organizations

JAMES D. THOMPSON

Complex organizations—manufacturing firms, hospitals, schools, armies, community agencies—are ubiquitous in modern societies, but our understanding of them is limited and segmented.

The fact that impressive and sometimes frightening consequences flow from organizations suggests that some individuals have had considerable insight into these social instruments. But insight and private experiences may generate private understandings without producing a public body of knowledge adequate for the preparation of a next generation of administrators, for designing new styles of organizations for new purposes, for controlling organizations, or for appreciation of distinctive aspects of modern societies.

What we know or think we know about complex organizations is housed in a variety of fields or disciplines, and communication among them more nearly resembles a trickle than a torrent (Dill, 1964; March, 1965). Although each of the several schools has its unique terminology and special heroes, Gouldner (1959) was able to discern two fundamental models underlying most of the literature. He labeled these the "rational" and "natural-system" models of organizations, and these labels are indeed descriptive of the results.

To Gouldner's important distinction we wish to add the notion that the rational model results from a *closed-system strategy* for studying organizations, and that the natural-system model flows from an *open-system strategy*.

CLOSED-SYSTEM STRATEGY

The Search for Certainty

If we wish to predict accurately the state a system will be in presently, it helps immensely to be dealing with a *determinate system*. As Ashby observes (1956), fixing the present circumstances of a determinate system will determine the state it moves to next, and since such a system cannot go to two states at once, the transformation will be unique.

Fixing the present circumstances requires, of course, that the variables and relationships involved be few enough for us to comprehend and that we have control over or can reliably predict all of the variables and relations. In other words, it requires that the system be closed or, if closure is not complete, that the outside forces acting on it be predictable.

Now if we have responsibility for the future states or performance of some system, we are likely to opt for a closed system. Bartlett's (1958) research on mental processes, comparing "adventurous thinking" with "thinking in closed systems," suggests that there are strong human tendencies to reduce various forms of knowledge to the closed-system variety, to rid them of all ultimate uncertainty. If such tendencies appear in puzzle-solving as well as in everyday situations, we would especially expect them to be emphasized when responsibility and high stakes are added.

Since much of the literature about organizations has been generated as a by-product of the search for improved efficiency or performance, it is not surprising that it employs closed-system assumptions—employs the rational model—about organizations. Whether we consider *scientific management* (Taylor, 1911), *administrative management* (Gulick and Urwick, 1937), or *bureaucracy* (Weber, 1947), the ingredients of the organization are deliberately chosen for their necessary contribution to a goal, and the structures established are those deliberately intended to attain highest efficiency.

Three Schools in Caricature

Scientific management, focused primarily on manufacturing or similar production activities, clearly employs economic efficiency as its ultimate criterion, and seeks to maximize efficiency by planning procedures according to a technical logic, setting standards, and exercising controls to ensure conformity with standards and thereby with the technical logic. Scientific management achieves conceptual closure of the organization by assuming that goals are known, tasks are repetitive, output of the production process somehow disappears, and resources in uniform qualities are available.

Administrative-management literature focuses on structural relationships among production, personnel, supply, and other service units of the organization; and again employs as the ultimate criterion economic efficiency. Here efficiency is maximized by specializing tasks and grouping them into departments, fixing responsibility according to such principles as span of control or delegation, and controlling action to plans. Administrative management achieves closure by assuming that ultimately a master plan is known, against which specialization, departmentalization, and control are determined. (That this master plan is elusive is shown by Simon, 1957a.) Administrative management also assumes that production tasks are known, that output disappears, and that resources are automatically available to the organization.

Bureaucracy also follows the pattern noted above, focusing on staffing and structure as means of handling clients and disposing of cases. Again the ultimate criterion is efficiency, and this time it is maximized by defining offices according to jurisdiction and place in a hierarchy, appointing experts to offices, establishing rules for categories of activity, categorizing cases or clients, and then motivating proper performance of expert officials by providing salaries and patterns for career advancement. [The extended implications of the assumptions made by bureaucratic theory are brought out by Merton's (1957) discussion of "bureaucratic personality."] Bureaucratic theory also employs the closed system of logic. Weber saw three holes through which empirical reality might penetrate the logic, but in outlining his "pure type" he quickly plugged these holes. Policymakers, somewhere above the bureaucracy, could alter the goals, but the implications of this are set aside. Human components—the expert officeholders—might be more complicated than the model describes, but bureaucratic theory handles this by divorcing the individual's private life from his life as an officeholder through the use of rules, salary, and career. Finally, bureaucratic theory takes note of outsiders—clientele—but nullifies their effects by depersonalizing and categorizing clients.

It seems clear that the rational-model approach uses a closed-system strategy. It also seems clear that the developers of the several schools using the rational model have been primarily students of performance or efficiency, and only incidentally students of organizations. Having focused on control of the organization as a target, each employs a closed system of logic and conceptually closes the organization to coincide with that type of logic, for this elimination of uncertainty is the way to achieve determinateness. The rational model of an organization results in everything being functional—making a positive, indeed an optimum, contribution to the overall result. All resources are appropriate resources, and their allocation fits a master plan. All action is appropriate action, and its outcomes are predictable.

It is no accident that much of the literature on the management or administration of complex organizations centers on the concepts of *planning* or *controlling*. Nor is it any accident that such views are dismissed by those using the open-system strategy.

OPEN-SYSTEM STRATEGY

The Expectation of Uncertainty

If, instead of assuming closure, we assume that a system contains more variables than we can comprehend at one time, or that some of the variables are subject to influences we cannot control or predict, we must resort to a different sort of logic. We can, if we wish, assume that the system is determinate by nature, but that it is our incomplete understanding which forces us to expect surprise or the intrusion of uncertainty. In this case we can employ a natural-system model.

Approached as a natural system, the complex organization is a set of interdependent parts which together make up a whole because each contributes something and receives something from the whole, which in turn is interdependent with some larger environment. Survival of the system is taken to be the goal, and the parts and their relationships presumably are determined through evolutionary processes. Dysfunctions are conceivable, but it is assumed that an offending part will adjust to produce a net positive contribution or be disengaged, or else the system will degenerate.

Central to the natural-system approach is the concept of homeostasis, or self-stabilization, which spontaneously, or naturally, governs the necessary relationships among parts and activities and thereby keeps the system viable in the face of disturbances stemming from the environment.

Two Examples in Caricature

Study of the *informal organization* constitutes one example of research in complex organizations using the natural-system approach. Here attention is focused on variables which are not included in any of the rational models—sentiments, cliques, social controls via informal norms, status and status striving, and so on. It is clear that students of informal organization regard these variables not as random deviations or error, but as patterned, adaptive responses of human beings in problematic situations (Roethlisberger and Dickson, 1939). In this view the informal organization is a spontaneous and functional development, indeed a necessity, in complex organizations, permitting the system to adapt and survive.

A second version of the natural-system approach is more global but less crystallized under a label. This school views the organization as a unit in interaction with its environment, and its view was perhaps most forcefully expressed by Chester Barnard (1938) and by the empirical studies of Selznick (1949) and Clark (1956). This stream of work leads to the conclusion that organizations are not autonomous entities; instead, the best laid plans of managers have unintended consequences and are conditioned or upset by other social units—other complex organizations or publics—on whom the organization is dependent.

Again it is clear that in contrast to the rational-model approach, this research area focuses on variables not subject to complete control by the organization and hence not contained within a closed system of logic. It is also clear that students regard interdependence of organization and environment as inevitable or natural, and as adaptive or functional.

CHOICE OR COMPROMISE?

The literature about organizations, or at least much of it, seems to fall into one of the two categories, each of which at best tends to ignore the other and at worst denies the relevance of the other. The logics associated with each appear to be incompatible, for one avoids uncertainty to achieve determinateness, while the other assumes uncertainty and indeterminateness. Yet the phenomena treated by each approach, as distinct from the explanations of each, cannot be denied.

Viewed in the large, complex organizations are often effective instruments for achievement, and that achievement flows from planned, controlled action. In every sphere—educational, medical, industrial, commercial, or governmental—the quality or costs of goods or services may be challenged and questions may be raised about the equity of distribution within the society of the fruits of complex organizations. Still millions live each day on the assumption that a reasonable degree of purposeful, effective action will be forthcoming from the many complex organizations on which they depend. Planned action, not random behavior, supports our daily lives. Specialized, controlled, patterned action surrounds us.

There can be no question but that the rational model of organizations directs our attention to important phenomena—to important "truth" in the sense that complex organizations viewed in the large exhibit some of the patterns and results to which the rational model attends, but which the natural-system model tends to ignore. But it is equally evident that phenomena associated with the natural-system approach also exist in complex organizations. There is little room to doubt the universal emergence of the informal organization. The daily news about labor-management negotiations, inter-agency jurisdictional squabbles, collusive agreements, favoritism, breeches of contract, and so on, are impressive evidence that complex organizations are influenced in significant ways by elements of their environments, a phenomenon addressed by the natural-system approach but avoided by the rational. Yet most versions of the natural-system approach treat organizational purposes and achievements as peripheral matters.

It appears that each approach leads to some truth, but neither alone affords an adequate understanding of complex organizations. Gouldner calls for a synthesis of the two models, but does not provide the synthetic model.

Meanwhile, a serious and sustained elaboration of Barnard's work (Simon, 1957a; March and Simon, 1958; Cyert and March, 1963) has produced a newer tradition which evades the closed-versus open-system dilemma.

A NEWER TRADITION

What emerges from the Simon-March-Cyert stream of study is the organization as a problem-facing and problem-solving phenomenon. The focus is on organizational processes related to choice of courses of action in an environment which does not fully disclose the alternatives available or the consequences of those alternatives. In this view, the organization has limited capacity to gather and process information or to predict consequences of alternatives. To deal with situations of such great complexity, the organization must develop processes for *searching* and *learning*, as well as for *deciding*. The complexity, if fully faced, would overwhelm the organization, hence it must set limits to its definitions of situations; it must make decisions in *bounded rationality* (Simon, 1957b). This requirement involves replacing the maximum-efficiency criterion with one of satisfactory accomplishment, decision making now involving *satisficing* rather than *maximizing* (Simon, 1957b).

These are highly significant notions, and it will become apparent that this book seeks to extend this "newer tradition." The assumptions it makes are consistent with the open-system strategy, for it holds that the processes going on within the organization are significantly affected by the complexity of the organization's environment. But this tradition also touches on matters important in the closed-system strategy: performance and deliberate decisions.

But despite what seem to be obvious advantages, the Simon-March-Cyert stream of work has not entirely replaced the more extreme strategies, and we need to ask why so many intelligent men and women in a position to make the same observations we have been making should continue to espouse patently incomplete views of complex organizations.

The Cutting Edge of Uncertainty

Part of the answer to that question undoubtedly lies in the fact that supporters of each extreme strategy have had different purposes in mind, with open-system strategists attempting to understand organizations per se, and closed-system strategists interested in organizations mainly as vehicles for rational achievements. Yet this answer does not seem completely satisfactory, for these students could not have been entirely unaware of the challenges to their assumptions and beliefs.

We can suggest now that rather than reflecting weakness in those who use them, the two strategies reflect something fundamental about the cultures surrounding complex organizations—the fact that our culture does not contain concepts for simultaneously thinking about rationality and indeterminateness. These appear to be incompatible concepts, and we have no ready way of thinking about something as half-closed, half-rational. One alternative, then, is the closed-system approach of ignoring uncertainty to see rationality; another is to ignore rational action in order to see spontaneous processes. The newer tradition with its focus on organizational coping with uncertainty is indeed a major advance. It is notable that a recent treatment by Crozier (1964) starts from the bureaucratic position but focuses on coping with uncertainty as its major topic.

Yet in directing our attention to processes for meeting uncertainty, Simon, March, and Cyert may lead us to overlook the useful knowledge amassed by the older approaches. If the phenomena of rational models are indeed observable, we may want to incorporate some elements of those models; and if natural-system phenomena occur, we should also benefit from the relevant theories. For purposes of this volume, then, we *will conceive of complex organizations as open systems, hence indeterminate and faced with uncertainty, but at the same time as subject to criteria of rationality and hence needing determinateness and certainty.*

THE LOCATION OF PROBLEMS

As a starting point, we will suggest that the phenomena associated with open- and closed-system strategies are not randomly distributed through complex organizations, but instead tend to be

specialized by location. To introduce this notion we will start with
Parsons' (1960) suggestion that organizations exhibit three distinct
levels of responsibility and control—*technical, managerial,* and
institutional.

In this view, every formal organization contains a suborganization whose "problems" are focused around effective performance of
the technical function—the conduct of classes by teachers, the
processing of income tax returns and the handling of recalcitrants
by the bureau, the processing of material and supervision of these
operations in the case of physical production. The primary exigencies to which the technical suborganization is oriented are those
imposed by the nature of the technical task, such as the materials
which must be processed and the kinds of cooperation of different
people required to get the job done effectively.

The second level, the managerial, *services* the technical suborganization by (1) mediating between the technical suborganization and those who use its products—the customers, pupils, and so
on—and (2) procuring the resources necessary for carrying out the
technical functions. The managerial level *controls,* or administers,
the technical suborganization (although Parsons notes that its control is not unilateral) by deciding such matters as the broad technical task which is to be performed, the scale of operations, employment and purchasing policy, and so on.

Finally, in the Parsons formulation, the organization which consists of both technical and managerial suborganizations is also
part of a wider social system which is the source of the "meaning,"
legitimation, or higher-level support which makes the implementa-
tion of the organization's goals possible. In terms of "formal" controls, an organization may be relatively independent; but in terms
of the meaning of the functions performed by the organization and
hence of its "rights" to command resources and to subject its customers to discipline, it is never wholly independent. This overall
articulation of the organization and the institutional structure and
agencies of the community is the function of the third, or institutional, level of the organization.

Parsons' distinction of the three levels becomes more significant
when he points out that at each of the two points of articulation
between them there is a *qualitative* break in the simple continuity
of "line" authority because the functions at each level are quali-
tatively different. Those at the second level are not simply lower-
order spellings-out of the top-level functions. Moreover, the articula-

tion of levels and of functions rests on a two-way interaction, with each side, by withholding its important contribution, in a position to interfere with the functioning of the other and of the larger organization.

If we now reintroduce the conception of the complex organization as an open system subject to criteria of rationality, we are in a position to speculate about some dynamic properties of organizations. As we suggested, the logical model for achieving complete technical rationality uses a closed system of logic—closed by the elimination of uncertainty. In practice, it would seem, the more variables involved, the greater the likelihood of uncertainty, and it would therefore be advantageous for an organization subject to criteria of rationality to remove as much uncertainty as possible from its *technical core* by reducing the number of variables operating on it. Hence if both resource-acquisition and output-disposal problems—which are in part controlled by environmental elements and hence to a degree uncertain or problematic—can be removed from the technical core, the logic can be brought closer to closure, and the rationality, increased.

Uncertainty would appear to be greatest, at least potentially, at the other extreme, the institutional level. Here the organization deals largely with elements of the environment over which it has no formal authority or control. Instead, it is subjected to generalized norms, ranging from formally codified law to informal standards of good practice, to public authority, or to elements expressing the public interest.

At this extreme the closed system of logic is clearly inappropriate. The organization is open to influence by the environment (and vice versa) which can change independently of the actions of the organization. Here an open system of logic, permitting the intrusion of variables penetrating the organization from outside, and facing up to uncertainty, seems indispensable.

If the closed-system aspects of organizations are seen most clearly at the technical level, and the open-system qualities appear most vividly at the institutional level, it would suggest that a significant function of the managerial level is to mediate between the two extremes and the emphases they exhibit. If the organization must approach certainty at the technical level to satisfy its rationality criteria, but must remain flexible and adaptive to satisfy environmental requirements, we might expect the managerial level to mediate between them, ironing out some irregularities stemming from external sources, but also pressing the technical core for modifications as conditions alter. One exploration of this notion was offered in Thompson (1964).

Possible Sources of Variation

Following Parsons' reasoning leads to the expectation that differences in technical functions, or *technologies,* cause significant differences among organizations, and since the three levels are interdependent, differences in technical functions should also make for differences at managerial and institutional levels of the organization. Similarly, differences in the institutional structures in which organizations are imbedded should make for significant variations among organizations at all three levels.

Relating this back to the Simon-March-Cyert focus on organizational processes of searching, learning, and deciding, we can also suggest that while these adaptive processes may be generic, the ways in which they proceed may well vary with differences in technologies or in environments.

RECAPITULATION

Most of our beliefs about complex organizations follow from one or the other of two distinct strategies. The closed-system strategy seeks certainty by incorporating only those variables positively associated with goal achievement and subjecting them to a monolithic control network. The open-system strategy shifts attention from goal achievement to survival, and incorporates uncertainty by recognizing organizational interdependence with environment. A newer tradition enables us to conceive of the organization as an open system, indeterminate and faced with uncertainty, but subject to criteria of rationality and hence needing certainty.

With this conception the central problem for complex organizaions is one of coping with uncertainty. As a point of departure, we suggest that organizations cope with uncertainty by creating certain parts specifically to deal with it, specializing other parts in operating under conditions of certainty or near certainty. In this case, articulation of these specialized parts becomes significant.

We also suggest that technologies and environments are major sources of uncertainty for organizations, and that differences in those dimensions will result in differences in organizations. . . .

REFERENCES

Ashby, W. Ross: *An Introduction to Cybernetics*, London: Chapman and Hall, Ltd., 1956.

Barnard, Chester I.: *The Functions of the Executive*, Cambridge, Mass.: Harvard University Press, 1938.

Bartlett, Sir Frederick: *Thinking: An Experimental and Social Study*, New York: Basic Books, Inc., Publishers, 1958.

Clark, Burton R.: *Adult Education in Transition*, Berkeley, Calif.: University of California Press, 1956.

Crozier, Michel: *The Bureaucratic Phenomenon*, Chicago: The University of Chicago Press, 1964.

Cyert, Richard M. and James G. March: *A Behavioral Theory of the Firm*, Englewood Cliffs, N.J.: Prentice-Hall, Inc., 1963.

Dill, William R.: "Desegregation or Integration? Comments about Contemporary Research on Organizations," in W. W. Cooper, Harold J. Leavitt, and Maynard W. Shelly II (eds.), *New Perspectives in Organizational Research*, New York: John Wiley & Sons, Inc., 1964.

Gouldner, Alvin W.: "Organizational Analysis," in Robert K. Merton, Leonard Broom, and Leonard S. Cottrell Jr. (eds.), *Sociology Today*, New York: Basic Books, Inc., Publishers, 1959.

Gulick, Luther, and L. Urwick (eds.): *Papers on the Science of Administration*, New York: Institute of Public Administration, 1937.

March, James G.: "Introduction" in *Handbook of Organizations*, Chicago: Rand McNally and Company, 1965.

March, James G. and Herbert A. Simon: *Organizations*, New York: John Wiley & Sons, Inc., 1958.

Merton, Robert K.: "Bureaucratic Structure and Personality," in Robert K. Merton (ed.), *Social Theory and Social Structure* (rev. ed.), New York: The Free Press of Glencoe, 1957.

Parsons, Talcott: *Structure and Process in Modern Societies*, New York: The Free Press of Glencoe, 1960.

Roethlisberger, Fritz J., and W. J. Dickson: *Management and the Worker*, Cambridge, Mass.: Harvard University Press, 1939.

Selznick, Philip: *TVA and The Grass Roots*, Berkeley, Calif.: University of California Press, 1949.

Simon, Herbert A.: *Administrative Behavior*, 2d ed., New York: The Macmillan Company, 1957a.

————: *Models of Man, Social and Rational*, New York: John Wiley & Sons, Inc., 1957b.

Taylor, Frederick W.: *Scientific Management*, New York: Harper and Row Publishers, Incorporated, 1911.

Thompson, James D.: "Decision-making, The Firm, and the Market,"

in W. W. Cooper et al. (eds.), *New Perspectives in Organiza-
tion Research,* New York: John Wiley & Sons, Inc., 1964.
Weber, Max: *The Theory of Social and Economic Organization,*
A. M. Henderson and Talcott Parsons (trans.), and Talcott
Parsons (ed.), New York: Free Press of Glencoe, 1947.

20   Community Interorganizational Problems
in Providing Medical Care and
Social Services

SOL LEVINE, PAUL E. WHITE, and BENJAMIN D. PAUL

Facilitating communication among local health and welfare organizations has been a major objective of public health administrators and community organizers. Their writings contain many assertions about the desirability of improving relationships in order to
reduce gaps and overlaps of medical services to recipients,[1] but, as
yet, little effort has gone into making objective appraisals of the
interrelationships that actually exist within any community. Nor
have sociologists done much in paving the way for the practitioner.
Although sociologists have devoted considerable attention to the
study of formal organizations, their chief focus has been on patterns
within rather than between organizations. Only recently have they
begun to investigate the area of interorganizational relationships.[2]

During the past four years we have been studying relationships
among health and welfare agencies in four northeastern communities. Some of our findings appear to have fairly clear implications
for the general objective of mobilizing community health and welfare services.

MULTIPLE SOURCES OF AUTHORITY AND CONFLICTING GOALS

Looking at the health and welfare system in the community, we
quickly become aware of an array of diverse organizations, each of

Reprinted from the *Journal of Public Health,* 53 (August 1963): 1183–95 by permission of the American Public Health Association and of the authors.

which is relatively autonomous and has a separate locus of authority. There are, for example, different levels of official government represented in most large-size American communities. We may find a local health or welfare department, a district or regional health office, a state rehabilitation agency, and a U.S. Veterans Administration clinic. Voluntary agencies within the community also show variation with respect to the locus of their authority. On the one hand are what might be termed the "corporate" health agencies like the National Foundation, American Heart Association, and the American Cancer Society, where authority is delegated from the national or state organization to the local chapter or affiliate. On the other hand, there are "federated" organizations like the Visiting Nurses Association and the Family Service, which delegate authority to the state and national levels, are less bound by their national associations, and are more oriented toward the problems and conditions of the specific communities in which they operate.[3] There are other instances which could be cited, but these examples will suffice for our purposes. Social scientists have used the term "political pluralism" to refer to the multiple sources of authority which exist within the American scene—a term which has special relevance for the health and welfare agency field.

Given such diverse and multiple sources of authority, it is understandable that maximal interagency cooperation is not always attained. As a result of the pluralistic or divergent sources of authority, and for other reasons as well, health and welfare organizations in the community have varying goals and specific objectives which may conflict with one another, even though all of them share fundamental values, such as the promotion of health and the prevention of disease. Agencies differ in the standards they employ to evaluate their success and the means they use to achieve their objectives. Consider, for example, an official state rehabilitation organization whose objective is to rehabilitate or return to employment persons who have suffered some serious illness. The local community branch of this organization, to justify its existence, has to present a successful experience to its parent organization and to the state legislators, namely, that a given number of persons have been successfully rehabilitated. The goals of the organization cannot be fulfilled, therefore, unless it is selective as to the types of handicapped persons it accepts as clients.

Other community health and welfare agencies, consequently, are often frustrated in their efforts to get the rehabilitation agency to accept their particular clients for rehabilitation. In the judgment of these frustrated agencies the state organization is remiss in fulfilling its purpose. The state agency, on the other hand, is reluctant to commit its limited personnel and resources to the lengthy and time-consuming task of attempting the rehabilitation of what seem to be very poor risks. While the state agency may share the values of the local community with regard to the desirability of rehabilitating the serious cases, and while it wants acceptance and approval from the local community, it is the state parent agency, the state legislators, and governor on whom it relies for its financial support.

UNITED FUND VS. SINGLE DRIVE

The importance of conflicting goals, especially those which emanate from outside the local health agency system, also is evident in the widespread controversy over fund-raising. As Hamlin has noted, "Of all the controversies currently surrounding voluntary agencies, certainly the most strident has been the debate between advocates of independent and federated fund-raising."[4] It is well known that such corporate agencies as the American Heart Association and the American Cancer Society resist pleas of federated fund-raising advocates and carry out their own fund-raising campaigns. Moreover, these and other corporate agencies often incur the resentment of agency personnel and board members and of community leaders for not spending a greater proportion of their collected funds for local services.

Information obtained from executives of 68 voluntary agencies in four communities indicate that, in comparison with agencies of the federated type, corporate organizations do indeed allocate a smaller proportion of funds for services on the local level (Table 20.1).

Although the fund-raising issue is an important one and while fundamental values can be invoked to support either position, a more detached view of the problem reveals that underlying much of the clamor and controversy are the varying goals and objectives of the different health agencies. The fulfillment of certain organizational functions (e.g., research) requires concentration of considerable resources on the national level. Organizations specializing in research, therefore, characteristically have a predominantly corporate form of organization whereby authority is delegated from the national to the local. Corporate organizations, requiring greater

TABLE 20.1
Per cent of Funds Expended Locally by Corporate and
Federated Agencies in Four Communities

	Per cent of Funds Expended Locally*			
	0–25	26–50	51–75	76–100
Corporate				
(N = 28)	5	6	10	7
Federated				
(N = 48)	1	0	5	42
Total = 76				

* When categories are collapsed, Chi-square value = 30.14 and is significant at 0.001 level.

centralization of resources on the national level, are understandably alert to any activity in the local community which may impede the flow of sufficient funds to the national body. In short, the national single drive agencies view the health picture from a national vantage point and, while their local chapters or affiliates are oriented partly to their respective local communities, the authority of these local chapters or affiliates is relatively limited and circumscribed by priorities established by the national bodies. By contrast, the Community Chests and Councils and the United Funds, comprised of predominantly federated agencies, are more geared to the local community, per se. They want to establish "maximal rationality" in the allocation of resources, and they want the fruits of their fund drives to be delivered on the local scene. In large part, then, the United Fund-single-drive controversy can be seen as a contest between two sources of authority which, in turn, are inextricably linked with the varying objectives and functions of the respective organizations.

NEEDS AND PROBLEMS OF ORGANIZATIONS

In order to understand why organizations do or do not cooperate with one another it is necessary to focus on the organizations themselves and to consider their respective needs and requirements.* Every organization has some kind of goal or objective toward which it directs its activities: A health department may have as its goal the promotion of health and the prevention of disease; a tubercu-

* For a more complete statement of our conceptual framework see reference 6.

losis agency may have as its primary goal the eradication of a specific disease; a child and family service may aim at the development of psychologically and emotionally healthy children and families. In order to achieve these goals an organization must have three main elements or resources. It must have recipients to serve (directly or indirectly); it must have resources in the form of equipment, specialized knowledge, or funds; and it must have the services of personnel to direct these resources to the recipients. Few, if any, organizations have access to enough of these elements to attain their objectives fully. Under realistic conditions elements are scarce, and organizations must select the particular functions, services, or activities which permit them to achieve their ends as fully as possible.

Although an organization limits itself to particular functions because of scarcity, it can seldom carry out even these without, to some extent at least, cooperating and establishing relationships with other agencies in the health and welfare world. The reasons for this are clear. To carry out its functions without relating to other local agencies, an organization must be able to obtain all the necessary elements—clients, labor services, and other resources—directly from the community or from outside it. Approximating this ideal case is the corporate health agency, as we have mentioned, which conducts research on a national level and does not provide direct services locally. In fact, by discouraging its affiliates from providing direct services on the local level, the national is assured that its locals will be less dependent on other local health and welfare agencies, and, hence, less influenced by them.[5] Certain classes of hospitals treating a specific disease and serving an area larger than the local community can also operate fairly well without actively relating to other local agencies. Even in this case, however, other agencies usually control some elements that facilitate carrying out its functions. Most agencies, especially those offering direct services, are unable to obtain all the elements they need from the general community or through their individual efforts. The need for a sufficient number of clients, for example, is often more efficiently met through interaction and exchanges with other organizations than through independent case-finding procedures.

Because ideas of coordination and cooperation are embedded in powerful social values, clear understanding and objective study of interagency relationships are rendered difficult. Who, for example, would admit opposing cooperation when the welfare of a patient might be involved? The cooperative theme which pervades much of

American life is even more prescribed for personnel of nonprofit agencies whose *raison d'être* is the promotion of human welfare. The foregoing discussion casts a different light upon the question of interagency coordination and cooperation. Instead of considering "good will" among agencies and the personalities and affability of individual executives, however important these may be, our attention is directed to the organizational factors that affect the flow of specific and measurable elements (i.e., patients, personnel, and nonhuman resources) which are the lifeblood of organizational activity and maintenance. Accordingly, the student of health and welfare agencies must not take at face value generic comments about the desirability of greater coordination and cooperation but must try to ascertain (1) the problems of health and welfare agencies, (2) the specific types of cooperation sought, (3) by whom, and (4) from whom.

It is not surprising that a large proportion of personnel in the health and welfare agencies report shortages of money and personnel as their main problems (Table 20.2).

Most of the executives and supervisory personnel also indicate that they would expand their services or offer different types of services if they had sufficient resources. While hardly any agency

TABLE 20.2
Responses of Health and Welfare Personnel in Two Cities Regarding the Greatest Problems of Their Agencies

Problems	City A (79 Respondents)		City B (68 Respondents)	
	No. of Times Mentioned	Percent	No. of Times Mentioned	Percent
Lack of sufficient personnel	22	15.0	14	12.0
Lack of qualified personnel	22	15.0	27	23.1
Lack of money	35	23.8	23	19.6
Lack of facilities	19	12.9	21	17.9
Lack of understanding by other agencies	14	9.5	5	4.3
Lack of understanding by public	23	15.7	20	17.1
Lack of coordination and planning	3	2.0	2	1.7
Lack of use by other agencies	4	2.7	2	1.7
Other	5	3.4	3	2.6
Total responses	147*	100.0	117*	100.0

* Multiple responses were given. Information was obtained from all but one of 34 agencies in City A and all but one of the agencies in City B.

indicates outright that getting recipients constitutes one of its main problems, concern with additional or more selective referrals is evident in discussions with personnel on the need for interagency cooperation.

THE SEARCH FOR COOPERATION

A content analysis was made of the responses of all executives and other agency personnel in two cities concerning the cooperation they would like to have with other health and welfare agencies. We were able to classify the types of cooperation sought into the following seven categories:

1. More referrals
2. More or better case information
3. More or better personal services to patients
4. More nonhuman resources (equipment, technical information, etc.)
5. More money
6. More information on agency services
7. More planning and/or coordination

Although there is considerable difference in the amount of co-operation sought in the two communities, the patterns are quite similar when the seven types of cooperation are ranked (Table 20.3).

In the two communities a large percentage of respondents express their desire to have greater planning and coordination with other agencies. These statements reflect widely different organizational needs and conditions. First, there are those agencies which interact considerably with one another but have not attained complete consensus. For example, whereas a family service agency and a department of welfare may have frequent contact with each other, their relationship may be characterized by considerable attrition. The family service agency may decry the lack of professionalism and the failure of the welfare agency to pay attention to psychological factors. The welfare agency, in turn, may accuse the family service agency of being supercilious and of failing to share case information with other agencies. These differences are not inexorable and in many instances welfare departments and family service agencies have succeeded in achieving effective and har-

TABLE 20.3

Responses of Personnel in Health and Welfare Agencies in Two Cities as to Type of Cooperation Sought with Other Organizations

	Number of Responses		Ranking of Responses	
Type of Cooperation Sought	City A	City B	City A	City B
(1) More referrals	55	25	3	3
(2) More or better case information	30	22	5	4
(3) More or better personal services to patients	54	26	4	2
(4) More nonhuman resources (equipment, technical information, etc.)	16	7	6	7
(5) More money	13	8	7	6
(6) More information on agency services	113	16	1	5
(7) More planning and/or coordination	96	46	2	1
Total responses	377	150		

monious relationships. At any rate, it is evident that these organizations are already involved in a series of cooperative relationships with one another and are seeking more and better means of cooperation.

Second, there are agencies which have little contact with one another but for whom there is a functional need for working together. For example, an osteopathic hospital has many patients who could use the services of the Visiting Nurses Association. Because of the particular status of osteopaths with the medical and nursing profession at the present time, however, there is very little contact between the two organizations. When personnel of an osteopathic organization express the need for more cooperation and coordination with the VNA, they are asking, in fact, that their agency obtain legitimacy from the rest of the health community.

Third, the search for more coordination may reflect a vague notion that some mutual value would accrue from greater contact with another organization. Included here would be organizations struggling for survival which are seeking further justification for their existence and hoping to improve their lot by becoming linked with the activities of other agencies.

In addition, there are organizations which, in stating the need for greater coordination with other agencies, are not only seeking the resources accruing from interagency exchange, but are also expressing their avowed organizational goals. A good example is the community council or planning council, one of whose main explicit objectives is to effect greater interagency coordination. Another case is the health department which is charged with the responsibility for the health of its constituents and which, in the minds of some health officers, should promote the most effective utilization of agency resources within the community.

While only a small percentage of personnel express the desire for money from other organizations, this does not mean that finances are a matter of little concern to health and welfare agencies. As we have seen, the lack of funds and personnel are the two problems most often cited by agency personnel. Rather, it can be inferred that agencies are not random or anarchic in their search for cooperation. What they seek from other organizations is tempered by the realities of the situation. Money is sought in almost all cases only from organizations which normally provide funds to individuals or agencies (e.g., the Welfare Department, the Office of Vocational Rehabilitation, the Cancer Society and the National Foundation).

The functions of an agency determine its need and capacity for interaction. Nondirect service agencies have less need than do direct service agencies for elements from other local organizations. Of the nine agencies in two communities which are without patients or clients, eight do not express the need for any additional cooperation with the other agencies of the study. The one exception is a United Community Service which expresses a desire for more information about, and for more coordination with, other agencies.

One clear category of agencies seeking all types of additional cooperation with other agencies, particularly referrals, is the local federated voluntary agency which provides direct services. Included in this group are such agencies as the Visiting Nurses Association, the Family Service Agency, and the United Cerebral Palsy. These agencies are almost totally dependent upon the local community and the agencies within it for clients and other elements. Although they operate with relatively low budgets, they generally enjoy considerable prestige and have outstanding community leaders on their boards. Yet, despite their modest needs and the support of community leaders, they are not completely assured of their continued existence and, therefore, constantly seek elements from other agencies.

The search for new clients is not always dictated by an immediate need. Additional clients are an important organizational asset in a different sense: They help to demonstrate to board members, the general community, and other legitimizing bodies the value and demand for the services of the agency. In bargaining for support to expand its domain or add specialized personnel to its roster, an agency's case is strengthened if it can point to an impressive waiting list.

These general statements are, of course, dependent upon such factors as the objectives, functions, and needs of the individual agencies. A hearing and speech center, for example, offering needed specialized services which have waiting lists of more than six months, seeks less referrals than are sought from it. Yet, it is intent in obtaining case information and other types of cooperation from the rest of the agency world. Another illustration may be found in a Jewish social service agency which maintains a kind of natural monopoly over a good number of its own clients. The agency appears to be relatively content in the scope of its operations and does not seek much interaction with the rest of the agency system.

In almost all cases, the hospitals of our study tend to seek co-operation less than it is sought from them; and in all cases, other agencies seek referrals from hospitals more than hospitals seek referrals from them. Hospitals, of course, tend to have the highest budgets and caseloads and are generally assured of a large number of patients from physicians. Moreover, they tend to receive more referrals from health and welfare agencies than do other agencies of the health system. In fact, hospitals and other agencies with full caseloads often either discourage the input of too many patients or, depending on their specific functions, develop selective criteria for screening patients. Altogether, they are less desperate for additional elements from other agencies than are other types of organizations.

Yet, the continued flow of sufficient clients may even pose a serious problem for agencies enjoying an abundance of them at a particular time. Consider, for example, the concern of a large voluntary teaching hospital about the changing function of a municipal hospital. When the voluntary hospital learned that the municipal hospital might modify its program from care of the chronically ill to the care of medically indigent acute cases, it expressed concern that its own supply of ward cases would be depleted, its teaching activities impeded, and its ability to attract the better internists and residents thereby harmed. This points up the fact that even organizations which normally have a sufficient number of clients still depend upon a continuation of this salutary state. It appears that patients are a familiar and everyday resource that tends to be taken for granted except when there is a serious danger of curtailment.

Most of the relationships among health and welfare agencies, then, center around the flow of elements and, as we will see later, the rights and obligations with respect to these elements. It is necessary to add a practical note here. Interorganizational activity naturally is not confined to obtaining elements but also involves sending them to other organizations. Since no single organization can provide the total spectrum of services required by all patients or clients, an organization, to fulfill the general objective of having care provided to the patient, may have to direct the client to other relevant organizations. In doing so, the sending agency is linking itself with the services of the receiving agency and, to the extent the referral is a successful one, may enjoy the good will of the satisfied client, of the receiving agency, and, consequently, of the community as a whole.

There are times when the referral process has less desirable consequences for the agencies, the patient, or the community as a whole. Agencies which are overloaded, or which for one reason or another are incapable of rendering the services expected of them, may merely be concerned with removing the load or, in less respectable terminology, "getting rid of the client." In such instances, the agency may refer the patient to another organization which is not in a position to accept him. In two communities which we studied, the voluntary hospitals supported the establishment of government-sponsored chronic disease hospitals in the expectation that a hospital for medically indigent, long-term patients would free a number of beds for patients who could pay for services. In one of the communities it was the frequent practice of physicians to arrange for patients to be transferred to the chronic hospital when the patient could no longer pay for medical services. The eager efforts of physicians to transfer patients resulted in persistent conflict between the voluntary hospitals and the welfare department which administered the chronic disease hospital.

DETERMINANTS OF ORGANIZATIONAL INTERACTION: FUNCTION, ACCESS, AND DOMAIN CONSENSUS

We have already suggested that the kinds and degrees of interactions that go on among agencies are affected by (1) the functions they carry out which, in turn, determine the elements they need; (2) their access to elements from outside the system of health and welfare agencies or, conversely, their relative dependence upon the local system of other health and welfare agencies. A third factor which affects interaction among local agencies is the degree to which what may be termed domain consensus exists within the system of health and welfare agencies.

As we have indicated, organizational relationships directly or indirectly involve the flow of elements. Within the local health and welfare system, the flow of elements is not centrally coordinated, but rests upon voluntary agreements and understandings. Obviously, there can be little exchange of elements between two organizations which do not know of each other's existence or are completely unaware of each other's functions. Our research findings indicate that agency personnel are often ignorant about the kinds of services provided by other agencies in the system. In a given community where 34 agencies were studied, each agency was asked to comment about the scope of services provided by all other agencies in the sample, and data were tabulated in the form of a matrix, 34 by 33. More than 50 per cent of the matrix cells were filled in by "don't knows." In another community where 33 agencies were studied, about 40 per cent of the matrix cells were filled in by "don't knows." It is not surprising that, in general, agencies with little familiarity about each other's services do not interact much with each other and, in most cases, not at all.

Also, there can be little exchange of elements between two organizations without at least some implicit agreement or understanding. These exchange agreements are contingent upon the organizations' respective domains. The domain of an organization consists of the specific goals it wishes to pursue and the functions it seeks to undertake in order to achieve these goals. In operational terms, organizational domain in the health and welfare field refers to the claims which an organization stakes out for itself in terms of (1) problem or disease covered, (2) population served, and (3) services rendered. "The goals of an organization constitute in effect the organization's claim to future functions and to the elements requisite to these functions, whereas the present or actual functions carried out by the organization constitute de facto claims to these elements."[6]

When we speak of domain consensus between two agencies we are referring to the degree to which they agree and accept each other's claims with regard to problems or diseases covered, services offered, and population served. Unless organizational domains are clarified, competition may occur between two agencies offering the same services, especially when other agencies have no specific criteria for referring patients to one of these rather than the other. If all the services are operating at capacity or near capacity, competition between the two agencies tends to be less keen; if services are being operated at less than capacity, however, competition and conflict between the two agencies are often in evidence. Vying for patients or clients, contesting the right of another organization to offer particular services to certain classes of patients or clients, and, in fact, sometimes questioning the organization's very right to exist —all these are often the bitter fruits of conflicting domains. If not resolved quickly, these conflicts gain the attention of the rest of the health agency work and of the general community who begin to deplore what they regard as unnecessary duplication of services.

In a good number of cases, two organizations may resolve the conflict between them by agreeing to specify the criteria for the referral of patients to them. The agreement may often take the form of the two conflicting agencies handling the patient consecutively. For example, age may be used as a criterion. One conflict in which three rehabilitation agencies were involved was resolved by one agency taking preschool children, another school children, and the third, adults. In another case where preventive services were provided one agency took preschool children and the other children of school age. The relative accessibility of the agencies to each of the respective age groups was a partial basis for these divisions. Consecutive treatment of patients is also possible when patients are allocated on the basis of disease stage. One agency provided physical therapy to bedridden patients; another handled them when they became ambulatory.

Organizational conflict results not only from an organization expanding its domain or intruding on that of another, but also occurs when it is judged as not doing as much as it should. If the general goals of a specific agency are accepted by others, they may encourage it to expand its functions or serve new population groups. There is some evidence that agency personnel sometimes may even make "incorrect" referrals to other organizations in order to encourage the latter to expand their domains. Over time, however, should an agency not respond to this encouragement, it may be forced to forfeit its claim to a particular part of its domain.

It is important to note that particular organizations may find it more difficult to legitimize themselves to other parts of the health agency system than to such outside systems as the community or the state. An organization can sometimes obtain sufficient support from outside the health system long after other organizations within the system have challenged or rescinded its domain. In one community, a social service agency was pressed by other agencies to go out of existence because it was believed that the services it was offering were being delivered more effectively by another agency. However, the agency in question suddenly became the recipient of a large bequest which assured its continued survival for some time. Instances of this sort sometimes make it difficult for other health agencies to encourage or coerce a particular agency to be more cooperative and "rational" in its relations with other agencies.

While much of our analysis has focused on the "exchange" value inherent in organizational interaction, we should avoid committing a rationalistic fallacy. We should not assume that executive personnel always know their organizational self-interest and are ever acting in its behalf. In fact, overconcern with the immediate acquisition of elements may have long-run negative consequences. In one community, for example, a sheltered workshop, supporting itself from the sale of products, began to exclude the more seriously handicapped in order to maintain a high rate of production. Accordingly, it refused to accept referrals from a number of community agencies and, over time, lost their approval—a factor which resulted in the failure of the sheltered workshop to obtain voluntary grants of funds necessary for its operations. Today, the workshop is barely operating. Yet, it seems likely that had the workshop accepted the more serious cases from other community agencies, they would have lent their support to its continued existence.

It is our impression that, even in terms of organizational survival, a number of agencies have overlooked the usefulness of relating to the rest of the health and welfare system and have been preoccupied with obtaining support from three main sources: (1) the general community; (2) local governing boards; and (3) their parent bodies or policy-making groups outside the community. This orientation often results in exaggerated concern with organizational identity, the publicizing of dramatic instances of organizational achievement, and the devising of glowing statistics to attract community attention and impress board members. The assumption that underlies this orientation is, of course, that it is the best means of insuring continued support. It can be easily understood how this orientation can produce a keen and jealous competitive spirit among individual agencies. While this orientation may be feasible for corporate agencies which are not oriented toward the local com-

there is a limit to which changes in their policy can be effected by pressure on the local level. While there may be little point in investing time and energy locally in criticizing their organizational goals, some headway may be made by working on the state or national levels where basic organizational policies are formulated.

2. Improve the knowledge organizations have regarding one another—The goals, functions, problems, and restrictions under which organizations operate should be made explicit. We have found that an agency is sometimes taken aback when its overtures for cooperation with another agency are not met with immediate favorable response. The reason for this often lies in the failure of the initiating agency to appreciate the problems and goals of the organization it is approaching. Obviously, there is little likelihood of obtaining cooperation when only one organization will benefit. Yet, many organizations seek to enter into exchanges with other organizations and bemoan the lack of cooperation from others when only their own goals can be furthered by the proposed activity. A clearer knowledge of the problems and goals of the other organization would appear to be a first step in developing cooperation between two organizations which is based on mutual benefit.

The usual listings of agencies and their functions which exist in communities provide little guidance in this respect, either for other agencies or for the recipients of services. These lists appear to be developed more for public relations purposes than for guides to intelligent utilization by other organizations or clients. As a result, clients are sent to inappropriate agencies and others who should be referred are not referred. It would help if the caseload and capacity of each organization were known to all. So often an organization is listed in most impressive terms with a yearly caseload of ten people and a capacity not much beyond ten. If the list of agencies contained some information about the agencies' main problems (e.g., getting volunteers, transportation, and so on) and about the resources they possess which might be made available to other organizations, it would provide a useful guide for others in the health system.

3. Recognize and analyze domain differences and related tensions between organizations and develop mechanisms for the solution of these differences—In our study of domain consensus, we learned that conflicts were often resolved when agencies agreed on criteria by which others could distinguish their respective functions. Such delineation of function can result in greater efficiency in the health and welfare system by permitting greater professional

specialization and by facilitating the referral of patients and the flow of information.

4. Educate the boards and community leaders to recognize the interdependence of the health and welfare agency system—One of the major tasks for the agency professional staff is the reorientation of board members to the fact that direct service organizations (1) can no longer survive solely by depending on large individual private sources in the community, and (2) that agency continuity can best be assured by contributing to the rest of the health and welfare system. Once the boards adopt this view, professional staffs will be freer to redefine their roles and objectives to include greater cooperation with other agencies.

5. Means and mechanisms must be developed whereby professional personnel are provided appropriate rewards or incentives—Because the average health worker has internalized broad professional norms, he tends to act to safeguard the welfare of his clients and, when necessary, to refer them to other appropriate agencies. However, unless the health worker's positive behavior toward clients and other agencies is valued or approved by the individual agency by which he is employed, there is a limit to the degree to which his professional norms can sustain him. In short, it is not sufficient to plead with professionals to modify their behavior; incentives must be introduced within each organization to foster desired courses of action (i.e., cooperating with other agencies).

6. Establish some formal mechanism by which specific professionals would be charged with the main responsibility of studying and assessing community needs and of stimulating and coordinating the activities of various health agencies—Who would this person (or persons) be? It should be someone who views the community as a patient and is intent on developing maximal rationality among the system of health and welfare agencies; someone steeped in community organization and the sociology of organization and familiar with the scope of each of the health and welfare professions; someone able whenever necessary to reach outside the community to achieve more effective coordination. It should be someone capable of dealing with official and voluntary organizations and various kinds of hospitals.

Contrary to the beliefs of many public health people, the health officer is not often recommended as the person most suitable for this role. In two communities the head of the Community Council or United Community Service is cited more frequently by agency personnel. Even when the question is posed in terms of coordinating only health agencies, the health officer does not receive an impressively large percentage of mentions. On the other hand, the Community Council is mentioned most when the question is restricted to welfare agencies. This would indicate that having the health department accepted as the principal coordinator of health and/or welfare agencies is not shared by the rest of the health and welfare agency personnel. It also suggests that most agencies are not as yet prepared to invest in a single person or agency the responsibility of coordinating their work with one another. Another point of interest in this respect is that there is even less acceptance of the welfare department as the potential coordinator of welfare activities. This may be due in part to the fact that many of the welfare department's personnel are without graduate training.

Our findings indicate that the choice of a coordinator and the delineation of his role is still problematic; yet, we trust that our other recommendations provide bases for an approach to solution of the problem.

CONCLUSION

In this paper we have discussed the goals, needs, and problems of individual agencies and how these may impede interorganizational relationships. At the same time, we have pointed up that agencies, in fact, cooperate with one another considerably and actively seek cooperation in order to acquire necessary resources. In short, there is a patterned interplay among health and welfare agencies which stems largely from their respective functions. However, since these functions have arisen in a laissez-faire manner with each agency independently attempting to meet its specific objectives, various barriers to greater interorganizational cooperation have developed. We have suggested various approaches by which these barriers may be overcome. But increased cooperation among agencies does not automatically guarantee that the health needs of the community are being met. An even more important objective challenges the skills and ingenuity of health leaders and community organizers: how to direct the natural interplay among agencies so that their functions are congruent not only with one another but also with the needs of myriads of recipients?

NOTES

1. Haldeman, J., and Flook, E. "The Development of Community Health Services," *A.J.P.H.* 49:10–21 (Jan.), 1959.
2. Etzioni, A. "Organizations and Society: Three Dimensions of Recent Studies." Paper presented to the Annual Meeting of the Eastern Sociological Society (Apr. 11–12), 1959, New York, N.Y.
3. Sills, D. L. *The Volunteers: Means and Ends in a National Organization* (Glencoe, Ill.: Free Press, 1957).
4. Hamlin, R. H. *Voluntary Health and Welfare Agencies in the United States* (New York, N.Y.: The Schoolmasters' Press, 1961).
5. Briggs, J. L., and Levine, S. "Control Over Local Affiliates by National Health Organizations." Paper presented at Meetings of American Sociological Association, St. Louis, Mo., 1961.
6. Levine, S., and White, P. E. "Exchange as a Conceptual Framework for the Study of Interorganizational Relationships." *Admin. Sc. Quart.* 5:583–597 (Mar.), 1961.

21   Bureaucracy and the Lower Class

GIDEON SJOBERG, RICHARD A. BRYMER, and BUFORD FARRIS

Bureaucratic structures, so our argument runs, not only encounter major difficulties in coping with the problems of the lower class but also serve to maintain and reinforce patterns that are associated with the "culture of poverty." Here we shall focus upon the relationships between client-centered bureaucracies[1] and the lower class in American society.

Sociologists have devoted little attention, on either the community or national level, to the impact of bureaucracy upon the stratification system. Yet our experience, based on research among lower-class Mexican-Americans in San Antonio,[2] points to the critical role of bureaucratic organizations in sustaining social stratification. Sociologists frequently compare lower- and middle-class culture patterns, but they fail to recognize that bureaucratic systems are the key medium through which the middle class maintains its advantaged position vis-à-vis the lower.

Reprinted from *Sociology and Social Research*, 50 (April 1966): 325–37, by permission of the authors and of the publisher.

Our analysis of the effect of the client-centered bureaucracy upon the lower class is cast in rather theoretical terms. However, illustrative materials from our research project and the writings of other scholars indicate the kinds of data that support our generalizations. After delineating the main elements of the bureaucratic model, we discuss the lower class from the perspective of the bureaucratic system and then bureaucracy from the viewpoint of the lower class. These materials set the stage for a consideration of various emergent organizational and political patterns in American society.

THE NATURE OF BUREAUCRACY

In the post-World War II era various sociologists[3] have questioned the utility of Weber's analysis of bureaucracy. Nevertheless, sociologists continue to assume that bureaucracy (as conceived by Weber) is positively associated with the continued development of an advanced industrial-urban order and that this bureaucracy is more or less inevitable.

Modern bureaucracies lay heavy stress upon rationality and efficiency. In order to attain these ends, men are called upon to work within a hierarchical system, with well-defined lines of authority, and within a differentiated social setting, with an elaborate division of labor that stresses the specialization of function. This hierarchy and division of labor are, in turn, sustained through a complex set of formalized rules which are to be administered in a highly impersonal and standardized manner. There is considerable centralization of authority, and as one moves from top to bottom there is greater specialization of function and adherence to the rules.

What is not as clearly recognized is that efficiency and rationality are predicated upon an explicit statement of the organization's goals. Only when an end is clearly stated can one determine the most efficient means for its attainment. Thus, because the corporate structure has had an explicit goal (i.e. profit), it has been quite successful in measuring the efficiency of its programs (i.e. means).

The corporate system has been the model that other bureaucracies have emulated. As a result, there has been considerable concern with efficiency within, say, the Federal Government. McNamara's reorganization of the U.S. Defense Department in the 1960's is a case in point. It is significant that McNamara has drawn heavily upon the work of Hitch and McKean[4] in developing his program, for Hitch and McKean argue that organizational goals must be spelled out in rather concrete terms in order to measure the effectiveness of various programs. An understanding of the interrelationships among measurement, objectification of goals, and efficiency and rationality is essential if we are to assess the impact of bureaucratic structures upon the lower class.

ORIENTATIONS OF BUREAUCRACIES TOWARDS THE LOWER CLASS

Bureaucratic organizations frequently reinforce the class structure of the community and the nation through their staffing procedures. When a bureaucracy serves both upper- and lower-class groups, as does the school, the poorly qualified teachers tend to drift into lower-class neighborhoods, or, as frequently occurs, beginning teachers are placed in "hardship" districts, and then the most capable move up and out into upper-status school districts where higher salaries and superior working conditions usually prevail. Thus, the advancement of lower-class children is impeded not only because of their cultural background but because of the poor quality of their teachers.

In welfare bureaucracies, social workers have struggled to escape from their traditional identification with the poor, either by redefining their functions in order to serve middle-class clients or by moving away from clients into administrative posts. Once again, evidence suggests that the lower class comes to be served by the least qualified personnel.

In addition to staffing arrangements, the bureaucracy's method of selecting clients reinforces the class system. At this point we must remember that bureaucracies are under constant pressure to define their goals so that the efficiency of their programs can be measured. But unlike corporate systems, client-centered bureaucracies experience grave difficulties in specifying their goals and evaluating their efficiency. The client-centered bureaucracies meet the demands placed upon them through the use of simplified operational definitions. Universities, for instance, do not judge their effectiveness in terms of producing "educated men" but according to the ratings of their students on national tests, the number of students who gain special awards, etc. These operational criteria reflect the orientation or view of persons in positions of authority within the bureaucracy and the broader society. In turn, these criteria become the basis for the selection of clients. Through this procedure, a bureaucratic organization can ensure its success, and it can more readily demonstrate to the power structure that the community or society is "getting something for its money." The bureaucracy's success is likely to lead to an increase in funds and expanded activities. It follows that client-centered bureaucracies often find it advantageous to avoid lower-class clients who are likely to handicap the organization in the attainment of its goals.[5]

Several illustrations should clarify our argument. The Federal Job Corps program has been viewed as one means for alleviating the unemployment problem among youth, especially those in the lower class. This program has sought to train disadvantaged youths in various occupational skills. The success of the Job Corps is apparently to be evaluated according to the number of trainees who enter the industrial labor force. Consequently, the organization has sought to select those youths who have internalized some of the middle-class norms of upward mobility and who are likely to succeed in the occupational system. The Job Corps by-passes many persons who in theory stand in greatest need of assistance; for example, potential "troublemakers"—young men with criminal records —are not accepted as trainees. Because of this selection process the Job Corps leadership will likely be able to claim success and to convince Congressmen that the program should be continued and perhaps broadened.

A more subtle form of client selection can be found in child guidance clinics. Here clients are often accepted in terms of their "receptivity" to therapy.[6] However, this criterion favors those persons who have been socialized into the middle-class value orientation held by, for example, the clinic staff and the social groups who pay the bill. The poor, especially the families from ethnic groups within the lower class, who according to the ideal norms of these agencies should receive the greatest amount of attention, are quietly shunted aside. Moreover, one study has indicated a positive association between the social status of the client and the social status of the professional worker handling the case in the agency.[7]

The procedures by which school systems cope with their clients are perhaps central to understanding the community and national class system, for the educational variable is becoming increasingly significant in sustaining or advancing one's status. At this point we are concerned with the differential treatment of clients by the organization once they have been accepted.

School systems frequently employ IQ tests and similar instruments in their evaluation of pupils. These tests, however, have been constructed in such a manner that they articulate with the values, beliefs, and knowledge of the middle class and the demands of the power elements of the society. That these tests are used to make early judgments on the ability of pupils serves to support the existing class system. Lower-class pupils often come to be defined as "dull," and, through a kind of self-fulfilling prophecy, this definition of the situation structures the students' future career. In fact, school counselors frequently interpret test scores according to their middle-class expectations; they, therefore, tend to discourage lower-class pupils from attending college even when their scores are relatively high.[8]

It is significant that the New York City school system has been forced to abandon the use of IQ tests.[9] It appears that the traditionally disadvantaged groups such as Negroes and Puerto Ricans have attained sufficient political power to challenge those methods that the school bureaucracy has used for determining success, methods that have been oriented to middle-class rather than lower-class norms.

Bureaucratized school systems place the lower-class clients at a disadvantage in still other ways. Various types of standardization or categorization, which are a product of middle-class expectations and which are viewed as essential for maintaining efficiency, limit the school's ability to adjust to the "needs" of lower-class pupils. We know of a special class, for example, that was established for the purpose of teaching lower-class and problem children, but in which the rules demanded that the teacher follow the same teaching plan employed in other classes in the school.

Actually, bureaucratic structures socialize the incumbents of roles in such a manner that they are frequently incapable of understanding the world-view of the lower-class client. Discussions of the bureaucratic personality, such as those by Merton and Presthus,[10] have given but scant attention to the difficulty of the bureaucrat's taking the role of the lower-class other. For as a result of his role commitment, the bureaucrat tends to impose his own expectations and interpretations of reality upon the client. He often comes to view the norms of the system as invariant. And bureaucrats in the lower echelons, those who have the greatest amount of contact with lower-class clients, are also the most bound by the rules. Faced with recalcitrant clients or clients having divergent value orientations, the typical office holder will say in effect, "If only clients would act properly, everything would be all right, and we could get on with our work."

The bureaucrat, oriented as he is to the middle- or upper-class life styles, usually lacks knowledge about the lower-class client's subculture. Moreover, he finds it difficult to step outside his formalized role. If he seeks to take the role of the client—in the sense of understanding the latter's belief and value system—he will ultimately have to challenge or at least question some of the rules that govern the operation of the system of which he is a part. For if he understands why clients act the way they do, he is likely to recognize that they have valid reasons for objecting to his conception of reality or, more specifically, to some of the bureaucratic regulations. Consequently, bureaucratic organizations tend to penalize those of their members who "overidentify" with clients.

Social workers who overidentify with their clients or teachers who overidentify with their students are considered to be indulging in nonprofessional action. Such action, so the reasoning runs, makes it impossible for the professional to adhere to the ideal norms of universalism and objectivity and thus to assist his clients effectively. Professional norms such as these reinforce those bureaucratic norms that impose barriers upon the lower-class person's advancement in the social order.

The controls exerted by the bureaucrats over members of the lower class are intensified because the office holders are constantly called upon to normalize and stabilize the system with an eye to maintaining the proper public image. One means of stabilizing and rationalizing the system's performance is to work within the context of established rules or categories. But to cope really effectively with such deviants as juvenile delinquents, the schools would have to alter radically their time-honored categories. Our experience suggests, however, that school systems stifle the grievances of deviant or lower-class groups, for these grievances, at least implicitly, challenge the bureaucratic norms that are supported by the groups that determine public policy.

The general insensitivity of bureaucracies to lower-class persons and their problems is highlighted in the "custodial function" adopted by many mental hospitals and even slum schools.[11] Because the bureaucracy's normative system runs counter to (or at best ignores) the norms and values of the lower class, a minimum of attention is given to socializing clients into the bureaucratic—or broader societal —norms. Bureaucratic systems adjust to this situation through the caretaker function.

ORIENTATIONS OF THE LOWER CLASS TOWARDS BUREAUCRACIES

Just as significant as the bureaucracy's orientation towards the lower class is the latter's orientation toward the bureaucracy. Our investigations, particularly depth interviews of Mexican-American families in San Antonio, support the conclusion of other social scientists—that members of the lower class encounter serious difficulties when they attempt to understand or to cope with the normative order of bureaucratic systems.

First and foremost, the lower-class person simply lacks knowledge of the rules of the game. Middle-class persons generally learn how to manipulate bureaucratic rules to their advantage and even to acquire special "favors" by working through the "private" or "backstage" (as opposed to the "public") sector of the bureaucratic organization. Middle-class parents teach by example as they intervene with various officials—e.g. the police or school teachers—to protect the family's social position in the community. In contrast, the lower-class person stands in awe of bureaucratic regulations and frequently is unaware that he has a legal and moral claim to certain rights and privileges. More often, however, it is the lack of knowledge of the system's technicalities and backstage regions that is responsible for the lower-class person's inability to manipulate a bureaucratic system to his advantage.

We mentioned earlier that in its lower echelons the bureaucracy is highly specialized and governed by numerous regulations. Therefore, the lower-class person, whose knowledge of the system is least adequate, must interact with the very officials who are most constrained by the formal rules. This situation is complicated by the fact that the problems the lower-class person faces are difficult to treat in isolation. The lack of steady employment, of education, and of medical care, for example, interlock in complex ways. Yet, the lower-class client encounters officials who examine only one facet of his difficulties and who, in the ideal, treat all cases in a similar fashion. After one agency (or official) has dealt with the special problem assigned it, the client is then referred to another agency which will consider another facet of the situation. It follows that no official is able to view the lower-class client as a whole person, and thus he is unable to point up to the client how he might use his strengths to overcome his weaknesses.

Middle-class persons, on the other hand, are in a position to deal with higher-status office holders, who are less encumbered by the rules and thus can examine their clients' problems in holistic terms. Delinquents from middle-class homes, for instance, are more apt than those from lower-class surroundings to be judged by officials according to their overall performance—both past and present.

The cleavage between modern bureaucracies and the lower class is intensified by various cultural differences. Gans,[12] for example, has found that lower-class persons typically relate to one another in a personal manner. Middle-class persons are better able to relate to others within an impersonal context. Thus, members of the lower class face a greater gulf when they attempt to communicate with middle-class bureaucrats who ideally must administer rules according to impersonal, universalistic norms.

This divergence between the lower class and bureaucratic officialdom in patterns of social interaction simply makes it more difficult for a lower-class person to acquire knowledge of how the system operates. It is not surprising that under these circumstances members of the lower class often experience a sense of powerlessness or alienation. This alienation in turn reinforces and is reinforced by the sense of fatalism that is an integral part of "the culture of poverty."[13] That is, those who live in the world of the lower class account for events in the social sphere in terms of spiritual forces, chance, luck, and the like; they have little or no sense of control over their own destiny.

Because bureaucratic officials find it difficult to understand the perspective of lower-class clients and because lower-class persons must increasingly cope with highly specialized and technically oriented systems, the social distance between the bureaucratically skilled members of American society and some elements of the lower class may well be increasing rather than decreasing.[14] A kind of "circular causation," in Myrdal's terms,[15] is at work, as various social forces tend to exaggerate the schism between at least some sectors of the lower class and the upper socioeconomic groups who control the bureaucratic organizations.

ORGANIZATIONAL IMPLICATIONS

The dilemmas of client-centered bureaucracies which deal with lower-class persons are reflected in a variety of programs designed to eliminate poverty, juvenile delinquency, and other social problems. By examining these programs we can clarify some of the relationships between bureaucracy and the lower class discussed above and can bring to light other issues as well.

There have been two broad strategies for resolving the problems faced by the lower class on the national, state, and local levels. The dominant strategy emphasizes increased bureaucratization. The second approach, of theoretical rather than practical import at the present time, calls for a fundamental restructuring of client-centered bureaucracies.

1. The primary means of overcoming the problems that have been associated with the lower class has been more and more bureaucracy. This pattern has taken two forms.

a. The social problems of the lower class that have resisted solution (in terms of the values and beliefs of the dominant groups in society) are to be resolved through expansion of existing bureaucratic structures or the addition of new ones. This has been the main thrust of most legislation on both the national and the state levels since the 1930's. The programs initiated during the New Deal era have reached their fruition in President Johnson's "Great Society." In one sense the problems generated by bureaucracy are to be met by more bureaucracy.

The efforts to resolve social problems through bureaucratization have proliferated in the nongovernmental sector as well. For example, some programs—e.g. the Y.M.C.A. Detached Workers Program in Chicago[16]—seek to combat delinquency among lower-class groups by fitting youth into an organizational apparatus.

The sociologist Glazer[17] views this organizational revolution as the basis of the new utopia. It is the model towards which men should strive. He, like many other sociologists, considers an industrial-urban order to be equivalent with a bureaucratic social order.

b. A small group of persons believe that the problems of the lower class require a counter-organizational solution. The Mobilization for Youth program in New York—at it has been interpreted by some social workers—is an instructive case in point.[18] Here a number of social workers, perhaps as a reaction to their traditional over-identification with middle-class norms, have been attempting to organize the poor in order to counter the problems generated by entrenched bureaucracies. In theory the new bureaucratic systems should side with the poor against the established bureaucracies which are controlled by the upper socioeconomic groups.

2. Along with this trend towards bureaucratization, there have been increased efforts to remake bureaucratic structures or to create nonbureaucratic systems in order to attain certain ends.[19]

a. Although the therapeutic community in the mental health field has not been specifically designed for lower-class clients, this development has been spurred by the sociological descriptions of custodial hospitals that have cared for lower-class patients. These highly bureaucratized systems have fallen far short of their stated goals; indeed, they have done much to stifle communication between therapists and patients.[20] The therapeutic community, which in extreme form calls for a complete breakdown of status barriers between therapist and patient, has thus emerged as a new organizational form in order to further the treatment of patients.

Somewhat similar communities have emerged in other areas as well. The Provo Experiment[21] with juvenile delinquents has displayed some of the characteristics of the therapeutic community. In at least the early stages of their contacts with delinquents, the workers in this project have placed considerable reliance upon informal groups (in sharp contrast to, say, the bureaucratized reformatory) as a mechanism for revising the delinquent's orientation.

b. In a similar vein, there have been efforts to set up organizations along collegial lines. Some writers, like Litwak. seem to regard this type of system as a "professional bureaucracy."[22] But if we take the Weberian model as our starting point, the very notion of a professional bureaucracy is a contradiction of terms. The collegial organization and the bureaucratic system are built on divergent principles. The former stresses, for example, equality among office holders and the need for generalists rather than specialists. The generalist, unencumbered by highly formalized rules, can view clients in holistic terms and thus examine their weaknesses relative to their strengths. There emerges here a type of rationality that is not encompassed by Weber's notions of "formal rationality" (typical of bureaucratic systems) and "substantive rationality" (typical of traditional paternalistic systems).[23]

Some mental hospitals are apparently being built along collegial lines—as a compromise between a bureaucratic system and a therapeutic community.[24] Our experience in a neighborhood agency indicates that a collegial organization is necessary if social workers are to function as "mediators" between divergent class elements.[25] Workers within a bureaucratic welfare agency, as depicted by Wilensky and Lebeaux,[26] must take the class structure (as defined by the upper socioeconomic groups) as their frame of reference. Because bureaucratic functionaries find it difficult to understand the role orientations of lower-class others, they can not mediate effectively between elements of different social classes.

Overall, the trends in the development of nonbureaucratic organizations suggest a close association between the system's internal structure and its relationships with clients. These trends also support our contention that bureaucratic systems have not been successful in working with lower-class clients.

POLITICAL IMPLICATIONS

The tensions generated by the bureaucratic solution to current social problems are highlighted by the efforts to resolve the difficulties encountered by the Negro lower class. The debate generated by the "Moynihan Report" is of special theoretical interest.[27] (This Report, issued by the U.S. Department of Labor, was written by Daniel P. Moynihan, although he is not formally listed as author.) Moynihan argues that the family structure of the lower-class Negro —which is mother-dominated and highly unstable by societal standards—must be revised if Negroes are to adapt to the industrial-urban order or the bureaucratic school systems, economic organizations, etc.

Elements of the Negro leadership have sharply attacked the Moynihan Report. They believe that instead of restructuring the lower-class Negro family we must remake modern bureaucratic systems so that these will be more responsive to the "needs" of the Negro lower class.

Moynihan's position is in keeping with that of many sociologists who accept present-day structural arrangements as more or less inevitable. Sociologists often argue that social problems arise because lower-class individuals or families are committed to sociocultural patterns that make it difficult for them to accommodate to the demands of industrial-urban organizations. Although some scholars have analyzed the dysfunctions of bureaucratic systems,[28] they rarely, if ever, assume that basic structural reorganization is necessary or possible. But the Weberian model may not be a rational or efficient organization for coping with many of the problems that have emerged (and will emerge) in an advanced industrial order where the problems of production have been resolved and the issues dealt with by client-centered organizations loom increasingly larger.

Sociologists must re-examine their basic premises if they are to grasp the nature of current social trends. For one thing, politics in a post-welfare, advanced industrial-urban order may become oriented around pro-bureaucratic and anti-bureaucratic ideologies. The rumblings of minorities (including some intellectuals in England, the United States, and Sweden) suggest that this type of political struggle may be in the offing. It is of interest, for example, that in the United States elements of the New Left—e.g. Students for a Democratic Society—share a common "devil"—the bureaucratic system

—with elements of the right wing. We would hypothesize that some relationship exists between these ideological concerns and the problems of client-centered bureaucracies. Certainly, these developments are worthy of serious sociological investigation—and before, not after, the fact.

CONCLUSIONS

Evidence indicates that modern bureaucracies, especially client-centered ones, stand between lower-class and upper-status (particularly middle-class) persons. These groups do not encounter one another within a vacuum but rather within an organizational, bureaucratic context. Even when they meet in relatively informal situations, the bureaucratic orientation of the middle-class person structures his response to the lower-class individual. It is through their positions in the key bureaucracies that the higher-status groups maintain their social advantages and even at times foster bureaucratic procedures that impede the advancement of lower-class persons into positions of privilege. While our illustrative data are limited to the United States, many of our generalizations seem to hold for other industrial-urban orders as well.

The social and political implications of the dilemmas that face bureaucratic systems require far more attention than they have received. Weber's conception of bureaucracy may have deflected sociologists from some significant concerns. There are, after all, other intellectual traditions to draw upon. For example, Spencer's[29] analysis of how "military organizations" emphasize the contributions of individuals to the system and of how "industrial organizations" emphasize the contributions of the system to individuals is of considerable relevance for an understanding of the link between formal organizations and their clients and, ultimately, formal organizations and social stratification. But whatever one's source of inspiration, the study of the impact of different kinds of formal organizations upon social stratification is central to the sociologist's major concern—that of understanding the nature of order.

NOTES

1. The term "client-centered bureaucracy" is derived from the classification scheme of Peter Blau and W. Richard Scott, *Formal*

Organizations (San Francisco: Chandler Publishing Co., 1962). They employ the term "service organizations" for this type of structure.

2. Our main project, which focuses upon the evaluation of an action program for the prevention of juvenile delinquency, is supported by the National Institute of Mental Health: Grant No. R11-MH-1075-02 and 02SI. This project has, as a result of a grant from the Hogg Foundation, University of Texas, been broadened to include a study in depth of lower-class Mexican-American families.

3. Peter Blau, *The Dynamics of Bureaucracy* (rev. ed. Chicago: University of Chicago Press, 1963), and Alvin Gouldner, *Patterns of Industrial Bureaucracy* (New York: The Free Press, a Division of the Macmillan Co., 1965).

4. Charles J. Hitch and Roland N. McKean, *The Economics of Defense in the Nuclear Age* (Cambridge: Harvard University Press, 1960).

5. See e.g. Martin Rein, "The Strange Case of Public Dependency," *Transaction*, 2 (March–April, 1965), 16–23.

6. Based on the personal observations of Buford Farris who, as a social worker, has had extensive contact with these agencies.

7. Raymond G. Hunt, Orville Gurrslin, and Jack L. Roach, "Social Status and Psychiatric Service in a Child Guidance Clinic," *American Sociological Review*, 23 (February, 1958), 81–83.

8. Aaron Cirourel and John I. Kitsuse, *The Educational Decision-Makers* (Indianapolis: Bobbs-Merrill Co., 1963). For a general discussion of the bureaucratization of the school system see Dean Harper, "The Growth of Bureaucracy in School Systems," *American Journal of Economics and Sociology*, 23 (July, 1965), 261–71.

9. Fred M. Hechinger, "I.Q. Test Ban," *New York Times*, March 8, 1964, Section E, p. 7; Fred M. Hechinger, "Testing at Issue," *New York Times*, November 1, 1964, Section E, p. 9.

10. Robert K. Merton, *Social Theory and Social Structure* (rev ed. New York: The Free Press, a Division of the Macmillan Co., 1957), 195–206 and Robert Presthus, *The Organizational Society* (New York: Vintage Books, 1965).

11. See e.g. Ivan C. Belknap, *Human Problems of a State Mental Hospital* (New York: McGraw-Hill Book Co., 1956); Fred M. Hechinger, "Poor Marks for Slum Schools," *New York Times*, December 12, 1965, Section E, p. 9; Kenneth Clark, *Dark Ghetto* (New York: Harper and Row, 1965), chap. 6.

12. Herbert Gans, *The Urban Villagers* (New York: The Free Press, a Division of the Macmillan Co., 1965).

13. See e.g. various essays in Frank Riessman, Jerome Cohen, and Arthur Pearl (eds.), *Mental Health of the Poor* (New York: The Free Press, a Division of the Macmillan Co., 1964).

14. U.S. Bureau of the Census, *Current Population Reprint Series*

P-60. No. 47, Income in 1964 of Families and Persons in the United States (Washington, D.C.: U.S. Government Printing Office, 1965).

15. Gunnar Myrdal, Economic Theory and Under-Developed Regions (London: Gerald Duckworth and Co., 1957), 16–20.

16. Charles N. Cooper, "The Chicago YMCA Detached Workers: Current Status of an Action Program," Paper presented at a joint session of the annual meeting of the Society for the Study of Social Problems and American Sociological Association, Los Angeles, California, August, 1963.

17. Nathan Glazer, "The Good Society," Commentary, 36 (September, 1963), 226–34.

18. See e.g. Charles F. Grosser, "Community Development Programs Serving the Urban Poor," Social Work, 10 (July, 1965), 15–21.

19. There has been considerable interest in reorganizing corporate bureaucracy in recent years, but this material does not bear directly upon the problems at hand.

20. See e.g. Belknap, op. cit.

21. LaMar T. Empey and Jerome Rabow, "The Provo Experiment in Delinquency Prevention," American Sociological Review, 26 (October, 1961), 679–95.

22. Eugene Litwak, "Models of Bureaucracy Which Permit Conflict," American Journal of Sociology, 57 (September, 1961), 177–84.

23. From Max Weber, trans. and ed. by H. H. Gerth and C. Wright Mills (New York: Oxford University Press, 1946).

24. Research being carried out by James Otis Smith, J. Kenneth Benson and Gideon Sjoberg as part of the Timberlawn Foundation Research Project, Dallas, Texas, will bear directly upon this issue.

25. Gideon Sjoberg, "The Rise of the 'Mediator Society'," Presidential address delivered at the annual meeting of the Southwestern Sociological Association, Dallas, Texas, March, 1964, examines the overall role of mediators in modern society.

26. Harold L. Wilensky and Charles N. Lebeaux, Industrial Society and Social Welfare (New York: The Free Press, a Division of the Macmillan Co., 1965), 238–40.

27. U.S. Department of Labor, The Case for National Action (Washington, D.C.: U.S. Government Printing Office, 1965). For reactions to this essay see: "The Negro Family: Visceral Reaction," Newsweek, 60 (December 6, 1965), 38–40 and John Herbers, "Moynihan Hopeful U.S. Will Adopt a Policy of Promoting Family Stability," New York Times, December 12, 1965, 74.

28. See e.g. Harry Cohen, The Demonics of Bureaucracy (Ames, Iowa: Iowa State University Press, 1965).

29. Herbert Spencer, The Principles of Sociology, 3 vols. (New York: D. Appleton and Co., 1899).

Chapter Seven

DIRECTIONS OF SOCIAL WORK

It would be a remarkable bit of prophecy to set down the direction social work will take in the final quarter of the 20th century. Therefore, in entitling this chapter we have taken care to end the word "direction" with an evasive "s." Like Leacock's irrepressible Gertrude the Governess who always "jumped upon her horse and rode off in all directions," social work in the 1970s seems to be moving in several ways at once, presenting a dizzying array of practices, problems, and programs. Some prognostications are dour: Social work is doomed. Others are ebullient: *Real* social work is just about to begin.

Checking through the issues of the past year's *Journal of the National Association of Social Workers* at the time of writing, we found that the list of topics covers a fantastic range. Apart from articles aplenty on professional business such as ethics, accountability, methodology, and supervision, there appeared to be no corner of community life untouched by social work. There were articles about social work in police departments, in industry, and in disasters. Descriptions of practice included social work with addicts, alcoholics, and victims of sickle cell anemia. There were discussions of social work in relation to women's lib, lead poisoning, legal services, and legislative action. And that is only a sample.

claimed and others it should never have claimed. The criticism of casework is, in a nutshell, that social casework has made *no difference* in efforts to relieve social stress.[5] While we cannot here undertake an evaluation of the many evaluations of social casework, neither can we pass this subject by without comment. Most of the studies cited in the literature of criticism are not well suited to the task of evaluating casework. Many of them (particularly those cited by Joel Fischer)[6] deal with client populations who suffer from problems caused by extreme economic deprivation; moreover, many of these client populations did not request the kind of help proffered by the social caseworkers who served them. (Some studies of outcomes of therapeutic interventions have found that casework *does* make a difference with client groups who have voluntarily sought help.[7]) In many evaluative studies, the nature of the casework intervention is not clear, and in some studies where control groups are used it is not clear as to how the stimulus given to the experimental group (i.e., casework) differed from what was given to a control group.[8] By and large, most of these studies have searched for changes in individual and family functioning brought about as the result of clinically-oriented intervention, a highly unrealistic expectation in light of the evidence that interpersonal and intrapersonal factors are not the cause of many of the problems treated.

These comments, we hope, will encourage some skepticism of critiques of casework. But it is even more important, as Briar indicates, that there be redefinition and clarification of the goals and functions of casework, along with development of methods to increase effectiveness and techniques to measure effects realistically.

During the period of the late 1960s, in which devastating critiques of casework (and, to a lesser extent, of the entire profession) became a pervasive theme in the literature, the profession was changing in numerous ways. The breadth and scope of the change are described in Pins's article "Changes in Social Work Education and Their Implications for Practice" (Reading 23). Pins's focus is on training, and the training is for a profession rapidly expanding on many fronts. The number of schools and programs is increasing; enrollments for degrees and programs ranging from the two-year community college course to the doctorate are growing; training programs are being revised in almost every way imaginable; increasing attention and resources are being devoted to disadvantaged groups and racial and ethnic minorities. And all this, Pins indicates, is taking place at a time when social work and social work education face a major fiscal crisis because of government cutbacks in funds. There seems to be a great deal of activity in the field, but it is difficult to determine whether this is because the engine of change is running very fast or merely running down.

In contrast to these papers which deal with the expansiveness of social work, in Reading 24, "Toward a Model for Teaching a Basic First-Year Course in Methods of Social Work Practice," Allen Pincus and Anne Minahan are concerned with the question of how to bring it all together. Their attempt is to create a unified model of practice by "examining the tasks of the social worker in action and isolating and identifying the basic elements of social work practice reflected in these tasks."

The attempt to integrate method and theory in social work is part of a general concern in our society to integrate knowledge and practice. Interest in general systems theory and ecological approaches, it appears, is pervasive in all of the professions and disciplines, as well as in the general community. The intellectual efforts to understand the ways in which "everything is related to everything else" are motored by a desire to grasp and to exercise greater control over technology and knowledge which has grown to a size and degree of complexity that is beyond people's comprehension. These efforts are reflected in Pincus and Minahan's text, *Social Work Practice: Model and Method*, in which their ideas are developed more fully.[9] Students preparing for careers in the direct services will find this conception of social work practice useful.

The usefulness of a unitary method of practice is that it enhances social workers' abilities to communicate with one another. This is not an insignificant point because, at present, caseworkers, group workers, and community organizers talk different languages, based on the varied theoretical sources of knowledge they use. There is, for example, a considerable language difference among the caseworker who may use Sigmund Freud or Erik Erikson, the group worker whose discourse is cast in concepts taken from George Homans or Robert Bales, and the community organizer whose terminology may come from Saul Alinsky, Amitai Etzioni, or Alfred Kahn. A unitary approach that is based on goals and objectives common to all social work practice might have both a clarifying and a unifying effect.

However, generalizations about a phenomenon as complex and wide ranging as social work can be hazardous. When practice is conceptualized at a high level of generalization, it is possible that practitioners may fail to perceive the important subtleties and differences among the human phenomena with which they deal. This failure can occur because it may take all of the worker's energy and intellect to deal with the larger system and its dynamics. The uniqueness of individual units (i.e., people) in larger systems may become too distracting to deal with. Furthermore, although all phenomena can be cast in systems terms, because everything that moves is a system, there is a considerable difference between person systems, group systems, organizational systems, and institutional systems. These differences cannot be thoroughly appreciated by one theory of systems.

Given these questions about systems theory, we believe that a unitary method of social work practice, while offering a useful perspective, should be viewed with caution because it may jeopardize such social work values as the belief in the integrity and uniqueness of individual persons. In addition, certain practical issues are raised by the unitary approach. Should all social workers be trained as "generalists" who are prepared to deal with all types of problems? Or, if the jack-of-all-trades social worker is not acceptable, what sorts of specializations ought to be developed? Should specialization occur at an advanced level of training, in which case the integrating functions will be carried by the less well trained, who will all be generalists? Or, should social resources be concentrated on preparing the larger corps of less well-trained professional workers to give immediate and concrete services, leaving the integrating function to more highly trained people?

Finally, while the integration of methodological approaches has many benefits, it runs counter to some of the strong trends reflected in other papers in this volume, by Haug and Sussman (Reading 18), Sjoberg et al. (Reading 21), and Martin Rein (Reading 25), each of which calls for a professional practice that is more responsive to client control than the profession has heretofore been. But a unitary practice is far more complex than anything the profession has used to date. The social worker who masters Pincus and Minahan's integration of methods must have the knowledge and skill to deal with the interrelated social problems of individuals, families, groups, and communities. His use of theory must be wide ranging, and the variety of decisions he must make staggers the imagination. All of this complexity will not, we think, produce a social worker superperson who will reach hitherto unknown heights of competence. But the purview of the practitioner and the technology he will use will be far broader and more varied than before; and, therefore, clients and the community-at-large will have *less* control in social work decision making than they have now.

We do not point up this contradiction to suggest that it is a reason for rejecting the unitary approach; we simply want to make clear that it is not possible to move in all directions at once. Social workers cannot become more technically and theoretically sophisticated and at the same time less professionally autonomous.

This issue is joined in the last two selections. In Reading 25, "Social Work in Search of a Radical Profession," Rein describes some of the features of the kind of social work practice that is responsive to current social issues and community concerns. Rein's description of types of radical and traditional social work captures the major theoretical perspectives on professions, social problems, and social change as they bear upon social work. The "traditional casework" Rein describes represents elements of the repressive, reactionary, and unattractive features of practice; much of the description is of a kind of casework that hardly exists anymore. The new and more socially oriented elements in the past 25 years of casework practice are viewed as characteristics of the "radical casework" in Rein's matrix. "Community sociotherapy" focuses on one objective of the field of activity known as community organization and social planning. That objective, Rein says, is the "transformation of individual personality." This is a somewhat narrow interpretation of the activities in this field. The examples to which Rein refers in his article—Haryou and Mobilization for Youth—cannot be described merely as "community sociotherapy," although this was one of the many objectives of those programs. A review of the current literature of community organization suggests the broader range of activities and objectives in the field.[10]

Finally, what Rein designates as "radical social policy" reflects sets of activities related to social action and social reform; these are activities that have been a concern of the profession from days of yore. As Rein indicates, this set of activities is somewhat removed from the kinds of things to which the majority of social workers providing direct services can pay attention *in their jobs as professionals:* "Individual social workers may, of course, function as reformers in the areas of employment, income distribution, and political power, but these activities are marginal to their professional tasks. In this sense, they are professionals who are radical rather than members of a radical profession." Rein's paper brings us back, full circle, to the problem of duality in the profession, which will always be present because it inheres in the relationship between social welfare and social work.

In the concluding paper, Reading 26, "The Deprofessionalization of Social Work," Specht challenges the vision of a radical profession for which so many yearn. He describes four ideological currents that, in his view, will undermine professionalism in social work: activism, anti-individualism, communalism, and environmentalism. These currents are well represented in other papers in the text. In Specht's view, the accommodation that has been made to these currents, both in practice and in social work education, erodes what is professional in social work.

The resolution of some of the strains that are currently working in the profession, Specht suggests, may lie in social work's becoming less professional, while some of the social welfare and indirect-service functions of the field become more a part of the profession. From a practical viewpoint, it is probably the case that for many years social work has put most of its educational resources at too high a level, thereby overproducing MSW's to carry out a range of tasks, many of which do not require advanced training. This is a somewhat reluctant acknowledgment that Dr. Abraham Flexner was at least half-right. The increasing numbers of BSW programs and the use of subprofessional personnel are salutary in this regard. Ultimately, these developments should force education at the master's degree level to become much more selective in the objectives of training and selection of students and curriculum content.

We would have liked to conclude this book with a clear and unequivocal statement about how society's best interests can be served by social work. We do have some preferences, which we have presented in the selections we have authored and in introductory statements to the chapters. Nonetheless, the arguments for radicalization, deprofessionalization, and decentralization are as well presented and persuasive as what can be said for professionalization, unification, and rationalization in social work. The uncertainty which is apparent in regard to every significant aspect of the profession is, we think, indicative of the fragile vitality of social work in this era.

NOTES

1. Henry Meyer, "Profession of Social Work: Contemporary Characteristics," *Encyclopedia of Social Work, II*, ed. Robert Morris (New York: National Association of Social Workers, 1971), pp. 959–72.

2. U.S. Bureau of Census, *Census of Population: 1970*, Vol. 1, *Characteristics of the Population* (Washington, D.C.: U.S. Government Printing Office, 1973), Table 222, p. 725.

Most studies of social workers have been carried out by the National Association of Social Workers (NASW) and therefore are usually focused on the membership of that association, which had approximately 50,500 members in 1969. Although NASW changed its regulations in 1970 to allow those with Bachelor of Social Work (BSW) degrees to membership, most of the knowledge available about social workers pertains to NASW members with Master of Social Work (MSW) degrees. This situation will very likely change over the next few years as the number of BSWs increases.

3. Dorothy Bird Daly, "Social Work Manpower," in *Encyclopedia of Social Work*, ed. Robert Morris (New York: National Association of Social Workers, 1971), pp. 1481–86.

4. For descriptions of the three traditional social work methods, see the following: *Social Casework*—Sister Mary Paul Janchill, R.G.S., "Systems Concepts in Casework Theory and Practice," *Social Casework*, February 1969, pp. 74–82, and Ann Hartman, "But What Is Social Casework?" *Social Casework*, July 1971, pp. 411–19. *Social Group Work*—Catherine P. Papell and Beulah Rothman, "Social Group Work Models: Possession and Heritage," *Journal of Education For Social Work*, Fall 1966, pp. 66–77. *Community Organization*—Jack Rothman, "Three Models of Community Organization Practice," *Social Work Practice, 1968* (New York: Columbia University Press, 1968), pp. 16–47.

5. Edward J. Mullen et al., *Evaluation of Social Intervention* (San Francisco: Jossey-Bass, Inc., Publishers, 1972), and Joel Fischer, "Is Casework Effective? A Review," *Social Work*, Vol. 18 (January 1973): 5–20.

6. Fischer, "Is Casework Effective?"

7. Steven Paul Segal, "Research on the Outcome of Social Work Therapeutic Intervention: A Review of the Literature," *Journal of Health and Social Behavior*, 13 (March 1972): 3–17.

8. For example, see Edwin Powers and Helen Witmer, *An Experiment in the Prevention of Delinquency—The Cambridge-Somerville Youth Study* (New York: Columbia University Press, 1971), and Gordon E. Brown, ed., *The Multi-Problem Dilemma: A Social Research Demonstration with Multi-Problem Families* (Metuchen, N.J.: The Scarecrow Press, Inc., 1968).

9. Allen Pincus and Anne Minahan, *Social Work Practice: Model and Method* (Itasca, Ill.: F. E. Peacock Publishers, Inc., 1973).

10. For example, see Rothman, "Three Models," and Robert Perlman and Arnold Gurin, *Community Organization and Social Planning* (New York: John Wiley & Sons, Inc., 1972).

22   The Current Crisis in Social Casework

SCOTT BRIAR

It is said that social casework is in deep trouble. It is said that caseworkers are destined for extinction. It is said—and this criticism cuts deepest of all—that casework is not responsive to the needs of the persons it claims to serve. These criticisms, with many variations, can be heard from persons outside the profession, from other social workers, and even, though more softly, from some of our fellow caseworkers. In fact, just a few months ago, Helen Perlman felt moved to ask whether casework is dead.[1]

As a teacher and practitioner whose professional career has been centered on social casework, I am distressed by these criticisms. Unfortunately, what distresses me most is that I find myself compelled to agree with many of these criticisms. Casework *is* in trouble. And unless casework cures its own ills, it could very well be destined to become, at worst, a relic of a past era or, at best, a marginal activity in the profession. But I am not willing to stand idly by to watch this prophecy come to pass. The initial vision that gave rise to social casework was based on an important insight into the human condition in modern society, namely, the realization that if social welfare programs are to be genuinely responsive to the needs of persons, they must be individualized. If that insight is forgotten, the profession as a whole will be the worse for it.

The recent criticisms of social casework have taken two principal forms. One questions the very existence of casework by arguing that a case-by-case approach to social problems is at best inefficient and at the worst, hopeless and perhaps even harmful. The second declares that casework simply is not effective, a criticism that is perhaps even more fundamental than the first.

The argument against the case-by-case approach to social problems has appeared partly as an accompaniment to the rising tide of interest in social change and social reform. I want to emphasize that I see no grounds for anything but enthusiasm and optimism about this trend and the promise it portends for the profession and

From National Conference on Social Welfare, *Social Work Practice, 1967* (New York: Columbia University Press, 1967), pp. 19–33. Reprinted by permission of the author and of Columbia University Press.

for social welfare. It is a welcome development, not only because social reform activities have too long been neglected, but also because there can be no doubt that many of the problems of concern to the profession will not yield to direct service alone but require intervention at other systemic levels in the social order.

In some of the burgeoning literature on the need for social reform, however, there has appeared a strand of strong and sometimes shrill criticism of social casework. Some of this criticism is well deserved, but some of it heaps on social caseworkers responsibilities they never presumed to carry, and some of it reflects a disquieting naïveté about what social change can realistically be expected to accomplish. But more important is that the growing emphasis on social change as a strategy for alleviating social problems has evoked from many caseworkers a defensiveness about their own activities. And this defensiveness threatens to block more constructive responses by caseworkers to the changes occurring in the profession.[2]

It is important at the outset to be clear about the legitimate grounds for a critique of the casework enterprise. It is fair to criticize casework—or, for that matter, group work, community organization, and social reform—for failing to accomplish what it claimed it could do; in other words, for not being effective. If caseworkers have claimed to be able to help persons with certain kinds of problems and the evidence shows that they have not done so, then caseworkers better return to the drawing board and look for other ways to accomplish their aims. It also is fair to criticize caseworkers if they lose sight of the problem, the need, the person, and the task in a preoccupation with techniques, ideologies, and theoretical concepts. In other words, if it is true, as some have argued,[3] that caseworkers, rather than devising methods tailored to the client's needs and expectations, have expected clients to adapt to the caseworker's methods, then caseworkers should pause to remind themselves that their first commitment is to the client. And, finally, it is fair to criticize casework if it cuts itself off from persons who need its services. That is, if it is true, as it appears to be, that persons who could benefit from the services of caseworkers are systematically deprived of them, then we must alter the methods of delivering and offering casework services so that they are available to such persons.

It is *not* responsible, on the other hand, to criticize social casework for failing to fulfill responsibilities it never promised to discharge—for failing, for example, to eliminate poverty, do away

with delinquency, or end illegitimacy. It is possible that some caseworkers have made such rash and immodest claims, but I do not
believe the field of social casework has seriously taken these responsibilities upon itself. Consequently, it is absurd to point to the
continued existence of social problems as a sign of the failure of
casework. Nevertheless, the misconceptions implicit in this line of
argument point to the need for a clearer statement of what it is that
caseworkers are supposed to do.

The dominant preoccupation of social casework over the past
thirty-five to forty years has been devoted to the development of
the therapeutic function of social casework, or what has come to
be called "clinical" casework. I have no quarrel with clinical casework—most of my own practice is of this sort—except that I do
not think clinical casework is nearly as effective as it ought to be.
Caseworkers can no longer afford to ignore the implications of
studies such as the recently published Girls at Vocational High.[4]
The findings of that study may seem discouraging, but they cannot
be written off as due to inadequacies in research design and technology. For what confronts us is not one study but a long list of
studies with equally distressing results. Hunt, Kogan, and their co-
workers labored long and hard at the Community Service Society in
New York City to measure the outcome of casework and found an
average movement of only one step on the movement scale, a result that, at the least, should have stimulated a searching recon-
sideration of the clinical casework approach developed in that
agency and widely promulgated in the field.[5] This is not to say that
casework is never effective, and it is important to be clear about
that. Any caseworker can cite cases from his own experience to
show that casework is effective, sometimes dramatically so. What
the research indicates is simply that our batting average is too low
—not that we never succeed but rather that we succeed too infrequently.

The research on the effectiveness of casework is only a small
part of the story. Research on the effectiveness of psychotherapy is
both more extensive and, in some respects, more rigorous than the
outcome studies of casework.[6] I know that many caseworkers are
quick to insist on the difference between clinical casework and
psychotherapy, but it is demonstrable that the theory and techniques of treatment that inform clinical casework practice were not
developed independently but carry a heavy debt to psychotherapy,
and to psychoanalytic psychotherapy in particular. Thus, studies that
question the efficacy of dynamic psychotherapy also challenge the

foundations of clinical casework. And the plain facts are that the effectiveness of the traditional psychotherapies, the so-called "dynamic" psychotherapies, is in grave doubt. Even defenders of the traditional psychotherapies who have surveyed this body of evidence can find only weak support in a few isolated studies and for the remainder can only question the validity of the research itself, a weak and no longer sufficient defense.[7]

Moreover, at least as far as casework is concerned, it is not simply that effectiveness is less than satisfactory, but other research has shown that the model of clinical casework dominant for many years is suitable for no more than a fraction of the clients who come to us. We now know that even in the presumably ideal conditions of the private family service agency, the conception of casework as a prolonged series of interviews between the caseworker and an individual who is seeking help with emotional or interpersonal problems appears to be applicable to at most 25 percent of the clients who seek help from such agencies.[8]

But the findings I have all too briefly summarized here should not be viewed as cause for despair. The response required is of quite another sort. The message of these findings is that caseworkers should embark on a period of active and vigorous innovation and experimentation, in a search for more effective models and methods for the conduct of clinical casework. Fortunately, some promising directions for experimentation have already appeared. Caseworkers in many places are experimenting, for example, with short-term methods of intervention. But experimentation with short-term approaches has not proceeded at a pace commensurate with their obvious relevance to the reality that a large proportion of the encounters between caseworkers and clients are of brief duration. If we are to give short-term methods the attention they deserve, we have to modify our tendency, as Lucille Austin notes, to regard them "chiefly as a matter of expedience."[9] Family treatment represents another area of active experimentation in social casework. Unfortunately, however, the family therapy movement also illustrates a characteristic weakness of innovative efforts in social work, namely, the failure to conduct systematic evaluations of effectiveness. Despite the enormous effort that has been devoted to family diagnosis and treatment over the past ten to fifteen years, the number of attempts to assess its effectiveness systematically can be counted on the fingers of one hand.[10] Thus, we continue to expand family treatment only on the basis of faith and the missionary zeal of the practitioners who have become committed to it. Faith, however, is not enough. The crucial questions to be asked of an intervention method are not "Does it sound good?" or "Is it fascinating?" but "Does it work?" and "Is it more effective than other methods?"

Appearing on the horizon are some even more fundamental innovations in treatment models and techniques. I have in mind a variety of new therapeutic strategies based on theories that depart radically from the psychoanalytic formulations that have dominated psychotherapy and casework for the past thirty to forty years. One illustration of these new departures is the attempt to apply sociobehavioral theory to social work practice. When one first hears it, the language and metaphors of this approach may seem strange or even disagreeable, but do not turn away if they do. Or, at first glance, it may seem that this theory simply puts new labels on old, familiar ideas, but that impression, too, would be invalid. The sociobehavioral approach has already had wide application and is based on theories that are backed by extensive research.[11] The results thus far are impressive, sometimes dramatically so, and perhaps the most promising aspect of sociobehavioral theory is that it suggests a strategy for the development of practice knowledge that is more systematic than those we have followed in the past. We cannot afford to ignore any perspective that is demonstrably successful or that appears to promise a more effective strategy for developing the body of knowledge we need in order to improve our effectiveness. Finally, I would mention the important innovations now being formulated in response to our increased understanding of the realities of casework with the poor.

My intent in these comments on clinical casework is to make two general points. The first is that current attempts to disparage the therapeutic function of social casework are invalid and misdirected. Clinical casework represents an essential function carried out in relation to important human problems. For that reason, the demand for caseworkers to perform this function should continue to increase, if—through more vigorous innovation and systematic experimentation—caseworkers can discover ways of performing this function more effectively.

My second point is that the general field of psychotherapy is in a state of exciting ferment and experimentation. Unfortunately, however, many caseworkers are effectively isolated from these developments, for it still is true that caseworkers by and large keep abreast primarily of those developments in psychotherapy that are within the psychoanalytic tradition, broadly defined. This restriction is becoming increasingly dysfunctional for clinical casework, since, as Ford and Urban recently concluded in their excellent review of developments in psychotherapy, "the innovative steam has gone out of the psychoanalytic movement. Major theoretical and technical advances in the future will probably come from other orientations."[12] In order that we can benefit from those advances in the general field of psychotherapy that may be applicable to casework practice, it is essential that we find ways of keeping informed about the many new developments in that closely related field.

I said that the disparagement of clinical casework is misplaced. The proper target of these critics, in my opinion, is the strong tendency to equate clinical casework with casework, the tendency to regard the therapeutic function as the *only* function of casework. To make this equation is to constrict the range of functions of casework and thereby to make it less flexible and less responsive to changing needs and conditions. The founders of social casework had no such narrow conception of the functions of the social caseworker. (By founders, incidentally, I have in mind persons such as Mary Richmond, Porter Lee, Edith Abbott, Shelby Harrison, and Bertha Reynolds.) The therapeutic function was part of their vision of social casework, but it was only one of several functions they thought caseworkers should perform. However, the history of social casework is in large measure a history of progressive constriction, elimination, and reduction of the functions of casework to the therapeutic or clinical function.[13] The other functions of the casework enterprise envisaged by its founders have either atrophied or have been relegated to marginal activities subsumed under the catch-all phrase, "environmental manipulation." I believe this trend ought to be reversed, not simply because the founders had a broader conception of the caseworker's mission, but because changing conditions and changing conceptions of the problems facing the profession require an expanded conception of casework.

Two functions that were explicit components of the casework enterprise in its early history have since atrophied. I select these two functions only as examples: they are not the only functions that have been neglected.

One is a function that currently is being revived under the rubric of "social broker."[14] The justification for this function resides in the fact that there are many persons who need services but do not know that these services are available; many others know that the services are available but do not know where to obtain them; others who know where to obtain services do not know how to get them or else face obstacles in seeking and obtaining them; and still others do not know how to gain the maximum benefits available to them. This function is vastly more important today than it was when Mary Richmond and her colleagues were preoccupied with it, because the maze of social welfare programs is far more complex and the social agencies are larger and more bureaucratic than they were in her day. Fortunately, however, we have an advantage not available to Mary Richmond, namely, a substantial body of knowledge concerning the dynamics of the welfare system and its constituent agencies. This body of knowledge could be applied—though by and large it has not been—to the performance of the social broker function, much as we have applied social and psychological knowledge in our performance of the therapeutic function.

The problem of getting what one wants and needs from the public welfare agency, the health department, the vocational rehabilitation agency, the psychiatric hospital, the public school—and on and on through the array of organizations with which persons must negotiate to get what they need—is no simple matter, as everyone knows from his own encounters with large, complex organizations. Increasingly, if a person is to gain from these agencies the benefits to which he is entitled, he requires an informed and skilled guide who knows the social welfare maze, knows the bureaucracy, and knows how to move it to get what the client needs and deserves. In our personal lives, we may be able to negotiate effectively with the organizations that directly affect us because we know how, the businessman is able to hire specialists to deal with the organizations on which he depends for services and benefits, but many of the persons we seek to serve lack the knowledge, skills, or resources to negotiate effectively with the organizations on which the satisfaction of their needs may depend.

Currently, the broker function is being revived, but only to a limited extent. As an outgrowth of the war on poverty, new careerists are being trained to perform this function. But evidence already is accumulating to indicate that subprofessionals can perform this function effectively only with professional guidance and direction and that in some instances they cannot perform it very effectively at all, partly because some of the problems encountered require the application of considerable skill and knowledge.[15] Recognition of the importance of this function also is evident in the growing interest in the creation of neighborhood information and referral centers. Thus far, however, discussion of such centers has been focused more on organizational considerations than on the roles to be performed and the knowledge and skills required for their effective performance.

Another function that was highly visible early in the history of social casework subsequently not only declined in significance but came to be regarded by some as inconsistent with the proper conduct of casework practice. Some of the early leaders in casework saw one function of the caseworker as that of a person who actively fought on the side of his client to help him meet his needs, realize his hopes and aspirations, and exercise his rights. The caseworker was to be his client's supporter, his adviser, his champion, and, if need be, his representative in his dealings with the court, the police, the social agency, and the other organizations that affected his well-being. In other words, the caseworker was to serve not only as a therapist or as a social broker, but also as an active advocate of the client's cause in relation to the various social organizations.[16] Currently, we are being told by lawyers, who at last are becoming interested in social welfare problems in sufficient numbers to make a difference, that performance of the advocacy function by social workers is essential both for the client to get what he is entitled to receive and for the social welfare system to operate as it is supposed to, especially as it becomes more institutionalized. For instance, fair and equitable procedures in an organization will remain such only if its clients are able to insist that the procedures be honored and to call the organization to task when it becomes lax. But many of the persons whom caseworkers seek to serve, especially among the poor, will not exercise their rights, press their claims and needs, or appeal actions that adversely affect them unless someone performs the role of advocate, because many of these clients are too apathetic, feel too powerless, or are too uninformed to do so. Moreover, effective performance of the advocacy function would help to insure that agencies are attentive and responsive to the needs and desires of clients.

One example will illustrate the importance of the advocacy function. The California State Department of Social Welfare provides a fair hearing procedure to be used by a welfare recipient when he believes that the welfare agency has erred or has taken improper action in his case. There are over one million welfare recipients in California. During a one-year period, from 1965 to 1966, only 1,098 recipients, or less than one tenth of one percent of all recipients, used the fair hearing procedure. There is no doubt that the proportion of recipients who have legitimate grounds for requesting a hearing is substantially greater than one tenth of one percent. For one thing, this proportion is substantially below the rate of error in the agency's favor typically found in sample case record audits. What prevents more recipients from using this procedure? Based on some research I am currently completing, I would say one reason is that only a tiny fraction of recipients know about the fair hearing or how to apply for it, in spite of the fact that they are routinely given information about this procedure.[17]

A substantial proportion of recipients who obtain fair hearings win their appeals. And the recipient's chances of winning are doubled if he brings along someone to represent him. The recipient can select anyone he wants as his representative; rarely does he bring a lawyer, but the hearings are informal and a lawyer's skills and knowledge ordinarily are not necessary to represent the client. The client's caseworker frequently is required to be present, but he is expected to represent both the client and the agency, which prevents him from serving as his client's advocate. Bear in mind that the stakes for the client may be quite high, namely, the means to feed, house, and clothe his family. I suggest that the caseworker ought to be free to represent his *client's* cause in such situations. And the agency should want to have this function performed in order to discharge its commitment to the welfare of its clients.

Finally, it should be emphasized that performance of the advocacy function to the point where the client has the experience of making his wishes felt and having them acted on can enhance, sometimes dramatically, his sense of confidence, competence, and mastery and reduce the feelings of apathy and impotence many of our clients experience in their dealings with the organizations that affect their lives.

It also is important to see both the social broker and the advocate functions in a somewhat broader context. In my view, these functions must become institutionalized if the social welfare system is to operate as it should, no matter how well planned or enlightened it is otherwise. It would be a naïve and tragic mistake to view these as residual functions that need to be performed only because the social welfare system has not yet been perfected. On the contrary, the social welfare system cannot be perfected unless these functions are performed effectively. To argue otherwise is analogous to arguing that the fact that plaintiffs and defendants still need attorneys when they go to court is symptomatic of imperfections in the court system, that if the court system were perfected, lawyers would be unnecessary. The opposite is, of course, the case. That is, the court system as a system cannot operate properly unless the functions assumed by lawyers are performed.

I have discussed three functions that originally were conceived to be integral components of the caseworker's mission: the therapeutic function, the social broker function, and the advocacy function. Subsequently, casework became preoccupied with the therapeutic function at the expense of the others. The therapeutic function flourished and underwent sophisticated theoretical development to the point where it seemed to some that this was the *only* function of casework. Recently, research has raised grave questions about the effectiveness with which caseworkers perform their therapeutic function. I have argued that our response to these questions should be vigorous innovation and systematic experimentation. I have also argued that we need to expand our conception of the casework mission to include other functions, not simply because they are part of our historic heritage but because the needs of our clients and the conditions of their lives require that we assume these responsibilities. Moreover, we should devote to these other functions the same measure of thought and skill we have long devoted to the therapeutic function, for the tasks these other functions impose on us are no less difficult or demanding than those we encounter in our therapeutic work.

I do not mean to imply that these three functions are the only ones I have in mind in calling for an expanded conception of social casework. I discussed the social broker and advocate functions as crucial examples to make the case for an expanded conception of casework. But there are other functions that caseworkers need to perform. For example, there is the vital and indispensable role that social caseworkers should be playing, as practitioners, in social policy-making. Caseworkers have virtually unique access to information indispensable to the development of sound social welfare policies and programs.

Moreover—and I cannot emphasize this point too strongly—I have in mind no fixed list of casework functions, because the central point is that these functions arise in response to the needs of the persons we seek to serve, the conditions of their lives, and our understanding of these needs and conditions. Consequently, as these needs and conditions and our knowledge of them change, our responses to them should be modified accordingly. It also follows from that, of course, that not all these functions are needed by every individual or family nor will any one caseworker necessarily perform all of them.

An expanded conception of social casework has many implications that deserve more detailed discussion than is possible here. However, two general implications are of crucial importance. First, vigorous innovation and experimentation in treatment methods and participation in the activities required in performing the advocate and social broker functions require that caseworkers have much greater professional autonomy and discretion than now prevail in many, if not most, social agencies. Ninety percent or more of all caseworkers practice in bureaucratic organizations, and the demands of such organizations have a tendency to encroach upon professional autonomy. Every attempt by the agency to routinize some condition or aspect of professional practice amounts to a restriction of professional discretion, and for that reason probably should be resisted, in most instances, by practitioners. But it will not be enough to resist bureaucratic restriction. We will need to roll back the restrictions that already constrain practice in order to gain the freedom essential to experiment, to discover new and better ways of helping the clients to whom we are primarily responsible. There are, of course, realistic limits to the amount of autonomy and discretion an organization can grant to the practitioner, but no one knows just where that limit is, and we cannot know until we have tried to reach it. It may be that when this limit is reached we will find it still too confining to engage in the kind of practice required to help some of our clients.

The second general implication is that the remedies I have proposed require a much closer relationship between practice and research than we have achieved thus far, because research is an indispensable tool in our efforts to improve the efficacy of casework. The relationships between the practitioner and the researcher continue to be problematic. There are good reasons to believe that in the long run the best solution to these problems may be to develop both sets of skills in the same person.

A brief quotation from Alfred Kahn concisely expresses a basic assumption underlying everything I have said:

> Crucial to social work is an integrative view of needs . . .
> The real commitment, and the unique nature of the entire social work institution . . . is not to any one method or even one concept but rather to human need. The role is dynamic—and never completed. The danger is the loss of that flexibility essential to the recognition of new horizons and the undertaking of consequent responsibilities.[18]

If we take seriously the view that the central commitment is to human need and if we keep our attention focused squarely on the needs of persons and the responsibilities these needs impose on the profession at all levels of systemic intervention, I believe the result must be an expanded and dynamic conception of the scope and multiple functions of the endeavor we call social casework.

NOTES

1. Helen Harris Perlman, "Casework Is Dead," *Social Casework,* XLVIII (1967), 22–25.
2. Berthe Gronfein, "Should Casework Be on the Defensive?" *Social Casework,* XLVII (1966), 650–56.
3. Richard A. Cloward and Irwin Epstein, "Private Social Welfare's Disengagement from the Poor: The Case of Family Adjustment Agencies," in Mayer N. Zald, ed., *Social Welfare Institutions* (New York: Wiley, 1965), pp. 623–44.
4. Henry J. Meyer, Edgar F. Borgatta, and Wyatt C. Jones, *Girls at Vocational High: An Experiment in Social Work Intervention* (New York: Russell Sage Foundation, 1965).
5. For a review of this research, see Scott Briar, "Family Services," in Henry S. Maas, ed., *Five Fields of Social Service* (New York: National Association of Social Workers, 1966), pp. 16–21.
6. The literature on research on psychotherapy is too vast to be summarized here. A recent review of major studies of traditional psychotherapy is available in Hans J. Eysenck, *The Effects of Psychotherapy* (New York: International Science Press, 1966). An excellent source for current developments in research on psychotherapy is the chapters on psychotherapy in the *Annual Review of Psychology* published each year by Annual Reviews, Inc., Palo Alto, Calif.
7. See, for example, Robert Wallerstein, "The Current State of Psychotherapy: Theory, Practice, Research," *Journal of the American Psychoanalytic Association,* XIV (1966), 183–225.
8. Briar, *op. cit.*
9. Howard J. Parad, ed., *Crisis Intervention: Selected Readings* (New York: Family Service Association of America, 1965), p. xi.
10. One of the better exceptions is Robert MacGregor, *et al., Multiple Impact Therapy with Families* (New York: McGraw-Hill, 1964).
11. See, for example, Leonard Krasner and Leonard P. Ullmann, eds., *Research in Behavior Modification* (New York: Holt, Rinehart and Winston, 1965); and Leonard P. Ullmann and Leonard Krasner,

eds., *Case Studies in Behavior Modification* (New York: Holt, Rinehart and Winston, 1965).

12. Donald H. Ford and Hugh B. Urban, "Psychotherapy," in *Annual Review of Psychology: Volume 18, 1967* (Palo Alto, Calif.: Annual Reviews, Inc., 1967), p. 333.

13. Bertha Reynold's autobiographical book, *An Uncharted Journey: Fifty Years of Growth in Social Work* (New York: Citadel Press, 1963), is in part a chronicle of one person's efforts to maintain a broader conception of the casework mission in the face of her colleagues' more successful attempts to constrict it.

14. For other discussions of this concept, see Charles F. Grosser, "Community Development Programs Serving the Urban Poor," *Social Work*, X, No. 3 (1965), 15–21; and Paul Terrell, "The Social Worker as Radical: Roles of Advocacy," *New Perspectives: the Berkeley Journal of Social Welfare*, I, No. 1 (1957), 83–88.

15. Sherman Barr, "The Indigenous Worker: What He Is Not, What He Can Be," Fourteenth Annual Program Meeting, Council on Social Work Education, 1966.

16. For other discussion of the advocacy role, see Grosser, *op. cit.*; Terrell, *op. cit.*; Earl C. Brennan, "The Casework Relationship: Excerpts from a Heretic's Notebook," *New Perspectives: the Berkeley Journal of Social Welfare*, I, No. 1 (1957), 65–67; and Scott Briar, "The Social Worker's Responsibility for the Civil Rights of Clients," *ibid.*, pp. 89–92.

17. Scott Briar, "Welfare from Below: Recipients' Views of the Public Welfare System," *California Law Review*, LIV (1966), 370–85.

18. Alfred J. Kahn, "The Function of Social Work in the Modern World," in Alfred J. Kahn, ed., *Issues in American Social Work* (New York: Columbia University Press, 1959), p. 16.

23   Changes in Social Work Education and Their Implications for Practice

ARNULF M. PINS

It is currently fashionable to bemoan the shortcomings of social work education, but teachers, students, practitioners, and consum-

Reprinted with permission of the National Association of Social Workers and of the author from *Social Work*, 16, 2 (April 1971): 5–15.

ers all agree that it will change—and should. There are—and there should be—differences of opinion about the nature, direction, and timing of this change. There is—but there should not be—lack of knowledge and misinformation, especially on the part of practitioners, about the changes that are occurring or have already taken place.

A graduate of a school of social work or an undergraduate program in social welfare ten years ago or before might not today recognize the educational program of his own school, or any other for that matter. More changes have taken place in social work education in the recent past than in any other similar time period. For example, a description of social work education prepared only five years ago is already outdated.[1] Major modifications and innovations have been occurring at a constantly accelerating pace—changes that have important implications for social work practice and ought to be the concern of all social workers.

This paper presents a brief overview of recent developments, identifies major changes in both graduate and undergraduate social work education, and indicates some of the implications of these changes and developments for practice and practitioners.

AN OVERVIEW

First of all, it is important to note some relatively new assumptions and some outdated conceptions. At this point in time—April 1971—social work education is *not* synonymous with the master's degree programs in graduate schools of social work, graduate social work education is *not* primarily directed to preparation for casework, and treatment no longer is the exclusive or even major emphasis. At both the graduate and undergraduate levels social work education not only prepares students for social work practice as it exists now, but has been placing greater emphasis than before on helping students learn to analyze this practice critically and to be responsible and effective agents of change.

There is general consensus that not every job in social welfare requires a professional social worker with a master's degree from a graduate school of social work; others can do certain tasks as well and maybe better. So even if there were no shortage of master's-degree social workers, personnel with different or lesser social work educational preparation would and should be used to deliver social services. A decade ago, even five years ago, many social workers thought that some day, even if in the distant future, an adequate supply of MSWs would fill every social service job. This view is gone today not only because of necessity but also because the way of thinking about utilization of personnel and the job to be done has changed. Thus employing personnel for social welfare who do not have a master's degree is no longer a temporary expediency.

Today social work education operates on several levels:

1. The doctoral degree, offered in graduate schools of social work to prepare students for leadership roles in policy development, administration, planning, advanced practice, research, and teaching.

2. The master's degree, offered in graduate schools of social work to prepare students for professional practice, administration, and policy and planning functions.

3. The baccalaureate degree (generally called "undergraduate programs in social welfare"), offered by four-year colleges and universities to prepare students for beginning practice in certain areas.

4. The associate degree, offered in two-year community colleges to prepare students for community and social service technician roles.

5. Continuing education, offered by schools of social work, university extension services, the professional association, and agencies to update social workers' knowledge and skill and/or to prepare them for new and more advanced responsibilities. (Continuing education tends to be more generic than in-service training, which prepares staff for a particular task or a variety of tasks related to a specific setting.)

The changes in social work education and the development of programs at different levels have been rapid and often piecemeal. As yet no generally accepted relationship has developed between the different levels. Various efforts are under way to consider effective linkages between associate and baccalaureate degree programs and between baccalaureate and master's degree programs. These efforts at developing a "continuum" seek to minimize overlap and to provide various exit points from education to employment.

UNDERGRADUATE EDUCATION

Undergraduate social work education is currently offered at both the baccalaureate and associate degree level. Baccalaureate programs have had a long history of conflict and confusion, starts and stops, feelings and problems.[2] In the last few years, however, there has been growing clarity about and acceptance of these programs. The guide for undergraduate education, issued by the Council on Social Work Education (CSWE) in 1967, already under review for revisions, identifies four objectives for undergraduate social work education.[3] The first is *the enrichment of liberal education*. The view that today nobody in our society can be considered liberally educated without an understanding of social welfare is similar to the realization a decade or two ago that one could not have a liberal education without some knowledge of political science, economics, sociology, and psychology. A second objective is *preparation for graduate social work education*. Although graduate schools of social work have not limited admission or even given preference to students with undergraduate social work education, they have, more and more, modified their programs or requirements for them. The third purpose is *preparation for practice and employment in social welfare*. This purpose was first stated officially in 1967—in contrast to the earlier guide (in 1962) which reflected the view that undergraduate programs were preprofessional. The fourth purpose of undergraduate programs is to *contribute to preparation for other human service professions and occupations* (either for employment or for graduate education).

In the four years since the revision of the CSWE guide, the third objective—preparation for practice in social welfare—has assumed greater importance. A growing number of undergraduate programs give major or exclusive priority to the preparation of students for certain areas or levels of practice. This trend has been reinforced by employment policies of public and voluntary agencies and more recently by the action of the professional association—the National Association of Social Workers—to admit as full members individuals who hold baccalaureate degrees from undergraduate programs in social welfare that are approved by CSWE.

The CSWE guide recommends that undergraduate programs in social welfare consist of a liberal arts base with emphasis on the social sciences plus some social welfare courses and field experience. The social welfare content generally includes (1) the study of social welfare as a social institution, which builds a bridge from the social sciences and social problems to application of this knowledge to social welfare, (2) the area of social work as a profession, which includes emphasis on the role of the social worker and the teaching of skills for beginning practice, and (3) field experience in direct service roles under educational direction to enhance both cognitive understanding and practice skills.[4]

There are about 750 undergraduate programs in social welfare in the United States, ranging from one course to a full sequence. Of these, over 200 programs meet requirements for CSWE constituent membership, which call for a sequence of courses, field experiences, full-time faculty, and identification of programs in college catalogs. These requirements were established in 1967, and all existing member programs were required to meet them by 1970. Thus CSWE's new list of undergraduate programs no longer includes those programs that, for example, offer only single courses or provide no field experience.[5] Such programs still have value for liberal arts education, but they are not considered adequate for any kind of preparation for practice.

CSWE is recognized by the U.S. Office of Education and the National Commission on Accrediting as the official accrediting body for social work education. In keeping with this responsibility, the CSWE Board of Directors voted in the spring of 1970 to initiate standard-setting for undergraduate programs in social welfare in addition to carrying forward its ongoing program of accreditation of graduate social work education. It approved new requirements and procedures, which become effective on July 1, 1971.[6] According to the new criteria, colleges and universities are asked to identify and describe their undergraduate program in social welfare in their catalogs, to provide a broad liberal base for the social welfare program with content in the areas specified in the CSWE guide, to require educationally directed field experience with direct engagement in service activities for students preparing for practice, and to indicate on the transcript or diploma or otherwise certify that a student has completed a program in social welfare.

The 1971 criteria require for the first time that one of the objectives of the program be preparation for practice, administration of the undergraduate program be assigned to a full-time faculty member, the full-time faculty of the undergraduate program include a social worker with a graduate degree from an accredited school of social work, and a social worker with a graduate degree from a school of social work teach the content on social work practice.

The forthcoming list of CSWE–approved undergraduate programs in social welfare, to be issued in the summer of 1971, will make it possible for agencies employing baccalaureate-degree social work staff to identify workers who are graduates of an approved undergraduate social welfare program that prepared them for practice and to give them appropriate preferential work assignments and salaries. Also graduate schools of social work will find it easier to consider advanced placement or other special treatment for students who enter graduate education after completing an approved undergraduate program in social welfare.

Another relatively recent development in undergraduate social work education is the training of community and social service technicians in two-year community colleges, sometimes called junior colleges. Community colleges today are the fastest-growing level of higher education. In the past 1½ years CSWE has conducted a study of community college social service programs and has developed and issued a guide for community colleges planning to prepare community and social service technicians.[7] The guide urges that community colleges planning to start such a social service program work with the agencies in their geographic area in order to enhance the early and effective utilization of their graduates.

The goals for community college programs in the social services area, as identified in the CSWE guide, are to provide sound general education, to prepare for employment in the human services and in social welfare, and to provide a base either for further general education or for social work education. Efforts are being made to make these programs generic and liberal even though they are and should also be vocational. The liberal arts base, even of the technical education component, should be protected so that it may provide the broad knowledge social work personnel need and allow for transferability of credits or courses taken. Students who enter a community college generally are not sure at the outset whether they will be ready or have the financial resources to go on to a third and fourth year of college education. Therefore it is important that those who decide to study for a baccalaureate degree or higher should not have to start over again; this was often necessary for students in the earlier vocational programs in junior colleges.

In a certain sense community colleges are inverting the educational pyramid. Formerly the idea was that a student starts his college education with a broad liberal base, then concentrates on one of the basic disciplines, and only at the end of the four-year education does he take any specialized or how-to-do-it courses. By inverting the pyramid, which is just as sound educationally, a student starts with specific practice skills, then "builds in" the needed social science and social welfare knowledge, and at the end takes basic general liberal arts courses. CSWE's guide for community colleges suggests a curriculum in which at least half the courses should be general education (English, sociology, history, political science, and the like) and no more than about a quarter of the courses should be designed to give the students beginning practice skills with people and institutions (e.g., interviewing). CSWE also recommends field experience for students preparing to become social service technicians. Social agencies will in time get requests, depending on the need in their location, to provide field learning for community college students in addition to field placements for baccalaureate and master's degree social work students.

GRADUATE EDUCATION

Changes in graduate social work education have been both quantitative and qualitative. The number of graduate schools of social work, the size of their enrollments, and the number of graduates have increased dramatically.[8] As of July 1, 1970, there were seventy accredited schools of social work in the United States; this includes nine new schools opened in the past five years. In addition, ten other graduate schools have opened and are working toward accreditation. Several more new schools have just appointed deans and are planning to open in the near future, with another fifteen projected schools at various stages of progress, actively committed to the development of a graduate social work education program.

Enrollments have likewise grown. Graduate schools of social work have exceeded the 13,000 mark in full-time master's degree enrollment and are nearing 6,000 in the number of graduates each year, about double that of five years ago. The doctoral programs have also increased; 23 graduate schools of social work—almost one-third—have doctoral programs and several others are planning such programs. The graduates of these programs have grown in number in the last ten years from only 30 doctoral degrees to about 90 granted each year.

There have been several major qualitative changes in graduate social work education including shifts in objectives, curriculum content and organization, and the nature and methods of instruction. The new CSWE "Curriculum Policy Statement" gives increased freedom and responsibility to schools of social work in identifying their mission and in determining their curriculum organization.[9] The earlier 1962 and 1952 statements listed sequences and specified method concentrations; the new curriculum statement allows and encourages schools to develop and define their own approach to teaching practice for different social work roles.[10] As a result, the traditional triad of casework, group work, and community organization is no longer the key organizing factor in teaching practice (formerly called the methods courses). Schools are developing other ways of teaching social work practice, based on various types of service and different kinds of settings.[11] Until recently, schools of social work tended to offer programs that were alike—if not identical. Today there is great diversity.

In the past few years graduate schools of social work have sought increasingly to prepare students to be more knowledgeable and competent in policy, planning, and service delivery roles dealing with rural and inner-city problems, ethnic minority group concerns, and problems of institutional racism. This is observable in the changing nature and content of class and field instruction, faculty and student research, and extension programs and special projects.[12] The needs of the poor continue to be reflected in the curriculum, and increased emphasis is being given to concern about employment/unemployment. Schools of social work have also enriched their class and field teaching with more content about drug addiction, alcoholism, crime and delinquency, family planning and with increased attention to the needs of the handicapped, the young, and the aging. In general the teaching approach to these and other major social problems and deprived population groups emphasizes systems-change, not only amelioration. These changes in curriculum content and the new patterns of teaching social work practice are also reflected in the students' choices of concentration. In the past four years, the proportion of students in graduate schools of social work who concentrated their studies in casework decreased from 85 percent to 36 percent. Students' choice of group work remained steady at about 10 percent. The percentage of students in community organization increased from about 1 percent to almost 10 percent.

This changing pattern of teaching social work practice and students' preferences is also evident in the number of students in programs that taught social work practice in a generic or combined way, which moved from 4 percent to 37 percent in the same three-year period.[13] It should be noted that some of the programs now called "combined" or "generic" are often still basically casework, group work, or community organization programs with some reorganization and different labels. However, if the new designations do not fully describe the content, they do reflect the intent and direction of curriculum development. In general, graduate schools of social work are giving increased emphasis to prevention and institutional change in addition to treatment, which received primary attention in an earlier period.

Of special interest to practitioners will be the change in field instruction, which for the past 15 years has increasingly become an integrated part of the total educational program of schools of social work.[14] This has enhanced the unity and effectiveness of the students' education, but it has also brought more headaches to the agencies. As a result of the greater integration of class and field teaching, not only practice skills are learned and taught in the field, but a variety of other subjects. More than that, the traditional division between class and field is beginning to disappear. What we used to believe could only be taught in the field is being taught in the classroom, or in laboratories, or with new technology, and what we thought obviously belonged in the classroom is taught in many places in the field. Many different patterns of field instruction have been developed that move away from dependence on the one-to-one instructor-student relationship to the use, in addition, of group teaching and a variety of other people within the agency. New settings are being utilized for field instruction, including some that are not social agencies—neighborhood membership organizations, mayors' and governors' offices, unions, and so on. In addition to agency-based field instruction, students are also placed in campus-based field instruction units or school-directed training centers. In some places, students have—in addition to or in place of year-long field placements—a variety of brief short-term or satellite experiences in various settings. In such cases, the field instructor often accompanies the students to the different placements.

New and changing needs in our society and the shifting focus and image of social work education have brought to graduate schools of social work a new type of student who is more interested in social change and has a different conception of the student role in professional education. These students tend to be more critical of their education than their forebears and to express their views and make recommendations (or demands) for change more readily. Students are currently serving on various committees of schools of social work and are actively participating in reviews and revisions of curricula.

Not only have the objectives, curriculum content, and methods of instruction of schools of social work changed in recent years, but also the length of graduate social work education is being questioned once more.[15] Current accreditation standards require that a student must have a baccalaureate degree for admission to a graduate school of social work and that the graduate program be for two academic years with no diminution of credit for special groups. At the present time, three schools have the approval of the CSWE Commission on Accreditation to experiment with combining graduate and undergraduate education in a 3-year/2-year pattern or a 4-year/1-year pattern. Since many other schools want to introduce changes in the length of the master's degree program, a special committee on the length of graduate social work education, established by the CSWE board, is studying the issues and considering alternatives. Final action is expected by April 1971.[16]

In view of changing social needs and social service delivery patterns, the knowledge and competence of social workers in practice also require updating and enrichment. Schools of social work in recent years have increased and expanded their efforts in this regard. A recent CSWE study on the role of the school of social work in continuing education found that two-thirds of the schools have such programs and that half of the schools either have or are looking for full-time directors of continuing education.[17] The survey revealed that over 15,000 people in 500 different offerings were involved during the 1969–70 year in continuing education provided by schools of social work. One needs to add to this total the number of individuals who obtain continuing education from local and regional institutes sponsored by NASW, from city-wide workshops and courses sponsored by a variety of agencies, and those who are part of continuing education programs not related to social work and offered in various units of the university or in other places. Continuing education, more than any other level of education, seems to respond more rapidly to new needs and local priorities.

MINORITY GROUPS' CONCERNS

The past few years have witnessed increasing attention and priority by graduate schools of social work and undergraduate programs in social welfare to the concerns and needs of the major disadvantaged ethnic minority groups, especially Asian-Americans, American Indians, blacks, Mexican-Americans (Chicanos), and Puerto Ricans.[18] The number of students from these groups in graduate schools of social work has increased substantially. The number of nonwhite first-year students in master's degree programs for 1970– 71 is over 1,600, representing almost one-fourth of the total first- year student enrollment. This total is substantially higher than the number of nonwhite first-year students enrolled last year. Slightly over 14 percent of all first-year students in 1970–71 are black. The percentage of first-year students who are Chicano or Puerto Rican is only 4.3 percent; first-year students who are Asian-American total only 1.5 percent and only 0.6 percent are American Indians. While this is much too small, the number of first-year Chicano students enrolled in the past two years was 2½ times larger than the total who entered in 1968.[19]

There was also major growth in the number of doctoral students from minority groups.[20] No comprehensive data are available on minority group students in undergraduate programs in social wel- fare. In addition to recruiting more minority group students, a major national effort is also under way to recruit and develop more minor- ity group faculty and to enrich the curriculum with content about ethnic minority groups. In November 1970, 17.4 percent of full-time faculty members in accredited schools of social work were non- white. There were 259 black, 32 Puerto Rican, 17 Chicano, 43 Asian- American, and 2 American Indian teachers. Although no comparable data is available for earlier years, inquiries received by the CSWE office suggest that the appointment of nonwhite teachers on all faculty levels has increased markedly in the past year or two. In- creasing attention has been given in social work curricula to the causes and consequences of discrimination and racism and the role and responsibility of social workers to deal with these problems. All social workers need to know more about the strengths, life-styles, problems, and priorities of ethnic minority groups to be effective in working with minority group concerns at both the policy and prac- tice levels.

In 1968 CSWE established a new accreditation standard requiring schools to give evidence of special efforts to assure cultural diversity in their student body, faculty, and staff. This new standard supple- ments an existing standard, approved early in the1950s, prohibiting discrimination in student and faculty selection. CSWE has also launched several special projects to help schools attract more minor- ity group students, to recruit and develop more minority group faculty, and to enrich the curriculum with content about minority groups.[21]

OTHER MAJOR CHANGES

Another development affecting both graduate and undergraduate social work education is the increased application of learning theory and the use of new teaching methods and media. There is more individualized and independent learning in social work education today than ever before. Equipment devised through educational technology (e.g., video tapes, overhead projectors) is used more frequently and effectively. There is growing use (or are we returning to a past practice?) of people from the community (especially practitioners, administrators, consumers of service, laymen, government officials) for one, two, or more sessions to teach specific content to students. The use of new media and new people in teaching is due to the fact that we know more about learning, that educators want to bring students into closer contact with "real life" problems, and that students are seeking (demanding!) more "relevant" and immediate experiences.

A variety of new patterns is developing to link graduate and undergraduate social work education and to relate the schools of social work more closely to other units of the university. Graduate schools of social work are more frequently relating to undergraduate programs in social welfare in the same college, university system, state, or geographic area. Similar arrangements are being developed by some graduate schools of social work with community colleges in their proximity. Graduate schools of social work are exchanging faculty and course offerings for students in other professional schools and academic programs on the same campus. One can begin to see schools of social work establishing these and other relationships with schools of education, law schools, medical schools, schools of public health, departments of urban affairs, ethnic studies, and so forth. Some schools are moving into relationships with other countries for regular fieldwork, summer experience for graduate students, or "two semesters abroad" for undergraduate students.

Social work education may be facing a major fiscal crisis. There is already some and probably will be further cutback in federal aid to social work education, both to schools and to students. The cutback is in addition to an already narrower use of federal aid for social work education for specific categorical purposes. This reduction of federal support for social work education is occurring at a time when universities generally are losing state and federal aid in other areas (e.g., science and medicine) so that schools of social work find it more difficult to turn to the universities for "hard money." The worsening economic situation has made fund-raising and other activities to replace public funds with voluntary support most difficult. Unfortunately the fiscal problems for social work education come at a moment when there is great need to expand and change, when commitments for change at all levels of social work education have been made and need to be carried out—to revise curriculum, to seek and admit more students from various population groups, and to prepare graduates for varying social work roles. Public and voluntary agencies can expect social work education to turn to them for help in field instruction and student aid more often than they have in many years.

Changes in higher education throughout the country generally are also affecting social work education and the training of social work manpower. For example, the current ferment in higher education is affecting the focus and content of social work education and the nature and effectiveness of teaching patterns and methods. It is also changing and increasing the role of students in graduate schools of social work in matters affecting their education.

Another recent development is the way the university has come to the school of social work (and the school of education if there is one on the same campus) as the key unit to relate to the practical and urgent concerns and problems of the community. When a university that once ignored or was unrelated to the community in which it is located decides that it ought to concern itself with the needs of its surrounding population, it is not unusual for a president of the university to call in the dean of the school of social work and the deans of a few other professional schools and to ask them to use their know-how to help the total university relate to the community. This trend inevitably affects the class and field teaching of the school of social work and the use of local social agencies.

IMPLICATIONS FOR PRACTICE

Social work education is changing greatly and rapidly. It is changing at a time when practice is also changing, when NASW is changing, when CSWE is changing, and when unfortunately the government's support of social work and social work education is also changing. This requires that agencies be well informed about what is happening in education and that schools be knowledgeable about new trends and changing priorities in practice. Major new developments and changes in social work education and practice will inevitably lead to new strains and problems between them, but can also provide new opportunities and accomplishments. Agencies and educational institutions need to review, revise, broaden, and improve their relationships and contacts. Agency executives and social work practitioners need to update and continue to obtain more knowledge about current programs of social work education and to be clearer and more specific about their staffing needs. There is urgent need also to make differential work assignments to current graduates from the various levels of social work education.

The traditional relationship between graduate schools of social work and local agencies that employ graduates and/or are used for field instruction has been changing for some time.[22] Field instruction has become more school directed. In a period when educators and students need more knowledge about the rapid changes in practice and agencies and workers require more information about major new developments in social work education, the contact and communication between education and practice seem to have become less regular and meaningful. Agencies and their staff should, if necessary, reach out to social work education to make the needed input to help education stay relevant to practice needs and priorities. Teaching materials reflecting new and changing practice are especially needed. It will be increasingly important and necessary for practice to relate not only to graduate schools but also to colleges and universities with undergraduate programs and community colleges with programs to prepare community and social service technicians. Practice and education will need to explore together new clarifications and methods to provide students from the associate, baccalaureate, master's, and post-master's degree level with different and effective field instruction. Educators and agency executives will need to consider more and new ways to finance social work education and especially student aid, field instruction, and continuing education.

In view of the development of undergraduate social work education and the changes in graduate social work education, agencies need to seek more information and understanding about the knowledge and skill brought by graduates from different levels of social work education and to develop new and more appropriate staff utilization patterns. Students completing undergraduate social welfare programs in the future will have better preparation for beginning practice in certain areas than previously. MSW graduates will bring broader and deeper knowledge of environmental factors than before and will possess greater skill for, interest in, and commitment to policy formulation and institutional change.

Agencies frequently complain that social work education does not prepare students for practice. Educators complain that agencies have not been specific or consistent about the nature and degree of knowledge and skill they require of staff. Since graduate schools of social work may be expected to be less similar in their objectives, curriculum content, and patterns of instruction in the future, their graduates will possess competence and interests in different areas. Consequently agencies will need to be clearer than before about the kind of MSW social worker they will need and to interview and select graduates for their staff accordingly. In view of the varying needs of different public and voluntary agencies and their desire for many different types of staff, it will be difficult for any one educational program to develop a narrowly specialized curriculum for a specific setting. Most undergraduate programs have or are developing a generic curriculum; while the curricula of graduate schools are more specialized than in the recent past (with emphasis on social problems and/or practice areas), they generally still do not and will not prepare students for practice in any one specific agency setting. In view of both these factors, agencies need to give more attention to orientation and in-service training programs for new staff. Since knowledge in the social sciences is growing, program priorities and service delivery are changing, and recent graduates' knowledge base is broader and more up to date, agency staff development and other forms of continuing education for all staff are critical.

THE FUTURE

The new developments and trends in social work education described in this article are the result of many factors. They reflect our nation's growing concern about the major social problems of poverty, discrimination, and racism. The changes in education are also attempts to incorporate major revisions and stimulate further changes in the delivery systems of social services and the roles played by social workers. These require both more and better qualified social work staff with advanced education for clinical practice, planning, administration, and policy roles and others with baccalaureate degrees or less for many direct service roles. Recent developments in social work education have also been influenced by an increasingly diverse group of students, many of whom bring special life experiences and whose career motivations include changing dysfunctional systems in addition to ameliorating individual and group problems.

Further changes in social work education are certain in the next few years. The preparation of social service technicians in two-year community colleges will probably continue to grow and there will be more specification of curriculum and clarification about agency utilization of graduates from this level of education. The beginning practitioners, in many but not all areas of social work, will increasingly be prepared at the baccalaureate-degree level. Consequently both the class and field curriculum of undergraduate programs in social welfare will be expanded and enriched. Standard-setting at this level will enhance the quality of these programs but probably will also decrease their number. Postbaccalaureate-degree programs in the future most likely will concentrate on preparation for advanced clinical practice, planning and community organization, administration and policy, research and teaching. It is possible that in time the doctoral degree will become the common advanced degree. All social work education programs will provide their students with more and deeper knowledge about factors causing individual and social problems and about the roles and limitations of social welfare and social workers. Students will learn more generic skills but will also have increasing opportunities to specialize.

Social work as a profession seems to have a tendency to do one of two things when it comes to change. It is either slow to change, holds onto the familiar, makes small changes and studies and worries them to death or, under pressure of its own disgust, it tries to be radical and make too much change too fast without thought or planning. In social work education we need to learn better to anticipate the nature and quantity of required manpower, to move and change quickly when need makes action urgent, and yet to think and plan carefully when issues are complex and consequences serious.

Social work practice has an important stake and role in what happens in social work education in the years ahead. Social work education, in order to continue to change and improve, requires more frequent, consistent input from social work practitioners and agency executives and boards.

NOTES

1. Cordelia Cox, et al., *Contemporary Education for Social Work in the United States* (New York: Council on Social Work Education, 1966).

2. For details see Arnulf M. Pins, "Undergraduate Education in Social Welfare," *Social Welfare Forum, 1967* (New York: Columbia University Press, 1967), pp. 142–158.

3. *Undergraduate Programs in Social Welfare: A Guide to Objectives, Content, Field Experience and Organization* (New York: Council on Social Work Education, 1967).

4. For example, see the following syllabi: Richard H. P. Mendes et al., *Social Welfare as a Social Institution* (New York: Council on Social Work Education, 1969); Irving Tebor and Patricia Pickford, *Social Work: A Helping Profession in Social Welfare* (New York: Council on Social Work Education, 1966); Ralph Dolgoff and Frank Loewenberg, *The Teaching of Practice Skills in Undergraduate Programs in Social Welfare and Other Helping Services* (New York: Council on Social Work Education, 1970); Margaret Matson, *Field Experience in Undergraduate Programs in Social Welfare* (New York: Council on Social Work Education, 1967).

5. *Colleges and Universities with Undergraduate Programs in Social Welfare* (New York: Council on Social Work Education, 1970).

6. "New Requirements for Undergraduate Programs in Social Welfare," *Social Work Education Reporter*, September–October 1970, pp. 15–16.

7. Donald Feldstein, *Community College and Other Associate Degree Programs for Social Welfare Areas* (New York: Council on Social Work Education, 1968); *The Community Services Technician: Guide for Associate Degree Programs in the Community and Social Services* (New York: Council on Social Work Education, 1970).

8. For details see *Statistics on Social Work Education*, published annually by the Council on Social Work Education.

9. *Curriculum Policy Statement for Master's Degree Program in Graduate Schools of Social Work* (New York: Council on Social Work Education, 1969).

10. The 1952 statement described and permitted parallel and distinctive two-year concentrations for casework and group work. In the 1962 curriculum policy statement three methods were named —casework, group work, and community organization. Curriculum statements prior to 1952 listed specific courses.

11. For details see Lilian Ripple, ed., *Innovations in Teaching Social Work Practice* (New York: Council on Social Work Education, 1970).

12. Kurt Reichert, "Schools of Social Work and Inner-City Concerns, Racial Problems and Anti-Poverty Activities," *Social Work Education Reporter*, March 1968, pp. 2, 49–51.

13. Frank Loewenberg, ed., *1970 Statistics on Social Work Education* (New York: Council on Social Work Education, 1971).

14. For example, see Betty Lacy Jones, ed., *Current Patterns in Field Instruction in Graduate Social Work Education* (New York: Council on Social Work Education, 1969).

15. This was one of the factors that in the 1940s led to the development of two different and often competing spokesmen and accrediting groups for social work education. For a summary of earlier conflicts, see Ernest V. Hollis and Alice B. Taylor, *Social Work Education in the United States* (New York: Columbia University Press, 1951), pp. 38–39.

16. For a summary of issues and alternatives see "Open Meeting on Length of Graduate Social Work Education: Attendance and Views of Constituency Invited," *Social Work Education Reporter*, September–October 1970, pp. 7–9.

17. Deborah Miller, *Continuing Education Programs in Schools of Social Work: Report of a Survey* (New York: Council on Social Work Education, 1969).

18. For details see Harold Greenberg and Carl Scott, "Ethnic Minority-Group Recruitment and Programs for the Educationally Disadvantaged in Schools of Social Work," *Social Work Education Reporter*, September 1969, pp. 32A–32D; and Carl Scott, ed., *Ethnic Minorities in Social Work Education* (New York: Council on Social Work Education, 1970).

19. For details see Frank Loewenberg and Thomas Shey, "Ethnic Characteristics of Full-Time Master's Degree Students in U.S. Schools of Social Work," *Social Work Education Reporter*, June 1970, pp. 14–17; and *1970 Statistics on Social Work Education*, Table 207.

20. For details see Frank Loewenberg, "Non-White Doctoral Students and Graduates in Social Work," *Social Work Education Reporter*, December 1969, p. 13.

21. For details see James Dumpson, "Progress Report: Special Committee on Minority Groups," *Social Work Education Reporter*, March 1970, pp. 28–33.

22. For example, see *Potentials and Problems in the Changing Agency-School Relationships in Social Work Education* (New York: Council on Social Work Education, 1966).

24   Toward a Model for Teaching a Basic First-Year Course in Methods of Social Work Practice

ALLEN PINCUS and ANNE MINAHAN

INTRODUCTION

This paper will present a conceptual model which can be used in teaching a basic first-year methods course in graduate schools of social work. We will begin with a brief analysis of the shortcomings of the division of practice into three methods (casework, group work, and community organization) and the parallel division of methods courses into the same three areas.

Developments in the field over the past decade (for example, the growth of broad problem-focused agencies such as community-centered mental health clinics and experimental neighborhood-based multi-service centers) have strained the traditional boundaries between casework, group work, and community organization and have brought into question the adequacy of describing practice in terms of these three categories.[1] Critics of the traditional view of practice emphasize the necessity of working across different systems (e.g., individual, family, small group, organization, neighborhood, community) and defining services in terms of client needs rather than the other way around.

Aside from any new modes of practice which defy categorization as casework, group work, or community organization, there is also growing recognition that the social worker, despite his identification with any one methodological specialty, often becomes involved with a number of different systems in the course of his work.[2] For example, though we are accustomed to think only of the caseworker as working with individuals, group workers often do individual diagnostic studies before asking an individual to join a group; they also maintain contacts with individual group members outside group

Reprinted with permission of the Council on Social Work Education and of the authors from Lilian Ripple, ed., *Innovations in Teaching Social Work Practice* (New York: Council on Social Work Education, 1970), pp. 34–57.

meetings, reach out to existing groups through their leaders and other individual group members, and establish individual contacts with teachers, parents, judges, police, and other influential people in the life-space of the group and its members. Similarly, the community worker collects information from individuals, urges individuals to become active in a variety of committees or organizations, and seeks to influence attitudes and behavior in direct interviews with individuals. Examples of the caseworker's and community worker's involvement with groups, and the caseworker's and group worker's involvement with the community can easily be supplied.

It is noted that the organizational system is often ignored in moving from the group to the community, and only discussed in the context of administration. However, the organization is often a target of the worker's intervention in dealing with a problem and he must know how to operate in relation to this system just as he does in relation to the individual, the group, or the community. Further, if the worker's primary identification is with his profession rather than with a particular agency, in his own agency he should be prepared to effect changes which will enhance his practice.[3]

Even if a social worker does involve himself primarily with one system, the question can still be raised about the adequacy of defining methods in relation to the "size" of that system. As Schwartz has indicated:

> . . . the single variable embodied in the number of people one works with at the same time is simply not significant enough to be endowed with the designation of "method." Not significant enough, that is, if we reserve the term method to mean a systematic mode of helping which, while it is used differently in different situations, retains throughout certain recognizable and invariant properties through which one may identify the social worker in action. In this light, to describe casework, group work, and community organization as methods simply mistakes the nature of the helping process for the relational system in which it is applied.[4]

How have the schools of social work responded to the blurring of the boundaries between casework, group work, and community work? Some schools have not responded at all. They require the student to select a specialization in casework, group work, or community work before entering school, and the student receives little or no instruction in methods outside of his specialization.

A second group of schools have recognized that practitioners in one method specialty should know something about the methodologies employed by their fellow social workers. This development is reflected in the curriculum by such courses as "casework for group workers," and "group work for caseworkers." In many respects, such a methods curriculum might serve to reinforce rather than to loosen the existing distinctions between methods. By contrasting other methodologies with the one the student has elected to specialize in, identification with the unique aspects of one's chosen specialty, rather than identification with a common base of practice, may be enhanced. This approach does develop method specialists with some knowledge of another methodology, although this knowledge will be limited if not supported in the field course.

A third group has been busy abstracting common principles that apply to the three current methods and identifying and analyzing the similarities and differences among them. A shortcoming of this approach is that it basically accepts and leaves intact the traditional division of practice into casework, group work, and community organization, while at the same time it tries to build some bridges between them or "integrate" them within a common framework. Methods courses based on this approach usually are taught jointly by casework and group work (and sometimes community organization) instructors, each of whom presents material from his own area within some common outline which facilitates comparing and contrasting of material. However, the identity of each method is preserved and, to some extent, reinforced since the various methods are personified by the different instructors. In this approach, instructors often operate at a level more abstract than the methodological content from which they draw. This can result in courses which are too general and vulnerable to the criticism of teaching the student to be a jack of all trades and a master of none. Indeed, if the course is not planned carefully, the instructors may end up offering a watered-down version of the course they would ordinarily teach to students specializing in their area of practice. This approach can be especially frustrating to the instructors because of the opposite pull of trying to build something new while at the same time hanging on to the old.

To go beyond this stage and build a basic first-year course in methods of social work practice which is something different than a combination of casework, group work, and community work is difficult because there are few conceptual models to draw on and because it means giving up our old identities as caseworkers, group workers, or community workers before it is clear that a new identity can be found. But it is not until traditional identities are shed that we are free to find a new one.

It should be made clear that we do not consider a basic methods course as teaching an homogenized supra method, any more than a basic course in research methods could be considered as teaching a supra method of research, combining different research specializations. Rather, as in a basic research methods course, we began with the assumption that, regardless of the many forms that the practice of social work does or should take, there is a common core of specific concepts, principles, procedures, and skills which are necessary for the practice of social work and which all students should consequently acquire and master before pursuing any specialized form of practice. It should also be made clear that we do not view this course as preparing generalists as opposed to specialists. Depending on how it is combined with other methods courses and the rest of the curriculum, such a methods course can set the base for the development of a variety of kinds of practitioners such as the methods generalist, the problem specialist, the social actionist, etc.

Building a New Model

In building a new conceptual model for teaching social work practice we switched our focus from searching for a palatable way of combining existing definitions of the three methods and devising general principles that would fit them, to examining the tasks of the social worker in action and isolating and identifying the basic elements of social work practice reflected in these tasks. We sought to develop a "middle range" model, avoiding either too microscopic a view of practice (such as an analysis of the verbal interchanges of the worker in an individual interview) or too broad a view (such as generalizations about all workers following a problem-solving process, sharing a common set of values, utilizing relationships, etc.). In other words, we wanted a model which would be specific enough to be useful in teaching concepts and techniques that the student could apply in his field work and use to analyze his activities as a change agent, but general enough to be applicable to a variety of settings and situations and provide the student with an adequate overview of social work practice.

Our model has been built up by bits and pieces and draws on many existing formulations. It can be considered new only in the sense of consolidating segmented efforts and fitting them together in a different way.[5]

The three main components in our model for teaching methods of social work practice are listed below. They will be discussed in detail in the next section.

1. The types of systems in relation to which the social worker carries out his role: change agent systems, client systems, action systems, and target systems. These systems may be of varying sizes.
2. The phases of the planned change or problem-solving process over time that the worker goes through in performing his role.
3. The analytical and interactional skills employed by the worker: data collection, data analysis, and intervention.

Any task performed by the social worker in action can be analyzed in terms of the types of systems in relation to which the task is performed, the phase of the process at which the task is performed, and the skills utilized by the worker in performing the task. It should be noted that our model is not based on any single theoretical approach to analyzing behavior. For example, the *types of systems* component relies on social systems concepts while the *process through time* component draws on developmental concepts.

Although factors such as values, settings, etc. are not labeled as major dimensions of the model, they are integrated with the three main components. For example, the effects of the agency setting on practice are seen in relation to influences on decision-making, on the delivery of service, on the options open to the worker in negotiating a contract with the client system, etc. Value considerations, behavioral science knowledge, etc., are likewise interwoven in all components.

We recognize that no model can pretend to adequately convey the complexity and the art in social work practice. A model is merely an analytical tool. As a tool it can not be considered as right or wrong but must be judged in the light of its utility in serving its purpose (in this case, teaching a basic first-year course in methods of social work practice). The complexity and the art do come through as the student experiments in applying the model in his practice and discusses his experience in class.

EXPLICATION OF COMPONENTS OF MODEL

Type of System

When the social worker works with different-size systems, he must determine who the client is, identify the system that should be changed, and determine what system should be involved actively in the change efforts. The role of the social worker can be viewed in relation to four *types* of systems: change-agent systems, client systems, target systems, and action systems.

Change-Agent System.   The concept of change agent is borrowed from Lippitt, Watson, and Westley, who describe the variety of specialists who work with different type systems as change agents and "call all of these helpers, no matter what kind of system they normally work with, change agents."[6] Thus, we view the social worker as a type of change agent and the public, voluntary, or profit-making agency or organization that employs him as the *change-agent system.* We do this to emphasize that the change agent himself normally is not a detached professional worker, but is influenced in his change efforts by the system of which he is a part and which pays his salary. When his own change-agent system becomes a target for change, the social worker must understand how his relationship to the system will affect his change effort.

When, however, a social worker is a private practitioner, he alone composes the change-agent system unless he contracts on a regular or *ad hoc* basis to work together with other change agents such as other social workers, clinical psychologists, economists, and other social scientists.

Client System.   The term "client system" is also borrowed from Lippitt, Watson, and Westley, who refer to the specific system that is being helped as the client system.[7] We take a somewhat different view, shared by Brager, and consider the *client system* as the person, family, group, organization, or community which *engages the services* of a social worker as a change agent.[8] The client system, or some sub-part of it (one member of the family, one group in a neighborhood, the Board of Directors of an organization, one organization in the community), "contracts" with the social worker and is the *expected beneficiary* of the worker's services. The social worker may attempt to enlarge the client system by involving other members of a larger system in the contract or to reduce the client system by delimiting his contractual agreements.

The term "client" is then being used as it would be in relation to professions in general. As the term is used here, the client system is *not* necessarily the target of the social worker's interventions, although this is the sense in which the term is ordinarily used in social work. Sometimes in order to serve the client system, we "help" another system to change—thus, the distinction between our view of client system and the definition given above from Lippitt *et al.*[9]

Our view of the nature of the client system has many implications for such issues as sanctions and voluntary vs. involuntary clients. It is useful to think of two types of sanctions under which the practitioner works. First, there is the sanction which gives him the right or opportunity to make his services available to the public and certifies his competence. This sanction comes from his profession and, in some areas, from state statutes. Second, there is the sanction which gives the practitioner the right to engage in specific activities on behalf of a specific client. This sanction comes from the client himself when he voluntarily contracts for the services of the practitioner. For example, a surgeon may be licensed to practice medicine in a given community, but he cannot operate on Mr. Jones, a resident of that community, without Mr. Jones's permission. The same is true for social work, except that we often work with "involuntary clients," persons who have not requested or contracted for our services. Initially, a worker in child protective services, street-gang work, prisons, or organizing low-income neighborhoods does not have a voluntary contract with the parent, gang members, prisoners, or neighborhood residents. His initial sanction to engage in specific activities in these cases comes from the agency which employs him (the change-agent system), and, thus, indirectly from the community which supports the agency. The community, in a sense, is then the "client." In these cases, an important task of the social worker is to convince involuntary clients that they can benefit from his services and to get them to enter a contract with the worker, thus shifting as much as possible the worker's sanction from the community to those he seeks to work with directly.

Target System. The person, family, group, organization, or community (or some subpart or combination of systems) at which the social worker directs his change efforts comprises the *target system.* Thus, an important diagnostic task of the social worker in collaboration with the client system is determining those persons, processes, social conditions, etc. that he must change in order to benefit the client system. The terms "target" or "target system" have been used often by others. Burns and Glasser have noted that it may be helpful to consider the primary targets of change as distinct from the persons who may be the primary clients.[10]

The social worker may work with or on behalf of the client system, and may intervene through direct interaction with the target system or bring influences from other systems to bear on the target system. Very often the client system and target system partially overlap as, for example, when a mother (client) comes to an agency for help with a problem child and the worker seeks to change the way the mother disciplines the child in addition to working with the child himself. At other times, the client system and target system are the same, as when a worker accepts an individual client for help in solving a personal problem. In other cases the target and client systems are separate, e.g., in trying to open up jobs in the community for ex-mental patients, the large employers might be thought of as the target system and the ex-mental patients as the client system. When the social worker seeks to change certain practices or policies of his agency in order to better serve the community or his own clients, the change-agent system itself may overlap with the target system.

Action System. Warren uses the term *action system* to describe new systems created to perform community action tasks.[11] Broadened, the term includes the system the social worker works with and through to influence the target system, whether the target is an individual, group, organization, etc.

Action systems are composed of all those persons and processes engaged in influencing the target system. An action system may be: (1) a new system put together by the worker with the expectation that members will be placed in direct interaction with each other (e.g., a formed-treatment group), (2) an existing system already in interaction (e.g., a family, a teen-age gang), or (3) several people who may not at any one time be engaged in direct interaction with each other but whom the worker will coordinate and/or attempt to influence on behalf of a client system (e.g., representatives of several agencies involved with a client).

In individual therapy we have the smallest possible action system composed of the change agent and the client (who is also the target). The social worker in the mental hospital who forms a pre-discharge group is putting together an action system to help the members of the group (who are both clients and targets). When a committee is formed in the community to develop day care centers, the action system (the committee) may include some part of the client system (those mothers who want day care facilities) and may not at all overlap with the target system.

Implications of Systems

The first component in our model of practice, *type of system*, helps us to locate the activity of the worker in relation to the several types of systems he becomes engaged with in performing his change-agent role. In turn, the various combinations of separate and overlapping types of systems present him with different demands, opportunities, and dilemmas. We recognize that in actual practice any one problem confronting the worker may involve multiple client, action, and target systems. Further, in any given problem, the client system may be considered the target system with respect to certain goals, but with respect to other goals the target system may lie outside the client system. For example, in working with a local neighborhood organization which wants the city to set up a playground, the worker may help set up an action committee of local residents (action system) to influence the city. However, the low self-esteem of the committee members and their fearfulness in talking with city officials may require the worker to offer support to the groups and help them overcome these feelings. With respect to this second goal, the client system may also be considered a target system. Another example would be the worker in a community mental health center who may be working with a mother to change her way of handling her children (client system also the target system) and may also be serving as her advocate in getting the welfare department to increase her ADC grant (client system not the same as target system). The issue that often comes up in social work about process (system maintenance) vs. task (goal achievement) orientations is relevant here. The worker may adapt one orientation in relation to one type system but a different orientation in relation to another type.

Some of the implications of our framework for viewing the *type of system* component of our model of practice can be briefly stated:

1. No *a priori* assumption is made that the system which brings the problem to the worker is to be the major target for intervention. As Purcell and Specht have pointed out, "too often . . . the client system presenting the problem becomes the major target for inter-

vention and the intervention method is limited to the one most suitable to that client system."[12]

2. No a *priori* assumption is made that any size action system or particular mode of intervention for the action system is the most appropriate to deal with the problem presented by the client system. The appropriate action system can be identified only after the target and goals for change have been established.

3. The appropriateness of given strategies and change-agent roles is determined by the particular configuration of overlapping and separate types of systems the worker must deal with in a given problem. For example, if the client system, target system, and action system overlap, the worker may act simultaneously as enabler, communication builder, guide, etc. The social worker may be a partisan advocate and attack the target system only if it does not overlap with the action system and client system. Thus, the worker may establish one type of relationship and be guided by traditional social work values of honesty and self-determination when he is working with his client system, and maintain other relationships which reflect other values when he is attempting to influence a target system which lies outside his client and action system.[13]

4. The deliberate focus on the agency (change-agent system) as a potential target of change emphasizes the need to understand the process of changing agencies from within as well as from without.

5. The transfer and organization of knowledge relevant to working with different size systems and with different objectives are facilitated. For example, some of the same principles of group formation apply in the formation of an action system for group therapy as well as in the formation of a community action committee. It is useful to compare and contrast the considerations the worker takes into account in forming these two different kinds of groups.

6. The necessity for diagnosing the functioning of the action system is highlighted. If the action system the worker has chosen to work with is not operating in a way conducive to achieving the desired change, the worker will need to determine the cause of the dysfunction and then alter the composition, size, or patterns of operating the action system.

Phases of Planned Change Process through Time*

The second component of our conceptual model of practice is the problem-solving process through time. Social work practitioners and educators are familiar with this concept. A number of writers have described the activities of a change agent against a framework of a logical sequential series of phases.[14] The implication appears to be obvious that any successful change agent must follow and go through these phases or, similar to a person whose normal growth pattern has been faulty, the desired end state will not be achieved satisfactorily.

There are We have identified five phases adapted from models presented by Lippitt and Warren which help determine and order the various tasks involved in carrying out the change-agent role with different-size client, action, and target systems.[15] The five phases are:

1. Recognition of problem and initiating engagement of change-agent and client system.
2. Identification of client system, target system, change-agent system, and action system related to problem and establishing a contract with the client system.
3. Formation of the action system.
4. Operation of the action system.
5. Evaluation, termination, or transformation of the action system.

Each of these five phases can be analyzed by considering what must be accomplished at each phase, the focus of the data collection and data analysis engaged in by the worker and the system involved, the intervention skills employed by the change agent, the knowledge base guiding the change agent, and the value considerations that come into play.

We recognize, in describing the planned change process in the context of five phases, that the worker may be operating in one or more phases at the same time. As Lippitt *et al.* have noted:

> Most change processes probably proceed by a kind of cyclic motion, starting over and over again as one set of problems is solved and a new set is encountered; hence the different

---

* Eds.' note: The authors' conceptions of the phases of planned change and intervention skills are treated somewhat differently in their recent book *Social Work Practice: Model and Method* (Itasca: F. E. Peacock Publishers, Inc., 1973).

phases become mixed up and the final objective may be achieved by a process which seems rather muddled to the observer who is looking for a clear-cut developmental sequence.[16]

The five phases can be said to overlap in the sense that the end product of one phase represents the beginning point of the next phase. For example, the end-point of phase one—initiating engagement of client system—represents the starting point of phase two, which is concerned with arriving at a working agreement or contract with the client system. In some cases, two or more phases may overlap to the point of merging into one another. For example, phases two and three may merge when the worker continues to work in a one-to-one action system with the same client he saw for an initial intake interview.

The implications of using this framework for analyzing and teaching process through time can be summarized as follows:

1. The use of all practice skills in all phases becomes obvious and explicit. In the old intake-study-diagnosis-treatment-termination model, it is difficult to escape from the implication that data collection occurs primarily at the intake and study phases and treatment occurs only at a later phase.

2. Relevant knowledge from social science can be plugged in at the appropriate time in the change cycle. For example, motivation theory from psychology and social psychology becomes particularly relevant at the first phase as we examine the motivations and resistances of change agents, change-agent systems, and client systems to engaging in a change effort. Theories of natural stages of group development become particularly relevant at the fourth phase, when the action system begins to operate.

3. The tasks that should be accomplished at each phase in order for the change process to proceed as well as the nature of the client-worker relationship that should be established, can be identified. For example, a major task in phase two is arriving at a contract or working agreement with the client system. Though the type of relationship the client can expect to have with the worker may be spelled out in the contract, the kind of relationship he experiences with the worker in working out the contract provides him with an actual demonstration.

4. Important value considerations that influence the worker in his

work with different types of systems can be identified at each phase. For example, the issue of the rights and sanctions of the worker to initiate contact with a client system is stressed at phase one. Questions of client self-determination arise particularly at phase two when the contract is established and at phase three when the action system is being composed.

5. The worker may be at different phases in the process with different sub-parts of the client system. For example, if, in the course of working with a family, it is decided to include "grandma" in the regular treatment sessions, then with respect to grandma the worker must be concerned with the issues of the earlier phases, such as grandma's motivations and expectations, how to initiate contact with her, etc. In such cases, we also have to be concerned with the effects of changing the action, target, or client systems on the systems with which we are already working. Another illustration is when an action system, such as a committee to establish a neighborhood center, is enlarged. The new members may be concerned with issues with which the old members have already dealt. Thus our framework of sequential phases helps the worker understand the problems and conflicts he will have to deal with as additional systems and subsystems become involved in the change process.

The Skills of the Social Worker

The skills the social worker utilizes in carrying out his change-agent role comprise the third component of our conceptual model of practice. As with most change agents, the skills of the social worker can be categorized into three broad areas: (1) data collection, (2) data analysis and decision-making, and (3) intervention. As indicated earlier, all three skills are used at all phases of the planned-change process, and with all the types and size systems with which the worker is engaged.

Though much of the practice of social work is an art, one of the hallmarks of the professional social worker is his ability to rationally and purposefully select and use his different skills to meet different demands and situations. We have developed frameworks for studying each of the three skill areas which are useful in teaching the student how this is accomplished. To be sure, the three skill areas are highly interrelated in actual practice and our distinctions between them are analytical ones. However, we have found that an exploration and analysis of the separate skill areas is a prerequisite for understanding the interrelated nature of skills as they are utilized in performing various social work tasks.

DATA COLLECTION

Most problems confronting the social worker will require data collection on and from a variety of different systems. The approach used here for analyzing the data collection skills of the social worker draws heavily from research methods literature.

Data collection techniques can be divided into three main categories: (1) questioning, (2) observing, and (3) using existing written material. Each of these techniques can be applied in studying different sizes and types of systems.

1. Questioning
    A. Direct verbal questioning (e.g., individual and group interviewing)
    B. Direct written questioning (e.g., application forms, survey questionnaire)
    C. Projective and other indirect verbal and written techniques (e.g., role playing, sentence completion tasks)
2. Observing
    A. Observing behavior and social interaction
        (1) Participant observation
        (2) Non-participant observation
    B. Observing inanimate objects
3. Using Existing Written Materials
    A. Materials intended for use by change agents (e.g., case records, minutes of committee meetings)
    B. "Raw" material not originally intended for use by change agents (e.g., newspaper stories, letters)
    C. Systematically organized data (e.g., population census statistics, budgets of agencies)

In using these various techniques the worker may have the option of structuring to some degree the system or phenomenon under study and/or the method used to record the data which are collected. Though there is a continuum from non-structured to structured, it will help to represent different approaches according to [the dichotomies shown in Figure 24.1].

FIGURE 24.1

		System Being Studied	
		Non-Structured	Structured
Method of Recording Data	Non-Structured	1	2
	Structured	3	4

Some examples may help to illustrate the kind of techniques which would fit into each cell.

1. An open-ended interview with a school teacher about a particular student.
2. A diagnostic group in a mental health clinic where the group sessions are purposefully structured to elicit certain behaviors and place certain demands on the children. The worker records his observations and impressions after each meeting, but does not follow any particular form in doing so.[17]
3. A systematic content analysis of the minutes of a local community action commission to determine who voted with whom on what issues.
4. Observing a family interact around a task supplied by the worker and recording the number of supportive acts each parent displays toward each child.

By structuring the system under study the worker is in a sense helping to generate the needed data.

Given this variety of approaches to data collection, the worker must select in a purposeful way the most appropriate collection techniques to obtain the needed data. Since each method of data collection presents its own unique advantages and disadvantages the worker must often think in terms of a data collection strategy, combining two or more approaches. The suitability of a given technique will depend on a number of factors such as:

1. Type of data needed.
2. Size and type of system under study.
3. Demands placed on the system under study by the particular technique.
4. Relationship of worker to the system under study.
5. Degree of client involvement desired.
6. Speed with which the data must be obtained.

In summary, this approach to viewing data collection in social work practice emphasizes the techniques of data collection rather than *what* data should be collected. (The latter will depend on the particular problem confronting the worker and the phase of the planned change process in which he is working.) Except for discussions of interviewing, the social work literature generally is sparse on actual techniques of data collection. While interviewing is perhaps the most important data collection tool of any social worker, it must be placed in perspective with other techniques. Our approach to data collection helps to supply this needed perspective. The various techniques outlined here can be adapted to fit many different sizes and types of systems that the worker may wish to study.

DATA ANALYSIS

The skills categorized under the heading of data analysis are basically analytical skills and are used by the worker at all phases of the planned change process. These analytical skills encompass (1) using theories, concepts, and theoretical orientations to interpret or "make sense" out of data, and (2) decision-making, which would include judgment, prediction, selection among alternatives, and goal setting.

The first skill (making sense out of **data**) not only requires a substantive knowledge of the theories, concepts, or theoretical orientations being used (e.g., ego psychology, learning theory, role concepts, group dynamics, power structure, etc.) but also an ability to connect the conceptual realm with actual situations through inductive and deductive thought processes. This skill will be exercised in making many "on the spot" interpretations of data in addition to more leisurely studying of data without the pressure of supplying immediate feedback to client, action, or change-agent systems. Lehrman and Meehl are examples of writers who have dealt with these issues.[18]

The second analytical skill is decision-making. Considering its importance in practice and the amount of attention it has received in psychology, administrative science, and organizational theory, it is surprising that so little attention has been paid to it in the social work literature. In viewing decision-making, we have borrowed heavily from these other disciplines. To understand the decision-making skill of the practitioner one must have knowledge of:

1. Factors which affect the judgment of the practitioner, such as amount of information, anchoring effects, lock-in effects, and organizational context.[19]
2. Different models underlying the decision-making process, from the operations research or pay-off matrix models which account for all factors entering in the decision in a highly rational manner[20] to the less structured "muddling through" type of model as described by Lindblom.[21]
3. Characteristics of decisions which will affect the applicability and desirability of using different decision-making approaches, such as complexity, reversibility, degree of risk or uncertainty, and time allotted to make decision.

It should be noted here that in discussing the data analysis skills of the social worker we are referring only to the analytical activity of the individual practitioner. His involvement of others in his decision-making, or the help he may provide to individuals or groups in arriving at decisions, are tasks which require a combination of intervention skills and analytical skills. (Knowledge of his own decision-making processes will, of course, help him in these tasks.)

It should be further noted that we have purposely steered away from talking about "diagnosis." The writing of a diagnostic statement about the functioning of the client, action, or target system may be a task at some phase in the planned change process. But we emphasize again that what we are concerned with here are the analytical data analysis skills of the practitioner which are utilized at all phases of the planned change process and in relationship to all systems with which he is engaged.

INTERVENTION SKILLS

Intervention skills are those techniques used by the worker to influence and effect change in action and target systems on behalf of client systems. As with the other skill areas, there are two main aspects to the development of a framework for studying intervention skills. The first is a scheme for describing and classifying different intervention techniques. The second is a systematic approach for studying the parameters which determine the applicability and appropriateness of a given technique in a given situation.

Because of the complexity of this skill area we have not been able to devise any one classification scheme which has proved adequate. For example, the size of the system in which the intervention skill is employed does not provide a satisfactory basis for classification since many techniques (e.g., rational persuasion, confrontation, supporting feelings, reinforcing behavior, etc.) can be employed in different size systems. Similar difficulties are presented by schemes based on other distinctions, such as the level at which intervention skills are directed (e.g., behavior, effect, cognition, etc.), theoretical systems or orientations from which the techniques derive (e.g., learning theory, psychoanalytic theory, socialization theory, conflict models, etc.), person-environment dichotomies, and roles played by the worker (e.g., enabler, advocate, teacher, expert, etc.).

We have found Vinter's distinction between direct and indirect modes of influence to be helpful.[22] Though Vinter is referring to working with groups, his concept has wider applicability. Adapting his definitions, *indirect means of influence* are those interventions utilized to modify the conditions of an action system which subsequently affect one or more members. For example, through modification of the size, composition, operating procedures, or programming of an action system the worker can indirectly influence the behavior of the members of that system and consequently its ultimate success.

Direct means of influence are those interventions utilized by the worker to effect change through his immediate personal interaction with one or more persons or members of an action or target system. These immediate interactions may influence an individual directly or create further interactional situations where members of a system will influence each other. Indirect intervention skills might be thought of as analytical skills because they represent planning done by a worker in determining the conditions for the operation of an action system. Direct intervention skills are interactional skills.

By necessity we are operating with a multiple perspective on ways of classifying intervention techniques and we encourage the student to use any approach or combination of approaches which he finds most useful in analyzing and describing his intervention efforts in a given case.

As for the second aspect of our framework for this skill area, factors which determine the use of given intervention techniques in a given situation, we are currently exploring the following approach. We are examining a variety of intervention techniques (e.g., giving information, demonstrating behavior, confrontation, interpretation, persuasion, reinforcement, desensitization, crisis prov-

FIGURE 24.2
Examples of Situations in Which Intervention Skills Are Utilized

		Type of System Being Influenced			
Size of System in Which Influence is Exerted	Client(s) Who Is (Are) Also the Target System	Target(s) Which Is (Are) Outside the Client System and Action System	Target(s) Which Is (Are) Part of the Change-Agent System	Target(s) Which Is (Are) Part of the Action System
Dyad	Helping a client discuss a marital problem	Getting a landlord to reduce the rent of a client	Convincing your agency director to support a change in the intake policy	Teaching a foster mother how to deal with a child's behavior problem
Small Group	Helping members of a treatment group share their experiences	Trying to get a social club at a community center to admit a handicapped client of yours as a member	Convincing the other "team" members at a staffing that the patient should be discharged	Trying to get a committee to postpone voting on an issue
Organizations and Other Larger Social Systems	Guiding a neighborhood self-help organization in selecting an appropriate project	Trying to get the city to adopt a better building code	Getting the welfare department where you work to fix up its waiting room	Persuading participants in a demonstration to avoid violence

ocation, coercion, providing feedback, etc.) which derive from a variety of change models and theoretical orientations, and we are studying the various situations in which different techniques are utilized. On a general level we are defining "situation" in terms of the *size* of the system in which the influence effort is being exerted (dyad, small group, organization, and other larger systems) and the *type* of system being influenced (change-agent system, client system, target system, action system, or some combination thereof). The chart [in Figure 24.2] gives some examples of how we classify different situations.

As we discuss different examples in each of the 12 categories from the students' field work and explore the kinds of intervention techniques used by the students, we are beginning to identify the kinds of techniques which are applied in the different situations. If we look across the rows in the chart we can see within a given *size* system which techniques are applied with all *types* of systems and which seem to be unique to a given type. Similarly, if we look down the columns, we can begin to identify within a given *type* of system those techniques which can be applied in all *sizes* of systems and which are unique to a particular size system. On a more specific level, as we discuss different examples within the same category we are making note of those variables which form the "context" of the situation, such as the status of the others in the system *vis-à-vis* the worker, resources available to the worker, expected duration of the relationship with the worker, age of the others in the system, etc., and studying how they influence the choice of techniques within and across different situations.

If we combine any of the categorizations of intervention skills discussed earlier with the chart, we can further refine our distinctions. For example, within each situation we can classify techniques according to whether they are direct or indirect, or if aimed at the cognitive, affective, or behavioral level, etc. With this kind of a scheme the student can talk about the different sizes and types of systems he must influence in working on a given problem, define the situations he will confront, the contexts of these situations, and plan an appropriate strategy of action.

SUMMARY OF CONCEPTUAL MODEL

Our model enables us to view the essential unity of the change-agent role in social work. In place of abstract generalizations regarding similarities and differences in casework, group work, and community organization, we have attempted to identify the specific components underlying all social work practice. Our model thus allows us to talk about the specific activities of the social worker without running into jurisdictional disputes as to which of the three traditional methods of practice they fit into. For example, all social workers employ interviewing skills in collecting data. Indeed, a good part of the community worker's time is spent in individual interviews. Is interviewing to be considered a casework skill if taught in a casework course and a community organization skill if taught in a community organization course? Similarly, what about the community worker who, seeking to influence a certain member of the community to change his attitude about a community project, uses such techniques with him as logical discussion and exploration, clarification, acceptance, support, ventilation and verbalization of feelings, and reassurance and encouragement. Is the community worker "caseworking" this person? And what about the caseworker who is running a diagnostic group or an intake group at a community mental health center? Is he a caseworker practicing group work? Or is he to be considered a caseworker when working with individuals and a group worker when working with the group? We can of course add many more such examples. The point we wish to emphasize is that all of these activities can be understood as *social work* tasks performed by *social workers* who utilize certain skills in relation to different sizes and types of systems, at a given phase in the planned change process. Our model makes explicit that any skill utilized with any system is a social work skill. A diagnosis of why an action committee is unable to work together is a task of the same order as a diagnosis of why Johnnie wets his bed. Likewise, trying to get a school teacher to change her perception of a child is a task of the same order as getting the mother of the child to interact differently with her child.

Our model is congruent with a problem-centered approach to social work practice. Problems do not come neatly wrapped into individual, group, and community-size packages. Our model allows us to approach a given problem situation without any *a priori* assumptions and to determine on the basis of the given specific situation, the size and types of systems we must work with and through to achieve desired changes. We also can alter and redefine any of these systems at various points in the process through time as we move with the problem across different size systems.

We do recognize that individual social workers have developed specialized knowledge and skills and have opted for different theories of causation and models for changing behavior. They may concentrate on service to one size or type of client system, to particular problem areas, and to a particular field of practice. We also recognize that when an agency or worker is engaged in problem-centered practice that more than one change agent may be involved in activity focused around a particular problem situation. For example, in a neighborhood multi-service center, one worker may be engaged with family members in working on emotional problems and another worker may be engaged with members of the same family in a community action enterprise. However, our model of practice enables both workers to view the total problem, determine with the client system the various tasks that need to be done, and determine what tasks each worker will do with what system to provide a unitary approach to the problems.

While we do not believe that all social workers need to be all things to all people, we do believe that all social workers must at least be social workers to all people. As we begin to move away from primary identifications as caseworkers, group workers, and community workers, we are quickly substituting new identities as problem area specialist, people helpers, as opposed to system changers, etc. However, if there is such a thing as a profession of social work, the worker must bring to his particular kind of practice an identification as a social worker, and further, this identification must have some methodological basis or content. In other words, what is the base or core from which specialization is taking place? This is the issue we tried to address in developing our model for teaching a first-year methods course. We are sympathetic with the views of Overton, who believes that specialization in social work has perhaps been premature.

> Until we have sufficiently developed and explicitly described the social worker-in-action, we are not in a position to say what form specialization should take or what the proper mix of generic and specific ought to be.[23]

Implications for Teaching Methods

Our conceptual model was purposefully designed to serve as a blueprint for a basic first-year (two-semester) course in methods of social work practice. We started the course almost two years ago with an embryonic version of the model presented here. The model was actually developed along with the course and our ideas have been greatly modified as the result of feedback from our students. In translating this model of practice into a teaching plan for a course, there are a number of factors to be considered, such as:

1. The order in which the components of the models are taught.
2. The relationship of the methods course to the field course.
3. The relationship of the course to second-year methods courses.
4. The use of team teaching.

We will comment briefly on each of these areas.

Order in Which Components of Model Are Taught. In our first attempts at teaching the course (we are now in the midst of our second time around) we concentrated on data collection and data analysis skills the first semester, and focused on integrating these skills with intervention skills in the phases of the planned change process during the second semester. Our purpose in doing this was to acquaint the student with such basic skills as interviewing which are used almost immediately in field work. We were also overreacting to our concern that the skills be taught separately from the phases of the process over time so that no one skill became identified with any one phase. In addition, it is easier to present the conceptual framework for each skill area when the skill is taught as a separate unit than when the skill area is divided up among the many phases, e.g., covering data collection skills used at each phase as these different phases are taught.

However, the dysfunctions of teaching the skill areas as separate units apart from the phases have become apparent. It is difficult to talk about these skills without considering the context in which they are used in the planned change process. It has also been difficult to postpone discussing intervention skills until the second semester.

The next time around we are considering using the process-through-time component of our model as the major variable in structuring the course. We would divide the phases over the two semesters and teach the three skill areas as they are utilized at each phase. This approach also would have the advantage that the content of the first phase, such as identification of problems and needs, expectations and motivations of client and change-agent systems, getting client and change-agent systems together, etc., fits in well with the concerns of the beginning social work student. We could continue to present the conceptual material on types of sys-

tems at the beginning of the semester, though we must keep referring to it and illustrating it throughout the semester in order for
these concepts to take hold. A major problem that would result
from teaching the course this way would be how to present the
frameworks for viewing each of the three skill areas, if these areas
are no longer taught as a unit but scattered throughout the course.
This remains an unresolved problem at this time.

Relation to Field Course.   There are two observations to be made
about the relationship of the methods course to the field course.
First, much of the value, indeed most of the value of a basic course
in methods of social work practice is lost if the approach to viewing
practice taught in the course is not carried over in the field, and if
the field does not permit a range of experience in working with
different sizes and types of systems. With almost all of our students
in field units taught by faculty field instructors who also are teaching courses and seminars on campus, this problem is to some extent
alleviated, but far from resolved.

Our second point, related to the first one, is that in our many attempts to relate the methods course to the field course we are
moving closer to the point of view that the classroom and field
course are actually inseparable parts of a methods course. In class
we present conceptual material, but illustrate and highlight concepts with case examples, role playing, films, and other teaching
devices. The field provides live experiences, but they are related
to conceptual realms by the field instructors. We are exploring ways
of combining the methods and field course. One project now in
progress is a multi-methods video tape laboratory in which students
from four different field units (who are also in one section of the
first-year methods class) spend part of their field work time practicing skills in the laboratory with the aid of video tape feedback.
Instead of maintaining the current division and boundaries between
field and classroom, we must begin to look at our model of practice
and identify the mode(s) of instruction (e.g., lecture, field experience, etc.) which are best suited for learning the different components of the model and relating experiential and conceptual
realms. Our undergraduate program has moved further In this
respect than our graduate program, and plans have been made
for combining the undergraduate methods and field experience
course in a single two-semester course on theory and methods of
social work practice.

Relation to Second-Year Methods Courses.   As mentioned earlier,
our model is meant to serve as a blueprint for a basic first-year

course in methods of social work practice. It is important that this course be taught in the first year rather than being offered as a kind of integrative course in the second year. The kind of orientation to social work practice which is taught in the course provides. the student with a perspective from which subsequent methods courses can be understood and stresses his identity as a social worker, rather than a caseworker, group worker, or community worker. When the course is offered in the first year it also gives the student some time to explore different areas of practice and helps to prevent premature specialization in any one area.

Another important reason why this course should precede other methods offerings is that the course is designed to provide a knowledge base which is essential to doing more advanced work. We see the course as being analogous to a basic course in research methods where students acquire the basic principles, concepts, and skills in research methodology before going on to more advanced and specialized courses such as research methods in personality assessment, demographic methodology, etc.

There are a variety of approaches to second-year methods courses which can build on the base of the first-year course. One alternative is to continue with the same model and "broaden and deepen." Another alternative is to organize special courses along a number of different lines, e.g., different size systems, different intervention models, different problem areas, different age groups, etc. At our school we have recently instituted an approach in which we offer three groupings of second-year methods courses; one grouping is based on system size (individual, family, group, neighborhood, community); one is based on processes within an agency (administration, consultation and supervision, program development, etc.); and the third is based on special interventive approaches (behavior modification, crises intervention, etc.). The student elects four courses with at least one from each grouping. His selection depends on his own interest and learning needs. We are just beginning to evaluate this approach, but so far the student reaction has been favorable, and they enjoy the freedom of selection of different courses. We also are offering a course the second year which follows the approach developed in the first year for those faculty and students who want to continue down this avenue.

Team Teaching. We have found the team teaching approach very useful in developing and teaching our course. It is important however, that the co-teachers see themselves as contributors to a mutual pool of experience and ideas rather than as representatives of the casework, group work, or community organization point of view. Team teaching, of course, is not without its pitfalls and requires compatible personalities if the venture is to be a successful one. While we cannot discuss here all the pros and cons of team teaching, we have observed that the advantages tend to diminish over time while the disadvantages become accentuated. When the course is taught a number of times, a point of diminishing returns may be reached after which the results may not warrant the large amount of time and effort the team approach requires.

It is often said that to be able to teach a basic social work methods course an individual must be some kind of super human being who is equally expert in casework, group work, and community organization. Those who hold this point of view fail to understand, as we have pointed out throughout this paper, that a basic social work methods course is not the same as a combination of casework, group work, and community work. When new practice courses are being developed and tested in the classroom, a collaborative teaching approach may be advantageous. However, once a course has been developed, the task of teaching it alone is not beyond the capability of an ordinary human being.

NOTES

1. Herbert H. Aptekar, "Some Models of the Social Work Generalist," paper presented at the National Conference on Social Welfare, San Francisco, 1968; Werner W. Boehm, "Toward New Models of Social Work Practice," *Social Work Practice, 1967*, National Conference on Social Welfare (New York: Columbia University Press, 1967); Boehm, "Common and Specific Learnings for a Graduate of a School of Social Work," *Journal of Education for Social Work*, Vol. 4, No. 2 (Fall, 1968); Mary E. Burns and Paul H. Glasser, "Similarities and Differences in Casework and Groupwork Practice," *Social Service Review*, Vol. 34, No. 4 (December, 1963); Michael March, "The Neighborhood Center Concept," *Public Welfare* (April, 1968); Helen Northern, "An Integrated Practice Sequence in Social Work Education," *Social Work Education Reporter*, Vol. 16, No. 2 (June, 1968); Alice Overton, "The Issue of Integration of Casework and Group Work," *Social Work Education Reporter*, Vol. 16, No. 2 (June, 1968); Robert Perlman and David Jones, *Neighborhood Service Centers* (Washington, D.C.: U.S. Department of Health, Education, and Welfare, 1967); Helen Harris Perlman, "Social Work Method: A Review of the Past Decade," *Social Work*, Vol. 10, No. 4 (October, 1965); Francis P. Purcell and Harry Specht, "The House

on Sixth Street," *Social Work*, Vol. 10, No. 4 (October, 1965); Elliot Studt, "Social Work Theory and Implications for the Practice of Methods," *Social Work Education Reporter*, Vol. 16, No. 2 (June, 1968); William Schwartz, "The Social Worker in the Group," *The Social Welfare Forum, 1961*, National Conference on Social Welfare (New York: Columbia University Press, 1961); Hyman J. Weiner, "The Hospital, the Ward, and the Patient As Clients: Use of the Group Method," *Social Work*, Vol. 4, No. 4 (October, 1959).

2. Ronald Lippitt, Jeanne Watson, and Bruce Westley, *The Dynamics of Planned Change* (New York: Harcourt, Brace & World, 1965).

3. We are indebted to Virginia Franks, our colleague at the University of Wisconsin, for the development of this concept as well as for her early conceptualizations of a multi-methods practice and curriculum. See Virginia Franks, "The Autonomous Social Worker," School of Social Work, University of Wisconsin—Madison, March, 1967. (Unpublished mimeo.)

4. Schwartz, *op. cit.*, pp. 148–149.

5. Though we developed our own conceptual model independently of the work carried on by Studt (Elliot Studt, *op. cit.*), we find her emphasis on "task" to be both compatible and in many ways parallel to ours. There are many differences, however, in our elaboration of the basic components of practice.

6. Lippitt *et al.*, *op. cit.*, p. 12.

7. *Ibid.*

8. George A. Brager, "Advocacy and Political Behavior," *Social Work*, Vol. 13, No. 2 (April, 1968).

9. Lippitt *et al.*, *op. cit.*

10. Burns and Glasser, *op. cit.*

11. Roland Warren, *The Community in America* (Chicago: Rand McNally & Co., 1963).

12. Purcell and Specht, *op. cit.*, p. 71.

13. Brager makes a similar point in his discussion of the appropriate use of manipulative behavior in social work practice (Brager, *op. cit.*).

14. See Lippitt *et al.*, *op. cit.*; Henry Maier, *Three Theories of Child Development* (New York: Harper and Row, 1965); Helen Harris Perlman, *Social Casework: A Problem Solving Process* (Chicago: The University of Chicago Press, 1957); Warren, *op. cit.*

15. Lippitt *et al.*, *op. cit.*; Warren, *op. cit.*

16. Lippitt *et al.*, *op. cit.*, p. 130.

17. For an example of this technique, see Sallie Churchill, "Social Group Work A Diagnostic Tool in Child Guidance," *American Journal of Orthopsychiatry*, Vol. 35, No. 3 (April, 1965).

18. Louis Lehrman, "The Logic of Diagnosis," *Social Casework*,

Vol. 35, No. 5 (May, 1954); Paul Meehl, *Clinical versus Statistical Prediction* (Minneapolis: University of Minnesota Press, 1954).

19. Henry Miller and Tony Tripodi, "Information Accrual and Clinical Judgment," *Social Work*, Vol. 12, No. 3 (July, 1967); Herbert Simon, *Administrative Behavior* (New York: The Free Press, 1959); Ben Orcutt, "A Study of Anchoring Effects in Clinical Judgment," *Social Service Review*, Vol. 38, No. 4 (December, 1964); Tony Tripodi and Henry Miller, "The Clinical Judgment Process: A Review of the Literature," *Social Work*, Vol. 11, No. 3 (July, 1966); Martin Wolins, "The Problem of Choice in Foster Home Finding," *Social Work*, Vol. 4, No. 4 (October, 1959).

20. See, for example, A. Z. Arthur, "A Decision-Making Approach to Psychological Assessment in the Clinic," *Journal of Consulting Psychology*, Vol. 30, No. 5 (October, 1966).

21. Charles Lindblom, "The Science of Muddling Through," *Public Administration Review*, Vol. 19, No. 2 (Spring, 1959).

22. Robert Vinter, "The Essential Components of Social Group Work Practice," *Readings in Group Work Practice* (Ann Arbor: Campus Publishers, 1967), p. 18.

23. Overton, *op. cit.*, p. 47.

25   Social Work in Search of a Radical Profession

MARTIN REIN

There is a great deal of interest today in the radicalization of professions. A restless search for relevance to public policy is being undertaken in social work, psychiatry, psychology, city planning, sociology, and political science, to name a few fields. One form that the radicalization is taking is to question afresh the role of the professional association in the area of public policy. In the last few years, this reassessment has been most striking. At the 1968 National Conference on Social Welfare, for example, black activists pressed the conference to change its preamble which defines the conference as a forum for discussion that "does not take an official position on controversial issues." The city planning profession has split recently into what Gans calls

Reprinted with permission of the National Association of Social Workers and of the author, from *Social Work*, 15 2 (April 1970): 13–28.

. . . the progressive and conservative wings: with the former calling for social planning to reduce economic and racial inequality, and the latter defending traditional physical planning and the legitimacy of middle class values.[1]

Sociologists seem especially vigorous in calling for a radical sociology. Gouldner's review of Parsons' book *American Sociology* captured the discontent seen at the 1968 Conference of the American Sociological Association. He quotes one angry sociologist who asserted:

The profession of sociology is an outgrowth of 19th century European traditionalism and conservatism wedded to 20th century American corporation liberalism. . . . The professional eyes of the sociologists are on the down people, and the professional palm of the sociologists is stretched toward the up people.[2]

Gouldner and Seeley define a radical social science as one critical of the emerging forms of the welfare state, which they view as a new social control system seeking "conformity as the price of welfare." Reform should not be limited to "melioristic efforts within the system," they hold, but should "develop alternatives to the *status quo*."[3]

The press for radicalization has taken another form as well. It is directed not only at extending the role of the professional as citizen and member of a professional organization, but at changing the very essence of his professional activity. In this sense we are witnessing today a search for radical professionalism rather than a quest for the professional who acts as a radical. Reassessment of the professional role is taking two major forms. The first is a reexamination of the profession's sources of legitimacy, a process that has been accompanied by a growing disenchantment with its avowed role as gatekeeper of tested knowledge. Some social workers are now trying to derive their legitimacy—their right to intervene—from the clients to be served, rather than from the technology they have accumulated. It is not uncommon to find in the new professional literature a call for social workers.

. . . [to] join with . . . clients in a search for and reaffirmation of their dignity. . . . Let us become mercenaries in their service—let us, in a word, become their advocates. . . .

Let our clients use us . . . to argue their cause, to maneuver, to obtain their rights and their justice, to move the immovable bureaucrats.[4]

This principle of accountability to the consumer departs from traditional professionalism, which has always been colleague oriented rather than client oriented, a distinction captured by Everett Hughes who defined a professional as someone respected by his colleagues and a quack as someone respected by his clients.

The second broad approach to radicalizing professional activity has been to advocate intervention in larger systems, such as the community, rather than in the life of the individual. Today community intervention is an idea in good currency among the helping professions. Witness the growth of community psychiatry, community psychology, and community organization in social work. One need only read such journals as *Psychiatry and Social Science, American Psychologist,* or *Social Work* to recognize this shift in the professions to social action with neighborhood groups. This shift will be discussed in further detail later and the author will argue that, by itself, community intervention represents an inadequate index of radical activity.

These two trends suggest a basis on which to elicit the creed of social work as a profession. But before proceeding, the obstacles to formulating a professional belief system will be discussed. It is hoped that a review of these impediments will serve as an introduction to a discussion of the development of a radical social work creed.

OBSTACLES TO A PROFESSIONAL CREED

Throughout social work literature, one finds references to the fact that social work is a value-laden profession. Hence it might seem an easy task to summarize the values that comprise its belief system and then explore the relevance of this creed to today's urban problems. But the literature deals with values only globally; the discourse is confined to a high level of abstraction. For example, there is the widely held proposition that each individual has dignity and worth. Surely this is an important statement but, unless its implications and consequences are drawn for professional practice, it is not a useful frame for action.[5]

What is more, social work literature contains the implicit assumption that there is a consensus on professional values and one must join in this consensus as a precondition for professional practice. All values are presented as though they were mutually reinforcing. The possibility of a conflict in values is never suggested although, in actuality, opposite sets of values are often embraced simultaneously. Timms, a prominent British social worker, notes:

> Caseworkers have asserted a faith in the potentialities of the human being to change himself and his society, whilst on the other hand, espousing a group of psychological theories which appear to place severe limitations on the capacity of individuals to change.[6]

One obstacle, then, is to recognize that the values in a professional creed are problematic rather than self-evident and that they frequently conflict.

Another obstacle arises from the difficulty of defining the profession. What, after all, is social work? An exhaustive study of social work education in the early 1950s concluded that "social work and social workers should be looked upon as evolving concepts that are as yet too fluid for precise definition."[7] By the late 1960s this fluidity had hardly become solidified. Indeed, to the extent that social work is involved in a fundamental reassessment of its major organizing principles, it is even more fluid today than it has been in the past. Because social workers serve as policy planners, reformers, social critics, and clinicians, it is difficult to identify the single professional creed that binds together these diverse activities.

A further problem in identifying the professional creed arises from the inability to separate clearly the procedural and substantive aspects of professional activity. Social work, like other professions, was influenced by the pragmatism of John Dewey. Dewey stressed the continuity of experience and the importance of process. In accord with this formulation, means and ends became blurred, professional technology became defined in terms of process, and social workers came to emphasize method and neglect purpose. Hence it is exceedingly difficult to find out what social workers believe and what they are trying to accomplish. There is nothing more challenging to a social agency than to ask what its objective is. The emphasis on process rather than outcome tends to obscure the role of ideology. What social workers believe must be inferred from what they say and do.

The last obstacle to be discussed is the disparity between rhetoric and reality, between what professionals say and do. A failure to implement ideals runs through the history of social work. The field developed out of a deterrent ideology, which sought alternatives to sending poor persons to the workhouse and would permit them to stay in the community while at the same time keep welfare rolls low. A common practice underlying the celebrated Elberfield system in Germany, the work of Thomas Chalmers, and the later activities of the Charity Organization Society was the use of strict investigation and close supervision of paupers as a way of making life on the dole uncomfortable and intolerable. So harsh were the ideals of political economy on which the social work ideology of the nineteenth century was based that it is not surprising to discover that humanitarianism and common sense inhibited their full expression. Reality and rhetoric diverge today as well. For example, social workers may believe that a precondition of good casework is full employment, a decent income, adequate social services, and a sound physical environment. But if this rhetoric were insisted upon, there would be no casework for the poor.

From a review of these obstacles, it seems reasonable to conclude that the search for a single, common professional creed is illusory. There are many creeds and many belief systems. The question now becomes: What are the critical components of the multiple belief systems? The author thinks these may be found in an examination of the different orientations in social work to behavioral goals and change processes.

STANDARDS OF BEHAVIOR

Norms and standards can be examined from several perspectives —standards that judge client, professional, or organizational behavior. In this analysis, the primary focus will be on the standards or norms of acceptable social behavior to which social work clients are held accountable. From this focus, the author is examining the social purposes of social work practice. What then are these norms? As Titmuss has astutely observed:

The attitudes that society adopts to its deviants, and especially its poor and politically inarticulate deviants, reflects its ultimate values. . . . We must learn to understand the moral presuppositions underlying our action.[8]

One of the principal moral presuppositions underlying social work practice in this country has been acceptance of society's linkage of work and income. With the exception of keeping women and the aged out of the labor force during the Depression, social workers have supported those policies designed to get the able-bodied poor to work. Industrial society is organized around the preservation of the middle-class ethic that rewards the industrious. But are there criteria by which to judge men other than market-productivity standards? To respect the dignity of man and to assert that each man has inherent value must clearly repudiate these dominant norms.

Since the issue of conformity to established standards is so crucial a component of a professional creed, it requires further discussion. For example, school performance is judged by the individual's ability to meet competitive standards (based on mastery of a body of information) and socialization for achievement. The ideal of helping people reach whatever level of performance they are capable of, i.e., self-actualization without reference to minimum standards, is a radical ideal that challenges accepted social standards. Teachers and social workers know that educational attainment largely determines life chances and they strive to do what they can to equip their pupils and clients to compete. Hence they are naturally attracted to those most likely to succeed, those whose achievements will reward the social workers' and teachers' efforts. It is, after all, not perversity but realism that leads professionals to make this assessment. The school cannot care equally for the education of every child, whatever his skill, unless society values all men for whatever contributions they can make. And this, our performance-market-productivity-oriented society is unwilling to ensure.

Social workers must choose whether to help individuals meet prevailing standards or whether to challenge the standards themselves. If they choose to challenge values, they cannot do so by creating new ones. As professionals they must show that established norms conflict with other still more fundamental values in the society or that they are inconsistent or irrelevant to the specific task at hand.

In most situations, there is an overwhelming urge to bypass the issue altogether, with the argument that happiness and self-fulfillment can only be achieved when individuals conform to the standards of the society. Thus, helping people conform to the work ethic in our society assures their contentment because the conforming man is the happy man. This dubious proposition is lucidly challenged in The People Specialists, a book about the human relations movement in industry. Personnel men share much in common with social workers. The personnel movement has two conflicting roots—one in scientific management, which was concerned with the study of men at work to determine how their material output could be best increased, the other in social welfare, which was concerned with improving the workers' levels of living. Which aim were the personnel workers to accept: "to make workers more productive or to make them happier?" Personnel theory, like social work theory, proceeded under the assumption that to do one is to do the other. But as the author shows, "there is no clear evidence to support any direct relationship between high morale and high productivity." Indeed, there is some contradictory evidence:

> In most corporations maturity is not a prized quality. On the contrary, the infantile qualities of passivity, dependence, submissiveness seem to be the hallmarks of "good employees."[9]

This is not an abstract philosophical debate. Most social work practice whether in industry, prisons, probation, public welfare, or mental health must accept the conflict between the individual's needs and the imposed and often arbitrary standards of society. When such conflicts arise, social workers must decide whether they support or challenge these established standards. Of course, some may try to define themselves as neutral arbitrators between contending parties. A radical ideal holds that the social worker must choose sides and is obliged to protect the individual against the system.

Industrial social work, which never fully blossomed in the United States, had to make such a choice. The difference between the French and Indian schemes illustrates the general dilemma. The French hired social workers on the assumption that happy workers were productive because they came to work regularly and were not distracted by marital, health, or other problems. In India it was assumed that the firm had more power than the individual and there was a natural tendency for power to corrupt. Hence the individual needed to be protected against this more powerful system. The social worker's role was to even out the odds.

INTERVENTION STRATEGIES

Theories of change can be divided into two broad categories.[10] There are those that accept social conditions as a constraint and conclude that change must start within the individual. They are based on the premise that if the individual himself would only change, he would be able to move toward altering the external resources in the social environment. By contrast, other theories treat external conditions as the targets of change, rather than as constraints. Their argument is that man cannot change until the world he lives in is transformed. His material circumstances must change first because man's emotional responses are adaptations to the external circumstances in which he lives.

This distinction should be made as concretely as possible because what is implied are two alternative courses of action. As an example, the dichotomy just drawn will be applied to the area of manpower policy for disadvantaged groups. One approach emphasizes the necessity of direct efforts to modify the attitudes of the disadvantaged before introducing them into job situations. This is based on the principle of preparing people in advance for a change in their environment. The other approach brings the subemployed into a job situation first, thus changing their occupational environment as a precondition for individual change. Social services are then looked upon as supports to help the individual handle the demands of his new environment. This shift from preparation to support is important in understanding the role of social services and social work in manpower training programs.

One further approach must be mentioned. It is the position that change in the character of the individual can be brought about by the process of social action. As man organizes to change his world, he changes himself. This change theory is more subtle than the others. It appeals to the conservative-traditional camp as well, where it is more popularly known as a self-help ideology, by which individuals take action on their own behalf. There is radical and revolutionary support for it as well. In a thoughtful report on "Race Relations and Social Change," Coleman explains the revolutionary argument for participation, as revealed in the writings of Sorel, Sartre, and Mao Tse-Tung:

> Participation in revolutionary action transforms the previously apathetic masses, by giving them a goal and the hope of achieving the goal. The revolutionary action itself and the rewards of success it brings to hard work create men who are no longer bound by traditional customs, inhibited by ascribed authority patterns, and made apathetic by lack of hope. This psychological transformation, according to these authors, is a necessary prerequisite to the social and economic transforma-

tion. Applied to the case of Negroes in the United States, it would state that the real benefit of the civil rights movement is the psychological change it has produced and is producing in those Negroes active in it. A more radical application would be that only by engaging in a real revolution will Negroes be psychologically transformed in such a way that they can achieve their goals.[11]

But what if the external conditions do not succumb to action programs? This approach is not altogether explicit about this awkward question and how it might be resolved. One interpretation holds that even in failure, personality change can be achieved. The self-help position could argue that personal dignity is won by the process of striving to better one's conditions. Character is forged by the activity, rather than the outcome. The more radical position would appear to suggest that change can be brought about by the total submission of the individual in the collectivity. Although his material circumstances may not be altered, his social-psychological environment has nevertheless been dramatically altered. Although social change approaches are often considered inherently radical, they are not. The purposes of social intervention theories, whether revolutionary or conservative, can either be directed at freeing men to build new standards or encouraging them to accept standards of proscribed behavior. It is for this reason that an intervention strategy, separated from the *purposes* of intervention, does not provide the basis for a creed.

Carried to its logical conclusion, this distinction between changing individuals and changing social conditions tends to break down. A theory which asserts that the starting point for change is the individual is incomplete if it leaves out the political and hence environmental processes that have led to the creation of an organized effort to induce change in the individual. Moreover, the availability of an authentic helping person is in itself a change in the external environment if other human beings are accepted as environmental resources. Similarly, only considering a change in social conditions leaves out the intervening processes by which an altered world produces individual change. Why are some groups and individuals able to exploit changes in the external environment and others are not? Thus, when applied to specific situations, the distinction becomes less convincing, and most reasonable men prefer a more differentiated argument that specifies the conditions under which one or another theory of change is more appropriate. But in the absence of a scientific theory of change, passion and ideology have a rich soil in which to blossom. It is for this reason that in this paper these theories are treated as elements of an ideology.

It should be emphasized again that the important generalization which arises from these observations is that both individual and social change theories can be used either to accept or repudiate established standards of behavior. Strategies of change can be used for different goals and, therefore, both goal and process become inseparable components of an ideology.

By dichotomizing the two dimensions of standards and theories of intervention in a two-by-two table, it is possible to identify four major professional creeds. They are (1) traditional casework, (2) radical casework, (3) community sociotherapy, and (4) radical social policy. (See Figure 25.1.)

FIGURE 25.1
A Typology of Social Work Ideologies

Theories of Change

		Individual			Social Conditions
	Accept	Traditional Casework			Community Sociotherapy
Standards of Behavior			1	3	
			2	4	
	Challenge	Radical Casework			Radical Social Policy

TRADITIONAL CASEWORK

The literature of social casework abounds with references to helping the marginal, deviant, and mentally ill meet standards and, thereby, achieve self-actualization and fulfillment. That conformity is viewed as the road to self-fulfillment is evident.

As Davis pointed out, advice about life problems is given in terms of moral ideals rather than actual practice. It is assumed that "one can best secure mental health, best satisfy one's needs, by conforming."[12] The social worker is thus trapped into what Hughes has called the "fallacy of one hundred percentism"—the refusal to admit the possibility of less than complete acceptance of moral, legal, respectable norms for behavior.[13] It is not surprising then to find that Hamilton, perhaps the leading modern casework theoretician, describes the function of diagnostic casework as "adaptation to reality."[14] As Keith-Lucas pointed out, diagnostic casework "can be used to justify the caseworker's desire to urge or dwell on the moral standards of the community through identifying these with the client's 'reality.' "[15] Biestek makes the implications explicit:

> The important fact to a caseworker is that these standards
> are realities in the client's life. . . . The client's personal ad-
> justment must include a sound, realistic social adjustment, be-
> cause as an individual he lives in a definite social community.
> . . . The function of the caseworker is to help the client ac-
> cept and adjust to these standards.[16]

Thus, by falling prey to the fallacy of one hundred percentism, many caseworkers hold their clients to a higher standard of morality than the one to which the community itself adheres.

Throughout the literature of social work, a discerning reader can note that many social workers believe the task of social work is

> . . . to reconcile the poor to their station in life . . . to
> plaster up the sores of an unjust society . . . to get the grit
> out of the administrative machinery—to persuade recalcitrant
> old ladies to go into institutions, to empty urgently needed
> hospital beds, to chivvy rent arrears from difficult tenants.[17]

These are, after all, the various realities to which the clients of social work must adjust—the realities of the economy, racial injustice, and bureaucracy.[18] In an effort to discredit this interpretation of the social worker's function, Titmuss has pointed out that two question-able assumptions underlie the insistence on adaptation to reality.

> The first is that reality is something which the caseworker
> knows, but the client does not; the second is that if adaptation
> is genuinely to take place, reality must genuinely be accepted
> by the caseworker. The ultimate logic of this is to make the
> caseworker a prisoner of the collective *status quo*; conse-
> quently, she will have little or nothing to contribute to the
> shaping of the social policy; she will not, in fact, desire to do
> so.[19]

But this discussion of traditional social work is theoretical, being based only on what social workers say. Obviously, the literature may be subject to other interpretations. Only scattered empirical evidence is available on the attitudes and behavior of social workers, but these seem to support the author's exposition. The author has found no study directly concerned with the issue of getting clients to meet standards of behavior; studies deal with agency rules or, more generally, with personal values.

In 1967 Rossi et al. analyzed welfare workers in fifteen cities who worked primarily with Negro clients. They reported that their sample

> . . . came out about evenly split on making decisions largely based on agency rules or largely on the circumstances of the client. However, the breakdown by race showed the whites considerably more rigid, with fifty-four percent (as compared with forty percent of the Negroes) saying they usually obey the agency rules.[20]

Billingsley, in his study of professional child welfare workers in Boston, obtained data on the choices social workers make when their assessment of the needs of their clients conflicts with agency procedures. He discovered that "in spite of the social worker's intellectual and emotional commitment to meeting the needs of his clients," more than three-quarters complied with agency rules even when these conflicted with "the workers' own estimation of the needs of the client."[21]

McLeod and Meyer at the University of Michigan conducted a study in which they compared the values of professionals, nonprofessionals, and social work students on a number of issues. One of these dealt with belief in change versus tradition, that is, "the willingness to accept change as contrasted with the orientation that is committed to the traditional ways of the past." Their findings are suggestive. They found that the nontrained were oriented to the status quo (71 percent), but what was of special interest was the shift in values between those who were in training and those who were fully trained. Most students supported innovation while in training (54 percent), while most trained workers were committed to the status quo (52 percent).[22]

These findings are suggestive only, and it is hazardous to make firm generalizations based on them. They do appear however to indicate that the dominant value commitment and behavior of professional social workers supports in theory and practice a posture of getting others to meet standards of acceptable behavior. They reveal the extent to which social workers personally comply with bureaucratic norms even when these conflict with clients' needs.

RADICAL CASEWORK

Not all social workers are prisoners of the collective status quo when they work with individuals. Many overtly and covertly resist these pressures. Resistance to established norms can, as has been already suggested, take several forms. It can challenge the standards, either by appealing to other standards with which they conflict or by showing that the standards themselves are inconsistent and lead to contradictory and unintended consequences. A latent functional analysis, when properly done, is, after all, a form of muckraking or social criticism. Gouldner's critique of practices in adoption offers an illuminating example.

> Adoption agencies require or recommend that adoptive parents be of the same religion as the mother of the adopted child. What proof is there that this practice is desirable or effective either for the child or for the parents? In this instance, it seems probable that the policy derives not from evidence of its effectiveness at all but from the pressure of various interest groups.
>
> It may well be most injurious to a child to be adopted by parents of a religious persuasion similar to that of his biological mother, if members of this denomination regard illegitimacy with moral revulsion. . . . Yet, here, as in many other instances, agencies' practices are shaped by community pressures and legal requirements and do not rest on evidence of their effectiveness for the clients.[23]

Gouldner presents the hurtful consequences of certain adoption procedures in such a way that his statement becomes a useful instrument of social criticism. Critiques of this kind offer one framework from which a radical casework practice might emerge.

More typically, social workers try to activate those values that they accept as morally right and society accepts but fails to act on. They then organize their research and action to serve as moral witnesses, documenting the failure of society to implement the ideals it has already asserted in law or policy.

Another approach is suggested in the writing of Lichtenberg. In a discussion of the prerequisites necessary for the cure of the psychotic, he asserts:

> If we compare the organizing principles relevant to a therapeutic community with those embodied in the present day organization of the society, we discover that the principles underlying the therapeutic community are superior. . . . Equality, cooperation, openness and frankness between persons at all levels of authority, two-way flow of communication with whatever hierarchies exist, control of the governed not only over themselves but over those who govern, preoccupation with one's true feelings rather than with masking one's attitudes, confrontation with poor communication so that it does not escalate difficulties, sexual freedom, . . . all of which have been found to be essential ingredients of [the] therapeutic community.[24]

It is the structure of the community that is faulty, since it lacks what the psychotic requires for his cure. Lichtenberg clearly insists that the world must be changed if the emotionally disabled are to be cured. Of course, Freud's work, which had an enormous influence on social work practice, is a brilliant example of a systematic critique of and challenge to society's standards of sexuality and its principles of individual responsibility.

Casework practice then can challenge the standards of society by showing that they are irrelevant or have hurtful consequences, that valid and relevant standards are not implemented, or that the standards men live by are faulty.

But the discerning reader might well ask: Is radical casework an empty cell, logically plausible but nonexistent in reality? The author resists accepting this formulation, for he is convinced that radical casework does exist. One form that it takes is when the caseworker acts as an insurgent within the bureaucracy in which he is employed, seeking to change its policies and purposes in line with the value assumptions he cherishes. Caseworkers can act as rebels within a bureaucracy, humanizing its established procedures and policies. One cannot read the literature in social casework today without finding some examples of radical casework. In the writings of Briar, Miller, and Piliavin, one finds caseworkers repudiating the traditional norms of helping clients adapt to reality. They are at the frontier, trying to find ways to make a radical casework live.[25]

COMMUNITY SOCIOTHERAPY

Community sociotherapy has to do with the belief system which holds that such processes as organizing groups for self-help, protest, access to community facilities, or even revolution can create a transformation of the individual personality. Participation in social action is viewed as a sociotherapeutic tool. HARYOU-ACT, the Community Action Program in Harlem, put the argument as follows:

> If it is possible to establish a core program of social action, it would be reasonable to expect that the energies required, and which must be mobilized for constructive and desirable social change, would not then be available for anti-social and self-destructive patterns of behavior.[26]

The report claims, for example, that crime in Montgomery, Alabama, declined during the period of the civil rights protest.

This energy displacement theory was in an earlier period used to justify the notion that recreation reduced crime. It is a theory that explains how activism can be transformed into compliance. Other theories are also at hand, including claims for the positive effects on personal health of power, integration, cohesiveness, community competence, identity, and so forth. All of these have in common the proposition that as man tries to change his social condition, *he* changes in the process.

The attempt by sociologists to get social workers to use social action and self-help as strategies for promoting individual conformity has a long history. Part of the history that spans the twentieth century yet has a consistency in ideology which would almost suggest a linear theory in its evolution will now be reviewed. The first example is drawn from Znaniecki and Thomas's study of the Polish peasant written in 1918. The authors explain:

> It is a mistake to suppose that a "community center" established by American social agencies can in its present form even approximately fulfill the social function of a Polish parish. It is an institution imposed from the outside instead of being freely developed by the initiative and cooperation of the people themselves. . . . Its managers usually know little or nothing of the traditions, attitudes, and native language of the people with whom they have to deal . . . [Although] the

"case method" which consists in dealing directly and separately with individuals and families . . . may bring efficient temporary help to the individual, it does not continue the
social progress of the community nor does it possess much
preventive influence in struggling against social disorganization. Both of these processes can be attained only by organizing and encouraging social self-help on a cooperative basis.[27]

The argument is clear. Organizing and encouraging self-help will
reduce social disorganization. The failure to help the Polish immigrant conform to American standards, according to the authors'
criticism, is based on two factors—imposition by alien institutions,
which today is called "welfare colonialism," and the individual case
approach.

In the 1930s, the prescription for action took an organized form
in the Chicago Area Project under the leadership of Clifford Shaw
and Henry McKay, when a social action program was launched to
reduce crime and delinquency. It is perhaps of interest that Saul
Alinsky was a student of sociology at the University of Chicago at
the same time and, according to Morris Janowitz: "Some of his
notions of community action and organization are strikingly parallel
to those developed in this project."[28] Perhaps so, but it seems that
the distinguishing feature of this and the later programs the
Chicago project inspired is the absence of a political ideology and
the commitment to sociotherapeutic aims. In the 1940s, New York
University supported a project directed by Rudolph Wittenberg that
was designed to promote personality change through social action
in East Harlem. In the 1950s, New York City's Youth Board Gang
Project turned to community organization as a strategy to help
create an integrated community that could reduce crime and delinquency. In the 1960s, community organization as sociotherapy
can be found in Mobilization For Youth's program, which was
originally conceived as a delinquency prevention program and was
financed by the National Institute of Mental Health and the President's Committee on Delinquency and Youth Crime.[29]

The critique of social work in these examples was not directed
at the purposes of intervention, but at its effectiveness. Sociotherapy
was not a new ideology, but a new technology for getting marginal groups to meet standards. Znaniecki and Thomas's criticism
is not the established orthodoxy accepted by community psychiatry
and community psychology. Dumont, a psychiatrist at NIMH, com-
menting on the role of mental health programs in Model Cities,

asserts that "community organization is itself a major mental health service, an end in itself."[30] Scribner, while stressing the varied interests of "social action" pychologists, makes evident their common commitment to "social action without . . . political movements as forces of change." While the purposes of change are varied, they all center on different aspects of the problem of compliance—"correcting deviant behavior which interferes with individual progress, . . . controlling mass hysteria . . . or changing child-rearing practices. . . ."[31]

The concern for compliance through social action now seems to be taking a new turn. It is calling for an indirect strategy of involving the middle classes to control the lower classes, in whom it is assumed the roots of nonconformity to established standards grow. Glazer describes the Negro bourgeois as "the missing man in the present crisis." According to this thesis, black power, black capital, and black participation must mean the involvement of the Negro middle class rather than the Negro poor and disaffiliated groups.[32] Long develops the argument. He explains:

> The key question is whether there exists or can rapidly be produced sufficient middle class cadres to govern the black governed city. . . . The greatest fear clearly is that the middle class Negroes cannot dominate the lower class culture of Ghetto life.[33]

A change in social conditions is being called for to enable the middle-class Negro leadership to police its own poor more effectively. Apartheid in South Africa is justified on much the same grounds: by walling off the Negroes from white society, Negro leaders must police their own lower class. Social stability is more effective when imposed by indigenous institutions than by welfare colonialism.[34]

RADICAL SOCIAL POLICY

The link between social action and sociotherapy has been stressed in this paper because the author believes it is not widely understood and because it is the dominant pattern of the social environmentalist position today. But there is also evidence of a social action program that challenges the established standards of behavior and

also tries to replace existing institutions rather than merely trans-
ferring organizational slots from white to Negro leaders.

Perhaps the best known example of radical social action by a
social worker and a city planner who teach at a school of social
work is the work of Cloward and Piven in the welfare rights movement. Wilbur Cohen, Elizabeth Wickenden, and Winifred Bell
dominated the intellectual leadership in welfare policy. They were
committed to incrementalism as a strategy of change and liberalism
as a social philosophy. Cloward and Piven substituted a more radical
approach to social policy. Their *immediate* aim was not to improve
the social conditions of the welfare poor; they were not trying to
strengthen the welfare system, but rather to replace it. They believed that this apparent conflict of aims between improving conditions, which inhibits the urgency to introduce more fundamental
change, and disrupting the performance of an intolerable system
could be avoided in the case of welfare because an improved welfare system would be politically unacceptable. Amelioration would
lead to metamorphosis.[35]

While these are important tactical issues, they should not obscure
the essence of their radical creed, which is the commitment to redistribution, reducing inequalities, and altering social conditions—
political, economic, and social—as a precondition for individual
change. Cloward and Piven are not primarily concerned with the
problems of compliance, of getting individuals to meet standards or
promoting social stability. Rather, their emphasis is on altering institutions, redefining norms and purposes, and reassessing the
standards by which professional performance is judged.

The ideals of a radical profession must be able to find expression
in specific forms. Social workers already perform a great variety of
professional roles as reformers and organizers, policy analysts,
planners, researchers, consultants who are inside the bureaucracy,
critics who are outside the established system, and "insider-
outsiders," a role that enables them to be relevant, but critical. Like
all creeds, the radical creed may contain inconsistencies and contradictions. When rigidly applied, it can become dogma and theology. The function of a belief system is not to provide answers but
to offer goals and objectives toward which one's professional activities can be oriented.

Of the four professional creeds discussed in this paper, the author
has given more attention to traditional casework and community
sociotherapeutic ideologies because they are better developed and
experience has sharpened the understanding of them. It is not al-

together surprising that the more radical doctrines have failed to win wide support and hence remain at the margin of the profession. But the margin in one era may become the center of another.

PROFESSIONAL CREED AND URBAN PROBLEMS

Which of the professional creeds seems most appropriate to urban needs? America faces many urban crises—the crises of race, class, managerial competence, and financing services. While the problems overlap and reinforce each other, they must also be distinguished from each other.

The problem of race cannot be solved without a redistribution of authority, resources, and power. The problem of poverty requires a redistribution of income and resources. The issues of race and class need to be sorted out, and the trade-off between redistributing income and power (those aspects of the one goal that would be acceptable to proponents of the other goal) have to be clarified. The movement for school decentralization in New York City has by and large not demanded more resources for the ghetto, but only a different decision-making system.

What can be said about the relationship between professional doctrine and urban-racial problems? Which creeds are most relevant to this problem? In the search for a better solution to the problem of race, the liberal ideology, from which the spectrum of professional creeds previously examined are derived, has been assaulted. That the cherished beliefs about integration have been challenged is evident, but the insistence on separatism opens new issues. That the distribution of power among the social services is ethnically determined is a disquieting reality which has been long forgotten. Irish control of police, Italian control of sanitation, Jewish control of education, and perhaps Negro control over the new social services in community action agencies illustrate the neglected relation between service control and ethnicity. A redistribution of power may alter these established patterns. It has been relatively easy in ideological terms to accept a redistribution of power at the neighborhood level. A nineteenth-century leader of the settlement house movement asserted:

> Poverty, pauperism and other social evils could not be cured by alms, or by a redistribution of wealth, but only by creating [a] genuine neighborhood reestablished as a feature of civic life.[36]

Many still believe that creed today; for them the neighborhood remains a tool for sociotherapy.

But the great racial crisis will emerge as Negroes and other ethnic groups insist on a redistribution of power not by "turf," but by function. The struggle for power over education in New York City has already opened up the question of who controls the social services. For many Negroes, control of the social services offers a much better leverage for the redistribution of power than does control over economic institutions. The accountability system in the social services has always been vulnerable. The demonstrated weaknesses of elite accountability, democratic accountability, and professional accountability are already evident. We may be witnessing a new demand for ethnic and racial accountability.

The traditional and community sociotherapeutic belief systems, on which professional social work ideology rests, will not be able to cope easily with ideological issues that the crisis of race has already presented. A more adequate creed will have to be developed if the profession wishes to be relevant to the issues of race.

Poverty cannot be dealt with simply in terms of overcoming apathy through more intelligent service or through social action programs, however dedicated. What is needed is a national redistribution of resources that deliberately redresses the imbalance of opportunities between rich and poor communities, between Negro and white communities. Sociotherapeutic approaches, whether individual or social, run the risk of deceiving themselves and others if they function without a complementary national reform.

A dispassionate analysis of current social policy would confirm the conclusion that social work programs have been used as a substitute for more searching policies to redistribute income, power, and resources. There is a perverse tendency in American social reform to repudiate social work and then to embrace the very ideals that have been rejected. The Economic Opportunity Act stressed institutional change initiated by the poor. Shriver harshly reprimanded the social work community at the 1965 National Conference on Social Welfare for social work's preoccupation with individualized methods and failure to reach the poor.[37] Yet as Kahn observed:

> The heart of the community action program is in the field of individual remediation help, retraining, counseling and aid. . . . A social-change strategy, thus, continues to require case

and individual elements, and political realities may even render individual services primary despite ideological commitment.[38]

Community sociotherapy and traditional casework appear to have a stubborn vitality. The more they are rejected, the more they seem to survive, flourish, and expand. In the author's judgment, the viability of the professional doctrine that emphasizes therapeutic solutions has produced a great dilemma in American society insofar as the solution of poverty is concerned because it seems that social policies have been based on it. Accordingly, we have tried to stimulate the economic participation of the poor through training to support the work ethic, employability and counseling programs, and citizen participation, but have failed to develop an economic policy to achieve social objectives. In short, social policies have been generated to meet economic aims, but economic policies have not been used to meet social ends. Thus America lacks a policy of using up its available labor force or redistributing income among poor individuals and resources among low-income communities. Social work doctrine has inhibited the profession from openly repudiating the claim that casework can reduce dependency and social work can contribute to the reduction of poverty.

CONCLUSIONS

Social work, by itself, has almost nothing to contribute to the reduction of the interrelated problems of unemployment, poverty, and dependency. Therefore, if you interpret social work as radical social policy committed to altering political and economic institutions that affect well-being (on the assumption that social welfare activities to compensate individuals for the diseconomies generated by the political and economic system have been insufficient), then it ceases to be social work. Individual social workers may, of course, function as reformers in the areas of employment, income redistribution, and political power, but these activities are marginal to their professional tasks. In this sense, they are professionals who are radical rather than members of a radical profession. In recognition of this dilemma, some social workers have urged that the present profession be forsaken and a new one built that is committed to the problems of inequality of wealth, power, authority, and so forth and to strategies of redistribution. These major unresolved problems of public policy also touch the limits of the contribution of social science to social purpose. Hence it is especially crucial that the problem not become subordinated to methodology. But in this broader area of social reform, social work will need to compete with new programs that have been developed at such universities as Harvard, the Massachusetts Institute of Technology, the University of Michigan, the State University of New York at Buffalo, and the University of California at Berkeley and have been variously called public policy, public affairs, social policy, and urban policy. Can social work recruit able students, attract competent faculty, and win institutional resources and support to embark on this new venture and compete with these new centers of training? It clearly has not done so in the past. Whether past history is a prelude to the future must remain an open question.

What can social work do short of full repudiation of its present mission? It can contribute greatly to improving the quality of urban life, humanizing institutions, and altering the priority of social values. It can perhaps implement these objectives by defining its present mission more broadly, and it must do so in terms of the way it interprets its clients' needs. A radical casework approach would mean not merely obtaining for clients social services to which they are entitled or helping them adjust to their environment, but also trying to deal with the relevant people and institutions in the clients' environment that are contributing to their difficulties. That is to say, social workers must get the school to adjust to the needs of poor children as well as getting poor children to adjust to the demands and routines of the schools. They must force landlords to maintain their clients' housing as well as helping poor families to find somewhere to live. They must get public welfare agencies to change their procedures to make it easier to use welfare as a resource for help, as well as helping clients fulfill the requirements of the welfare bureaucracy. In short, then, a radical casework approach would mean not merely obtaining for the clients the services to which they are entitled or helping them adapt to the expectations of their environment, but it would also encourage the individuals to alter their external circumstances as well as seeking directly to change the framework of expectation and the level of provision that are contributing to these difficulties. Social workers need to emphasize skill in practicing casework in a hostile rather than a benign environment—casework that is directed not so much at encouraging conformity (adjustment to reality) but to marshaling the resources of clients to challenge "reality."

As social work moves away from altering the environment on behalf of a given client to altering the environment in general without reference to a specific client, it moves to social reform and to the boundaries of its main concern. Action at the boundary is crucial and should be encouraged, but it should not lead, as it has done, to the neglect of its center. If we try to redefine the present margin so that it becomes the new center of social work activity, then we accept the position that social work must move toward a radical social policy approach. However, a radical casework approach may prove, in the end, to be the more enduring strategy to pursue.

NOTES

1. Herbert Gans, "Social Planning: Regional and Urban Planning," *International Encyclopedia of the Social Sciences*, Vol. 12 (New York: Macmillan Co. & Free Press, 1968), p. 135.

2. Alvin Gouldner, book review of Talcott Parsons, ed., *American Sociology* (New York: Basic Books, 1968), *Science* (October 11, 1968), p. 247.

3. Letter by Alvin Gouldner and Jack Seeley to Frank Riessman, New York University, September 10, 1968. A conference on "Revitalizing Social Science" was held at New York University on October 14, 1968, to discuss the letter. This conference may be considered as a first meeting of representatives of the radical caucuses of the various social science associations. There is interest in creating a policy-oriented magazine and an organization. Unity on the left may be hard to maintain, as it always has been, but a start appears to have been made.

4. Henry Miller, "Value Dilemmas in Social Casework," *Social Work*, Vol. 13, No. 1 (January 1968), p. 33. Social workers are also dismayed by the criticism that casework "*systematically* excludes many of the persons most in need of attention [and even] when properly applied to persons disposed to use it," is ineffective. See Scott Briar, "The Casework Predicament," *Social Work*, p. 6, same issue. To meet these charges, the field has shifted its emphasis from the application of tested knowledge and accepted standards of "sound" practice to experimentation. Demands for innovation, experimentation, and accountability to service-users all illustrate a willingness to challenge established standards of practice.

5. Consider the recent debate on whether war-injured Vietnamese children should be brought to the United States for medical treatment. The National Association of Social Workers' Commission on International Social Welfare asserted that such a plan disregards a basic child welfare principle that "children have the right to grow

up in their own families in their own cultures." Such a conclusion, Kelman explains, has political consequences, for it supports the United States "government's desire not to call attention to civilian casualties of the war in Vietnam." Moreover, the preservation of life is a more important value, Kelman asserts, than respect for cultural diversity. Rose B. Kelman, "Vietnam: A Current Issue in Child Welfare," *Social Work*, Vol. 13, No. 4 (October 1968), p. 20.

6. Noel Timms, *Social Casework, Principles and Practices* (London, England: Routledge & Kegan Paul, 1964), p. 61.

7. Florence V. Hollis and Alice L. Taylor, *Social Work Education in the United States* (New York: Columbia University Press, 1951), p. 54.

8. Richard Titmuss, Foreword, in Noel Timms and H. F. Philips, *The Problem of the Problem Family* (London, England: Family Service Units, 1962), p. vi.

9. Stanley M. Herman, *The People Specialists* (New York: Alfred A. Knopf, 1968).

10. For this distinction the author has relied heavily on James S. Coleman, "Conflicting Theories of Social Change." (Mimeographed by the author, 1967).

11. James S. Coleman, "Race Relations and Social Change" (Baltimore: Johns Hopkins University, July 1967), p. 17. (Mimeographed.)

12. Kingsley Davis, "Mental Hygiene and the Class Structure," in Herman D. Stein and Richard Cloward, eds., *Social Perspectives on Behavior* (Glencoe, Ill.: Free Press, 1958), p. 334.

13. Everett Hughes, unpublished lecture, Brandeis University, 1961.

14. Hamilton is sensitive to the awkward moral problem that arises when casework practice emphasizes adjustment. Therefore, she tries to distinguish between adjustment and acquiescence, emphasizing that casework helps "the client to identify what is real." But there is no systematic treatment of what is reality or how acquiescence could be achieved without adjusting to one's situation. See Gordon Hamilton, *Theory and Practice of Social Case Work* (2d., rev.; New York: Columbia University Press, 1951), p. 237.

15. Alan Keith-Lucas, *Decisions About People in Need: A Study of Administrative Responsiveness in Public Assistance* (Chapel Hill: University of North Carolina Press, 1957), p. 143.

16. Felix J. Biestek, "The Principles of Client Self-Determination," *Social Casework*, Vol. 32, No. 9 (November 1951), p. 374.

17. D. V. Donnison in a book review of Barbara Wootton, *Social Science and Social Pathology* (New York: Humanities Press, 1959), *The Almoner*, Vol. 12, Nos. 4, 5, and 6 (July, August, and September 1959), p. 172, notes that "the social workers who have to resist these pressures often work in isolated and exposed positions."

18. For a similar criticism, see C. Wright Mills's famous study, "The Professional Ideology of Social Pathologists," *American Journal of Sociology*, Vol. 35, No. 2 (September 1949), pp. 179–180. Pathologists are sociologists who write textbooks about social problems. Mills believed that "these writers typically assume the norms which they use and often tacitly sanction them. There are few attempts to explain deviations from norms in the terms of norms themselves, and no rigorous facing of the implications of the fact that social transformations would involve shifts *in them*. . . . If the 'norms' were examined, the investigator would perhaps be carried to see total structures of norms and to relate these to distributions of power."

19. Richard Titmuss, *Commitment to Welfare* (London, England: Allen & Unwin, 1968), p. 42.

20. Peter Rossi et al., *Between White and Black: The Faces of American Institutions in the Ghetto* (Baltimore: Johns Hopkins Press, 1968), p. 144.

21. Andrew Billingsley, "Bureaucratic and Professional Orientation Patterns in Social Casework," *Social Service Review*, Vol. 38, No. 4 (December 1964), pp. 402–403.

22. Donna L. McLeod and Henry J. Meyer, "A Study of the Values of Social Workers," in Edwin J. Thomas, ed., *Behavioral Science for Social Workers* (New York: Free Press, 1967), Table 30–2, p. 409.

23. Alvin Gouldner, "The Secrets of Organizations," *The Social Welfare Forum, 1963* (New York: Columbia University Press, 1963), p. 167.

24. Philip Lichtenberg, "And the Cure of Psychosis Is for Us All," pp. 12–13. Unpublished manuscript, Bryn Mawr, Pa., 1968.

25. See, for example, Briar, *op. cit.*, pp. 5–11; Miller, *op. cit.*, pp. 27–33; and Irving Piliavin, "Restructuring the Provision of Social Services," *Social Work*, Vol. 13, No. 1 (January 1968), pp. 34–41.

26. *Youth in the Ghetto: A Study of the Consequences of Powerlessness* (New York: Harlem Youth Opportunities Unlimited, 1964).

27. Florian Znaniecki and W. L. Thomas, *The Polish Peasant in Europe and America*, Vol. 11 (Boston: Gorham Press, 1918), pp. 15–26.

28. Many of the observations in this section are based on an interview with Morris Janowitz. He later developed his insights in "A Note on Sociology and Social Work" (Chicago: University of Chicago, undated), p. 3. (Mimeographed.)

29. For a further analysis of community organization as sociotherapy, see Peter Marris and Martin Rein, *Dilemmas of Social Reform* (New York: Atherton Press, 1967), p. 167.

30. Mathew P. Dumont, "A Model Community Mental Health

Program for a Model Cities Area" (Washington, D.C.: Center for Community Planning, U.S. Department of Health, Education & Welfare, August 1967), p. 3. (Mimeographed.)

31. Sylvia Scribner, "What Is Community Psychology Made Of?" American Psychological Association, Division of Community Psychology, Newsletter, Vol. 11, No. 1 (January 1968), p. 5.

32. Nathan Glazer, "The Problem with American Cities," New Society, March 21, 1968, p. 3.

33. Norton Long, "Politics and Ghetto Perpetuation," in Roland L. Warren, ed., Politics and the Ghettos (New York: Atherton Press, 1969).

34. For a discussion of the conservative argument for Black Power, see Martin Rein, "Social Stability and Black Ghettoes," in ibid.

35. See, for example, Richard A. Cloward and Frances Fox Piven, "A Strategy to End Poverty," The Nation, Vol. 202, No. 18 (May 2, 1966).

36. Quoted in Roy Lubove, The Professional Altruist: The Emergence of Social Work as a Career (Cambridge, Mass.: Harvard University Press, 1965), p. 15.

37. Sargent Shriver, "Poverty in the United States—What Next?" The Social Welfare Forum, 1965 (New York: Columbia University Press, 1965), pp. 55–66.

38. Alfred J. Kahn, "From Delinquency Treatment to Community Development," in Paul Lazarsfeld et al., eds., The Uses of Sociology (New York: Basic Books, 1967), p. 497.

26   The Deprofessionalization of Social Work

HARRY SPECHT

The social work profession is undergoing fundamental change and may even be approaching its denouement. The purpose of this article is to explain this dour prognosis by examining ideological currents in which the profession is adrift—activism, anti-individualism, communalism, and environmental determinism—and to conclude with some comments about possible reclassifications of pro-

Reprinted with permission of the National Association of Social Workers, from Social Work, 17 (March 1972): 3–15.

fessional social work should these currents carry us in the direction indicated.[1]

What evidence supports these dismal prospects for social work? First, increasing numbers of social work functions are being performed by non-MSWs, such as new careerists, paraprofessionals, subprofessionals, and social workers with bachelor's degrees. The great expansion in social work training is not taking place at the MSW level, but at the BA and AA levels.[2] Government is increasingly reluctant to support graduate social work education or to hire professional social workers.[3] There is no reason to believe that when the economic and political situation improves, MSWs will be among those returning to their old jobs.

Second, there is no professional group about which there is such universal disenchantment. Who has anything positive to say about professional social workers? Clients? Certainly not the mainstay of social work clients—the poor and the minorities. Government? not likely. Once a reform era has ended, social workers—who were utilized as bureaucrats during the liberal reform period—are considered, in Lubove's phrase, "professional altruists," who serve government as ineffectual consciences-in-residence.[4] As caretakers for the lame and blind, they also serve an important social function, always well meaning and at times appreciated for their development of an ideology and set of practical skills geared to the amelioration of human suffering. More recently, however, many professional altruists have become political activists, and this is a transformation the government will neither accept nor forgive. Whom does that leave? The blue- and white-collar workers and the hard hats of middle America do not think the profession offers any benefit to them and probably perceive they are held in contempt by its more militant and outspoken members.

There is one other source to which social workers might have turned for support against their detractors, that is, the profession itself, through its official bodies—the National Association of Social Workers (NASW), Council on Social Work Education (CSWE), National Conference on Social Welfare, and schools of social work. But when political activism became fashionable, it was welcomed warmly from within.

The outcome of the downgrading of professionalism need not necessarily be feared and may prove to have felicitous consequences for social welfare services and the people who benefit from them. That is, one outcome of these trends may be the parting of social work and social welfare, the consequences of which will be discussed later.

Some readers may conclude that the vision of contemporary social work presented in this paper is shaped considerably by the author's location in Berkeley, California. And some, who live in areas that are not near a university, may find there is nothing in their current professional experience to which these comments are germane. However, Berkeley has more than once been the seat of an inauguration of trends, fads, and movements that have swept the nation. Armour, a poet, noting the premonitory significance of events in the Golden State, said:

> So leap with joy, be blithe and gay,
> Or weep, my friends, with sorrow.
> What California is today,
> The rest will be tomorrow.[5]

Special attention will be given to the effects and evidence of these trends in social work education. While life in the academy may not be the primary concern of the profession, it is the place where one must look to see what future professionals may be like. In a few years, the beliefs, attitudes, and behaviors of students will have an enormous impact on the field. Those who are unaware of the disarray and confusion that current trends have brought about in professional education are in for a few surprises when they meet the generation practicing the "new" social work.

ACTIVISM

Causes aside, it is the passionate but uninformed quest for "relevance" and activism that has helped convince others of social workers' naïvete. Stein has commented on these aims as follows:

> The cry for greater impact reflects the wish that the profession represent movers and shakers. . . . However, the frustration at our not having all that muscle leads not to scaling down our aspiration, but to intensifying our commitment to social change and social reform—in other words to enhancing the accent on ideology. Yet, ideology without the means to achieve ends—without competence and institutionalized means

to translate that competence into action—is futile for a profession. . . .

Vital and essential convictions . . . do not constitute ideology sufficient for purposeful direction.[6]

Compare this view with the fact that almost every candidate for national office in the 1971 NASW election was committed and ready to attack "institutional racism." Veblen referred to these kinds of words as "honorific," sentiments with which all would like to be baptized.[7] "Fighting institutional racism" is an excellent example of dogma without content, for we have yet to develop a clear understanding of what the term means.

Where is this so-called social work militance seen? By and large, not in the professional journals except the *Journal of Education for Social Work*. Although *Social Work* and *Social Service Review* have given space to divergent ideas, they maintain a balanced level of argument and their articles are thoughtful and critical. The trend is most evident in the public presentations of the profession, at conferences and institutes, and in the schools of social work. These provide the public forums that allow for personal confrontations, harassment, and intimidation—techniques that are particularly successful when used by a vocal minority against an opponent who is apologetic, confused, and timid.

It is extremely difficult for social workers to be critical of a left-oriented movement for social change today, especially one led by the young and the minorities. There is great pressure to remain united in our shared outrage over Vietnam and other imperialist ventures, racial and economic inequality in our society, lack of planning in the use of resources to solve urban problems, and the social system that supports these evils. But in the end we cannot expect the nation to become moral and responsible by treating issues immorally and irresponsibly. No matter how much we admire the moral fiber and courage of our children and our students—and even if one makes the *personal* choice to join them in their legal and illegal struggles for social justice—the profession can continue only as long as it assumes the responsibilities and authority of a profession.

The attributes of a profession, too complex to discuss in detail here, have been described by Greenwood.[8] They are (1) skills that flow from and are supported by a fund of knowledge organized into an internally consistent system called a "body of theory," (2) professional authority to practice specific functions, (3) sanction of the community, (4) a regulatory code of ethics, and (5) a professional culture. Professional politicians, lawyers, and social workers have this set of attributes, but the characteristics of each set differ. Advocacy and activism, if they are to be useful, must not be cast in the image of law or politics; rather, they must be developed as functions or techniques that are articulated with the knowledge, authority, sanction, culture, and professional ethics of social work. Advocacy and activism are still undeveloped as professional social work practice, but the profession nonetheless rushes to claim mastery of these new functions.

The political activists have a compelling rationale for revising the notions of what social work practice should be. This view encourages social workers to throw off the chains that have bound them to established institutions. But it embodies the notion of exchanging one set of chains for another. Miller makes a passionate plea for the new chains when he says:

> Let us become mercenaries in [our client's] service—let us, in a word, become their advocates. . . . Let our clients use us . . . to argue their cause, to maneuver, to obtain their rights and their justice, to move the immovable bureaucrats.[9]

Thus the social worker-advocate is as thoroughly bound by ideological commitments as the bureaucratic social worker is by organizational loyalties. Grosser discusses the practice of advocacy in more detail:

> The impartiality of the enabler and the functionalism of the broker are absent. Nor is the worker expert, consultant, guide or social therapist. He is, in fact, a partisan in social conflict. His expertise is available exclusively to serve client interests, since other actors in this social conflict may be using their expertise and resources against the client.[10]

Thus, the worker functions as a sort of half-baked lawyer or junior politician and the conception vigorously eschews the unique functions that professional social workers do have the expertise to handle. This attempt to borrow what appear to be the more potent knowledge and skills of professional lawyers and politicians is not unlike an earlier generation of social workers' efforts to fashion themselves in the image of psychoanalysts. The result, in this case, is likely to be even more disastrous.

The hallmark of a professional social worker is not his readiness to identify himself with a cause that supersedes fealty to any other. Rather, it is his desire and *ability* to proffer help to clients—rich or poor, black or white, oppressed, depressed, repressed, or whatever —within a *framework of ethics and values*.

Politicians and social workers operate from different knowledge bases and ethical frameworks, and these differences partly characterize the two groups. The distinction between politics and professional social work has become somewhat blurred in recent years because a self-righteous and sanctimonious "commitment to social justice" has replaced a rigid and sanctified "commitment to professional practice." There is no simple way to achieve professionalism that can avoid the struggle of complexities inherent in reconciling both sets of commitments. The new activist spirit in social work downgrades professional practice, which it defines as ineffective in dealing with social problems. In place of professionalism the activists offer the idea that revolution will create change more rapidly than social work practice, which may be correct. But this is not what the profession prepares one to do, nor should it.

ANTI-INDIVIDUALISM

Social workers are not responsible for the remarkable changes in society that have caused practice to be disparaged. But the profession has embraced all the trends that will lead to its undoing with a vigor not seen since Jane Addams's day.

Addams, however, was moved by a different spirit than today's social workers. She represented, above all, the spirit of individualism at its finest, a spirit that enabled her to spearhead many radical social ideas in the face of opposition from all political quarters. She frequently found herself alone, accused by an enraged community of abetting anarchy because she demanded justice for all or of being unpatriotic because she was a staunch pacifist throughout World War I. She knew the difficulty of living by principles:

> Partisans would never tolerate the use of stepping-stones. They are much too impatient to look on while their beloved scheme is unstably balanced, and they would rather see it tumble into the stream at once than have it brought to dry land in any such half-hearted fashion. . . . Life had taught me at least one hard-earned lesson, that existing arrange-

ments and the hoped for improvements must be mediated and reconciled to each other, that the new must be dovetailed into the old as it were, if it were to endure; . . . I discerned that all such efforts were looked upon as compromising and unworthy by both partisans.[11]

These ideas are cited as examples of individualism, although the term is more often used to refer to unbridled economic competition. Both aspects of individualism emerged during the Protestant Reformation, a time when capitalism freed the individual from the rigid confines of feudalism and left him the master of his own fate, to succeed or fail by his individual effort. The Protestant ethic, which developed after the Renaissance as part of a religious outlook consonant with the spirit of capitalism, views man's nature as evil and sees him powerless before God, required to strive incessantly to achieve so that he may gain salvation.

Fromm documented the psychological burdens that freedom and isolation impose on man and the various forms of escape men seek in communality. He saw nazism as a new bondage—as one means of fulfilling the emotional needs of a powerless and resentful population. But he thought, too, that some aspects of the fascist ideology are endemic to Western society:

> The fact of human individuation, of the destruction of all "primary bonds," cannot be reversed. The process of the destruction of the medieval world had taken four hundred years and is being completed in our era. Unless the whole industrial system, the whole mode of production, should be destroyed and changed to the pre-industrial level, man will remain an individual who has completely emerged from the world surrounding him. We have seen that man cannot endure this negative freedom; that he tries to escape into new bondage which is to be a substitute for the primary bonds which he has given up. But these new bonds do not constitute real union with the world. He pays for the new security by giving up the integrity of his self.[12]

There are many benefits to be derived from a shift away from individualism: the rejection of materialistic values, the refusal to measure man solely in competition with his brothers, the rejection of the notion that low social status reflects inherent inferiority, and the growing rebellion against national self-aggrandizement and war. But in supporting these changes, let us not rush headlong from the competition and alienation of individualistic ideology to a rejection of individual judgment and choice. For we will have lost a great deal if we abdicate responsibility for assessing our behaviors and for being aware of the dangers as well as the benefits to society of the alternatives we choose. The abandonment of responsibility results in the kind of glorification of deviant, criminal, and retreatist behavior that has become increasingly evident in the practice of some social workers, particularly those engaged in grass-roots organizing and community mental health.[13] It is difficult, but both possible and desirable, to support just and decent treatment of "street people" and drug-abusers, and to champion prison reform, while at the same time avoiding moral ambiguity in regard to socially destructive behavior.

COMMUNALISM

Just as anti-individualism rejects the authority of the old institutions to make judgments, so it exalts the values of a new communalism. The "group will" has become the higher value, and appeals made in its name often assume automatic priority, the lessons of history notwithstanding. The following statement shows the potential power of such an appeal:

Sometimes one is gripped by a deep depression. One can only overcome it, if one is in front of the masses again. The people are the fountain of our power.[14]

The quote is from Goebbels, Hitler's minister of propaganda. He might have added, "Power to the People!"

It is interesting to speculate further on the relationship of these trends to the current popularity of the encounter group, both in and outside the profession. Although offered as a means of achieving individual fulfillment, the encounter group clearly functions to relieve the burden of individual loneliness and gives primacy to the group as arbiter of how a person expresses himself and deals with others. Rogers, the high priest of the process, describes it as follows:

One of the threads is the increasing impatience with defenses. As time goes on the group finds it unbearable that any

member should live behind a mask or front. . . . The expression of self by some members of the group has made it
very clear that a deeper and more basic encounter is possible,
and the group appears to strive intuitively and unconsciously
toward this goal. Gently at times, almost savagely at others,
the group demands that the individual be himself, that his current feelings not be hidden, that he remove the mask of ordinary social intercourse.[15]

Throughout the new counterculture and even in the communes
themselves, the contradictory appeals to a new group identification
and to the old loyalties to the state are straining against the values
of individualism. Thus American individualism is not easily denied,
and much as the more politically minded revolutionaries and activists have tried to avoid it, they have often had to carry the burden
of such undisciplined allies as Jerry Rubin, a hazard with which
neither Mao nor Castro had to contend.

Although all the implications of such a movement are as yet unclear, some major questions have already emerged. According to
Marcuse, there is little possibility of utilizing democratic political
processes to achieve change. He says:

Certain things cannot be said, certain ideas cannot be expressed, certain policies cannot be proposed, certain behavior
cannot be permitted without making tolerance an instrument
for the continuation of servitude.[16]

Along with denying the right of free speech to groups that promote
ideas about war or discrimination on the basis of race or religion, he
would also deny the expression of ideas that are in opposition to his
own about the extension of public services.

The obvious question that follows was raised by Coles in a dialogue with movement activist Berrigan:

But who is to decide whether the government is fit to make
such judgments: Who decides whether the government is
hopelessly corrupt and evil or simply a government, hence like
all governments flawed somewhat? . . . You are saying that
our institutions are not fit institutions and therefore have no
right to exercise their authority as institutions and determine,
for instance, how to deal with violence, whether it be from the

Klan or from the Weathermen. But if those institutions don't have such authority, which institutions, which people do?[17]

"We do," answers Berrigan. "Who is we?" asks Coles, and the answer comes easily:

> Well, we are that small and assailed and powerless group of people who are nonviolent in principle and who are willing to suffer for our beliefs in the hope of creating something very different for those who will follow us.[18]

Berrigan's "we" is not lodged in the Church as representative of the will of God or in the Communist party as advanced spokesman for the proletariat, but rather in a self-selected group that shares an extraordinary degree of certainty and sanctimonious intolerance for any who express uncertainty. All wisdom is to be lodged in this self-defined group, and the burden of making individual judgments and assessing the utility of one course of action over another is removed.

Berrigan's "we" has gained some power and a following among the young by denying legitimacy to those institutions that, after the first granting of benefits to civil rights activists in the 1960s, became dilatory in granting broader participation in decision-making and in making further inroads against inequality. Legitimacy is denied when people no longer believe the myths of sovereignty. The threads that hold society together are easily untied once the binding is rent. Thus a small proportion of completely alienated people may, in their anger over institutional inequality, bring about some rather startling changes in the position of minorities, students, women, poor working-class whites, and the aged.

Berrigan's optimism regarding the nature of the new power is based on a passionate belief that men are naturally good and a corporate community personality exists that can set valid moral standards for its members. This is similar to Rousseau's doctrine of the "general will," with its implied reduction of government to a mere agent of the community's corporate personality. In this view there is no such thing as coercion because when an individual wants something different from what the social order ("the people") gives him, he is simply capricious, or in Rousseau's words:

> Whoever shall refuse to obey the general will must be constrained by the whole body of his fellow citizens to do so,

which is no more than to say that it may be necessary to compel a man to be free.[19]

Robespierre made the inevitable application of this doctrine when he said of the Jacobins: "Our will is the general will":

> They say that terrorism is the resort of despotic government. Is our government then like despotism? Yes, as the sword that flashes in the hand of the hero of liberty is like that with which the satellites of tyranny are armed. . . . The government of the Revolution is despotism of liberty against tyranny.[20]

Polanyi, discussing the prospects for scientific and intellectual development in Western society, observed that savagery is always lurking within us. But, he said, "it can break loose on a grand scale only when rebellious moral passions first break up the controls of civilization." Polanyi's comments, like Fromm's evaluation of the psychology of fascism, were prophetic. Writing in 1945, he described the effect of uncontrolled skepticism and undisciplined social passion on the youths of that era, which sounds frighteningly like our own:

> A generation grew up full of moral fire and yet despising reason and justice. Believing instead in what?—in the forces which were left for them to believe in—in Power, Economic Interest, Subconscious Desire. These they accepted . . . as the ultimate reality to which they could entrust themselves. Here they found a modern, acid-proof embodiment for their moral aspirations. Compassion was turned into merciless hatred and the desire for brotherhood into deadly class war.[21]

SOCIAL WORK EDUCATION

One is not helped to deal with these complexities by equivocation, which is what is too often heard from educators whose function is to train, orient, and socialize entrants into the profession. For example, Peirce asks that students be "involved in policy making at all levels, including final decisions." Lest there be any doubt that he is unequivocal about power-sharing, he further states that the concept "includes full voting rights, and an orientation which accords each member equal beginning position and power." But he also

says that the faculty is to have "ultimate responsibility for educational policy-making . . . [and] final responsibility for personnel
must rest with school administrators."[22]

The trick in avoiding the unpleasant matter of deciding where
final decisions, ultimate responsibilities, and authority shall rest is
to use the terms "participation," "decision-making," and "power"
interchangeably. Peirce is by no means alone in this sort of equivocation. Vigilante, for example, opts for shared power but with
final responsibility resting in the hands of the administrator.[23]
CSWE, spoken for by Vigilante as a member of the Committee on
Students, seems to have decided that students only want to gain
rights of participation and do not want to challenge the ultimate
authority of the faculty.[24] If CSWE is not aware of student-faculty
struggles for ultimate power (Vigilante says they do not occur),
they cannot have looked deeply into the matter.

Some students do seek ultimate power because they find their
views are antithetical to those held by the majority of the faculty
who are now in control. The viewpoint of faculty who are not willing to yield to student control is frequently based on what many
communalists consider an old-fashioned belief about education, expressed by Schreiber as follows:

> . . . the re-awakening of romanticism, the search for new
> or different values and meanings, the rejection of narrow, ma-
> terialistic and empty goals, the desire to go back to the funda-
> mental qualities in human and organizational relationships
> . . . are not, and they must not become the equivalent of
> Anti-Intellectualism. Nor, if there be any validity to the notion
> that working with people for human betterment requires skill
> and knowledge, can they substitute for the sustained and de-
> manding "involvement" in acquiring the theoretical, applied,
> and ethical foundations of methodology . . . none of which
> grow solely, and effectively, out of intuition and good inten-
> tion.[25]

The current ethos among some students and others in the movement is antithetical to Schreiber's notion. Carried to its extreme the
"new" social work says that nothing necessary to being a social
worker can be learned through self-discipline and study. Anyone
can do it, and any system for holding students accountable for
changing themselves—grades, examinations, evaluations—has
largely to be abandoned.

ENVIRONMENTAL DETERMINISM

The author's thesis is that the current movement embraces a fourth ideological current—environmental determinism—which displaces all problems and evil onto the "system," "the structure," or the "power elite." These constructs are useful when guided by a knowledge of their limitations and of individual behavior and complex social processes. But they are dangerously misleading when used without these mechanisms for self-correction. For then what is left is an ideology which says that there is nothing in us that must change, nothing that we must learn.

The struggle for control in education also involves the question of academic freedom. That is, the recent ideal-typical model of education views the university not as a political democracy, but as an institution supposedly insulated from the vagaries of politics and popular movements, with faculty free to judge one another solely on the basis of competence. This view is presently unpopular with the political Left and Right. Both assert that in reality the university is the political instrument of the other and both want the university to serve their own interests instead.

Boehm appears to reconcile this strain between academic freedom and the shift of power to a group with a differing ideology. It is a difficult feat, but he accomplishes it by the unique device of giving the professor freedom in his teaching only so long as he changes with the times.[26] He is not free to disagree with proposed changes because disagreement with change, which Boehm refers to pejoratively as "standing pat," is wicked and no one wants to defend that sort of thing.

However, academic freedom must include the freedom to teach a wide range of ideas from standing pat to proposing new alternatives. This does not require an ivory-tower variety of Berrigan's "we." Academic freedom can tolerate—indeed, it requires—open and free discussion among students, professionals, and faculty.

But freedom cannot survive an environment that measures ideas and knowledge on the basis of whether they support every political fad and professional peccadillo that looks attractive and modern. Depth of scholarship, persuasiveness of evidence, and degree of painstaking research are dreary, weighty criteria, but they are the appropriate ones—and they can only be applied by fellow scholars. Students and others should have their say, but to place responsibility—or even to share it—with a constituency of students, professionals, and the community-at-large will lead only to the further politicization of education and the profession.

There has been increasing pressure by students, faculty, and professionals to evaluate teachers on the basis of their political views. CSWE, by capitulating quickly to the demands of radical students, minority groups, and the political activists, has not distinguished itself for a concern with the quality of teaching or academic freedom. For example, the CSWE position statement on "Student Participation in Decision Making in Graduate Schools of Social Work" is as generous as Peirce and Vigilante in awarding power to students.[27] The CSWE accreditation manual is equally emphatic in stating that curriculum decisions are the responsibility of the faculty and that final responsibility for selection of faculty rests with the administrator. So far, they seem content to ignore the difficulties that flow from these contradictions.

SOCIAL WORK FUNCTIONS

What is the function of professional social work that, it is asserted here, is undermined by activism, anti-individualism, communalism, and environmental determinism? Briefly, social work is a set of practices (based on theory and knowledge of social processes and methods of intervention) by which people are helped to understand, utilize, and change social institutions. In its brief history these methods have come to include work with individuals, families, groups, organizations, and communities and thus cover a wide range of practices and problems.

Unfortunately, the predominant social work conception of "social institutions" was rather narrow for most of this century. For many decades, social work concerned itself largely with interpersonal and intrapersonal problems of social functioning and thus avoided entangling itself with the problems of large-scale institutional change. Those who implored the profession to "get into the political arena" and pay greater attention to the social structural aspects of social problems were either ignored or tolerated as gadflies.

It is quite remarkable how little was done in the more traditional clinical quarters of the profession for over thirty years to integrate social science knowledge into professional practice. Even today, in many schools, the teaching of psychiatric casework is not much different from what it was twenty years ago. Thus there is the curious situation of an agency like Community Service Society—a veritable bastion of psychiatric casework—floundering to find a program.[28] Vapidity and myopia are the villains, not activism or advocacy. But the Community Service Society example does cause one to wonder whether there is much difference between the two extremes of clinical myopia and mindless activism.

While there has been no great change in recent years in the knowledge base of the profession and the way in which knowledge about methods of change is integrated into practice, there has been a great politicization of social workers. If the profession had integrated knowledge of political systems, organizational operations, analysis of social welfare problems and programs, and theories of social change into the practice of helping people understand, utilize, and change social institutions, there might have been a significant development of social work practice. That integration never took place; rather, some individual social workers have become political activists.

If this political activity were limited to their own civic affairs, it would be meritorious. But when social workers become political activists in their own behalf, in their practice, in their professional associations, and in their roles as teachers, they misunderstand and abuse the function of the profession. For example, the Golden Gate Chapter of NASW has recently started giving political endorsements to candidates and referenda without respect to their specific relevance to social work and without even following the Chapter's own requirements for making endorsements.[29]

There may be some long-run rewards for those who made the profession a useful tool for political aspirants or groups attaining new positions of power, but the profession as a whole can expect no reward, for we will have only succeeded in persuading the public that any of the party faithful can do what professional social workers do. Activism can be used by anyone willing to "lay his body on the line." If we support environmental determinism in its extreme, there is nothing one needs to change in our clients or in ourselves, and, even if there were, we would be powerless to achieve that change as individual professionals. Thus there is no need for the profession as it is now defined.

Social work has always been an insecure profession, prone to seek alliances with others who appear to offer more security and status. It has flitted from one institutional alliance to another and from theory to theory. If psychiatry beckoned, we followed; if opportunity and "power" theory looked more likely, off we went. It is unfortunate that this willingness to follow current movements for change is not matched with as high a degree of ability to insist on standards for training and professionally competent programs. If it had been, we could be welcoming the growing number of minority social workers and young political activists into a profession that had a future. Instead, the profession may become the victim of ideological currents that, in demanding extremes of loyalty to political dicta, undercut professional development.

THE FUTURE

What, then, is likely to become of professional social work? First, the functions of social workers who practice in well-defined institutional service areas such as public health and public schools are likely to be absorbed by these institutions. Schools of public health and education are quite capable of training personnel in these functions.

Second, those professionals whose major tasks and functions are concerned with the planning, administration, and evaluation of social welfare services will probably continue as a professional group with their own identity. Graduate schools of social work would then become graduate schools of social welfare devoted to training this kind of professional.

Third, undergraduate schools of social work will, in all likelihood, continue their growth for a good long while, training people who will provide subprofessional personnel for institutional service areas like corrections and public assistance.

Moreover, there are those professionals whose major tasks and functions are identified with neither an institutional area of service nor with social welfare. They include private practitioners, "generalist" social workers, "advocates," and people who are identified with a specific method (caseworkers, group workers, community organizers) rather than by association with a specific institutional area of service. This large and diverse group has several options. The clinicians, particularly those in private practice, may be absorbed gradually into other therapeutic disciplines such as psychology or medicine. The others, if they are able, will select from among the other alternatives just outlined, but they will have much difficulty in readjusting to the changes that may come about.

What is the use of this sort of prognostication? Given the fact that it is impossible to predict such highly complex events with any degree of certainty, why bother at all? Schorr's editorial and Pins's article in a recent issue of *Social Work* are also predictions, but they, at least by implication, suggest an optimistic future.[30] However, if there is cause for optimism, the basis for it is not clear.

Although this kind of doomsday thinking might help turn the field around, this is the most dubious defense of all, because the causes of change in the profession are too much beyond our control. Further, as stated initially, the consummation that is forecast is probably devoutly to be wished. Although it may occur for the wrong reasons, it is likely to be a good thing. The only utility of this forecast is that is will allow some professionals and the organizations that train and employ them to consider how they might best prepare themselves if the profession is really drawing its last gasps.

Different groups may find this useful in different ways. The alternatives available to practicing MSWs have been mentioned, and those young people who are just entering the profession deserve at least one clear warning. Beginning students in schools of social work would be well advised to follow a course of study that will either prepare them for work in one of the institutional areas that is likely to employ people with social work training or for work in social welfare. For example, a beginning student would do better to study for public health social work than enter a "generalist" program. Or he might concentrate his studies on the social welfare field, which, in contradistinction to social work, is not a practice but an institution. Those who are experts in *social work* have developed their knowledge of and skill in methods of helping people. Experts in *social welfare* develop knowledge and skill about the different kinds of organizational and institutional arrangements by which society deals with specific problems like income maintenance, care of the aged, and so forth.

The study of social welfare has been greatly neglected by social work, which for almost half a century has considered itself the chief source of professional personnel for staffing social welfare institutions. The stranglehold of social work on social welfare has not served that institution well, and this is one of the reasons why the parting of social work and social welfare may be salutary.

Schools engaged in training for the MSW should begin planning for faculty, curriculum, and admissions policies that will prepare them to respond to the expectations the community will increasingly have of such professional schools. Their planning should be in the direction of training people to carry out those social welfare functions already mentioned, as well as developing a corps of professionals who can teach undergraduate social work majors and students in other professional schools about social welfare services and social work methods (whatever those methods may come to be called). The schools should also give high priority to related functions, such as supervision and consultation.

Furthermore, research should be the major area of knowledge around which all others are built. Schools preparing people to teach, administer, plan, and evaluate social welfare programs should insist that their curricula be founded firmly on knowledge and facts. Compassion and commitment in social welfare should be directed by well-defined competence, as it has not been in social work. These directions are not unlike those outlined by Schorr and Pins. However, whereas Schorr and Pins tend to foresee the continuance and growth of the *profession* of social work, the view held here is that it will diminish in stature and become a *subprofessional* service.

When C. Wright Mills—one of the great intellectual activists of our time and certainly exempt from the charge of political indifference—cautioned against the dangers of political activism by intellectuals, he could have been writing a caveat to the social work profession:

> We cannot create a left by abdicating our roles as intellectuals to become working class agitators or machine politicians, or by playacting at other forms of direct political action. We can begin to create a left by confronting issues as intellectuals in our work. . . . We must do so with all the technical resources at our command, and we must do so from viewpoints that are genuinely detached from any nationalist enclosure of mind or nationalist celebration.[31]

NOTES

1. In this article the profession refers to the nexus among those who have the knowledge and skills allegedly acquired by attaining the master of social work degree in schools accredited by the Council on Social Work Education. This nexus has acquired some legal sanction in the National Association of Social Workers, which, until recently, was their official instrumentality. Recently NASW changed its membership requirements to include bachelor's degreeholders from undergraduate schools of social work.

2. Kurt Reichert, "Current Developments and Trends in Social Work Education in the United States," *Journal of Education for Social Work*, Vol. 6, No. 2 (Fall 1970), pp. 39–50; Alvin L. Schorr,

"Moving Toward the Future," Editorial Page, and Arnulf M. Pins, "Changes in Social Work Education and Their Implications for Practice," *Social Work*, Vol. 16, No. 2 (April 1971), pp. 2 and 5–15, respectively.

3. Schorr, op. cit.; Pins, op. cit.; "Cuts in SRS Training Funds Deal Blow to Social Work Students," and "Chapters Find Job Hunt a Hard Job," *NASW News*, Vol. 16, No. 3 (March 1971), pp. 1–2; and "Human Resources and Social Work Training: The Case for Continued Federal Support" (New York: Council on Social Work Education, May 1971) (mimeographed).

4. Roy Lubove, *The Professional Altruist: The Emergence of Social Work as a Career 1880–1930* (Cambridge, Mass.: Harvard University Press, 1965).

5. Richard Armour, "I Loved You, California," *Look*, September 25, 1962, p. 54.

6. Herman D. Stein, "Reflections on Competence and Ideology in Social Work Education," *Journal of Education for Social Work*, Vol. 5, No. 1 (Spring 1969), pp. 83–84.

7. Thorstein Veblen, *The Theory of the Leisure Class* (New York: Modern Library, 1936), p. 17.

8. Ernest Greenwood, "The Attributes of a Profession," *Social Work*, Vol. 2, No. 3 (July 1957), pp. 45–55.

9. Henry Miller, "Value Dilemmas in Social Casework," *Social Work*, Vol. 13, No. 1 (January 1968), p. 33.

10. Charles F. Grosser, "Neighborhood Community Development Programs Serving the Urban Poor," in George A. Brager and Francis P. Purcell, eds., *Community Action against Poverty: Readings from the Mobilization Experience* (New Haven, Conn.: College and University Press, 1967), pp. 247–248.

11. Jane Addams, *Twenty Years at Hull House* (New York: New American Library, 1961), pp. 234–235.

12. Erich Fromm, *Escape from Freedom* (New York: Rinehart & Co., 1941), p. 237.

13. See, for example, John L. Erlich, "The 'Turned-on' Generation: New Antiestablishment Action Roles," *Social Work*, Vol. 16, No. 4 (October 1971), pp. 22–27; and Gerald R. Wheeler, "America's New Street People: Implications for Human Services," *Social Work*, Vol. 16, No. 3 (July 1971), pp. 19–24.

14. As quoted in Fromm, *Escape from Freedom*, p. 224.

15. Carl R. Rogers, *Carl Rogers on Encounter Groups* (New York: Harper & Row, 1970), p. 27.

16. Herbert Marcuse, "Repressive Tolerance," in Robert Paul Wolff et al., *A Critique of Pure Tolerance* (Boston: Beacon Paperbacks, 1969), p. 100.

17. Daniel Berrigan, S. J., and Robert Coles, "A Dialogue Under-

ground," *New York Review of Books*, Vol. 16, No. 4 (March 11, 1971), pp. 21–22.

18. Ibid.

19. Jean-Jacques Rousseau, *Social Contract* (New York: Oxford University Press, 1948), p. 184.

20. As quoted in George H. Sabine, *A History of Political Theory* (New York: Henry Holt & Co., 1937), p. 591.

21. Michael Polanyi, *The Logic of Liberty: Reflections and Rejoinders* (Chicago: University of Chicago Press, 1951), p. 5.

22. Frank J. Peirce, "Student Involvement: Participatory Democracy or Adult Socialization?" *Journal of Education for Social Work*, Vol. 6, No. 2 (Fall 1970), p. 23.

23. Joseph Vigilante, "Student Participation in Decision-Making in Schools of Social Work," *Journal of Education for Social Work*, Vol. 6, No. 2 (Fall 1970), pp. 51–60.

24. Ibid., p. 60.

25. Paul Schreiber, "Comments," *Journal of Education for Social Work*, Vol. 7, No. 1 (Winter 1971), pp. 5–6.

26. Werner W. Boehm, "Academic Freedom and Professional Education in Social Work," *Journal of Education for Social Work*, Vol. 7, No. 1 (Winter 1971), p. 41.

27. New York: Council on Social Work Education, November 17, 1970. (Mimeographed.)

28. "Social-Work Unit Changing Tactics," *New York Times*, January 29, 1971, p. 1.

29. See, for example, NASW Golden Gate Chapter mailing of May 26, 1971, as well as mailings for elections dated May 1970 and November 1971.

30. Schorr, op. cit.; and Pins, op. cit.

31. As quoted in Irving Louis Horowitz, "The Unfinished Writings of C. Wright Mills," *Studies on the Left*, Vol. 3 (Fall 1963), p. 10.

THE CONTRIBUTORS

Harriett M. Bartlett. Retired. Formerly Professor, Simmons College of Social Work, Boston.

Scott Briar. Dean, School of Social Work, University of Washington, Seattle.

Richard A. Brymer. Associate Professor, Department of Sociology, McMaster University, Hamilton, Ontario.

Richard Cloward. Professor, Columbia University School of Social Work, New York.

Buford Farris. Associate Professor, School of Social Service, St. Louis University, St. Louis.

Milton Friedman. Professor, University of Chicago.

Neil Gilbert. Associate Professor, School of Social Welfare, University of California, Berkeley.

Milton M. Gordon. Professor of Sociology, University of Massachusetts, Amherst.

Ernest Greenwood. Professor Emeritus, School of Social Welfare, University of California, Berkeley.

Oscar Handlin. Carl H. Pforzheimer University Professor, Harvard University, Cambridge.

Michael Harrington. Author, New York City.

Marie R. Haug. Associate Professor, Department of Sociology, Case Western Reserve University, Cleveland.

George Hoshino. Professor, School of Social Work, University of Minneapolis.

Kenneth Keniston. Professor of Psychology (Department of Psychiatry), Yale Medical School, New Haven.

Charles N. Lebeaux. Professor, Wayne State University, Detroit.

Sol Levine. Executive Officer, University Professors' Program, Boston University.

Samuel Mencher (1918–1967). Professor, School of Social Work, University of Pittsburgh.

Anne Minahan. Professor, School of Social Work, University of Wisconsin, Madison.

Benjamin D. Paul. Professor of Anthropology, Stanford University, Stanford, California.

Allen Pincus. Professor, School of Social Work, University of Wisconsin, Madison.

Arnulf M. Pins. Assistant Director-General, JDC-Malben, Tel Aviv, Israel.

Karl Polyani (1886–1964). Lecturer for Extramural Delegacy, University of Oxford, England.

Martin Rein. Professor, Massachusetts Institute of Technology, Cambridge.

Alice M. Rivlin. Senior Fellow, The Brookings Institution, Washington, D.C.

Gideon Sjoberg. Professor of Sociology, University of Texas at Austin.

Harry Specht. Professor, School of Social Welfare, University of California, Berkeley.

Marvin B. Sussman. Selah Chamberlain Professor and Director, Institute of the Family and Bureaucratic Society, Department of Sociology, Case Western Reserve University, Cleveland.

James D. Thompson (1920–1973). Professor, Department of Sociology, Vanderbilt University, Nashville, Tennessee.

Richard Titmuss (1907–1973). Professor, Social Administration, London School of Economics.

Paul E. White. Professor and Chairman, Department of Behavior Sciences, The Johns Hopkins University School of Hygiene and Public Health, Baltimore.

Elizabeth Wickenden. Social Welfare Consultant, New York City.

Harold L. Wilensky. Professor of Sociology, University of California, Berkeley.

Martin Wolins. Professor, School of Social Welfare, University of California, Berkeley.

INDEX

THE BOOK MANUFACTURE

The Emergence of Social Welfare and Social Work was typeset by hot metal linotype. Composition, printing and binding was by Kingsport Press. Internal design was by the F. E. Peacock Publishers art department. Cover design was by Simkin & Associates. The type in this book is Spartan Book with Century light and Spartan display.